THE
CHUNNEL

THE
CHUNNEL

The Amazing Story of the
Undersea Crossing
of the English Channel

DREW FETHERSTON

TIMES T BOOKS

RANDOM HOUSE

All rights reserved under International and
Pan-American Copyright Conventions. Published in
the United States by Times Books, a division of Random House,
Inc., New York, and simultaneously in Canada by Random House of
Canada, Limited, Toronto.

Grateful acknowledgment is made to Thomas Telford Publishing
for permission to reprint an excerpt from Chapter 7, "The Channel
Tunnel," from *Tunnel Design*, a paper written by G. S. Crighton
and L. Leblond (London: Thomas Telford Publishing, 1989).
Reprinted by permission.

Library of Congress Cataloging-in-Publication data is available.

ISBN 0-8129-2198-4

http://www.randomhouse.com/

Manufactured in the United States of America
9 8 7 6 5 4 3

FOR AMANDA

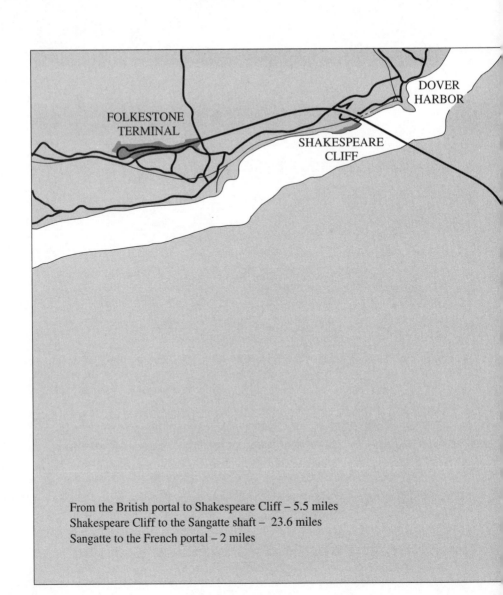

FOLKESTONE
TERMINAL

DOVER
HARBOR

SHAKESPEARE
CLIFF

From the British portal to Shakespeare Cliff – 5.5 miles
Shakespeare Cliff to the Sangatte shaft – 23.6 miles
Sangatte to the French portal – 2 miles

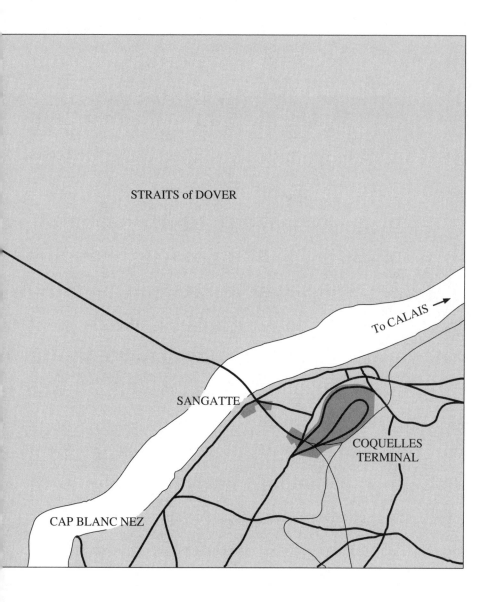

STRAITS of DOVER

To CALAIS →

SANGATTE

COQUELLES
TERMINAL

CAP BLANC NEZ

ACKNOWLEDGMENTS

This book, like its subject, is a narrow passage through a wide, deep, complex mass. In the tunnel's case, that mass is the stony seabed beneath the English Channel. In the book's case, it is the tunnel itself, the work of thousands of hands and minds whose labors, sprawled across two centuries, brought it into being.

Like the engineers who designed the tunnel, I had to make hard choices about size. They chose, for a great many reasons, to bore running tunnels that are 7.6 meters in diameter. I chose to build this narrative around the stories of a few dozen of the participants in this great undertaking. More generous dimensions might have improved both the narrative and the tunnel, but writers and engineers alike deal in the art of the possible.

Much of the narrative is drawn from interviews with fifty-eight men and women who played important roles in the tunnel project. Here I tried for as much depth as time and the goodwill of the subjects would permit; many of the interviews ran through several days and led to follow-up telephone calls. I also drew upon accounts that participants wrote themselves or gave to other interviewers.

Documents are the other great source of information about the tunnel, and I consulted them to the limits of my needs and capabilities. In the course of two hundred years, too much has been written about a Channel link for any single reader to scan, so I enlisted a daughter and a son to help me cast a wider net: I profited greatly from the months of searching that Sarah Fetherston did in the Channel Tunnel Association's archives in Churchill College, Cambridge, and from the work Andrew Fetherston did in various libraries in New York City.

I owe a great debt to Sir Alastair Morton and André Bénard, who, as the highest executives of Eurotunnel, gave me unconstrained permission to interview anyone I wished at Transmanche-Link, the contracting group that built the tunnel. Eurotunnel and TML were locked in an often bitter struggle. Under the terms of the contract then in force, they could have forbidden anyone at TML to speak to me. They did not, and I thank them for their courage and generosity.

The people at TML and Eurotunnel spent much time—precious time, because the workload was terribly heavy—educating me. So did they all—tunnelers, bankers, politicans, engineers, geologists, lawyers, consultants, financiers, archivists, historians—whom I approached with a notebook, tape recorder, curiosity and a great ignorance. They get the credit for all that is true and telling in this account; the blame for any deficiencies rests with me.

Frank Davidson's contributions, to the tunnel and to this book, cannot be overstated. Were it not for his vision and persistence, the former might not exist; without his memory and archives (and storytelling ability), the latter would be far poorer. I am grateful as well for the pleasure of his company.

Particular thanks also are due to John Reeve, John Noulton, Andrew McDowall and Howard Heydon, who provided me with access to a wealth of documents to supplement their rich recollections.

I benefited from the generosity of friends whose hospitality on occasion lifted the burden of logistics and let me work in comfort and ease: Roger and Odette Lemozy in France, Penny and Bob Atwood in England, and Hethy and Dick Nye in Barbados and Aspen. Penny Atwood also transcribed several hours of taped interviews, brutally boring work about which she never complained.

The staff at QA Photos in Hythe, particularly Margaret Matthews, spent many hours toiling in their files, pulling photographs for me. Daniele DeMori Calderon helped me arrange interviews in France. Their efforts are very much appreciated.

The book couldn't have been done without the help of several people. I owe special thanks to my agent, David Black, who brought the idea to me and steered the project through a number of difficult stages. His efforts always were directed toward making the book better. In this, he and I were both helped by several excellent editors at Times Books: Henry Ferris, Paul Golob, Steve Wasserman and Geoff Shandler.

Thanks also to my editors at *Newsday,* particularly Debra Whitefield and Mary Kuntz, whose understanding allowed me to earn my daily bread while pursuing this dream.

My deepest gratitude I give to my wife, Amanda Harris, whose strength and humor and love buoyed me in hard and easy times alike, and whose brilliant editing wrought much beneficial change in the manuscript.

THE
CHUNNEL

CHAPTER

I

Napoleon spoke of it: Courage, he observed from his confinement in St. Helena, was not often met nor easily summoned in the depths of the night.

On the dark night of October 30, 1990, Gordon Crighton understood this perfectly, felt it to the depths of his being: Hope and confidence flickering like a candle flame in a cold draft. The slow march of minutes across the impassive face of an office clock. Dawn—a dawn that might bring his disgrace—a lifetime away. Fear at the door, courage flown, a reputation in the balance.

The reputation for which Crighton feared was a considerable one. He was, at that moment, engineering director for United Kingdom Construction, Transmanche-Link Joint Venture, which meant that few ranked higher in the army that was laboring, this night as for more than a thousand before, to link Britain to Europe with a tunnel. He was a seasoned engineer, one of the best in the business of heavy construction.

Although it was getting on toward midnight, it was bright outside Crighton's office window; lights around the scatter of low buildings had pushed the darkness out of this small hollow, up into the lonely and bare hills along the Channel coast. This was Shakespeare Cliff, the gate into one of the biggest construction projects ever undertaken on the planet. It had not been dark or quiet for more than three years.

This Channel Tunnel, Crighton was fond of saying, was not just a hole in the ground. "You're talking about one of the largest engineering projects that's ever been built," he would say. "I would include the Panama Canal in that, and the Suez Canal. And, yes, even the pyramids." It was a keystone project for any career, the singular piece that would sit atop and secure the triumphal arch of a lifetime's work, and Crighton was within yards of that crowning achievement. Twenty-two kilometers from where he sat, deep below the tideswept floor of the Channel, a French tunnel-boring machine was grinding its way through waterlogged chalk, laboring the last few feet toward a hoped-for rendezvous with its British counterpart.

For all Crighton's pride, for all his feeling that the Channel Tunnel stood high among the great engineering works of mankind, his was still an engineer's view, and it understated the project's importance considerably. Much more was riding on the success of this titanic venture than engineers' boasting rights: Two governments had bet on it, wagering prestige if not currency, and failure here could translate rapidly into failure in public esteem. More than two hundred banks had money in the venture, and the careers of far-flung legions of executives were on the line. Merchant bankers had hawked shares to French and British citizens, and the worth of their promises would here be tested.

But the tunnel had still deeper meanings. The English Channel defines England. It is, in the English mind, as fraught a symbol as the Rubicon was to Caesar, the Hellespont to Alexander. The cliff upon whose height Crighton sat was the place to which Shakespeare's Gloucester, blinded and cast out to "smell his way to Dover," asked to be led in *King Lear*:

> *There is a Cliffe, whose high and bending head*
> *Lookes fearfully in the confined Deepe;*
> *Bring me but to the very brimme of it . . .*

That "confined deep" marked the profound and ancient cultural gulf that lay between England and France. Few other nations were so fascinated and repelled by each other than these whom the sea had long held apart. The Channel had made England, as Shakespeare noted to the enduring delight of his countrymen, "this precious stone set in the silver sea." The Channel served the nation "as a Moate defensive . . . against the envy of less happier lands."

And yet the Channel irked some by its very presence, and plans to breach it had been bruited for more than two centuries. They were of a remarkable variety: Iron bridges, undersea tunnels, sunken tubes, causeways and dams had been suggested, alone and in almost every possible combination. They had one thing in common: All but this last, the effort that now absorbed Crighton, were doomed never to be built.

It had not been easy to get this current project to this culminant point. The Channel Tunnel had proved to be a harsh master, and many who had worked on its behalf—bankers, politicians, engineers and executives—had undergone secular Gethsemanes. Now it was Crighton's turn for a night of agony. Governments, bankers, shareholders—these were abstractions now; they could be left for future discussions over a dram or pint at the Marquis of Granby, the preferred pub of the tunnel engineers. Tonight even the cathedral vastness of the tunnel seemed irrelevant. The drama to which Crighton was now a helpless spectator was focused on a hole, sixty millimeters in diameter and more or less horizontal, that extended 105 meters through the gray, sodden, clay-laden chalk out under the Channel.

A drill, probing ahead of a huge British tunnel-boring machine—a TBM, in the shorthand of the trade—had cut this narrow passage four days earlier. The drill had been sent forward on lengths of pipe and had naturally wandered a bit on its passage—sagging in response to gravity, veering to follow the texture of the rock. After some tests and measurements, the pipe was withdrawn, and the British TBM stopped. Now it lay silent and waiting as the French machine gnawed its way through the seabed, swallowing crushed rock like some great earthworm, searching for the hole left by the drill.

The moment captured the breadth of this project nicely: Here was this steel monster, 650 tons stretched over the length of two football fields, sucking in huge drafts of electric power, shaking the earth with its labors, groping for—a pinpoint. If everything had been done perfectly for the past three years, the French TBM (which was known fondly and familiarly to the workers as "Brigitte") would run onto the borehole exactly 41,612 meters from the British tunnel portal in Folkestone. When that happened, France and Britain would be linked by land for the first time in more than eight thousand years.

So much had been said and written about the precision of the tunnel works and the skill of the builders that the outcome of this exercise was (the world believed) guaranteed: The borehole would strike the French machine like a well-aimed English cloth yard arrow.

Crighton knew better.

He was no stranger to pressure. He was fifty-four years old and had spent years as a big-project engineer in every part of the world. He had built government buildings in Nigeria, bridges in Peru and road complexes in the Philippines for a string of major construction companies. In 1980, he had joined Balfour Beatty Construction, a big British firm whose particular strength was in power and transport systems, and had spent most of his first five years with the company in the Far East: a high-voltage network in Hong Kong, a transmission-line system serving a nuclear power plant in Guangdong Province, People's Republic of China.

He looked like a good engineer, on paper and in person. He was a product of that great nursery of British engineering, Scotland. "I grew up on a farm near Perth," he said. "And you know they say that every farm in Scotland produces an engineer, a doctor and a lawyer. It's the only way off the land, d'ye see? So I'm an engineer and my brother is a lawyer." Scotland had left neither his speech nor his attitude: He said "aye" for "yes," "wee" for "small" and "gaffer" for "boss."

He had a surpassing dislike for office life. "They don't know what to do with a hairy-arsed Jock in there," he would say. He wore a suit well, though, over a powerful stocky frame. He was nearly bald on top, but his eyebrows seemed to be striving to grow into the space. There was a pronounced streak of irony in his observations, and the eyebrows enhanced this, moving like semaphores to signal his feelings.

Like many British engineers, he had learned his trade in the field as well as in the classroom. It was a good process in many aspects; it created engineers whose ability to lead and direct came from an intimate personal knowledge paid for in sweat. British engineers tended to be democratic and approachable. This set them distinctly apart from their colleagues on the Continent. The French engineers with whom Crighton worked were technocrats, members of an elite, trained to lead as well as build.

In 1985, Crighton, by then head of civil engineering for Balfour Beatty, had been called to England to help his company and its nine partner companies—four British, five French—prepare a proposal to build an English Channel tunnel. It was a dangerously hurried process: On April 4 the British and French governments formally invited would-be promoters to submit proposals, with details of what sort of a fixed link—bridge, tunnel or a combination of the two—they proposed to build, over what period of time, with what sum of money, in the expectation of what profits. In this absurdly vague document, one of the very few firm, not-to-be-argued points dealt with finances: This was to be a private undertaking, with private funds. There would be no government funds, no government guarantees to investors. Bidders were told to have their proposals ready by October 31, 1985, less than seven months from the date of the invitation.

Crighton was sure it would all be wasted effort. He knew the history, knew that Napoleon had been interested in the idea of a Channel tunnel, as had Winston Churchill. Work had actually begun twice, but it had all come to naught, wrecked by a stubborn resistance that lay deep and all but unacknowledged in the English heart. Crighton did his part for the Submission to Government, then went back to China, to work on putting a subway in Beijing. He was there when, on January 20, 1986, the consortium of which Balfour Beatty was a part won the concession to build the Channel Tunnel. Nine months later, he was summoned back to London.

"I got back on the Saturday, and went into the office on the Monday, you know, and was told I'd be on the Channel Tunnel the next Monday," he recalled. "I said: 'I am not bloody going to take something that is going to last seven or eight years. I am not going.'" It would be far too long, he thought, to spend in one place, on one project. "In the construction world, projects last two or three years. Three is a very long project. You get used to moving on to something new every two years. You get bored with it. And I couldn't see myself digging a hole under the Channel, a long boring hole. And so I said no." He maintained that stance for a week, until his superiors at Balfour Beatty convinced him to accept the job. "I was told it would be good for me," Crighton recalled with a wry smile. "That it would keep me in finances for a wee while." He was far from being the only reluctant recruit on the tunnel job.

A Scot like Crighton had certain peculiar advantages on the Channel Tunnel job, the principal one being that he was British (which satisfied the British) but not English (a point of some importance to the French). "I don't think it's a big thing," he reflected. "But I do think it stood me in good stead now and again. And I played the card, between the French and the English. The French are very conscious of history. And of course Mary Queen of Scots was a French woman. There was the Auld Alliance—France and Scotland *against* England. We're talking, now, a few hundred years ago. But nonetheless, it's still there." So he did not hesitate to mention his birth to the French with whom he dealt.

He also suffered less from the odd but pervasive English prejudice against engineers and their creations, a prejudice that had acted as a drag on British technology for more than a century. It was another of the many things that divided British culture from that of France and the Continent, and it had contributed mightily to Britain's long opposition to the Channel Tunnel. Germany and France looked upon engineers as leaders and administrators; Britain looked upon them as grease monkeys.

For spiritual company on this evening, Crighton had two men: a French engineer named Laurent Leblond, who was his counterpart on the other side of the Channel, and John Hester, a hard-nosed second-generation American tunneler whose résumé included everything from piddling sewer tunnels to this grand undertaking. Crighton and Leblond had been opposite numbers from the earliest days of the project. Much separated Crighton from his French colleague: Leblond *was* a technocrat, a product of the École Nationale des ponts et chaussées, one of the most prestigious postgraduate schools for France's polytechnical elite. He was tall, fair, calm, soft-spoken, pleasant, confident. And he was not sweating out this night in his office, although the same fear was working on him. "Our surveyor had shown no signs of worry during the whole time," Leblond recalled. "Then, a few days before the breakthrough, he came to me and said, 'There may be a problem. . . .'" The worry had spread rapidly. Leblond decided to take his wife out for dinner that evening.

He and Crighton had been working opposite each other since the earliest days of the project, and, united by the problems they shared, came to regard themselves as an island of sanity and calm in a turbulent professional world. "He's got a sense of humor, and you will not build *any* job without humor," Crighton said. "The steam builds up, everybody gets uptight, and if you can't diffuse that, you're knackered. . . . Construction needs some humor about it, and a wee bit of flexibility, and Leblond was good at that. Unusual for a Frenchman." As usual for a Frenchman, Leblond spoke pretty good English; Crighton was entirely British in having no command of French.

Engineers figured that if the machines were less than 250 centimeters out of line, they could turn them easily enough to make a slightly kinked but serviceable linkup. If the error were greater, the problem would be more serious, because a TBM cannot back up. Brigitte and her British counterpart each cut a passage that was 5.38 meters in diameter. This raw hole, however, was lined with concrete segments that fit together to form a ring with an inner diameter of 4.8 meters. If the two TBMs were more than a diameter out of line, it would mean delay and an inundatory wave of bad publicity.

Delay was very costly: The best estimates at the time put the daily cost of the tunnel works at £1 million, and every day lost here meant a lost day of revenue after the tunnel opened. Bad publicity could be even more damaging. The banks that had backed the tunnel had grown terribly nervous about their investment. Not long before, the banks had forced a reorganization of the project that had cost several men their jobs—and had brought Hester and several other strangers to the scene.

If the tunnels were inconveniently far off, Crighton and Leblond were finished. Someone would have to bleed to atone for the mistake, and they were the most suitable victims. But even a smaller and less critical error would be enough, they knew, to disgrace them and destroy their professional reputations. Here again, success and failure in this enormous project would be measured in minute dimensions: A twenty-five centimeter error would be a marvel, seventy-five would be too much. A meter out of line would be bad, two would be shameful. Three meters—the rough equivalent of a lane change stretched over thirty-five kilometers of road—would be a disaster.

Both men were acutely aware of the stupefying complexity of the tunnel project. The Channel Tunnel was, in fact, a complex of a dozen tunnels. Six

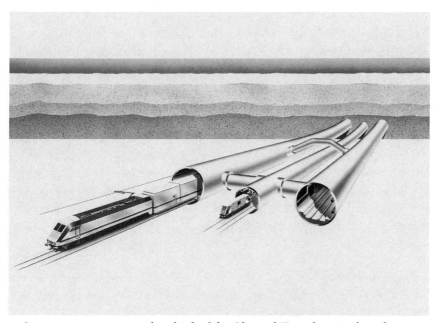

Investors were encouraged to think of the Channel Tunnel as simple and neat.

began directly under Shakespeare Cliff, at the bottom of a 110-meter-deep shaft outside Crighton's office. Three of these proceeded out under the Channel toward France; the others went in the opposite direction, back more than eight kilometers to the Folkestone portal. Similarly, on the French side, three tunnels headed for England from the bottom of a huge shaft at Sangatte; three others went east, under the land, more than three kilometers to the portal at Coquelles.

The twelve tunnels would string together to form three continuous tubes from Folkestone to Coquelles. Each of these would be more than forty-nine kilometers long. The tubes would be connected every 375 meters by cross-passages. If you cut through the tunnel complex at one of these cross-passages, the section would look like a dumbbell with a bulge in the middle of the bar. The ends would be the main running tunnels for trains, each with an internal diameter of 7.6 meters. The bulge in the center would be the 4.8-meter service tunnel. The entire dumbbell would be 37.6 meters across.

This dumbbell figure was familiar to anyone who had followed the Channel Tunnel's progress. Eurotunnel, the company formed to own and operate the tunnel, used it often to illustrate how the thing would look and function. Investment banks used it to explain the project to possible investors. Artists drew cutaway renditions that showed gleaming trains streaking through spotless tubes set in beds of handsome gray-white chalk. These illustrations were intended to reassure as well as instruct. To current or hoped-for sharehold-ers, to creditor banks or wavering politicians, they offered an image of a straightforward project. A big project, to be sure, one that would require a great deal of money and an enormous amount of labor and planning. But, the pictures suggested, nothing too complicated.

Again, Crighton knew better. The complexity of the tunnel was over-whelming. No untrained eye, no unschooled intellect could grasp or even imagine the underlying order in what seemed to be a perfect chaos of men, machines, muck and din. There weren't only cross-passages between the tunnels; other links, called piston relief ducts, arched over the service tunnel and connected the main running tunnels every 250 meters. These were de-signed to bleed away air pressure as the trains sped through the tunnels like enormous pistons, shoving a wall of air ahead of them. All of the cross-passages were cut by hand with air spades, brutally noisy pneumatic chisels that clamored day and night.

There were chambers everywhere, too, which ranged from small rooms for electrical equipment to huge crossover chambers where trains one day would be able to switch from one tunnel to another. There were two of these cathedral-like halls under the Channel; the one built by the British crews, almost eight kilometers out from the Shakespeare Cliff shaft, was 163 me-ters long, 15 meters high and 21 meters wide.

A steady rumbling flow of traffic was already moving through the tunnels: A stream of work trains trundled out to the TBMs; these were made up of flatcars bearing steel-reinforced concrete tunnel-liner segments and empty "muck skips"—hopper cars to carry back the excavated material—plus a "manrider" car to carry workers. Another stream ran in the opposite direction, with empty flatcars and full spoil cars. There were entire trains of manriders, too, that shuttled like a commuter railway, carrying workers to and from work. The manriders were Spartan affairs, steel-slab cars with slab benches and dim lights that occasionally functioned. They were about as luxurious as the muck skips. In the beginning the manriders had no doors whatever, but this caused too many injuries to tunnelers who slumped into a doze after a ten-hour shift and let a limb dangle outside. Now there were steel pipes welded on each side of the door; these were tracks for a net of heavy webbing that one lifted to enter or leave the car. They made the cars look and feel like animal cages, but they worked.

Crighton's chief surveyor was a calm man of reassuring appearance named Eric Radcliffe, a husky six-footer whose grizzled beard and perfect stand-up crew cut gave him the air of a piratical sea captain. He had surveyed tunnels all over the world during a career that was in its fourth decade when he took up the Channel Tunnel job in October 1987. He had gone out to Iran in

The reality underground was complex and messy.

1955 and had spent twenty years abroad—in East and West Africa, Morocco and Kenya—before returning to Britain to work on an ill-fated Channel tunnel project in 1974. When that job collapsed, Radcliffe resumed his overseas wanderings. He retired briefly to run a small restaurant in Majorca before coming back to Britain and to the tunnel.

The problems that confronted Radcliffe under the Channel were ancient and still far from solved. Passage tunneling—as distinct from mining—began more than four thousand years ago in the Middle East. The first towns needed to have water inside their defensive walls, and tunnels were the most secure way of assuring a supply. Thus were the waters of Perseus's spring led inside Agamemnon's citadel at Mycenae. These were not trivial operations;

the ancient water tunnel that served Aleppo, in Syria, was more than twelve kilometers long.

Hezekiah, King of Judah, learned of tunneling's difficulty around 700 B.C. when, faced with an impending siege by Sennacherib's Assyrian army, he ordered a tunnel dug to carry water from the Gihon Spring to the Pool of Siloam inside Jerusalem's walls. The aqueduct, like the Channel Tunnel, was dug from both ends toward the middle. The workers lost their way and had to dig several vertical shafts to the surface to see where they were. They wandered for 512 meters to cover the less than 200 meters between the spring and the pool. The tunnel is still in pretty good condition, though, and you can see, in its wall, the pick marks where laborers changed direction as they groped the last few meters toward each other.

Even rough success evoked great praise. Herodotos ranked a thousand-meter-long water tunnel on Samos, built in the sixth century B.C. by the engineer Eupalinus of Megara, as one of the greatest of Greek engineering feats—despite the fact that the tunnelers, working from both sides of a hill, missed each other by six meters in the horizontal and three meters in the vertical. The teams made sharp turns to find each other, leaving the tunnel with a kink.

Nothing was, or is, more difficult and dangerous than tunneling under water. History provides eloquent testimony to this: The first underwater tunnel, a 900-meter pedestrian passage under the Euphrates at Babylon, was finished in 2180 B.C. The *second* underwater tunnel, a 365-meter passage dug under the Thames at London by the great French-born engineer Marc Isambard Brunel, was finished in A.D. 1843.* Through all the centuries between, no tunnel ventured under water (although Leonardo da Vinci, in a résumé he submitted to Ludovico Sforza, Duke of Milan, said he thought he could dig one if it were necessary). The normal ration of danger was far greater under water. In the Hudson River railroad tunnels, built late in the last century to bring rail traffic into New York, each work crew of forty to fifty men could expect to have one fatality per month.

For the Thames Tunnel, Brunel sidestepped the navigation problem by digging from one side of the river to the other, from Rotherhithe to Wapping. It took sixteen years and two months, drained its public and private investors of money and broke Brunel's health and spirit. There was not enough money

---

* In fact, it is likely that the Thames Tunnel was really the first subaqueous tunnel, to use the term favored by engineers. There is much doubt about whether the Babylonian tunnel ever existed; the only mention of it was by Diodorus Siculus, a Sicilian-born Greek historian who was a contemporary of Julius Caesar. Diodorus cited a tradition that Semiramis, the legendary founder-queen of Babylon, had built such a tunnel, and he supplied some interesting details about its construction. But no trace of it has ever been found.

A collapse during construction of Brunel's Thames Tunnel.

even to complete the approach ramps that would have let vehicles use it. Without access for vehicles, this monument to endurance and fortitude became a gloomy pedestrian pathway. The toll was a penny, cheap enough to attract London's homeless, some of whom no doubt owed their poverty to the industrial revolution whose triumphs the tunnel echoed. The poor used the Thames Tunnel as a makeshift shelter for years, calling it the "Hades Hotel," until the East London Railway bought it in 1869, lined the roof with sheet iron and began running trains through it.

Railroads brought in the great age of tunneling late in the last century. The Alps quickly were riddled with rail tunnels: The Fréjus Tunnel, opened in 1871. The St. Gotthard, 1882. The Arlberg, 1884. The Simplon, 1906. The Lötschberg, 1912. These were only the largest tunnels, those judged worthy of a name. The 15.9-kilometer Lötschberg, for instance, was only one of thirty-four tunnels in a fifty-eight-kilometer stretch of rail that, in all, ran more than twenty-three kilometers underground.

But the problems that bedeviled Eupalinus lingered, as surveyors discovered in the 19.8-kilometer-long Simplon tunnel in 1901. Surveying by then was a demanding but reliable skill, at least on the earth's surface. Tunnels were different.

On land, surveying is founded on the "closed traverse," which a surveyor creates by walking around the perimeter of a polygon, carefully measuring its angles and the lengths of its sides. Land deeds often describe property in these terms, as a series of angles and distances. The polygon can be very complex—a small farm might have a hundred sides or more—but the geometry is simple and provides a perfect check on accuracy: The sum of the interior angles will be equal to the number of angles, less two, times 180 degrees. The surveyor attempts to make the figure "close"—that is, to have the angles and distances fit together so that the end of the last traverse line touches the beginning of the first. This only happens in theory, because no set of instruments can yield flawless measurements. The error in angles and distances is spread around the traverse.

A tunnel is too narrow for much of a polygon, however. One option is an open traverse, a series of lines and angles that simply zigzags through the passage, though this is notoriously prone to error and impossible to check for accuracy.

The Simplon engineers decided to use a sort of gunsight to keep their tunnel headings, which were to be driven straight toward each other, on line. They built two steel frames outside each portal; each of these had a steel plate with a slit in it. They were placed with the utmost care; surveyors measured more than nine hundred angles in setting them. Surveyors could peer from within the tunnel to see if the slits were aligned. This worked well for a while, but the tunnel face, following the earth's curve, appeared to descend one meter in each four kilometers. The gunsight had to be moved into the tunnel, and engineers worried that this could cause serious surveying errors.

After three years of work, when the miners stopped to celebrate the feast of their patron, Saint Barbara, the engineers moved in to make some accurate measurements. They were badly surprised by what they found.

The surveyors set up a light outside the portal and sighted back from more than five kilometers inside the tunnel. The earth's curvature and refraction—the bending of light as it passed through layers of air, the effect that makes a stick seem to bend where it enters a pool of water—depressed the image of the light almost two meters.

But instead of seeing one light, the observers saw two, one above the other. And the square tunnel opening, which the earth's curvature should have cut off to appear as a horizontal rectangle, instead appeared as a tall vertical rectangle. Further, this tall rectangle, two and a half times as high as it was wide, seemed to be leaning to the right. Persons passing the entrance also appeared to be bent over to the right, and so did the mysterious upper flame.

It dawned on the Simplon engineers that refraction in long tunnels created a very complex environment for a light beam. The air nearest the walls is warmer than the air in the center, because of ambient heat in the rock. This would not be a terrible problem in a perfectly round tunnel, with perfectly still air, if you could sight straight down the middle: The light would not be moving between layers of air, speeding up and slowing down as the density changed, pitching and yawing like a sailboat in heavy weather. But everything in a real tunnel—hot walls and cool center, cold air sliding in from the outside, hot air rising and eddying, air pushed in and pulled out by ventilating fans, air stirred by the actions of men and machinery—tended to toss light around in a most unpredictable fashion. In Simplon on that St. Barbara's Day, the engineers discovered that all of their measurements were wrong and had to be rethought, recalculated, redone.

Radcliffe had some considerable advantages over his professional forbears in the Simplon. First, he had the benefit of their painfully acquired experience. Second, he had much better tools. Navigation satellites, backed by some very careful triangulation work on the ground, could tell him where the tunnel's portals in Britain and France stood in relation to each other with an accuracy of one part in a million—in this case, a bit less than five centimeters, about the length of a wooden kitchen match. He had lasers instead of oil lamps, his instruments were better and the TBMs had onboard computer navigation systems.

This technology fascinated the press; a steady stream of news stories made it seem as if the satellites, lasers and computers steered the TBMs with inhuman precision. These stories irritated Radcliffe, to whom the limits of technology were as apparent as its abilities. They were still just tools, only as good as the hands that held them. And while the tools were better, the difficulties presented by the Channel Tunnel were far more challenging than anything surveyors had faced in the Alps.

For instance, the satellites could not tell Radcliffe much about how the tunnel portals related to each other in the vertical. To the satellites then available, the earth looked pretty flat. The usual way for surveyors to establish such things is by sight. The Simplon tunnel surveyors were able to survey their way from one portal to the other, across the Alps, with excellent accuracy by sighting from one reference point to another.

Radcliffe couldn't work point to point on the tossing waters of the Channel, of course. And while citizens of Dover could sometimes peer through a telescope and read the time on Calais's town-hall clock, the distance and the consequent atmospheric distortion were far too great to permit an accurate single sight. Nor could he use sea level on each side of the Channel as a starting point to relate the height of one tunnel entrance to the other. "Mean Sea Level is a slope across the Channel," he said. Winds, the spinning earth, the tides in the North Sea and the Atlantic—all conspired to slop the waters of the Channel around in a most disorderly and unpredictable fashion. In Britain, all heights were taken in reference to the Ordnance Datum Newlyn, an agreed-upon sea level. France measured its heights from a sea level established by the Institut géographique national. The trouble was, no one was sure where one stood in relation to the other.

There had been some work done on the problem. In 1963 two oceanographers computed the sea slope and concluded that Britain's Ordnance Datum Newlyn was 47.5 centimeters higher than France's Institut géographique national sea level. Later calculations came up with 44 centimeters and 44.2 centimeters. The Channel Tunnel engineers took the last figure and designated it Channel Tunnel Height Datum 1986; this became the basis for further refinement. In the end, the difference was judged to be 29.1 centimeters, which was rounded off to 30. Then, to avoid having to deal with negative numbers when they were underground, the engineers lowered it by exactly two hundred meters. All tunnel elevations were measured from this datum, the Nivellement Transmanche 1988, or NTM88.

But such precision was all on the surface. Radcliffe had to take it down into the tunnel through two adits, sloping access tunnels that led down from

Surveying in the Channel Tunnel.

the beach under Shakespeare Cliff to the underground chamber in which the British TBMs were assembled. From there, Radcliffe had to carry his exactitude through the tunnel as it progressed.

There were other complications. The Channel Tunnel, unlike the Simplon, was not straight. The seabed under the Channel contained many layers of rock that were unsuitable for a tunnel and one thin layer that was ideal. These layers unfortunately did not lie flat; in cross-sectional drawings they looked like rumpled covers on an unmade bed. The TBMs had followed the good rock, dipping down, banking left or right, rising toward the surface, their paths always dictated by the quality of the ground. Indeed, in these last nerve-racking moments, the two machines were not approaching each other head-on. Both TBMs were turning toward each other on a gentle arc, the British TBM edging to the left, Brigitte to the right.

In the tunnel, the complex path was easy to see. During construction, the tunnel had a row of fluorescent lights on either side, and a ride in a work train's cab was a hypnotic experience: The lights would descend in a gentle arc into the ground ahead, or climb into the roof, or bend into the walls. The horizon was where the lights disappeared, and this shifted and floated ahead of the train as it lumbered along at its regulation twenty-five kilometers per hour. In sections that were more or less straight, the horizon would move far ahead of the train. Then, as a bend approached, it would seem to pause as if waiting for the train. Then it would move on. This hypnotic effect was one of the reasons why this tunnel was being built for locomotives rather than automobiles: That languid play of light, the visual equivalent of white noise, had a tendency to overpower drivers, to alter the state of their attention to the road. In long road tunnels, some drivers are afflicted with the sensation that their vehicles are creeping sideways toward the wall or toward the oncoming traffic. Eventually, these drivers become paralyzed by fear and simply stop. In the Alps, long road tunnels kept motorcycle outriders on hand to scoot out and rescue these sufferers. Sometimes they had to peel a driver's rigid fingers off the wheel.

Radcliffe duly brought his line down into the tunnel and his crews began the long haul toward France. "Once we were underground, there was not much new," he said. "But it was a hell of a long way to go."

He did not have the wholehearted support of the tunneling crews, whose job was simply to move ahead as quickly as possible and who stood to earn bonus money for speed. "A good survey doesn't improve their progress or their bonus," Radcliffe said. He had arguments right from the first turn at the bottom of the adit, where he had built a solid, chest-high concrete plinth at the base of the wall to hold his instruments. When the tunnelers began laying rail for the work trains, they found the plinth sticking out into their path. The senior construction engineer came to Radcliffe and told him it would have to be moved. Radcliffe explained that it was absolutely necessary, that there was no other place for it. The engineer dug in his heels.

"I'm not setting out for France with a kink in my track," he said.

"If you move the plinth, you won't know where France *is*," Radcliffe replied. The plinth and the kink remained.

Surveying in the service tunnel was a nightmare. The 4.8-meter-diameter tube was utterly jammed: A flat concrete floor took up space at the bottom. Two train tracks lay side by side on this floor; the work trains they carried required a clear passageway three meters wide and two meters high. Water pipes ran along one wall, with trays for electric wires above them and power cable supports above those. Centered over the passageway was a big air duct, more than a meter in diameter. There were more power cables on the opposite wall. Workers shared a small catwalk halfway up one side of the tube with more pipes. The passage was so cramped that there were refuges provided on the catwalk where workers could shelter when trains passed. Even in the refuges, the passing trains were unpleasantly close, Radcliffe recalled.

In the end, Radcliffe's crews carried a series of zigzag lines down the tunnel, one the mirror image of another, so that a series of "scissors" forms were created. Because of refraction, the angles measured in the single-side traverse were all too large, but those in the zigzag were alternately too large and too small. They thus tended to cancel each other out, giving—the surveyors believed—a true overall reading.*

Hester, too, was troubled to the depths of his engineer's soul by the events that were taking place out under the Channel, but not because of any concern about the surveyors' accuracy. Instead, he was furious about what was going to happen when the TBMs found each other and the tunnels were finally joined. "I just hope and pray my father never sees what we're about to do," he had told a colleague. "Because he would recognize it as one of the dumbest fuckin' things anybody ever did."

Everybody in tunneling knew his father, Alabama Hester. "Probably the most famous tunnel superintendent that's ever been in the United States,"

---

* There was another surveying aid, the ZED computer navigation system on the TBM itself. This consisted of a laser in the tunnel aimed at a sensitive target on the TBM. A computer on the surface kept track of where the laser beam was shining, and a computer on the TBM kept track of the beam's location on the target. If the TBM wandered left, the laser would move to the right on the target, and the onboard computer would tell the driver (who worked blind in a small control room, seven meters back from the machine's cutting head) which way to turn, and how much. This system had its problems—computers aren't yet manufactured with subaqueous tunneling in mind—and, further, depended on the aiming of the laser, which depended on the surveyors.

said his son. "I'm not really from anywhere. I was born in White Plains, New York. My father was working on the airport down in Trinidad at the time, so when I was two months old we went down to Trinidad. I went to I guess a dozen different schools growing up. Went to high school in Australia; he was on the Snowy Mountain Project there. Came back, went to high school here. Little town called Hancock, New York, up in the Catskill Mountains." While John went to school, his father did the tunneling work for the Cannonsville reservoir.

He went to Rensselaer Polytechnic Institute in Troy, New York, until he hit a wrought-iron fence at fifty miles an hour on a 500-cc BSA motorcycle. "Totaled the bike," he said laconically. "Damn near totaled me." When he could walk again, he went to work in tunneling. "I started out on the end of a shovel," he said. "First job was the West Delaware Project, 43 miles of tunnel. Takes water to New York City from Cannonsville Dam. Worked on the Cannonsville Dam Intake, and I've been in it ever since. Managed to get a little education along the line. I'm a Professional Engineer and things like that but I spent close to fifteen years—as they say in England—'on the tools.' Mechanic, TBM operator. Worked for a TBM manufacturing company and taught people how to run TBMs for years."

Hester also had been a reluctant recruit to the Channel Tunnel. Hester's reluctance came from the same engineer's uneasiness about a long-lasting job that had spurred Crighton's brief rebellion. "I don't like driving to work on the same goddamned road every day. I want to do something different." He had been running a tunneling division for Morrison Knudsen, the big Idaho-based construction company and, practical man that he was, thought that the Channel Tunnel couldn't teach him anything useful. "Tunneling and the Channel Tunnel are not necessarily the same thing," he explained. "This is unique. The things that were done on this job are not really applicable to normal tunnel work."

Nevertheless, it was difficult to avoid the subject of the tunnel in Hester's circles, even in the United States. Wherever you went, to however insignificant a tunnel project, the conversation was about the Channel Tunnel. It had been that way for five years before Hester answered his telephone to hear an English voice invite him to come over to see if he'd like to be in charge of tunneling operations for Transmanche Link. "I thought it was someone winding me up," he recalled. "I mean, I had been pretty outspoken about the fact that there was nothing being done on the Channel Tunnel that's going to do any good anywhere else, so why should we pay any attention to it? You'll learn more from a little sewer job in Detroit than you will on the Channel Tunnel."

Hester visited, but continued to resist. Back at Morrison Knudsen, though, his boss encouraged him to sign on, promising to keep his job open in case things didn't work out. And so, on a chilly morning in December 1989, he stepped off a plane at London's Gatwick Airport and presented his permit to work on the Channel Tunnel to a British immigration officer. Hester's years of experience—and probably, he says, the example of his father—had given him a powerful sense of his own abilities. He radiated confidence the way a bonfire gives off heat. He knew his trade, he knew machines, he knew good men and he knew a fool when he met one. He knew how to give an order and how to fire anyone who deserved it. The French had particular problems with his directness; Hester was not above making harsh generalizations about the French national character, which he, like some other Americans, believed was more willing to assign blame than take responsibility for problems and errors.

The immigration officer looked over Hester's papers.

"They're certainly paying you a lot of money to be here," he said.

"Yes they are," Hester said.

The officer handed back the documents. "Too bad you're never going to get any of it," he said. "They're shutting down the project this afternoon."

On the surface, at least, the problem seemed to be about money: The cost of the tunnel had risen alarmingly; the bank loan was in technical default; the consortium of lending banks was reluctant to advance more cash. But as Hester would soon discover, money was, if not the least of the tunnel project's problems, simply one of several that were hounding it and threatening to drag it down. And while the project did not collapse before he could get to work, the money shortage was critical and quickly approaching mortal.

Hester was given broad authority over tunneling, and he sensibly left the other problems to those whose responsibilities they were. He was responsible for driving tunnel, and to this he put his hand and will. He did not like interference, and his considerable abilities had for the most part sheltered him from this.

Until now. This historic breakthrough would require ceremony, and that would mean ignoring several hallowed tunneling practices. In Hester's mind, there was only one right way to link two machine-driven tunnels: As the two TBMs approach each other, one dives downward and the other drives over it. The first machine is entombed in concrete and simply abandoned. The second machine is cut apart and removed, and the space in which it ended its life is lined with cast-iron rings.

Tunnel-boring machines do not, as Hester noted, "turn on a dime." A TBM diving into the seabed traces a very gradual curve. When the oncoming machine encounters this descending tunnel, it breaks through the sloping roof with the bottom of its cutting head. It then gradually eats away at the sloping roof of the first tunnel until, finally, it arrives at the point where the first TBM began its descent.

But not on this job, not for this breakthrough. History demanded that this be accomplished with ritual, to sanctify this still uneasy marriage between the nations. It could not be left to a machine to make the breakthrough. As with any marriage, there had to be a joining of hands. Humans would wield tools to open the passage, and when the rock had been parted, a Frenchman and an Englishman would reach through and shake hands.

So the breakthrough plan was this: The British machine would turn aside rather than down, until it was alongside the French machine, separated from it by several meters of intact chalk marl. As workers began to cut the French machine apart for removal, British tunnelers would hand-mine a narrow passage toward the face of the French tunnel.

Two tunnelers had already been selected by lottery for the honor of holing through and giving the ceremonial handshake. Philippe Cozette was a former heavy-equipment operator from Peuplingues, a village of 500 souls that was less than a kilometer from the tunnel portal in France. When he had learned, seven years earlier, that the tunnel would be built at his doorstep, he concluded that it might offer a secure livelihood—an important consideration in the Nord-Pas de Calais region, where both industry and agriculture were in deep trouble. The fact that Cozette had never worked underground made him typical in the French workforce, which was recruited from the region and trained for the work. Graham Fagg, who would share the honors with Cozette, was similarly typical of the British workforce: He was an experienced professional tunneler, who followed the work wherever it happened to be. Tunneling had taken him around the world; within months of the breakthrough, he would be working in Australia. By that time, Cozette would be studying to become a locomotive driver in the tunnel.

To Hester, "It was all bullshit. The whole scenario was stupid. A tunnel-driving nightmare. It was done for political reasons, and it was done wrong. Simple as that. There's no goddamned tunnel person in their right mind would do it that way." Sending the British TBM through the side wall of the tunnel would do terrible things to the structural integrity of the rock, Hester knew. It would require a huge amount of extra labor to seal up the hole, which would needlessly endanger the workers who did the sealing. It would delay a job on which very small amounts of time were worth a very great deal of money. Hester figured the extra tunneling would cost somewhere between £2 million and £3 million. On this historic night, he was home in his rented apartment in Folkestone.

·   ·   ·

Still, before there could be celebration of any kind, the tunnels *did* have to find each other. Radcliffe was down in the tunnel, in the TBM control room with David Denman, who had been service tunnel manager—or agent, as the post was more generally called in the business—for the last fifteen months and twelve kilometers. Denman was forty-four years old and had been tunneling for more than twenty-three of them. He loved his work, particularly when it was difficult and uncomfortable. He could recall jobs with fondness that others might have remembered with horror. "Five-foot tunnels, full of water," he said of a sewer-tunnel job in East London. "*Smashing* work, all muck and bullets."

He was a cheerful, sturdy man, with a sense of humor that stood well with the people above and below him. But when he spoke of his work, he came close to poetry. "Oh, it sounds lovely," he said of his TBM. "Magic. Like a good woman mewing in her sleep. You've got the throb of the hydraulic motors, the crunch and whirring of the cutter. You've got to take the *smell* into it—the smell of the ground, the smell of the hot hydraulic oil. To hear the pumps start up, oh, it's wonderful. You can *sense* when you've got a good shift going. You can *smell* it."

Denman had supervised drilling of the borehole for which Brigitte was now searching, so no one was better able than he to appreciate the uncertainty of the endeavor. Probe drilling had been going on ever since the TBM started, but only to check on conditions ahead of the machine and to make sure the chalk marl wasn't climbing or diving out of the machine's path. The probes went out on aluminum pipe, which tended to corkscrew, droop and otherwise take unpredictable turns, but close was good enough for everyday work.

When the probe was proposed as a tool for guiding the final linkup, Denman was told to get ready to do it. Steel would have to be used instead of aluminum to keep the drillrod as rigid and well-aimed as possible. The engineers wanted a 200-meter probe hole, if possible, to give them plenty of room to turn the TBMs if they were out of line. In late May, Denman did some test borings back near the British portal to see what sort of accuracy he might expect. He drilled from inside the tunnel toward the surface, 150 meters away. He angled the drill five degrees up to allow for droop. The drill missed its target by 12 meters. "Well, that made us realize that we had a problem," Denman recalled. Finding the French TBM "was going to be like picking up an air rifle and, without adjusting the sights, hitting a sixpence at a hundred yards."

After some tinkering, the drillers tried again, boring from one gallery below Shakespeare Cliff across to another, 230 meters away. The probe missed the gallery completely.

To try to chart its true path, technicians sent a clever Swedish-made device called a Reflex Maxibor through the hollow drillrod. The Maxibor was a forty-five-millimeter-wide tube, slender as a child's wrist, that had a video camera and a computer's microprocessor fitted artfully inside. As it snaked its way through the larger drillrod, the video camera watched three reflective rings on the inside of the tube and recorded what it saw in the microprocessor. After a trip to the end of the hole, the Maxibor was withdrawn and its microprocessor was connected to a portable computer, which digested the observations and produced a string of coordinates that, to a practiced eye, described the path of the probe.

The Maxibor had one important limitation: If the borehole turned too sharply, the camera would lose sight of one of the rings. When that happened, the turn didn't register and the rest of the information was of doubtful accuracy. That seemed to have happened in this latest test; Denman could only guess that the probe had ended up six meters high and two meters to the left of its intended target.

By October, the drillers were getting better results, and the tests shifted to the TBM itself. On October 5, the drillers sent a probe ahead one hundred meters, angling the drill up and to the right. The drillrod was pulled out, and

October 30, 1990: British tunnelers send a drill probe forward, searching for the French tunnel-boring machine.

the TBM then drove ahead, keeping track of the hole. "The first hole went out of the face and was lost after forty meters," Denman said. 'The second was lost as well. The third was just in the face at eighty meters. The fourth was just in the face at one hundred meters. And the fifth was the real probe."

He had done everything he could think of to make the probes accurate, even using the same drillers for all five holes to make them as alike as possible. But he knew that a wrinkle in the strata ahead, or a shudder in the drill frame, could nudge the probe entirely off course.

He drilled the hole. The Maxibor was shoved through, withdrawn and the digital contents of its electronic entrails were examined. It was sent forward again, to double-check the numbers. Denman then pulled the drillrod back ten meters and prepared to wait.

The British drill reaches the French TBM. The drill bit has been removed as a souvenir.

He had sent a British engineer over to the French machine. His name was Steve Cargo and his nickname was The Snail, because his gear was all marked "S. Cargo," which some linguist in the British camp had read aloud and translated. Denman and he were linked by telephone. When Brigitte was three meters from where the end of the hole was supposed to be, Denman, working on gut instinct and every calculation possible, drew a picture of where he thought the hole would appear in the rock face: in the upper right quadrant, about a third of the way in from the rim. He faxed the drawing to Cargo.

Brigitte drove to the point and stopped. Cargo said he couldn't see anything.

"Drive another foot," Denman said.

After a few minutes, Cargo came back on the line.

"I still can't see anything," he said. "But there's water coming through the face."

"I'll send the rod back," Denman said. It took another few minutes. It was getting toward 11 P.M., British time. "It should be coming through now," Denman said.

There was a pause.

"I've got it," Cargo said.

"Where was it?" Denman wanted to know.

"Just where it is on the picture," Cargo said. "Pull the rod back. We've taken off the bit."

England and France were linked.

2

The Dover Strait is one of the planet's younger bodies of water, although its precise age is impossible to tell and difficult to guess. Most theories agree that it formed about a half million years ago, when a huge glacial lake in the North Sea overflowed and broke through a chalk ridge that ran southeast from what is now Dover to Sangatte, nine kilometers down the coast from Calais.

The breakthrough created the original White Cliffs of Dover and Cap Blanc Nez. There is good evidence that the breakthrough was catastrophic; there is a great scar in the seabed, just south of the Channel Tunnel's path, that seems akin to a plunge-pool under a waterfall. Geologists call it the Fosse Dangeard; it is eighteen kilometers long, two kilometers wide and its deepest point is about 170 meters below the current level of the seabed. The rush of water widened the gap quite quickly and has continued to do so to this day, lengthening the distance between Dover's White Cliffs and their slightly less lofty French cousins at a rate that, over the ages, works out to nearly a meter every ten years.

Before the breakthrough, the land west of the ridge was a marshy tundra; streams snaked through it, joining and parting until they reached a deep single channel north of the Channel Islands. The sea occasionally encroached on this land, creeping slowly up and drowning the rivers over a few millennia, then receding at a similarly sedate pace. The breakthrough swamped the stream system and created, for a time at least, an English Channel that was a reasonable approximation of the one that exists today.

In the half million years since, it is likely that the Dover Strait has always had water flowing through it. For the first two hundred thousand years or so, it was seawater. Archeological evidence indicates that England was connected to the Continent during this time, and geologists think that a land bridge stretched from East Anglia to The Netherlands.

About a quarter of a million years ago, glaciers seem to have blocked the gap between Scotland and Norway, forcing the rivers of Northern Europe to find another outlet to the sea. The outlet was the Dover Strait and English Channel, and it is likely that the Rhine, the Thames and the Meuse all flowed through together, cutting a deep passage that remains as the Lobourg Channel, a sixty-meter-deep trough in the Channel bed. Shortly thereafter— say, 200,000 years or so—the first human beings probably made their way across to Britain. The sea invaded again when those glaciers melted, and this back-and-forth continued as glaciation waxed and waned. A borehole in the seabed six kilometers east-southeast of Dover produced a sample of peat that radiocarbon dating found to be 9,910 years old, plus or minus 120 years.

The peat lay thirty-six meters below current sea level. A thousand years or so after it was created in a bog on the margins of a narrow strait, the sea encroached again, leaving a last land connection, at least for a time, between Lincolnshire (north of the bulge of East Anglia) and The Netherlands. This was the last route by which travelers could walk (with perhaps a few stretches of wading or rafting) between Britain and the Continent. By about 8,300 years ago, full marine connection had been established between the English Channel and the North Sea. Britain has been an island since.

Youth shows clearly in the Strait's character: It displays a careless childish energy, pitting its strong tides against the winds that sweep between its bracketing cliffs (there are, on average, twenty-two gale-force storms a year), or running headlong with those winds, creating a confused, wicked, choppy sea. It is changeable, likely to turn from an easy amiability to a rough fury in minutes. This is a function of its shallowness; above the tunnel's course, it is nowhere deeper than seventy meters. If St. Paul's Cathedral were sunk in that uttermost depth not far from the French shore, the dome of that noble but not towering structure would rise above the wave like some rotund lighthouse. If the Eiffel Tower were sunk there, only the lower arches would be immersed.

While it is young in geologic terms, the Strait runs old and deep in human history. Richborough, now the site of a power station nineteen kilometers north of Dover, was the probable port of entry for several travelers who were to change the island's history: The Roman army that in fact subdued and occupied Britain—Julius Caesar's earlier trips across the Strait were little more than reconnaissances—is thought to have landed there in A.D. 43. Hengist and Horsa, who came (according to tradition) as invited allies and stayed as usurpers and conquerors, are said to have stepped ashore here in 477. In 597, St. Augustine landed at Richborough to begin his mission to Britain.

In 1168, Thomas à Becket tried to flee across the Strait to Rome, but contrary winds pinned him in Romney. Two years later, the four knights who came over from France to murder him in his cathedral landed at Hythe, four kilometers from what is now the Channel Tunnel terminal. The knights took the old Roman road up to Canterbury. The road still follows its ancient course, and one of the inns along its verge is named for a local smuggler, a notorious representative of a remarkable breed that flourished in the region well into the last century. Smuggling was so integral a part of the local economy that farmers struck a deal with the importers of contraband: The latter would let their helpers bring in the harvests, if the former neglected to lock their barns at night. This rough trade continued even during the times when England and France were at war.

The Strait was always a highway for war: The pivotal battle that decided the unhappy fate of the Armada began off the beach at Sangatte and swept up through the passage, whence the battered Spanish fleet commenced its disastrous attempt to reach home by sailing north around Scotland. The English captured Calais in 1347 and integrated it into their strategic thinking. *The Libell of Englyshe Polycye,* a book of naval strategy written in the middle of the fifteenth century by an Englishman (thought to have been Bishop Adam de Moleyns), said of Calais and Dover: "Keep these two towns sure to your majesty as your two eyes to keep the narrow sea. For if this sea be kept in time of war, who can here pass without danger and woe?" It was good advice; the British held onto Calais until 1553.

Shakespeare called it a moat, and while it didn't always preserve England from attack—the French burned Dover in 1295, doing so much damage that it took the town many years to recover—the image became rooted in the English mind. The water—and the line of castles, towers and bastions that stretched along its shore—was indeed a formidable barrier to would-be invaders. Napoleon, with one hundred thousand soldiers and a flotilla of more than two thousand ships assembled in Boulogne, said that six hours' mastery of the Channel would make him master of the world. He underestimated the task that faced him; his advisers thought that two weeks of absolute mastery—at an absolute minimum—might be time enough to prepare and launch an invasion, but neither nature nor the Royal Navy would allow it. After Dunkirk in 1940, Britain was defended from invasion by an army that had lost its arms, a Home Guard whose weapons included fowling pieces and souvenir spears from the days of Empire, a thin shield of fighter aircraft—and the Channel. The Wehrmacht looked across, paused, reconsidered.

Still, the Strait's chief importance, in wartime as in peace, was as a highway of commerce. Nature had not designed it with seafarers in mind—the tides ran swiftly, three knots and more; the bottom was strewn with sand ridges that rose uncomfortably close to the surface, it was entirely too narrow and the land on either side lacked safe harbors—but this did little to stanch the flow of vessels that passed through it. In 1966, a radar survey found that about 750 ships passed through the Strait each day. At times, because vessels like to pass through with a favorable tide, there would be as many as 120 ships in an hour.

This torrent of ships could choose between two channels, one on either side of the Varne Bank, a six-mile-long sandbar that divides the Strait like the center divider in a highway, and that rises to within 3.2 meters of the surface. Most preferred the English side, because the French side, though deeper, had a reputation for danger and was (perhaps as a consequence) less well marked. Dense fog filled the strait, on average, about one day in each fourteen, though in summer the incidence was often one day in five.

Modern radar, radio and navigation aids were not always equal to the task of regulating this flow, as events in early 1971 showed. On January 11, the tanker *Texaco Caribbean* collided with the Peruvian freighter *Paracas,* broke in two, blew up and sank in twenty-three meters of water near the Varne, taking nine of her crew. Before the next dawn, despite heroic efforts by the British lighthouse authority to mark the wreck and warn off other ships, the German freighter *Brandenburg* struck the tanker wreck and sank, with a loss of seventeen more lives. Although many more lights and buoys were strung about the wrecks, a Greek freighter struck one and sank on February 27. By

Tunnel-versus-bridge propaganda from the early 1960s.

Only a Tunnel can provide a dependable all-weather route between Britain and the Continent

this time, supertankers were an important part of Channel traffic. They traveled through the Strait, the big passenger ferries traveled across it; it was easy to imagine a nightmare scenario in which one collided with the other.

It was equally easy to imagine circumstances in which such a cataclysmic collision might have been welcomed aboard a ferry: The passage between France and England has a reputation, fully earned, for turning voyagers green with seasickness.

"We arrived in Dover on the 2nd [of January 1784] after a bad crossing," wrote François de la Rochefoucauld, a young French nobleman. "At Calais we had waited two days owing to the unfavorable weather and, when we made a start, we experienced one of the most violent sea-voyages possible. For twelve hours we were exposed to most disagreeable buffetings which

A 1904 French view of the Channel's horrors.

made me extremely ill during the whole period. Seasickness has an overwhelming quality; at every moment you think you are going to die and there is nothing that can bring you comfort. . . . One must indeed pay tribute to the sea—happy are they whom she spares."

The crossing was so dreadful that little seems to have been done to make it more comfortable. "Can anything be more barbarous and cruel than the arrangements which at present the public tolerate for crossing the 22 miles of sea between France and England?" wrote Mr. Felix Summerly to the *Times* in 1865. "If the day be wet—and throughout more than six months of the year this is the case—your feet are soaked through in descending the well-watered steps from Dover-pier to the steamer or across the pavement at Calais. When you arrive on board you have the choice between the cabin, detestably close and stinking, filled with human beings senselessly prostrate and sick, or the open deck, with the certainty of being soaked through by the rain and the spray."

Even the great suffered; Charles Dickens recalled the evil days when, after a comfortless night in a Folkestone lodging house, "At five in the morning you were blown out of bed, and after a dreary breakfast, with crumpled company, in the midst of confusion, were hustled on board a steam-boat and lay wretched on deck until you saw France lunging and surging at you with great vehemence over the bowsprit."

The fact that one could look across the Strait in good weather somehow made the sufferings less tolerable. It is thirty-three kilometers from Cap Gris Nez to the Dover harbor breakwater, a short enough distance for the British military authorities to have tried to barricade it with chain-anchored timber balks in early 1915. The conditions that made travel uncomfortable made this plan impossible.

Still, the narrowness of the Strait encouraged people to try to cross it in unusual ways. A French balloonist, assisted by an American scientist, crossed from Dover to Calais (and some distance beyond) in January 1785, a bit more than a year after the Montgolfier brothers made the first balloon ascent over Paris. Later that year, two Frenchmen were killed at Boulogne as they attempted a balloon flight in the other direction. The first recorded crossing by a swimmer dates to 1875. In 1909—less than three years after the first powered flight in Europe, a time when aviators sat on their machines rather than in them—Louis Blériot made his famous airplane crossing from what is now called Blériot-Plage, at the west end of Calais, to the grounds of Dover Castle. In 1979, an American pedaled a superlight aircraft across the Strait from Folkestone to the beach at Cap Gris Nez.

None of these venturesome means of travel promised much relief to the suffering everyday traveler, and while thousands gritted their teeth and made the voyage each year, few did not wish for some deliverance. These wishes flowed even before technology had anything to offer by way of answer; the sages of Amiens sponsored a competition to find a better way to cross the Channel in 1714. Nature seemed to invite some sort of a solution: The Strait was not very deep, after all, so a bridge might be able to stand in it, or a tunnel might pass beneath it. Indeed, events were to prove that the rock under the waters was peculiarly well-suited to those who preferred to think about a tunnel.

The water flowing through the Dover Strait cut through an ancient geological structure, the Weald-Artois anticline, like a knife through a many-layered cake. The anticline is a long oval hump that stretches across southern England and on into France. Its numberless layers of rock and sediment, laid down between 135 and 65 million years ago, were raised and distorted by the same geophysical events that formed the Alps. It is as if a many-layered cake had been set carelessly down on a loaf of French bread. If you slice away the top, as erosion has done to the rock over millions of years, the layers emerge as long ovals, with the lower ones—corresponding to the older layers of rock—in the center.

Dover's White Cliffs and Cap Blanc Nez are part of an oval that runs in a gentle arc toward London as the North Downs chain of hills, turns south and southeastward to form the South Downs and strikes the coast in the chalk headlands that stretch westward from Beachy Head. British geologists sort this thick bed into the Lower, Middle and Upper Chalks. The Upper and Middle Chalks are porous, and geologic movements have from time to time brought them to the surface, where weather cracked and damaged them. Water passes through them with great ease, making them unsuitable for a bored tunnel under the Channel.

But the Lower Chalk, deposited during a 6.5-million-year period that began about 97.5 million years ago, is different. It has a high clay content—as much as 40 percent—that gives it an overall gray color and, more to the point, seals it quite effectively against the passage of water. Near Dover the Lower Chalk is about eighty meters thick, but it thins to less than sixty-five meters near the French coast, where it also dips more sharply into the seabed.

Some of this gray chalk, nearer the bottom of the stack of layers, is particularly rich in clay, particularly water-resistant. This is called the chalk marl, and it has other wonderful qualities that are perhaps best appreciated by tunnelers. It is soft enough to cut with ease, but strong enough to stand without support. As one proponent of a Channel tunnel was to observe, "Providence has put in a continuous stratum of grey chalk underneath this Channel for the express purpose of our boring a tunnel through it."

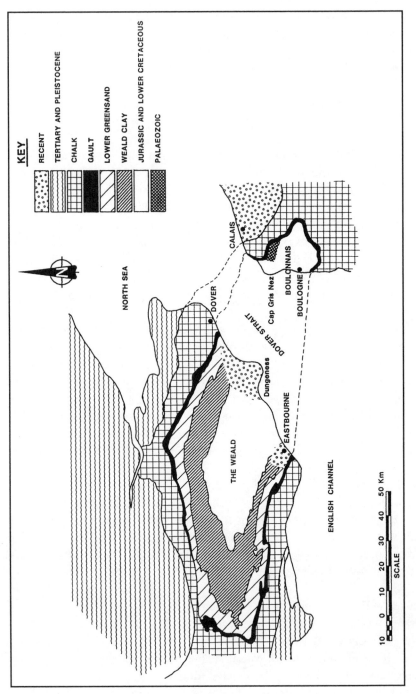

The geologic structure of the Straits of Dover.

Who first proposed—seriously proposed—a tunnel under this Channel? History accords the honor to a French engineer, Jacques-Joseph Mathieu, whose name is otherwise given as Albert Mathieu and Mathieu-Favier. Mathieu seems to have drawn plans for a double tunnel—one for horse-drawn traffic, with a parallel smaller tube, linked to the first by cross-passages, for ventilation—in 1802. A gutter was to carry any infiltrating water to pits at each end, whence it could be pumped to the surface. Mathieu submitted his plans to the minister of the interior, noting that it would seem impossible to persons who weren't accustomed to travel in the bowels of the earth. However, Mathieu had worked in coal mines that were more than three hundred meters deep, and the Channel was a mere sixty meters.

Mathieu's claim to this honor was extremely tenuous for a very long time. The drawings disappeared, and the plan was forgotten. For almost two centuries, the only evidence that remained was a rough and very inaccurate drawing of uncertain provenance, and the testimony of one man: Aimé Thomé de Gamond, a French engineer who himself lay claim to an important tunnel-related distinction: He was the first man to become so possessed by

An imagined French invasion of England by tunnel, sea, and air. Anonymous and undated, from about 1804.

the idea of a Channel link that he dedicated his life to creating one. And he was, inevitably, also the first—of many—to be used up, wrung out and ruined by that peculiar devotion.

Thomé—the "de Gamond" came from his marriage to a judge's daughter—was born in Poitiers in 1807, orphaned at sixteen and raised by an uncle whose revolutionary politics carried both into exile during the Bourbon restoration. He was therefore educated in Belgium and Holland. He began his life in engineering at a time of splendid optimism, when technology played Pegasus to every engineer's Bellerophon: One had but to mount the winged steed to conquer any problem or cross any chasm. Thomé was not the only engineer, surely, to have ignored the tale's ending, when Bellerophon tried to fly to join the gods on Olympus: Pegasus would not carry him thence, the gods resented his presumptuousness and he roamed the earth an accursed outcast. Thomé did not aspire to Olympus—although his thinking often was Olympian in scale—but his story came to much the same sad end.

By age thirty he had designed—by his account—no fewer than seven structures to link Britain and France: a tunnel in an immersed iron tube in 1834, another immersed tube the following year and five different bridges in the two years that followed. His imagination did not pause: In 1837 he proposed partially damming the Strait from each side and running an enormous steam ferry between the ends of these titanic breakwaters. In 1840, he proposed damming the Strait entirely from Shakespeare Cliff to Gris Nez, leaving three passages for ships.

These were really more dreams than plans—Thomé earned his living in mundane ways, including running a farm—and some had a decided sketchiness about them: One of his bridges was to have forty-meter-long spans between four hundred pilings set in the Channel bed. This works out to sixteen kilometers, about half the shortest distance between the two shores.

In 1851, Thomé later wrote, he began to study the Channel problem in earnest. The immediate result was an 1856 proposal for a tunnel from Eastware Point, about halfway between Folkestone and Dover, and Cap Gris Nez. The line connecting those endpoints passes over the north end of the Varne bank in mid-Channel, and here Thomé proposed building an artificial island, the Étoile de Varne. It was to have a port for ships on the surface and a railroad station at the foot of a large oval ventilation shaft. The station and the port would be connected by a spiral ramp in the shaft. The tunnel itself was to be circular in section, brick-lined, with two railroad tracks. Further ventilation would be via shafts running up through thirteen artificial islands strung across the Strait and adorned with lighthouses.

At the time, and on through the rest of the century, the idea of a fixed link between England and France was irresistible to dreamers and cranks. Their

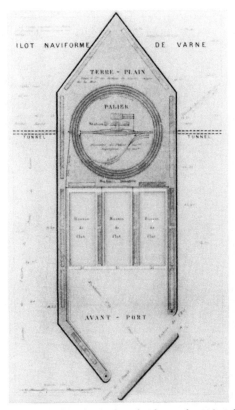

ILOT NAVIFORME DE VARNE

TERRE - PLAIN

PALIER

TUNNEL TUNNEL

AVANT - PORT

Thomé de Gamond's proposed mid-Channel artificial island.

proposals form a body of work that might interest psychologists as well as historians: bridges set in spun webs of steel tubes, tubes lying on the bottom of the sea or suspended between seabed and sea level, bare rails on the Channel bottom that would carry monster submarine locomotives, a dam whose top would be five hundred meters wide, large enough to accommodate a canal, several roadways and several railway lines—all this, plus scores of plans for bridges and tunnels that were conventional in design but delirious in scale and estimated cost.

This was the company that rational proponents of a link were forced to keep. At a century's distance, the thinkers and the dreamers tend to blur together in one mostly mad pack. And, truth to tell, a whiff of charlatanism hangs about Thomé. He tells tales, in his writings, that invite disbelief. For instance, he says that he made several dives in 1855 to the bottom of the Channel to collect rock samples. He made these descents naked except for a cloth band around his head and butter-soaked lint in his ears and nostrils, with a spoonful of olive oil in his mouth to keep water from forcing its way into his lungs, he says, with four 25-kilogram bags of stones to carry him down and a string of ten inflated pig bladders to whisk him back to the surface. On one dive, Thomé said, he was attacked and bitten on the chin by fish, which later observers think may have been conger eels. Pearl divers make such descents, but whether a forty-eight-year-old civil engineer could survive a plunge to thirty-three meters with such equipment—and whether conger eels would be there to greet him—is a matter of belief rather than proof.

Thomé did not restrict his schemes to the English Channel, but proposed similar crossings for the Irish Sea, the Strait of Gibraltar, the Strait of Messina between Italy and Sicily, the Dardanelles and the Bosporus, several of the bodies of water that isolated Copenhagen on its island and the Strait of Bonifacio between Sardinia and Corsica. There were multiple plans—three tunnels under the Irish Sea alone—and a certain carelessness of thought: The Gibraltar Strait is narrow but more than five hundred meters deep, so a tunnel with normal grades would surface nearly fifty kilometers inland.

It was therefore easy to think that his account of Mathieu's proposal might be an invention; researchers could find no evidence in any archives. Then, in 1993, the Université du littoral at Dunkerque acquired a single watercolored ink drawing: *Plans et coupes d'une communication souterraine entre Calais et Douvres par l'ingénieur des Mines J.J. Mathieu, 22 Frimaire an XII,* and Mathieu's place became much more firmly established.

Whatever the truth of his stories, Thomé did manage—eventually—to interest important people in his ideas, which he continued to spin with manic energy: A later version of his Étoile de Varne was to have a shaft three hundred meters in diameter, with a spiral track so that trains could ascend to exchange cargoes, at the surface, with ships that used the port. Queen Victoria is said to have given her blessing to his endeavor; he found English engineers of good reputation to join him in trying to get backing for his last design, which he brought forth in 1867. The idea was refined by his collaborators and seemed to be drawing near to reality—France liked the idea, and Britain did not object—when the Franco-Prussian War cruelly intervened. By the time France regained its feet, there were other plans vying for the approval of the governments. Over the next few years, Thomé was pushed aside. He died in 1876, worn out, destitute and pursued by creditors after spending 175,000 francs of his own money in pursuit of his dream.

One of the alterations that Thomé made to his later plans was to remove valves that would have made it possible to flood the tunnel. These were considered essential to calm British dread that a Channel tunnel would become a highway for an invading army. Thomé came to think that the British were no longer prey to such fears. He was entirely wrong, as Sir Edward Watkin was soon to discover.

Watkin, who was born to a well-to-do Manchester cotton merchant in 1819, was a man of many parts: an author, a host of literary soirees, a friend to Gladstone, a consultant who visited Canada at the British government's request to advise on forming the provinces into a dominion, a proponent of a shorter work week in factories. But before and above all he was a railroad man: He ran them. By 1866, he was chairman of two: the Manchester, Sheffield and Lincolnshire Railway and the South-Eastern Railway. In 1872 he became chairman of the London Metropolitan Railway. His ambition was to have a railroad that ran from England's north to Dover. Paris was an even more attractive goal, and as Thomé fell away, Watkin took his place as the most active advocate of a fixed Channel link.

Watkin knew railroads, politicians and money. He had the advice and help of good British engineers and—after a struggle with English competitors—the benefit of a solid French collaborator, the Société du chemin de fer sous-marin entre la france et l'angleterre, which had been organized in 1875. This had two million francs capital; a quarter of its four hundred shares were held by Rothschild Frères and twice that number by the Chemin de fer du nord, which the Rothschilds controlled. The Société was more advanced in its endeavors than anything on the English side: By 1876 it had taken thousands of soundings and seabed samples along the proposed tunnel route; by 1879, it was already at work on an access shaft at Sangatte. The Société also held a ninety-nine-year concession from the French government, which would go into effect in 1881 if by that time the company had an agreed English partner.

In 1880, Watkin sank a shaft at Abbots Cliff, near Shakespeare Cliff, and another at Shakespeare itself in early 1881. He soon had a very effective tunnel-boring machine hard at work, grinding away toward France. To clear the corporate air, still confused by the presence of a rival, the Channel Tunnel Company, he formed the Submarine Continental Railway Company in that same year, and in June told its shareholders that he expected to complete a pilot tunnel, seven feet in diameter, within five years. This would then be bored out to fourteen feet and fitted out to carry trains. Watkin's venture had the assent of the two governments—the British commitment was halfhearted, to be sure, but it was secure.

Watkin's confidence that he could finish a tunnel within five years made the British establishment uneasy. Thomé had claimed that Queen Victoria was in favor of a tunnel. Whatever the truth of that statement, the queen had, as early as 1875, let it be known that she did not now like the idea. In the same month that Watkin predicted success in five years, a *Times* editorial warned that the tunnel could be used to invade England—if not by France, then perhaps by Germany. If the tunnel were built, the *Times* said, "A design for the invasion of England and a general plan of the campaign will be subjects on which every cadet in a German military school will be invited to display his powers."

Watkin had proposed to the Board of Trade (the government department whose assent was needed for the tunnel works) that he build a mile of tunnel at his own expense, after which the government would participate in financing. He prepared a private bill for submission to Parliament that would allow him to buy land, build and operate a tunnel. In August 1881, the Board invited comment from the War Department, which set up a commission of inquiry, which invited testimony, which flowed in abundance.

The most important contribution came from Lieutenant-General Sir Garnet Wolseley, a well-known if slightly comic figure of the time: He was the model for the "model of a modern major-general" in Gilbert and Sullivan's *Pirates of Penzance*. Yet he was adjutant general of the British army, a veteran of the Crimean and several colonial wars. He was also entirely against the idea of a Channel tunnel. The *Times* had speculated that an enemy force could land on the beach, seize the tunnel mouth and quickly run a flood of troop trains through from the Continent. Wolseley suggested that the attack could come through the tunnel itself.

"A couple of thousand men might easily come through the tunnel in a train at night, avoiding all suspicion by being dressed as ordinary passengers, or passing at express speed through the tunnel with the blinds down, in their uniform and fully armed," Wolseley wrote in a memorandum to the commission, adding that 20,000 troops could follow in a dozen trains within four hours. Even a small band—say, 2,500 soldiers—"ably led by a daring, dashing young commander might, I feel, some dark night easily make themselves masters of the works at our end of the tunnel—and then England would be at the mercy of the invader."

These sentiments made Wolseley a still more comic figure to his age; he was shown in cartoons, in full-dress uniform, astride a terrified British lion, fleeing from a banty French cock that had emerged from a Channel tunnel. Derision did not diminish their effect, however. The attacks on the tunnel quickly spilled over into the press. A series of articles in the first half of 1882 in *The Nineteenth Century,* an influential monthly journal, was of particular importance in setting both official and public opinion against the tunnel. The chief antagonist here was a Navy man: Admiral Lord Dunsany, the grandfather of the literary Lord Dunsany.

The Nineteenth Century clearly did not discourage its contributors from writing at length, but even so, Lord Dunsany's exercises were unusually long.

Sir Garnet Wolseley flees the French cock astride the English lion. From the American humor magazine Puck.

His first broadside, in the February issue, ran to eight thousand words. The bulk of it purports to be a quotation from "a military officer occupying the highest position in the estimation and favor of the country." The officer (who is never identified) adopts the classic debating tactic of first stating his opponents' views in friendly fashion, the better to demolish them:

"Let us dispassionately discuss whether our pride in being an island is simply an affair of sentiment, or whether its roots stretch down to the strata where sound reasoning flourishes. Let me confess that it is difficult to do this, for does not the remembrance of the sufferings we have experienced in the Channel come vividly before us, and do we not contemplate with pleasurable anticipation the construction of a Channel tunnel which if made would save us from their recurrence whenever we again visit the Continent? The remembrance of the 'middle passage' to the African slave cannot be much more horrible than the idea of a Channel steamer is to the ordinary ease-loving Englishman. Let us confess therefore, at the outset, that we enter upon this discussion with a *prima facie* bias in favor of the scheme . . ."

The military man continued in this disarming way, noting that Wellington and other soldiers had long warned Britain against invasions that never came. "These soldier and sailor croakers have always been amongst us, and though we have never listened to them, Queen Victoria still rules over a free people."

Other nations didn't object to tunnels and bridges that crossed their borders, he noted, and the French did not worry that the British might use a tunnel to seize Calais.

He then moved to the attack, making most of the same points as Wolseley. Surely, he said, the prize was worth the gamble:

"Where in the world's history has there ever been such a reward, such a bait, as the possession of London, the conquest of England," he asked. "Four or five marches would enable [the enemy] to reach the Thames, and with the fall of London falls England, never to rise again." Even if the nation could be ransomed by the payment of huge sums, might not the conqueror insist on keeping Dover, and control of the tunnel, as a perpetual knife at England's throat?

Napoleon's ghost was summoned: Should his like ever rise to power in France, "is he likely to be restrained by conscientiousness or moral scruples from attempting to seize our end of the tunnel by a *coup de main* without any sign of warning whatever?" A civilized declaration of war, the writer thought, was too much to expect from such a scoundrel.

The article asked, rhetorically, why the great powers of Europe were "bowed down by the weight of military burdens," while England lived in safety and grew rich with a small army, no universal military service and no conscription.

"There can be but one answer: it is our 'silver streak.' A railway company now asks permission to make an easy way through that guardian girdle." Like Wolseley, he conjured the specter of a Britain exhausted by the financial burden of maintaining a huge standing army. Of course Paris was interested in the tunnel: It had an army of three quarters of a million trained men; England would need the same if a tunnel were built.

The next issue of *The Nineteenth Century* carried a reply from Col. Frederick E. Beaumont, Royal Engineers, whose interest in favor of the tunnel was well known: He had invented the tunnel-boring machine that was, at that moment, digging its way through the chalk marl under Shakespeare Cliff. Beaumont's machine was the progenitor of all modern tunnel-boring machines. It had a two-armed cutting head like an airplane propeller, rather than the full-face discs on later machines, and it held itself in place by gripping two beams set in the tunnel floor, but in other detail and overall principle, it was a model for all later TBMs. Beaumont had invented the machine in 1875, a year after a pneumatic rock drill of his design had performed marvels in a tunnel near Bristol, working three and a half times as fast as hand laborers.

Indeed, Beaumont's machine worked so well that it probably helped provoke the furious attacks by Dunsany, Wolseley and their legions: As an account in the *Illustrated London News* in March 1882 shows, the Submarine Continental Railway's project was well-planned, well-equipped and likely to succeed.

The *News* writer watched Beaumont's machine in action: Its cutting head made two or three revolutions a minute, each of which cut five sixteenths of an inch into the chalk—about an inch of progress per minute. Beaumont thought he could increase the revolutions to five per minute and cut three eighths of an inch per revolution, for a rate of two inches per minute. This worked out to an advance of six miles a year. A conveyor of buckets carried spoil to the back of the ten-meter-long machine, where it was dumped into wheeled skips, which carried it up to the surface. The compressed air that operated the machinery also provided fresh air to the tunnel.

Across the Channel, the French, too, were using a Beaumont-design machine, with comparable results. The effort in France prefigured the successful venture that was to follow in little more than a century. The French geologists recognized, from samples gathered from the Channel and test drillings on the shore near Sangatte, that the chalk marl lay rather deep beneath sea level, and that the white chalk above it was likely to leak unacceptable amounts of water into any tunnel sent through it.

They therefore sank a vertical shaft, 86 meters deep and 2.5 meters in diameter, near the beach just west of Sangatte. Work began in 1879 and took two years to complete, in part because the water problem was even worse than predicted. But finished it was, and the tunnelers soon built a 29-meter-long gallery at its foot. Another shaft, 5.4 meters in diameter, was sunk near the first to carry spoil to the surface.

The French Beaumont machine began work in the autumn of 1882 and made excellent progress; in some six-day weeks it carved more than a hundred meters of tunnel. If the British and French crews could maintain such rates, the tunnel might be finished in a few years.

The Beaumont tunnel-boring machine.

"THE ENGINEER"

. . .

Beaumont, for one, thought that it should be. It was true that he had a financial interest in the success—he and Thomas English (who had perfected and
actually built the boring machine) and a third partner had a contract to bore
a half mile of tunnel at a rate of at least two feet an hour, for which they would
be paid £2.10s per yard. But Beaumont also was an authority on the fortifica-
tions of Dover: He had, in fact, spent three years helping to design them. So
when he said that no new Napoleon could possibly seize the tunnel mouth,
his words carried some weight. They also carried some of the exasperation
that the tunnel's adherents felt. "I am really almost ashamed to have to argue
in such detail against a fear which is purely imaginary," Beaumont wrote.

If Wolseley and Dunsany wanted to wring their hands, Beaumont suggested they might better look across the Channel, to the great new harbor
works that France was building at Calais and Boulogne, which could shelter
a naval force—French or otherwise—that could truly menace England.

Beaumont's 3,500-word reply was swamped by the huge torrent of Dunsany's 9,000-word "rejoinder" in the same issue of *The Nineteenth Century*.
This time there were no debating tricks, no disarming banter: Readers were
treated to a purely isolationist tract in which Dunsany also noted that the
venture's shareholders came from all over the Continent and did not constitute a "patriotic body of Englishmen"—Englishmen who would presumably
not object if their asset were destroyed to thwart an enemy attack on Albion.

Two months later, *The Nineteenth Century* published a protest petition
against the tunnel, signed by about 250 men of substance and a few titled

An 1883 British antitunnel cartoon.

women. The signers included the Archbishop of York, five dukes, eleven earls, five viscounts, two bishops, a baroness and eleven barons, a Roman Catholic cardinal, eight lieutenant-generals, sixteen major-generals, six admirals, nine colonels and a small host of nobles and officers of lesser rank. The list also included Isaac George Bristow, president of the Barge-Builders' Trades Union, who thus became perhaps the first in a long line of maritime trade unionists to oppose a Channel tunnel.

The sole article in favor of the tunnel was headlined "A French Reply." The writer, Joseph Reinach, offered a witty and amused review of the controversy: "For us the Tunnel question is the question of the suppression of sea-sickness and of easier commercial intercourse," he wrote. "As to the military question, we should not have been conscious of its existence, had not Lord Dunsany given the sounding cry of alarm, had not Sir Garnet Wolseley honored it with his approval."

But Reinach did not hesitate to confront Dunsany on his xenophobia: "Will Lord Dunsany kindly allow us to put a question to him? What would he have said if a French Admiral had written as follows, in a French revue, respecting the Tunnel—'Be on your guard. England will make use of the Tunnel suddenly to invade France by surprise, without a preliminary declaration of war, on a dark night. She will take possession of Calais, where she will station her garrison. She will levy enormous indemnities. Perfidious Albion is as rapacious as perfidious.' "

Dunsany, he guessed, would have been properly shocked and offended. Reinach further shamed Dunsany by noting that any Frenchman who wrote so xenophobically would have been condemned by his own countrymen as "imprudent and frivolous, at the least."

British public opinion did not censure the opinions of its ruling estates, however, and Watkin was rebuffed by the authorities. He fought hard, used hard words and gentle hospitality—his dinners and tours in the tunnels were lavish and famous—but Wolseley and Dunsany's views prevailed. He was told not to drive his tunnel under Crown land. He nonetheless did so for a time, until the threats against him grew too harsh. The Beaumont machine was stopped on August 12, 1882, having dug 1,883 meters of tunnel. The French, baffled by such seeming folly, continued working for a few more months. Their machine halted on March 18 of the next year, having gone 1,669 meters.

One of the recipients of Watkin's subterranean hospitality was the Baron Frederick Emile d'Erlanger, head of an old banking family, head of the family's merchant bank and a board member of Watkins' enervated rival, the

Channel Tunnel Company. By 1886 the rival was dead, and the Submarine Continental Railway Company bought it and took over its more apt name. The new Channel Tunnel Company retained Baron d'Erlanger as a director. It also kept its mission, and Watkin tried again in 1887 to get a tunnel bill through Parliament, with the same result as before. Gladstone spoke out as a friend of the project, but yet another bill failed in 1888. Watkin gradually surrendered to the inevitable and looked away from the Channel Tunnel; like Thomé he had become interested in the possibility of a rail tunnel between Scotland and Ireland. He started work in 1889 on an iron tower at Wembley Park near London, which was to rival Eiffel's in Paris, but only one stage was completed, and that was torn down in 1907. By that time, Watkin was six years in his grave, and the Channel Tunnel's hopes had long since passed to d'Erlanger, as they had once passed to Watkin from Thomé.

Repeated defeats did not stanch the flow of new ideas for Channel links. The French and British tunnel companies continued to submit revised plans in the hope of silencing the military opposition; other venturers continued to pour forth a stream of new proposals, and the history that had begun a century earlier with Jacques-Joseph Mathieu grew ever more richly complex. But to understand this second century, one need look no further than the d'Erlanger family, which spent the energies of three generations on the idea and was repaid in disappointment.

A cycle developed that was interrupted only by larger calamities like the world wars: The Channel Tunnel Company would mount a campaign, secure some important support, strike down the arguments of its enemies—and then fail. It happened in 1906, when a new plan stirred the tunnel's old nemesis, *The Nineteenth Century*, now called *The Nineteenth Century and After* but still edited by the same man as in 1882, James Knowles. The journal reprinted the 1882 articles, and Knowles added his own view that the 1882 project had been "a scheme of private speculators and company-promoters" that common English sense had rejected.

Some prominent soldiers dismissed the idea that the tunnel was a security threat; one, Major-General Sir Alfred Turner, said that British military might was perfectly capable of turning back any attack through the tunnel. The idea that the French would attack Dover without declaring war, he said, was "too wild a hypothesis to be taken into serious consideration." Turner noted prophetically that the airplane, which had not yet shown itself capable of crossing the Channel, posed a far greater threat.

Nevertheless, Turner was ignored; the War Office opposed the project, and the Channel Tunnel Company withdrew its bills from Parliament in April 1907. Baron Frederick d'Erlanger died before another attempt could be mounted; his son, Baron Emile Beaumont d'Erlanger, succeeded him as

Two 1905 views of possible Channel crossings.

chairman of the Channel Tunnel Company in 1911. His tenure was marked by early success: The Channel Tunnel found important champions in the popular press and in Parliament, where Arthur Fell, a Conservative member, founded the Committee of the Members of the House of Commons in Favour of the Construction of a Channel Tunnel connecting England and France. Fell had more than eighty members behind him, and a reworked version of the 1907 proposal was set forth for government scrutiny. This time, the promoters made good progress in getting the public to grasp the tunnel's commercial benefits; the British Chamber of Commerce declared its support in September 1913. Nine months later, the government's Committee of Imperial Defence recommended against the tunnel. War broke out the following month.

The war was of particular assistance to the tunnel. Military men and strategists did not enjoy being derided for defending the silly fears of an earlier generation. "For my own part," one said, "I have never felt more humiliated than when I have had to meet the amused and contemptuous criticism of French military men on this subject."

During the war, military of several nations concluded that a tunnel would have aided the Allied effort in the conflict—a conflict that Britain entered, after initial reluctance, when Belgium was invaded and the other side of the Dover Strait and the Channel seemed likely to fall into unfriendly hands. The tunnel would have debouched just at the edge of Flanders's fatal fields. Marshal Foch said he thought a tunnel would have either prevented the war or brought victory to the Allies by 1916. German authorities held the same view; a war aim was to secure northern France "because the Channel Tunnel uniting Britain and France would be a danger to Germany."

Even the Committee of Imperial Defence acknowledged, during the war, that a tunnel would have been a good thing. But the insights of the war did not long endure, and though Fell and d'Erlanger continued to push for the tunnel, nothing happened. In 1922, Fell handed over the Channel Tunnel committee to Sir William Bull, who liked to compare himself to a bulldog. Few found reason to argue with the image; he and d'Erlanger fought hard and long through the rest of the postwar decade. In 1924, the Imperial Defence committee again doomed a tunnel by opposing it.

Why did d'Erlanger and Fell and Bull, and their faithful but battered legions, continue the fight? There was not much hope of political gain for the likes of Fell and Bull, nor financial gain for the promoters—d'Erlanger at one point offered to turn over his family's entire holding in the Channel Tunnel Company to the government, out of "patriotic motives" and the wish to make his "pleading on behalf of the numerous small shareholders who have stood true to this great project . . . more eloquent." In a speech to the Franco-

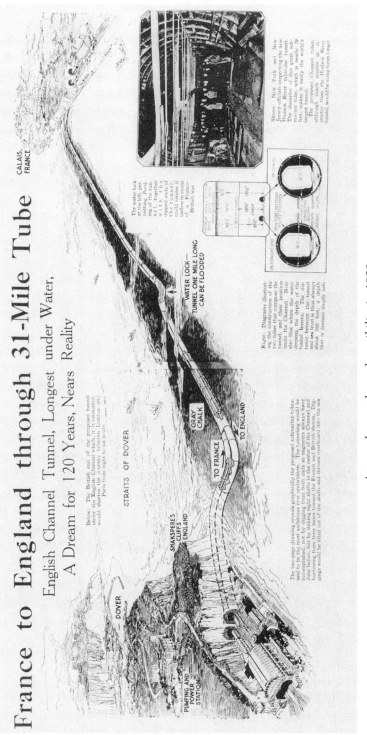

A tunnel seemed a real possibility in 1923.

British Travel Congress, he said, "Our aim is much higher than any possible monetary gain. The principal motive which inspires us is to indelibly engrave our names upon a page in the history of the civilization of the world."

And so, as the 1920s drew toward a close, Bull and d'Erlanger once more took the field. To stir support, d'Erlanger took a paid advertisement in the *Times,* noting that only two bodies had it in their power to bring about construction of a tunnel: Parliament and the press, and the former would not move until urged by the latter.

There was interest in the press, but there was an unfortunate blunder in the campaign for public support: Several newspapers and magazines took approving note of a new, serious book that proposed a direct, high-speed rail line between Paris and London, via a tunnel. Electric trains traveling at up to 120 miles per hour, the book said, would make the trip in less than three hours. The author (who was, in fact, proposing a one-track tunnel of his own) said the whole project, with new dedicated rail the whole distance, would cost £189,000,000, with the tunnel accounting for £31,000,000 of that. But the larger figure became associated with the tunnel alone, and opponents used it to attack the Channel Tunnel Company plan.

Despite such setbacks, the effort seemed to be going well. A model of the proposed Channel Tunnel drew favorable comment when it went on display in Selfridge's store on Oxford Street in January 1929. In that same month, Bull wrote to d'Erlanger, "We are going to offer a reward for the best article showing how the British end of the tunnel can be seized by force or treachery. There is nothing like getting down to the weak points of a case." Days later, the *Army, Navy & Air Force Gazette* came out solidly for the Channel Tunnel, and Lloyd's of London offered to discuss any insurance the Channel Tunnel Company might require.

The company began to receive requests for employment in the tunnel. One man wrote on his son's behalf, listing his six-foot, two-inch height as evidence of his merit and qualifications, to which d'Erlanger replied, "Your son has been placed on the list of those asking for employment when the Channel Tunnel is built, when I feel sure that the fact that he stands 6'2" will be taken into due consideration." A Mr. Bowen wrote to d'Erlanger, citing their youth together at Christ's College, Cambridge, as a preamble to asking for a job: "I think we were in the same year. I played for the College Rugby, but I think your long suit was tennis." D'Erlanger let a secretary reply that "Baron d'Erlanger was not educated at Cambridge."

Bull's committee invited comment on the tunnel from the British tourist trade and found a deep well of self-doubt in the soul of the English hotelier.

"I have often been told, especially by older people, that if it weren't for the crossing they would certainly spend their summers abroad," one wrote back, adding that a tunnel "would sound the death knell to the British Tourist trade . . . as it is the unpleasantness of the crossing which acts as the greatest deterrent to the majority of the people spending their vacations abroad."

J. J. Hewlett, manager of The Palace Hotel in Buxton, was similarly apprehensive: "In particular British Spas would suffer permanently. The combination of a Cure with the interests and experience of a visit to another country will appeal to many who have been so long deterred from going abroad by apprehensions of the discomforts of a sea trip, and the attraction will not be merely one of novelty, for Continental Spas, unlike our own, are centres of fashionable society and undoubted gaiety."

Some older and less commercial fears surfaced in the survey: One respondent worried that foot-and-mouth disease and "undesirable aliens" would invade England. "With our glorious traditions of the sea, it would not look well for Britons to enter the Continent by a rat-hole," he added. "I think its construction would be a calamity."

But feeling, both popular and official, was beginning to turn in favor of a tunnel. Bull polled both houses of Parliament and found majorities in support of the idea: fifty-five votes in Lords, sixty-nine in Commons. He was able to get the government to appoint a Royal Commission to study the tunnel; its finding would survive any change of administration. In October 1929, he wrote to d'Erlanger, "I think it is a question of now or never. I am positively certain that sooner or later the tunnel will be built, but I want, if possible, to see it started in my lifetime."

The Royal Commission examined every sort of fixed link from every angle: legal, financial, geologic, safety and general plausibility. Everything pointed toward the Channel Tunnel Company design, which had evolved into a double tube, each eighteen feet, six inches in diameter. Each would have a single rail line and would be linked to the other by cross-passages. There also would be a smaller drainage tunnel off to one side and lower than the others.

The commission's report, which went to the government in early 1930, was generally in favor of the tunnel. The government, however, seemed of a mind to disagree. Before the tunnel plan could be sent to its certain death before the Imperial Defence committee, one of the tunnel's adherents in Commons offered a motion that would have expressed the House's opinion that "every facility should be given for the project to be undertaken at the earliest possible opportunity." The government threw its weight behind the contrary view and prevailed, but just: The vote went 179 to 172 against the motion.

Both Bull and d'Erlanger professed to be pleased: The former said the narrow defeat was "enormously encouraging" because it showed that public support was swinging strongly toward a tunnel. The Baron's response was, "Alike to advocates and opponents of the tunnel scheme I say it cannot be killed—it can only be retarded. Sooner or later it will pass from conception into realization."

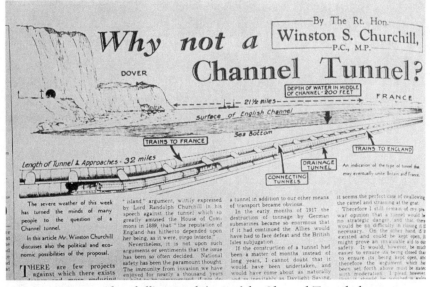

Winston Churchill's 1936 defense of the Channel Tunnel idea.

In private, though, both men were grievously disappointed. "I ought by now to have become inured to disappointment in connection with the Channel Tunnel," d'Erlanger wrote to Bull. "But I must confess that I had hardly expected so decisive a reverse, and I cannot but feel somewhat overwhelmed at what I can only regard as the final dissolution of the hopes and ambitions of a lifetime."

Bull replied the next day. "Let us both carry on the torch as long as we can and then, if we don't reach the goal in our lifetimes, we will hand it undimmed to our successors," he wrote. "I am as certain as I sit here that one day the tunnel will be made." Bull took this belief to his grave seven months later.

The tide that had run strongly for the tunnel since the end of the war now turned against it. The depression took hold. Car-ferry service started between Dover and Calais. Fell died in 1935. Baron d'Erlanger died in 1939. Late in that same year, the French Chamber of Deputies passed a resolution urging construction of a Channel tunnel; Neville Chamberlain—whose father, as president of the Board of Trade, had ordered Watkin to stop work in 1882—rejected the demand. In 1940, the Channel Tunnel Company's offices near London Bridge were destroyed in the Blitz with the loss of many of its records.

The d'Erlanger family's painful association with the tunnel did not end with the Baron's death; his nephew, Leo d'Erlanger, took his chair. He was an interesting man, well-liked and accomplished. The family's many connections and contacts were in him made flesh: His father was half-German, half-American and—having been judged too delicate to enter the hurly-burly of the family's banking business—an artist, author and architect of considerable accomplishments. Leo's mother was Italian, the daughter of Pope Leo XIII's chamberlain; the Pope was Leo's namesake and godfather.

Leo was the first of the family to be born in England. He went to Eton and Sandhurst, served in the Great War, where he suffered shell shock from which he slowly recovered. The tunnel was not his first and far from his only pursuit: His principal efforts went into aviation, where he and a partner formed the company that eventually became British Airways.

"I was brought up in a home where the Channel tunnel was a religion," he told an interviewer. "My grandfather used to talk about it when I came back for the holidays from Eton. 'Politics,' they all used to say. 'The only reason why the tunnel isn't built is politics.' I never paid much attention. I thought it was an old dodo and never had anything to do with it in my uncle Emile's lifetime."

He nonetheless honored the family tradition and took up the affairs of the Channel Tunnel Company. The Second World War pushed the idea of a tunnel so far into the background that it seemed in danger of fading even from memory. In 1947, the company's annual meeting lasted just one minute, during which one director suggested "that we wind up this whole joke." D'Erlanger talked him out of it. The annual meetings were held at the Charing Cross Hotel; there were times when it was difficult to get a quorum.

By the mid-1950s, military objections to the tunnel no longer existed. Ironically, the very machines that demolished these objections—airplanes

A lively 1949 Italian conception of a Channel Tunnel.

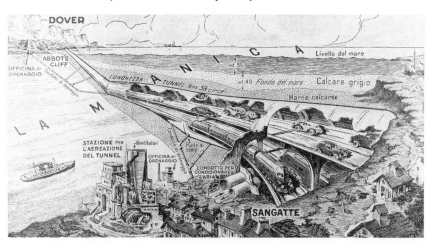

and rockets—now dominated most thinking about transportation. The Channel Tunnel that the Victorians had rejected as a technological threat to the nation now seemed sadly old-fashioned.

At least that was the view from shore. From the deck of a storm-tossed Channel ferry, things looked quite different. And so it was that the Channel Tunnel found yet another champion.

3

Istory likes a good story as much as any of us, and so it is that two French heiresses, Izaline and Henriette Doll, have become (in most tellings) the muses whose inspiration was almost sufficient to create a Channel tunnel.

Who would not be charmed by the tale: the lovely young sisters, on vacation in 1956, caught in mid-Channel by a brutal storm, tossed for hours on dangerous waves, rendered green as the seas that broke over their frail vessel. The twice-tasted breakfast, the safe landing, the welcoming arms of their rich and powerful husbands, the recounted horrors—and the teasing suggestion that those husbands ought to *do something* about the horrid crossing. Why not tunnel beneath all that disorder and discomfort on the surface?

Why not, indeed? Izaline's husband was Frank Davidson, a New York attorney, a Harvard-trained specialist in international law with an office on Fifth Avenue. Henriette's was Count Arnaud de Vitry D'Avaucourt, a brilliant graduate of the École polytechnique and Harvard Business School, the bearer of an advanced engineering degree from MIT and an ancient title in France. A few phone calls to well-placed contacts, a few meetings over drinks in clubs, and Technical Studies was born, with the House of Morgan and Dillon Read as its financial godfathers. Not many months later, Technical Studies produced a set of plans for a tunnel and, in time, came within an ace of actually building it.

The story of the two seasick wives, which is in most histories of the Channel Tunnel, is about half true, but the real story is rather more interesting than the fable: It leads, after many tortuous twists over nearly four decades, to the tunnel that exists today.

There *was* an unpleasant voyage, but Henriette did not share its discomforts. "We were staying at Blonville-sur-mer, a *plage de famille* on the Norman coast, and I had some law business in London," Davidson recalled. He and Izaline had two sons, the youngest only a few months old. "Izaline said, 'Well, I don't think you need to go by yourself; we can come along.' Unfortunately, there was an uncharted storm, and the ferryboat from Boulogne to Folkestone, instead of taking two and a half hours to make the crossing, took more than seven hours. This involved perhaps some risk to the baby, whom my wife was clutching for dear life."

A few months afterward, Davidson had lunch at Lüchow's in New York with Cyril Means Jr., a college friend, a former law professor at Stanford University who had gone on to become arbitration director of the New York Stock Exchange. Davidson told the tale of the dreadful voyage.

"The damned ship lurched and slithered, eh?" said Means, quoting Rupert Brooke's recollection in verse of the Channel's horrors. Davidson agreed that it had, for seven hours and more. And yes, Izaline had said *something* about not going back across the Channel if there wasn't a better way to travel. In fact, they made the return crossing by airplane, ran into another storm and ended up taking one of the boys to a doctor for treatment of a consequent earache.

The lunch table talk edged into speculation about whether a tunnel was possible. "Both of us recalled having read, as children of about twelve, an article in *Popular Mechanics* magazine about the attempt to build a tunnel in the 19th century," Davidson said. "We decided it was interesting enough to look up."

If one searches for the moment and place when the Channel Tunnel was conceived and took form, none has a better claim than this. Means and Davidson did not have quite as much wealth and power as certain British and French tunnel enthusiasts were soon to credit them. They were not without resources, however. They had good credentials, intelligence, ambitions and contacts. They were both in their late thirties—old enough to have some standing in the world, young enough to be unabashed by a task that more senior minds found daunting and dangerous. If they tried to build a Channel tunnel and failed, Means and Davidson—and de Vitry, too, for he soon joined the plot—would be more admired for their nerve than blamed for failing.

The three added a fourth member, Davidson's older brother Alfred. It was an interesting group; the members complemented each other quite nicely. Means was brilliant, affable, tireless, confident, a good judge of both enemies and friends, somewhat larger than life, a bon vivant with a talent for persuasion. De Vitry was very young, only thirty at the time, but he had graduated with high honors from the best schools that the United States and France could offer. Birth had given him rank as a member of France's old nobility; training had made him a *polytechnicien,* a member of the new nobility.

The Davidson brothers were Harvard-trained lawyer sons of a lawyer father, Maurice Davidson, whose activities in reform politics (he had helped launch the City Fusion Party, which had made Fiorello La Guardia mayor of New York City) had brought him friendship with, and the respect of, some quite powerful people. The brothers were seven years apart in age and quite different in manner and outlook. Alfred was hardheaded and practical; Frank was a visionary with a fondness for grand undertakings. They shared a certain can-do attitude, an ability to identify goals and move resolutely toward them. While he was still studying law at Harvard, Alfred wrote (and on occasion delivered) radio speeches for his father. Alfred later landed in the Roosevelt White House; when war broke out in Europe he helped draft the Selective Service legislation and worked in the Lend-Lease Administration. After Pearl Harbor, he was Roosevelt's liaison with Congress on the conduct of the war.

When Means and Frank Davidson launched the tunnel project over lunch, Al suggested recruiting a colleague from Lend-Lease: George Ball, whose longtime and continuing contact with government would shortly take him into the Kennedy Administration as undersecretary of state and, later, to the United Nations as the U.S. delegate thereto. Ball had superb contacts with the French—indeed, France had awarded him its Legion of Honor. He also had worked for Jean Monnet, the architect of France's postwar recovery, "the father of the Common Market," whose vision of a peaceful and united Europe had made him a secular saint of the period.

Frank Davidson graduated from Harvard in the difficult year of 1939. As the United States went to war, his father urged him to enroll in Harvard Law School. Davidson instead enlisted in the Canadian Army, became an officer and went ashore in Normandy two weeks after D-Day. During the fighting, Davidson passed within a kilometer of a chateau at St-Ouen-le-Pin that had been the birthplace of Izaline Doll, then a refugee in the United States, who would one day nudge him toward the project that would involve him for the rest of his life.

Davidson went dutifully to Harvard Law after the war and later worked as a lawyer in Houston for a time. There he met George Root, whose heavy construction company, Brown & Root, had invested heavily in the political career of Lyndon Johnson. Davidson thereafter returned to Cambridge, where he met Izaline. When the Doll family returned to France, Davidson wangled a job in the American embassy in Paris under Horace G. Reed, the counselor of embassy. "When Mr. Reed needed information in depth about anyone in France, he would send me around the corner to Mr. Dean Jay, who was head of the office of J. P. Morgan in Paris," Davidson said.

So when Davidson returned to set up his law practice in New York, he was a man who had seen some of the world and had met a number of the people who materially assisted in its operation. Undertaking to build a Channel tunnel therefore was not, for him and his circle, the fool's errand it might have seemed.

Means and Frank Davidson went to work quickly and in earnest. Davidson's first act was to contact George Brown, who knew as much as anyone about big public works projects. Brown took Davidson to lunch at the Pinnacle Club atop the Mobil Building in Manhattan and there gave him some very practical advice: Get some money or at least the promise of financial backing. Davidson took himself to the House of Morgan, the temple of commerce at the corner of Broad and Wall, whose influence was far greater than its modest size might have suggested. He went to see Dean Jay, who by then was back from Paris and preparing to retire. Davidson was looking for advice. Jay instead offered him an introduction to Thomas Lamont.

On Wall Street, Thomas Stilwell Lamont was called "Young Tom" to distinguish him from his father, Thomas William Lamont, who was an original partner of *the* J. P. Morgan and one of the men who had assumed command of the House of Morgan as the founder retired in stages after the Panic of 1907. Young Tom had followed his father into the business and into the world of investment.

At the time, the Morgan bank, like several of its august neighbors, still had its Partners' Room. Davidson's impression, as Jay ushered him in, was of a long, narrow space. "The first thing I saw were rolltop desks," he recalled. "There must have been a half-dozen or so of them in two rows, all facing a full-length oil portrait of J. P. Morgan on the far wall. The painting was over a fireplace, in which there was a log fire." Whatever warmth the fire brought to the room was offset by Morgan's chilling gaze. Once, when he presided in life, the men at the rolltop desks served solely at his pleasure; he could fire any of them at will. Now only his portrait oversaw the operations, but it captured the man's ferocity to a remarkable degree. A quarter of Morgan's face was in darkness; the eyes glinted in the shadows that pooled under the brows.

The partners who sat at the rolltops could, if they wished, escape from the founder's gaze and meet visitors in private rooms. But ordinary business was, by tradition, conducted in the Partner's Room, and Davidson's business did not require privacy. He accordingly took his seat next to Lamont's desk and explained his idea.

"Mr. Lamont turned across the aisle where, behind another rolltop desk, a man named Henry Alexander was reading a copy of *The New York Times*," Davidson recalled. Henry Clay Alexander was the son of a Murfreesboro, Tennessee, grain merchant. He had gone to work for J. P. Morgan Jr. as a young lawyer and had represented the House of Morgan well during the Congressional investigations of the 1930s. Alexander had become president of the bank in 1950 and its chairman in 1955.

"Henry," Lamont said, "this young man wants to build a tunnel between England and France. Do you think we should help him?"

Davidson recalled Alexander putting down his newspaper and turning to look him over. "After a few moments, Mr. Alexander said, 'Well, Tom, why not?' That was the only deliberation that the bank took before agreeing to back us."

Lamont visited Davidson's office a few days later—perhaps to make sure it existed—and offered to invest some of his own money in the venture. "Would twenty-five thousand dollars be all right?" he asked.

Davidson didn't hesitate to accept. "He took out his checkbook and wrote out a check for the amount," he said. "It was more than the company had at that time."

Lamont subsequently pointed out, in a meeting under the fixed gaze of Morgan's portrait, that federal law prevented banks, even J. P. Morgan's bank, from taking an equity position in such ventures. He asked if Davidson knew any investment bankers. Davidson did not.

"He said to me, 'Well, would you mind walking one block down the street to meet one?' " Davidson said. "He dialed a few numbers—he always made his calls himself—and said 'Henry, I'd like you to see a young man here who has a project I think you'd be interested in.' So I walked down and there was the chief owner and senior partner of Morgan Stanley, Henry Morgan."

Lamont also sent Davidson along to see the top people at Dillon Read, explaining, "I wouldn't want it to be thought that I was hogging all the business." Without Lamont's introduction, Davidson said, he never would have been able to approach the men who backed his plan.

In January 1957, Means took these promises of financing to Europe. He found a warm welcome in the very halls in which the Channel Tunnel had been so often condemned and doomed: the House of Commons.

Among Means's first contacts was Commander Christopher Powell, the aged secretary of the long-dormant Parliamentary Channel Tunnel Committee. Powell's job was to promote the tunnel—"to put together facts, figures and lunches," as Alfred Davidson summed it up—and he had had little enough to do for years. He therefore welcomed the brash young American who appeared in his office brandishing the names of some of the New World's most powerful financial institutions. Powell immediately set Means up to speak to the committee over dinner in the House of Commons dining room on February 28. The speech struck with such effect that within days the committee and Means approached a consulting engineer, Brian H. Colquhon, to commission a study of the project's history and prospects.

Colquhon was something of an outsider in London, Frank Davidson said. At that time, the inner circle of established British engineering firms was

Frank Davidson, left, *and Cyril Means.*

known collectively as "Victoria Street," since they all had offices on that thoroughfare between Parliament Square and Victoria Station. The fact that Colquhon's office was on Upper Grosvenor Street was notice enough that he hadn't yet broken into the ranks. His firm did a lot of work in Africa and had consulted on some tunnel projects. "The other firms wouldn't touch this," Davidson said. The engineer agreed to have a report ready in about four weeks, and he was as good as his word. It ran more than sixty pages and covered a great deal of familiar ground: There was a long section on history, there were remarks about the need for traffic and economic and cost studies to examine the financial viability of a tunnel, there was the scarcely needed caution that "of prime importance are the political considerations in England and France."

The biggest problem and source of danger, Colquhon found, was the dearth of geological information. "We have collated all the geological information, relating to this area, that is generally available," the report said. "Knowledge of the strata between the coasts is almost entirely conjectural."

Means received a distinctly chilly reception from Leo d'Erlanger, who presumably harbored proprietary feelings about the idea of a Channel tunnel and upon whose toes Technical Studies seems to have stepped. D'Erlanger had just contacted the Suez Canal Company in France to see if it was interested in participating in a Channel tunnel project. At about the same moment, Means and Davidson had written to the old Société concessionnaire du chemin de fer sous-marin entre la france et l'angleterre, not realizing that this had become a charge of the Suez Canal Company. Means's letter thus ended up on the spacious desk of Jacques M. C. Georges-Picot, the canal company's president and director-general. D'Erlanger was not pleased.

Recent events had made Georges-Picot receptive to suggestions that the Suez company might wish to broaden its business base. Its single major asset, the canal itself, had been seized by Egypt's General Gamal Abdel Nasser, and a Franco-British invasion had failed to retake it. Even if Nasser could be persuaded to ignore the invasion and restore the canal, the ninety-nine-year concession was due to expire in 1968. Georges-Picot had already put the idea of a Channel tunnel before his board of directors. The response to this was positive from all but the four Britons among the twelve members, who represented the shares held by the British government since 1875, when Disraeli had alertly bought them from the khedive of Egypt.

Georges-Picot replied politely to Means's letter and sent a representative to Davidson's office on an inspection visit. This took Means and Davidson by surprise. They did not, at that moment, have a letterhead. Indeed, they had not yet incorporated Technical Studies.

Their letter writing found another powerful French backer in Louis Armand, the head of SNCF, the French national railways company. Armand was a hero of postwar France; he had rebuilt his nation's war-ruined railway network, turning it into the most modern and efficient system on the continent. (But one that still, endearingly, paid for the meat with which the tenders of lonely grade crossings fed their companion cats.) He was a *polytechnicien,* an architect and pioneer of France's postwar resurgence, a national figure.

Armand liked Americans, apparently because he appreciated their war effort: He had played a key role in the actions of the *Résistance* on the railroads during the war and had narrowly escaped being shot by the Gestapo in the weeks after D-Day. "You could not say anything negative—even about the worst American crook—in Armand's presence," Frank Davidson said. "When we arrived—the brash Americans—he welcomed us and treated us as friends and defended us when necessary."

With those backers, things moved rapidly. On May 6, 1957, at the seventy-sixth annual meeting of the Channel Tunnel Company, d'Erlanger announced an agreement with the Suez Canal Company to once more attempt to breach Britain's watery barrier. By this time, d'Erlanger had come to accept American assistance: His announcement noted that the project now would have "the advantage of American finance and technical resources."

On July 26, 1957, a scant year after the Davidsons had endured their seven hours of mid-Channel purgatory, Technical Studies signed a Protocol of Agreement establishing the Channel Tunnel Study Group. D'Erlanger's Channel Tunnel Company held a 30 percent interest, as did the Suez Canal Company (by then an investment company, La Compagnie financière de suez) and a French group comprising the Société concessionnaire and La fédération routière. Technical Studies had 10 percent; the members agreed that "other North American participants" might be offered a 15 percent share, to be assembled by deductions from the other venturers. The partners agreed to put up £300,000 for initial studies.

Much of this was to go for geological studies of the Channel seabed, and Lamont cannily arranged to barter the information. At a meeting in Frank Davidson's office, he told his coventurers that he thought they should speak to some engineers about the project. Would Davidson host a lunch? Davidson, who had just joined the Harvard Club, agreed to stand for a meal and offered Lamont the use of his telephone.

"He made three calls," Davidson said. "The first was to Stephen Bechtel, the head of the Bechtel Corporation. He said, 'Steve, this is Tom Lamont. I want you to drop everything else and fly to New York and meet a young friend of mine who's involved in an important project. He needs your help and advice.'

"He then repeated the conversation with George Brown at Brown & Root and with Jack Bonny, the head of Morrison Knudsen in Boise, Idaho. At the time, I believe these were the three largest American construction companies. And the three men came, and we made a deal right then and there over lunch."

The construction companies agreed to design a tunnel and calculate how much it would cost to build. In return, they'd have full access to all geological information that the Study Group assembled—information that would help them a great deal in preparing a bid to build the tunnel.

There were only a few questions. Lamont asked the engineers, over the lunch table, if the tunnel could be built.

Brown noted that his company had just finished the Roberts Tunnel across the Great Divide to bring water to Denver. That was twenty miles long; Brown asked the distance across the Straits of Dover.

"A little over twenty-one miles," Davidson said.

"Well, I think we could do that," Brown said.

The Study Group was able to appoint as cochairmen two men who had just stepped down as permanent heads of their respective Foreign Offices: René Lucien Daniel Massigli, secretary-general at the Quai D'Orsay and former French ambassador to Britain, and Sir Ivone Augustine Kirkpatrick, a distinguished diplomat who had been the United Kingdom's high commissioner for Germany and was the permanent undersecretary in the Foreign Office. The group's technical operatives were René Malcor, France's former chief engineer of the port of Marseilles, whose name Armand put forward, and Harold B. J. Harding, vice president of the Institution of Civil Engineers.

The Study Group, thanks to history, comprised an unusually rich mix of shareholder-participants. The British government was represented, directly through the government's shares in the Suez Canal Company and indirectly through the nationalized British railways, which held about 26 percent of the Channel Tunnel Company's shares. The House of Rothschild in Paris owned a quarter of the Société concessionnaire, and the SNCF owned half.

The British government's representative in the Suez Canal Company was William Edward, the Second Viscount Harcourt. Lord Harcourt was to become cochairman of the Study Group in 1964 after Sir Ivone's death, but his later contributions to the Channel Tunnel came in part from an accident of birth that gave him strong American connections. He was J. P. Morgan's grandnephew and, in consequence, an officer of the merchant banking house of Morgan Grenfell, which over the next several decades would help create the Channel link. When at last a contract was signed to begin work on a tunnel, after many difficult days that then lay in the future, Lord Harcourt would be the one to sign it.

For the moment, though, there was much more basic work that needed doing. As Colquhon had discovered, there was a great deal of information available about the economics of a Channel link, but most of it was antique and unreliable. In the earliest days of Means's and Davidson's efforts, George Ball introduced them to Walter Headon, the chief economist of the Port of New York Authority, who produced a quick but professional assessment that found economic promise in the venture.

This was fine for lunch table talk but too thin to support real investment; more and deeper study was required. "We needed a professional assessment of the traffic and revenue prospects," Davidson said. "It was important to have the matter studied by firms trusted by the banks." Technical Studies found De Leuw Cather, a Chicago consulting firm that had been a pioneer in such studies. De Leuw in turn recommended that the French studies be done by SETEC—Société d'études techniques et économiques—that had been founded by De Leuw Cather alumni. Both companies went to work in 1958; they were to remain with the project, in one capacity or another, for more than thirty years.

Geological studies got under way, too. Some of the work was conventional; a drill rig came in during the summer of 1958 and bored holes in the Channel bed; the cores were taken ashore for study. Other holes were drilled on each shore, and these were used for seismic studies with explosives. The following spring, the Study Group began a series of sonar explorations of the seabed strata. Malcor summed up what the group had to know: "Did the grey chalk run in an unbroken layer from one side of the Channel to the other? How far was it folded and faulted? Were there valleys or gravel-filled pockets cutting into it which a tunneler would have to avoid? What was the dip of the chalk in this area?"

One great worry was that the tunnel would encounter an infilled valley, a gouge cut through the chalk marl by an ancient river, filled now with the sweepings from the bottom of the Channel: gravel, sand, silt. There were some vivid examples of what would happen if the tunnel struck an infilled valley. In the early morning hours of July 24, 1908, tunnelers digging the Lötschberg rail tunnel encountered one 300 meters beneath the known bed of the Kander River in the Alps; a torrent of muck and boulders rushed in and filled the tunnel back for nearly a mile toward the entrance, entombing all twenty-five men who had been working at the face.

The trouble with infilled valleys was that they were easy to miss if one relied on boreholes: Unless the drill penetrated the valley itself, there was no way to know one was there. Drilling in deep, quick water such as the Channel also was expensive, and sonar had little ability to penetrate rock deeply. Malcor and Harding therefore turned to a new device, nicknamed "Sparker." This was an apparatus, trailed from a workboat, that generated a twelve-thousand-volt spark under water. The spark, like lightning, produced a boom that traveled down through the water and into the seabed. Layers in the rock reflected part of the energy, which a trailing microphone picked up and caused to be charted on paper. The result was a series of horizontal lines that were a profile of the various layers of stone in the bed of the Channel.

In all, the Study Group's vessels would run more than a thousand kilometers of tests, crisscrossing the Channel in a rather broad band bounded on the north by Dover and Sangatte and on the south by Folkestone and Cap Gris Nez. The data was generally confirmatory: The chalk marl was continuous, though its path from England to France wasn't straight; it was in a sort of "W" shape, with a high point in the middle and low points near the shores. This was excellent news; such a configuration was perfect for drainage. Any water that seeped in would run naturally toward the low points, whence it could be pumped ashore.

The tests ended, for good and all, the idea of digging a tunnel under the Varne Bank, the route that had so beguiled so many planners since Thomé. There was no chalk marl there; the erosion that had produced the Channel had scoured it away. All that was left was Jurassic bedrock, and this was enough to warn off competent tunnelers; Jurassic rock throughout the Continent had been cracked and damaged by the geologic processes that created the Alps. It was the quintessential bad ground in a business founded on the axiom that good ground—not men, nor engineering, nor equipment—made good tunnels. *Jurassic,* wrote one expert, is "a word that makes the skin of experienced tunnelers creep."

Moreover, the Sparker surveys eventually did locate several infilled features in the seabed, including that seeming plunge-pool in the Channel bed, created when the chalk dam broke and the Dover Strait was formed a half million years ago.

As this work progressed, Technical Studies began taking political soundings. "Having served in British uniform in the Canadian army during World War II, I didn't want to go into this if British military opinion was against it," Frank Davidson said. He arranged an introduction to Lord Louis Mountbatten.

If the insular sentiments that had doomed the tunnel in Victoria's reign lived on, one would expect to find them in breasts such as Mountbatten's. Earl Mountbatten of Burma was Queen Victoria's great-grandson, Queen Elizabeth's confidant, Prince Philip's uncle, the last viceroy of India, a member of fourteen clubs and, ultimately, the victim of an IRA assassination. At the moment Davidson was ushered into his presence, he was Admiral of the Fleet—Churchill had appointed him to the post—and soon to be Chief of the Defence Staff, the senior military authority in Britain. He was also the embodiment of upper-crust Britishness.

Mountbatten's response to Davidson's inquiry about the British military's views on the tunnel was brief and encouraging. "That is entirely a *commercial* question," Mountbatten said. "Good luck to you."

Means and Davidson also engineered an invitation to visit Field Marshal the Earl Alexander of Tunis, Churchill's last minister of defense and the man who had commanded the withdrawal from Dunkirk.

"Lady Alexander served us a delicious tea, I remember, at their house in Windsor Great Park," Davidson recalled. "And Alexander said, well, he couldn't really answer our question right off the bat; he'd like to replay the battle of Dunkirk as if the tunnel existed. And throughout the tea he was moving teacups and glasses around, and finally looked up and said to us, 'Well, you know, I think it comes out all right. If the tunnel had been in existence, I simply would have drawn the perimeter around it, and we would have been thick enough on the ground to get out not only the men but the equipment as well. So I think you're on to a good thing.' "

Not all of Britain's military leaders were so ready to accept a Channel tunnel. Viscount Montgomery, the hero of El Alamein, knew the old song by heart: A Channel tunnel, in his oft-stated opinion, would be a dagger at

England's bosom. But surely, the press had asked Monty, surely a tunnel could be blown up if danger loomed?

"The lessons of history show that things that ought to be blown up never are, as Guy Fawkes discovered," he replied. "The Germans were supposed to destroy the bridges over the Meuse and over the Rhine at Remagen. But I think you will find that they never got around to it." Davidson and Means nonetheless made efforts to speak to Montgomery; they were unsuccessful.

Civilians as well as soldiers were divided on the question of a Channel link, and some of the naysayers were of distressingly high rank. Louis Armand kept encountering Sir Pierson Dixon, then the British ambassador in Paris, at the various official and social affairs to which they were both invited as a matter of course. Dixon never failed to give the assemblages the benefit of his thoughts, which were entirely negative, about the Channel Tunnel. Armand contacted Davidson to ask if there was any hope of winning over Dixon or, failing that, at least muting his criticisms.

Means, who had a politician's instincts and a private investigator's doggedness, began to inquire into Dixon's background and preferences. He soon turned up the fact that Dixon was an amateur but published writer of historical novels. One of these was set in ancient Rome; its protagonist was Julius Caesar's chief engineer, who had built road tunnels through the hills around the Eternal City so that its elite could more easily reach their country villas. Means prepared an erudite report on the history of tunneling; it made generous and approving mention of Dixon's book. Armand called Davidson not long after to say that there had been a remarkable change in the ambassador's views; he now had only kind words for the tunnel.

Davidson also pursued contacts in France, although the enthusiastic participation of such well-connected men as Armand and Georges-Picot made it rather less pressing. President de Gaulle was an Anglophile only insofar as France could take credit for British greatness ("Great Britain was conquered by men of our country," he once explained, "from whom sprang the British aristocracy, the force and grandeur of England. . . ."), but he *was* in favor of a Channel tunnel. Davidson, searching for an avenue to approach de Gaulle directly, went to see a well-connected officer at Rothschild Frères on rue Lafitte in Paris. Could he call the President?

He could not. "I never telephone the General," he said. "I wait. If the General wishes to see me, I'm of course at his disposal. But I cannot telephone *him*."

This sounded very much like a perfect standoff, since de Gaulle's regal refusal to consult anyone was well known. But as fortune would have it, the General *did* call within a few days—to inquire if Davidson's contact, Georges Pompidou, was available and of a mind to serve France as its prime minister.

*The Channel Tunnel's backers relax at the Lido in Paris in March 1959.
From left, Mrs. J. B. Bonny, Alfred E. Davidson, Ralph Olmstead, Mme.
Raoul de Vitry, J. B. Bonny, Mme. Arnaud de Vitry, Raoul de Vitry, Mrs.
Alfred E. Davidson, Arnaud de Vitry, Mrs. Ralph Olmstead.*

Pompidou accepted and in time showed himself to be a good, even crucial, friend of the Channel link.

The triumvirate of American construction companies kept its part of the bargain. They turned the design work over to International Engineering Company, a Morrison Knudsen subsidiary in San Francisco. The head of international engineering was a civil engineer named Charles Putnam Dunn, who was seventy-two years old when he was given the task of designing a tunnel under the English Channel. He was, Davidson recalled, "spry and active," and the work he produced in very short order suggests a vigorous mind and spirit.

A handsome thirty-page version of Dunn's plan appeared in November 1959, courtesy of the three companies, bound in black with stamped silver letters. It was really a précis—long on generalities, short on specifics, intended really as a sales document. After setting out the plans and the benefits to be reaped from a tunnel, the report noted that an important early step should be "to select a well qualified consortium of international construction firms." The document described two large railroad tunnels on either side of a smaller service tunnel, running 51.2 kilometers between terminals near

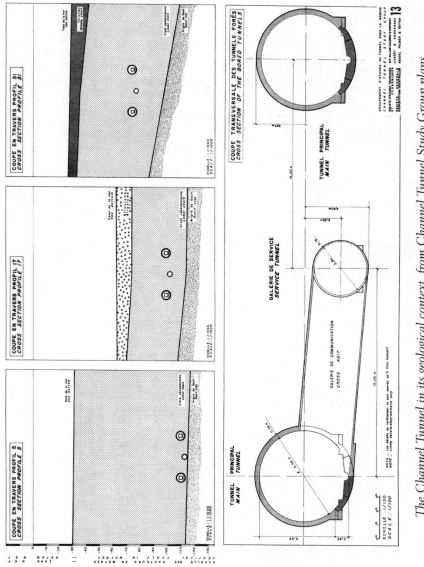

The Channel Tunnel in its geological context, from Channel Tunnel Study Group plans.

Folkestone and Coquelles. The tunnels were designed to accommodate rail shuttle cars carrying motor vehicles, and cross-passages linked the three tunnels at regular intervals. The rail tunnels met in four crossover chambers, two beneath the Channel and one under the land on each side. The plan showed access shafts on the cliff south of Dover and at Sangatte in France. It foresaw a ventilation system that would pump air down the service tunnel, through the cross-passages and out via the running tunnels. In sum, Dunn drew a set of plans that incorporated, quite precisely, all of the elements of the tunnel that was one day to be built.

Why the three-tunnel arrangement? Dunn argued that two small running tunnels, each with a single rail line, would cost about the same as a single big tube with a double rail line. The economy was principally one of time: The smaller ones could be dug faster by what were then still called "moles," but are now called tunnel-boring machines. Two small tunnels could more easily stay in the undulating bed of the Lower Chalk, whereas a large tunnel would probably have to break through into the fractured and porous rock above, or the weak and waterlogged ground below, to maintain the gentle grade and bends that high-speed trains required. And when the project was finished, one-way traffic in each of two tunnels would be safer than two-way traffic in a single large one.

The service tunnel, the Dunn plan said, "will serve many useful purposes." First, it would serve as a pilot tunnel to survey ground conditions ahead of the big running-tunnel TBMs. Next, the service tunnel would give access to the running tunnels without disturbing the flow of construction materials to the face and spoil to the surface. Finally, the service tunnel would be a crucial part of the necessary ventilation system. "The savings made possible by having the service tunnel approximately offset its cost," the plan noted.

If the project could get its final government approvals in a year, by November 1, 1960, Dunn said the tunnel could be ready by the end of 1964. The tunnels—less the rail lines and terminals, and excluding land cost and interest expenses—could be built for about £82.7 million, allowing for £5.7 million escalation over 1960 prices. Speed was essential, because delays cost money: "Interest during construction is a major item, amounting to several millions of pounds per year," Dunn's report said. "The total investment will be non-productive until the project is completed and placed in revenue-producing operation. The cost of the project would increase significantly beyond our estimate if the work were allowed to extend for a longer period of time. . . ." To get the tunnel operating quickly, he proposed installing the rail lines during the construction phase "on behalf of the two railroads."

That phrase summed up a major nontechnical difference between the 1959 idea and the one that came to be built. Bechtel, Brown & Root and

Morrison Knudsen wanted simply to build the tunnel. They assumed they would do so on behalf of a Channel tunnel company formed by the members of the Channel Tunnel Study Group. The tunnels, their report said, "will be built and owned by the Channel tunnel company. It is assumed that the Channel tunnel company will lease the tunnels to the British and French railroads, who will operate and maintain them." It was further assumed that the railroads would build and maintain, at their own expense, the rail lines in and near the tunnels and all terminal facilities.

In the end, Dunn's logic would not govern this aspect of the project, and the consequences would be drastic.

Dunn's report quickly proved sufficient to inspire competing proposals. One of these was for a huge £200 million bridge, with lanes for everything from bicycles to locomotives, and it provided an amusing sideshow.

It was a very serious proposal by a well-funded group, the Société d'étude du pont sur la manche, an Anglo-French-American combine of solid companies with good experience in heavy construction: Dorman Long of Britain, the Compagnie française d'entreprises from France and Merritt, Chapman and Scott from the United States. The group had recruited a redoubtable leader-spokesman in Jules Moch, a *polytechnicien* who was a marine engineer, a statesman, savant and author. Moch had been France's minister of public works before and after the Second World War, minister of the interior between 1947 and 1950 and minister of defense in 1950 and 1951.

For Moch, the bridge would forge a union of the two peoples. "What a splendid Anglo-French nation it could be," he wrote. "Imagine a sweep of land from Wick and Inverness in the north of Scotland to Perpignan and Menton, two thousand kilometers from North to South. It would marry Anglo-Saxon pragmatism to French Cartesianism, the perseverance of one to the passion of the other and, by mixing the two people, would create an almost perfect species!"

The bridge was to run from north of Dover to Cap Blanc Nez on the French coast. It would require 140 piers set in the Channel bed; these would carry a series of steel-framed spans. Ten of these would be 425 meters long, leaving a 400-meter-wide channel clear beneath them. The vertical clearance under these major spans would be 70 meters. The other spans would have 200 meters clear beneath them and vertical clearances of 51 meters. The surface of this titanic structure would be 38.5 meters wide. Railroad tracks, sheltered by specially designed wind baffles that would turn hurricane winds into pleasant breezes, would run along each side, bracketing eight lanes—four for four-wheel traffic, two for two-wheel traffic and two for disabled vehicles. There were to be two service areas perched out over the Channel, each with a restaurant, a hotel, a service station, a heliport (for rescue helicopters, in case of emergency) and parking for five hundred cars.

To critics who claimed that the bridge would render the Channel cluttered and hazardous to surface ships, Moch replied that it would in fact make navigation safer: The bridge pilings could serve as lane markers, and the long spans could be spaced so that skippers could steer in perfect confidence that the way before them was clear.

Moch's group attracted important support. By late 1961, when plans were officially submitted to the British government, it had fourteen major backers from industry, highway groups and banking. Among the banks were Crédit lyonnais, Société générale and Banque nationale du commerce et de l'industrie, now known as Banque nationale de Paris. The French public greeted a scale model of the bridge enthusiastically. The bridge group diplomatically had the model cars driving on the left while a model of the liner *Ile de France* steamed through the paper sea beneath the span.

What subsequently developed was a war between the Davidson and Moch forces for public opinion. As in any war, there were excesses. Moch himself committed some of these to print, in a 1962 book titled *Le Pont sur La Manche*.

The tunnel, he said, was "nothing more than a submarine ferry." Cars and trucks would congregate at the tunnel terminal, wait to be loaded on a shuttle car, then be hauled through to the other side. Train or ferry, drivers would still be slaves to a timetable. In the best of circumstances, passengers would be closed up in their vehicles for more than an hour. "One can foresee the little dramas that this will create," Moch wrote. "Children answering the call of nature on the seat cushions of automobiles . . ."

Less fortunate passengers might find themselves aboard a stalled train in the tunnel. Moch spared his readers none of the horrors that the sick, the infirm, the aged, the women and children would suffer as they debarked under the sea and slogged along the track bed to reach a rescue train—and, once they were out, to wait hours (or days, if their train had derailed) for their cars and baggage to be brought to the surface.

Even they could count themselves lucky: Moch summoned images of "the catastrophe on the Paris Metro, near the Couronnes station, the tenth of August 1903, [which] killed 84 people, most of whom were suffocated or trampled to death under the feet of the escapees."

Incredibly, Moch, who was eloquent about the benefits that Britain would reap from a solid transport link to a new and united Europe, nonetheless did not shrink from evoking the old bugaboo of invasion. If war came—he did not say whence—"it is clear that the British defense forces would wish to

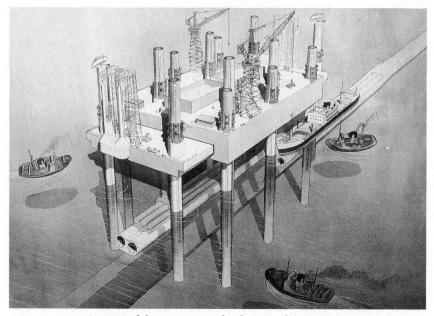

A proposal for an immersed-tube tunnel from 1962.

sever the link," he wrote. "Two cases must then be examined: One when the military isn't taken by surprise by the aggression and destroys the work before paratroopers try to capture it. Or the contrary: When the paratroopers capture both ends and find the link intact."

In either case, Moch argued, a bridge was better than a tunnel. In the latter, heavy guns or aircraft could more readily wreck the bridge than the tunnel. In the former case, either could be put out of commission with relative ease—the bridge could be rendered useless by blowing up a couple of pilings and a span or two.

"But once peace returns—and if there are any survivors of a nuclear war— nothing would be easier than to rebuild the destroyed bridge piling and to put up a new span," Moch wrote. If material had been stockpiled, the bridge could be back in service in a matter of months. Reboring a tunnel that had been blasted out of service, Moch suggested, would be a long, dangerous and perhaps impossible job. The tunnel might have to be entirely replaced.

Public and official opinion began to swing toward the bridge, particularly in France. But Moch's project was to be privately financed with loans to be repaid out of toll revenues. Opponents noted that the bridge group's own figures indicated a 3 percent return, not enough to make it attractive to investors.

In the end, an official Anglo-French panel decided in favor of the Dunn-design tunnel, and shares in the Channel Tunnel Company began to soar in

Hands under the sea, from The Observer, *1963.*

price even before the report was made public, rising from 17 shillings to £4 per share.

But politics again intruded. "We were wanting to get into the Common Market," said George Naylor, a lawyer in the City who was soon to be drawn into the tunnel effort. "The French were being obstreperous, and they wanted the tunnel." DeGaulle wouldn't admit Britain to the Common Market. Neither side would yield, and nothing could be done until someone did.

And so it stood for years. Frank Davidson did get to build a Channel tunnel—in miniature. It was a model, electric trains in a tube in a tubful of water, made to illustrate a talk to a boys' club in Connecticut. It became, for a time, a popular display on the House of Morgan's main floor. The Study Group carried out important geological surveys in the Channel that kept geologists in data for three decades. There was much activity, but no earth was ever moved.

4

Though they built nothing, Davidson and his associates had achieved one perfect success that saved the tunnel from another generation or so of neglect: They had persuaded investment banks in Britain and France that the venture had promise. By the time de Gaulle fell from power in 1968, more than a dozen of these banks led three separate tunnel consortia. When these managed to find common ground and merge, the pressure that they exerted was sufficient to nudge the British government into introducing a tunnel bill in Parliament. Although this provoked some heated opposition—one member complained that the government was trying to turn Parliament into the Reichstag—it did set the stage, by 1970, for another serious effort to build a link.

Perversely, the enthusiasm of Morgan Stanley and Dillon Read, the American investment banks that had backed Davidson's efforts, began to decline. "Bankers are hopeless people," recalled Al Davidson. "They had certain, quote, *standards*. Their idea was that you had to make twelve or fourteen per cent. Ours came out to maybe twelve, based on estimates of costs and expenses. This didn't please them very much."

As a result, the American houses made token investments. Since the strength of any partner was related to how much financing he controlled, the Davidsons' standing in the project diminished quickly and dramatically. Henceforth, Technical Studies would be relegated to the sidelines.

As elsewhere in the world, the board members of the British merchant banks sat on other boards as well. One such was Mark Turner of Kleinwort, Benson, who was also deputy chairman of a mining company that had been one of the great industrial success stories of postwar Britain: Rio Tinto Zinc.

Rio Tinto Zinc had been founded in Britain in 1873 as Rio Tinto Company, to acquire and operate the Rio Tinto mines in Spain, which had been producing copper since Roman times. It had some great successes in exploiting some of the Empire's mineral deposits, but ran into hard times in the 1930s. Turner was brought in in 1948 to turn things around, which he proceeded to do quite shrewdly. In the decades that followed, it became one of Britain's largest companies and a true multinational giant, with operations in Australia, North America, South Africa, Britain and Europe. Not all of its work was in mining, however. It worked as diligently and successfully to cultivate political contacts as ever it did to find the mother lode in any of its mines.

Turner proposed that, instead of a Bechtel or Brown & Root, RTZ be brought into the tunnel project. "He took the view, very rightly, that banks trying to build a tunnel was a no-good situation," said George Naylor, who became the banks' representative in the project. Turner was successful, and it was decided that RTZ would run the project while the banks would handle the financing.

Turner then brought in some excellent engineer-executives, among them Val Duncan—once described as "a suave, silver-haired Harrovian, who feels driven to expand and develop the wealth of the world with a Rhodes-type ardor"—and Alistair Frame, whom Naylor described as "a legendary engineer." For the political end, Turner brought in the Right Honorable Edward Arthur Alexander Shackleton, the Baron of Burley, O.B.E., son of the late Sir Ernest Henry Shackleton, the famous Antarctic explorer. The tunnel was put under RTZ Development Enterprises, and Shackleton was made its chairman.

"Eddie didn't have a clue about the engineering," said Nick Crossley, an RTZ engineer who worked on the tunnel. "But he was a hell of a good administrator. And he could communicate with the government." This last was something of an understatement; Lord Shackleton, who had been an RAF wing commander during the war, was the Labour Party's Opposition Leader in the House of Lords, minister in charge of day-to-day affairs of the Civil Service and a former Minister of Air Defence.

By late 1970, the British consortium had taken its final form, as what came to be called the British Channel Tunnel Company. The old Channel Tunnel Company had surrendered any role in administering the project, but still held 25 percent of the shares. The British investment banks each held 10.5 percent, except for Warburg, which had 5.5 percent. RTZ had 20 percent, British Railways had 4.74 percent and three American investment banks—Morgan Stanley, First Boston and White, Weld & Company—each had 0.92 percent.

The other members of the old Channel Tunnel Study Group, including Technical Studies, stayed only as financial participants. "We worked out a deal where the Study Group was to be paid £4 million, and Technical Studies would get £1 million of that," said Al Davidson. Payment depended, of course, on the successful financing and completion of a tunnel. Lord Harcourt, however, took a prominent place in the British group, in effect heading it.

Building a tunnel began to seem an achievable goal. On the French side, the Société française du tunnel sous la manche was a solid group comprising the Suez company, SNCF and nine big banks. Its leader was the formidable General Philippe Maurin, the architect of de Gaulle's nuclear deterrent, the *force de frappe.* "A very tough guy," Naylor recalled.

If all went according to plan, a traveler would be able to step or drive aboard a train on May 1, 1980, and be whisked under the English Channel to emerge, in a little more than a half hour, in a different country. The tunnel system that would accomplish this was based on Dunn's plans, which had been turned over to RTZ. There would be three tunnels cut side by side: two large running tunnels, each carrying a single rail line, straddling a smaller service tunnel. Cross-passages would connect the three tubes.

On the British side, the plan was to dig vertical shafts down to the tunnel level. On the French side, the plan was to build a long sloping adit northward, out under the Channel, from a point 175 meters back from the shore. Sangatte, then as now, was little more than one street, lined with houses, sandwiched between farm fields and a broad beach. The adit was to begin in a field at the southeast edge of the village. The French called this sort of adit *une descenderie,* and the British took up the term, merely adding the English definite article; it came to be called "The Descenderie." It would be the subject of much discussion, and worry, and hand-wringing, for decades to come.

There was one further change of substance to Dunn's plan: the addition of piston relief ducts between the running tunnels. In 1968, tests with models showed that there would not be enough room in the tunnel for air to flow smoothly around speeding trains; a locomotive would have to expend an immense amount of energy simply pushing air along, like a piston in a cylinder.

For the shuttles, the plan was to use special new locomotives based on SNCF's newest series, which delivered six thousand kilowatts of power. These 120-ton locomotives were expected to pull a 1,200-ton shuttle at 140 kilometers an hour on the flat. But the tests and calculation showed that the piston effect would reduce the maximum possible speed in the tunnel to 97 kilometers an hour. The piston effect was very sensitive to speed: The faster you tried to go, the more rapidly the opposing forces built up to resist your passage.

After model tests, and full-scale experiments in the Simplon Tunnel in the Alps and the Standedge Tunnel northeast of Manchester, the engineers concluded that the problem demanded piston relief ducts, cross-passages that linked the running tunnels directly, independent of the service tunnel passages. Tests showed that air in front of a speeding train would be pushed through the relief ducts and into the other tunnel. Behind the train, air would be sucked through the ducts in the opposite direction. In effect, there would be a circular movement of air through a two-kilometer stretch of the tunnels as a train sped through.

Ideally, the tests showed, there should be a 3.44-meter-diameter relief duct every 100 meters in the tunnel if the train speed was to be 140 kilometers per hour. (As a measure of how sensitive the piston effect was to train speed, if the trains slowed just to 130 kilometers an hour, the duct diameter could have been reduced to 1.27 meters.) Creating these 3.44-meter ducts would require the hand-mining of nearly a half million cubic meters of rock. The linings of these ducts would cover almost 125,000 square meters—more than thirty acres.

Economy demanded a compromise. The engineers calculated that you could get close to the ideal by putting 3.3-meter relief ducts each 250 meters. If you also made some small changes in the shape of the shuttle cars, they would be able to achieve level speeds of between 133 and 142 kilometers per hour. Passage times would increase by about thirty seconds to one minute, the report acknowledged, but this could be easily recouped by improving the terminal design and customs arrangements at both ends. If it later became essential to exceed those speeds, more powerful locomotives would be able to achieve it with relative ease.

The 250-meter spacing coincided with the planned distance between the regular cross-passages, so the RTZ engineers combined the two structurally: Each cross-passage would have a piston relief duct essentially built into its ceiling. There was a nagging worry, though, about the effect that a blast of air coming through a relief duct might have if it hit the side of a passing train in the other tunnel. Would it be powerful enough to rock the train dangerously? No one was certain, but the problem was put aside for the moment.

Moving trains of any sort created another concern among the engineers. Wheel and catenary friction, aerodynamic drag, waste heat from engines—all tended to dump heat, a lot of heat, in the running tunnels. It was a problem that would get worse with time, if traffic through the tunnel increased as anticipated. The heat load was expected to rise by about 3.5 percent each year.

No problem was anticipated in the service tunnel, which would be the duct through which fresh outside air was pumped to ventilate the tunnels. The service tunnel was expected to remain at a temperature of less than 15°C—rather cool, but excellent for anyone doing physical work. But if nothing were done to cool the running tunnels, the report said, "it is possible that the tunnel temperature could reach uncomfortably high levels within five years of opening." Piston relief ducts made the problem worse: Trains would not be pushing hot air out of the tunnel and drawing in cool air in their wakes.

Some heat would seep out through the walls. The lining, and the seabed rock beyond it, formed what the report called "an effective heat sink"—that is to say, the rock was a reservoir into which heat would naturally flow. But like any reservoir, it could be filled to overflowing; the rock would not be able to dissipate the heat as rapidly as the trains would be adding it. After ten years of operation, heat loss through the walls would be negligibly small.

The trains themselves (other than the engines) would soak up some heat during the passage, if they were at a lower temperature than the air in the tunnel—imagine a train coming from London on a freezing day plunging into the warm tunnel, absorbing heat during its passage, then dissipating the heat on the way to Paris. This effect was difficult to estimate, however; the RTZ engineers produced a formula for calculating heat removal by trains, but one had to know the tunnel temperature and the train temperature in order to use it. The temperature in the tunnel would, of course, vary from place to place, and the temperature of the entering trains would vary by the hour as well as the season. The engineers put this "train heat capacity" question aside as unanswerable, at least until the tunnel was in use.

Any water that seeped into the tunnel would be of enormous value for cooling. Seepage was certain: A dry tunnel anywhere is an anomaly, and a dry tunnel under a body of water is a practical impossibility. The RTZ engineers expected about 150 liters of water to leak into the underwater length of the tunnel each second. Not much was said publicly about this leakage, since 150 liters per second—a flow that would fill a railroad tank car in less than five minutes—sounds alarming. But the length of the three tunnel tubes, added together, was almost 150 kilometers, meaning that the leakage would amount, on average, to one liter per second *per kilometer of tunnel*—a trivial drip to even a confirmed worrywart, easily handled by a few pumps.

If the seepage were spread out over a long stretch of tunnel, that flow of 150 liters per second would carry a huge amount of heat with it when it was pumped to the surface. Under those conditions, the temperature in 1990 would be a full two degrees *lower* than the 22.5°C that the engineers considered optimum. Local leaks, even quite large ones, wouldn't help much at all, though. The water had to seep in, picking up heat over a large area.

The cooling effect of water was so profound that the engineers considered tapping the Channel for seawater to spray on the lining or to pump through heat exchangers. Other artificial cooling schemes were examined: Cold water could be pumped through finned piping (like the baseboard radiators used in houses) that would run the length of the tunnel. Cold water could be sprayed on the trains before they entered the tunnel. Ice chips could be sprayed on the trains, or a car full of ice chips could be made part of each train. "Finally," the report concluded, "it may be necessary to resort to air conditioning in the wagons." The heat question was left open to await further study.

Making the tunnel safe seemed fairly simple. There were four major concerns: flooding, fires, accidents and breakdowns. Flooding was a worry only if the ground was much worse than extensive geologic sampling suggested. Water would come in, to be sure, but the engineers designed big sumps, one at each shore and at the low points in the W.

For the other safety concerns, engineers plunged into the accident statistics of British Rail, SNCF and the London Underground. The relatively slight inconvenience of a locomotive breakdown or overhead power line failure, they concluded, might happen every two years. The same time would separate simple derailments, with more than ten years between more serious ones. Minor fires in the shuttle trains might happen, on average, once every six years; more than twenty years would separate serious fires. Through trains might have minor fires each twenty-eight years, serious fires once every fifty years or so.

The three-tunnel design all but removed the possibility of head-on collisions, and the confined space would prevent trains from overturning. In a long tunnel, however, the report said, the chances of fire "were not negligible." If there were a fire, the preferred course of action would be for the involved train to continue through and leave the tunnel. If that were impossible and the train had to halt, the ventilation system would keep the service tunnel a smoke-free refuge, to which passengers could be evacuated, if necessary, via the cross-passages. No evacuee would be more than 125 meters from an escape route.

All that anyone could do, the report suggested, was to work to reduce these risks. The signaling system was thus very important: Like the lighthouses that dotted the shores and shoals of the Channel, the signal lights would guide the hurtling trains to safe harbor. The state of the train-signaling art was fairly advanced. The basis was a system of "blocks," or lengths of track. The rails carried an electric current, and each block was insulated from the next. When a train entered a block, its wheels and axles completed the electrical circuit between the rails, permitting current to run to the trackside signal lights.

The simplest standard trackside signal had four lights, one above the other: green at the bottom, two yellow in the middle, red on top. When a train entered a block, all of the signals in that block showed red. When the train went on to the next block, these switched to show a single yellow light. When the train entered the block beyond that, both yellow lights went on. When the train cleared that block, the signal went green.

This was the system that RTZ proposed to use. All one had to do was calculate how much track was needed to stop the heaviest train traveling at the highest permitted speed, then place the signals the proper distance apart in blocks of the proper dimensions. This worked out to about 260 signals in the tunnel, plus about 40 in each terminal.

To back up this system, the engineers proposed sending information to the locomotive cab via a radio system installed between the rails. This would tell the train crew what signals were showing in the next block and what speed they might safely maintain. If necessary, the radio could be used to set the brakes automatically if the crew failed to take appropriate action.

And that, the designers in effect said, took care of safety and signaling. They threw in a batch of detection systems, to note any problems with ventilation, pumps, temperature, humidity, smoke, fire, chlorine, ozone or carbon monoxide. They talked things over with SNCF and the Inspectorate of Railways in Britain, and reached a tentative agreement among all parties.

The shuttle system was not intended to handle the peak traffic, but rather what statisticians call the "30th Peak Hour." Designing for peak traffic is wildly uneconomical, particularly for expensive links such as bridges and tunnels. Peak traffic hours tend to cluster in a few summer weekends. Think of any busy bridge or tunnel, then consider how many lanes it would need, and how wide a toll plaza, to handle the peak traffic on a summer holiday weekend without delay. Such a link would, by design, be underutilized for all but one hour of the 8,760 hours in a year. With this in mind, the shuttle system was to be designed around the anticipated traffic volume in 1990.

Before the plan for the shuttle system was even finalized, qualified builders ready and eager to start construction emerged. In Britain, three big construction companies—Balfour Beatty, Edmund Nuttall and Taylor Woodrow Construction—had already formed Cross Channel Contractors, a joint venture whose sole purpose was to build the tunnel. RTZ and the consortium had sensibly decided that the construction should be handled in the way that all experience suggested was best: By contract, awarded on the basis of competition, between a strong owner-client and a competent contracting group. Clear evidence of political commitment to the project appeared on both sides of the Channel; on October 20, 1972, the British and French governments, the British and French tunnel companies and the British and French national railways all signed a formal agreement to build the Channel Tunnel according to the schedule laid down in the report. The companies would raise the money, hire the contractors and oversee construction under a fifty-year concession from the governments. Most of the money would come from the sale of government-guaranteed bonds; a smaller part, to be raised first, would come from the sale of shares to private investors. An operating authority, controlled by the government but with representatives from all of the signatories, would run the tunnel once it opened.

Construction was to proceed in three stages, each of which would start with a formal agreement among the parties. Agreement No. 1, to be signed October 20, would cover £5 million worth of further planning, tests and surveys. Half the money would come from government-backed loans. If one or both of the governments canceled the project at this point, the governments would reimburse the companies.

If all went as expected, the parties would sign Agreement No. 2 on June 1, 1973, starting a phase that would see construction of adits and a "substantial part" of the service tunnel. This was to cost £20 million: £6 million from a private placement of shares, the other £14 million from government-guaranteed loans. If the project were canceled, the companies would be reimbursed with a profit by the governments.

Agreement No. 3 was to be signed in early 1975, after Britain and France signed a treaty, and after the legislative bodies of both nations gave formal approval to the tunnel. This final phase would take the project through to completion. Ten percent of the needed money would be risk capital, half of that from the sale of shares. The other 90 percent would come from government-guaranteed bonds. Here, too, the governments agreed to reimburse the companies if the project was killed.

It was clear, at the signing of Agreement No. 1, that the tunnel works would not move even a millimeter into the earth for months. But it was equally clear, to anyone who cared to look, that the companies were far from idle, and the events were more than enough to cheer the tunnel's longtime advocates. When Leo d'Erlanger proposed a sale of new shares to hold up Channel Tunnel Investments' share of the costs, the issue was oversubscribed. There was a genuine sense that *this time*—perhaps—the tunnel would actually be built.

With the game once more afoot, the usual ragtag English army assembled to stand against this threatened breach of their nation's islandhood: honest patriots and forthright xenophobes, Little Englanders and Kent-as-the-Garden-of-Englanders, seamen and ferry owners and port officials from Dover and

Tunnel construction cross section from the 1974 project.

other ports that faced Europe, history buffs who recalled Napoleon stymied in Boulogne and veterans who remembered Hitler and Dunkirk, farmers who feared for their livestock and suburbanites who feared for their rosebushes, their way and quality of life.

"Thousands of lorries will be carting material of all sorts around so that the roads will be permanently covered up, and doubtless covered with filth," ran one volley from the Channel Tunnel Opposition Association. "A large body of imported labour—not perhaps of the highest skills, or of the greatest honesty—will be dumped down in the area, with considerable risk to farm stock and to property generally."

This unhappy band saw hellfire leaping from the tunnel's mouth: "An absolute magnet to the attentions of Black September, IRA and similar organizations," their literature said on the subject of security. "It would be absolute madness to subject our vital cross-Continental traffic to such risks." On the effects of even a bomb scare: "The prospect is too horrible to contemplate, for the lorry flood would spread out all over East Kent."

It didn't matter that the ferries were freighted with many of these same problems—bombs would damage a ship far more than a tunnel, and East Kent had survived many a lorry flood caused by a few days of bad weather in the Channel. The ferry lobby didn't pause in its assaults; the chairman of one ferry line called the tunnel "a monument to the day when the British taxpayer put his hand in his pocket to improve a depressed area of France."

As in the past, the groups that opposed the tunnel drew their energy from a vast seething pool of antitunnel feeling that lay close beneath the calm, often cool surface of British society. That society—riven though it might be by divisions of class, geography, education, wealth, color and accent—wished, on balance, that the whole idea of a tunnel would simply go away. In France, there were islands of doubt among the sailors and dockworkers of Calais and shoals of Anglophobic resistance, but these were scattered in an ocean of enthusiasm. The French loved great projects, and a Channel tunnel, though it did not strike the eye as handsomely as would a grand bridge across the strait, was surely a *grand projet*. To appreciate it was to show intelligence and taste. In Britain, enthusiasm for the tunnel marked one as a crank. Insularity still lay in the heart and blood of every Englishman, a reservoir to fuel the activities of tunnel opponents.

This was usual and in the past had sufficed to turn back the threat to the virtues of insulation. But this time the issue seemed in doubt: The tunnel now had powerful friends in Britain, a nation that always had been guided, and often governed, by the wishes of its elite. Would the unease in every English breast be enough to thwart the serious effort of a group that comprised nobles both of blood and achievement?

It seemed unlikely, when one reviewed the ranks of the tunnel's proponents. They made a formidable crowd: Shackleton was there, of course, and Frame and Duncan. The merchant bank Hill Samuels had put forward Sir John Colville, who had been private secretary to three British prime ministers—Neville Chamberlain before, Churchill during, and Clement Attlee after the Second World War. When Princess Margaret married in 1947, Colville became her private secretary. When Churchill returned to 10 Downing Street, Colville rejoined him. George Naylor said simply, "He was immensely well connected."

As for Lord Harcourt, his pedigree made most of the realm's nobles look like parvenus. One of Harcourt's ancestors played a major role in establishing England's very sense of itself. Godefroy d'Harcourt, a Norman lord in exile in England, in 1346 urged Edward III to attack Normandy: "I will venture my head, that if you land there, you will find no opposition; for the Normans have not been used to war," Godefroy told the king, according to the great medieval chronicler, Jean Froissart. "There, Sir, you will find great towns, unwalled, which will afford your men great plunder."

Edward took the advice and with an army of 15,000 men sacked Barfleur, Cherbourg, Montebourg, Carentan and St-Lô. "In this manner they burnt many other towns," Froissart says, "And gained an immense quantity of riches. . . . The Englishmen burnt, destroyed, wasted, and pillaged the fine plentiful country of Normandy."

When the French finally assembled a huge army near Paris, the English fled northward, making for Calais. The English army was eventually brought to bay and forced to give battle on a low ridge near the village of Crécy, and the victory Edward won there echoes still in the English consciousness. Godefroy, guided by feudal rather than national loyalties, fought well in the English army's right wing.

Edward went on to Calais, besieged it, withstood a relief attempt by a French army (which camped at Sangatte) and forced the starving inhabitants to surrender after almost a year's privation. Edward drove out the *Calaisiens* and replaced them with English settlers. Calais remained part of England until Mary Tudor lost it to the French in 1558. So in seeking to build the Channel tunnel, Lord Harcourt was in a sense working toward the same end as that accomplished by his distant kinsman: to unite Calais once again with England.

With all that political, intellectual and financial power behind the effort, the Channel Tunnel supporters might well have considered adopting the motto of Harcourt's ancient family: *Le Bon Temps Viendra*. Certainly the City thought something favorable was in the wind for the tunnel; in the week ended May 5, before the RTZ report was officially presented to the governments, the price of Channel Tunnel Investments shares doubled.

For a time, too, the British government seemed to be gathering its resolve to stand behind the project. When the opposition grew clamorous, the government stunned it into silence on September 12 with a white paper that was a forthright and ringing endorsement of the project, as strong in support as the most enthusiastic tunnel backer might have dared hope.

France received the white paper enthusiastically. Pierre Billecocq, the deputy French transport minister, summoned the press to announce this "practically certain send-off" for the tunnel. His government would send a memorandum to the Assemblée nationale within days to prepare the path for a treaty between the two nations, which he said could be signed in November. This would coincide with the signing of Agreement No. 2 with the companies, which would authorize construction of short sections of the French and British service tunnels, to test both the TBMs and the assumptions on which the project was based.

Billecocq admitted that certainty would only come in April 1975, when Agreement No. 3 would irrevocably commit all parties to the project. "However, it will be almost impossible to put things into reverse after the signing of Agreement No. 2 and the treaty," he concluded.

But times were bad and growing worse in Britain, which was coming to the end of a difficult year. Wages had risen by 29 percent, prices by 16 percent, inflation by 22 percent, an additional 200,000 workers had lost their jobs, consumer spending had fallen and the balance of payments had skidded to a deficit of £3.75 billion. The Bank of England was having to prop up tottering banks everywhere. By November, the mighty National Westminster Bank was trying to quash rumors that it was in deep trouble.

Even the Trades Union Congress was alarmed and began talks with the government that eventually led to a moderation of wage demands in return for a government-ordered price freeze. "I looked over the precipice," one TUC leader said later. "And I didn't like what I saw."

This cooperation came with a price: The TUC wanted several government projects scrapped, and the Channel Tunnel was among them. When British Rail came in with a staggeringly high price estimate for a high-speed rail link between London and the tunnel, the tunnel opposition in government had the excuse it needed. The legislative process was halted.

Alistair Frame and his colleagues on both sides of the Channel did what they could to save the project. France had agreed, on December 9, to stop the clock to permit the British to try to work out the problems, and on December 17, the French National Assembly ratified the tunnel treaty. In the week after Christmas, Frame met with officials of the Department of the Environment to suggest that the project be shut down for two years, with the works maintained by a small crew, until the economic and political climate was better. He and his associates came away with a clear sense that the government had scant interest in keeping the tunnel alive.

On January 2, 1975, the British and French Channel Tunnel Companies notified the governments that they were in default, since the treaty had not been ratified. They did this, they said, only to protect their interests under Agreement No. 2. They didn't want to kill the project. Within days they had a proposal before Tony Crosland, head of the Department of the Environment, to have the tunnel bill reintroduced later that year so that construction could resume in late 1976.

There were some hopeful signs: British Prime Minister Harold Wilson met French President Valéry Giscard d'Estaing in Paris on January 3 and proposed delaying the tunnel project by perhaps a year; word reached the British press soon after that the French had agreed.

On Wednesday, January 15, British Rail's chairman, Richard Marsh, paid a social call on the French ambassador, in the course of which he expressed his confidence that the troubles besetting the Channel Tunnel would be soon solved.

On Thursday, the British government notified the ambassador that it was canceling the Channel Tunnel project. The announcement would be made the following Monday. This notice arrived after the embassy had transmitted Marsh's optimistic prediction.

On Friday, Marsh was hailed as he passed through the House of Commons lobby and was told that the tunnel was dead.

On Saturday, the French government sent a pleading letter to Britain, asking that no announcement be made Monday.

On Sunday, "clearly unhappy" British Rail planners released details of a simpler rail link that trimmed more than £105 million off the November estimate. Crosland notified the French that the decision to stop the project wouldn't be rescinded or delayed.

On Monday, the British tunnelers cranked up the Priestley TBM and began driving toward France. This was a gesture—the drive was supposed to start the next day—and it was futile. At 4 P.M., word came through that the project had been canceled, and the machine was stopped.

The British government, by canceling the project, condemned itself to buying up the Channel Tunnel companies and their works at a price that would give the private venturers a profit. The terms of Agreement No. 2 bound the French government to do the same: Each would have to pony up about £8 million. The reaction in Paris, in government, was a bitter compound of shock, horror, contempt, fury. The unfairness of having to pay for what was seen as British irresponsibility was particularly galling. "We carry no responsibility for any abandonment of the project," the foreign minister said in a radio broadcast after a Cabinet meeting on the fateful Sunday. "It would be abnormal that we should suffer any of the consequences."

In the end, the French paid. They paid enough to allow their tunnelers to complete The Descenderie, to store the unused TBM (which was still on the surface) and to seal up the works for possible use at some later date. The Descenderie, which in passing through some very broken, waterlogged chalk had cost the French engineers and tunnel crews much effort, was lined-out with cast iron and allowed to fill with water. The British companies got permission to drive their TBM forward about 250 meters, to cocoon it in the chalk marl to await a day when it might again be needed.

The symbolism of Britain's callous act was not lost on the French, of course; it was immediately seen as an indication of shallow commitment to the idea of a united Europe. "Without being too pessimistic, nor giving too much weight to symbols, one can't help but think that the abandonment of the tunnel is a bad sign," said *La Voix du Nord,* a regional newspaper published in Lille. "Is the future equally precarious for the economic and political links that bind the United Kingdom to its partners in the Common Market?"

But there was another note, too, in the French press: a philosophic acceptance of a sad and fated end that anyone might have predicted. "La Grande-Bretagne veut rester une île," said *Le Parisien Libéré,* a perfect elegy in very few words: Great Britain wishes to remain an island.

5

Frank Davidson was not as discouraged by these events as he ought to have been. He immediately set about trying to revive the Channel Tunnel.

This made good financial sense for him and his partners in Technical Studies. The project's collapse had brought down the 1972 agreement by which the members of the Study Group would receive about £4 million for their labors and expenditures; Technical Studies was to get a quarter of that payment.

It wasn't just the money that interested Frank Davidson, of course. He believed in the tunnel, believed in its value, believed in its inevitability. If costs had killed the project, he thought, cutting costs might bring it back to life. His idea was to build only the service tunnel. Its 4.5-meter internal diameter would be too small for trains, so Davidson proposed sending road vehicles through on a conveyor system like the people movers now common in airports.

In August 1975, De Vitry wrote to Roger Hutter, SNCF's deputy director-general, to suggest that a scaled-down version of the tunnel project be studied. Hutter responded with enthusiasm; the idea fell in perfectly with his own thinking and that of other officers of the French Channel Tunnel Company. Hutter asked CGE-Developpement, the company that had been overseeing the French tunnel work, to examine the single-tunnel salvage idea. He had the results of CGE's study by mid-September and invited the Davidsons, RTZ's Alistair Frame and a few other enthusiasts to a morning meeting— "followed by a friendly breakfast"—the next month in his office at 88, rue Saint-Lazare in Paris.

The study concluded that Davidson's conveyor wasn't a good idea, since it had never been tried and would be difficult to explain to the governments. A

better plan would be to increase the tunnel diameter slightly to 4.8 meters—
the TBMs could be easily modified—for standard British-gauge trains powered by standard British-style electric third rails. This tunnel would be too
small to carry vehicles on shuttle trains, so traffic would be limited to passenger and freight trains. It would accommodate only a single rail line, so
traffic would be one way at a time—westbound trains would have to wait at
the portal until all eastbound had cleared out, and vice versa. And, since
there couldn't be piston relief ducts in a single-bore tunnel, trains would run
more slowly, taking about fifty minutes to make the portal-to-portal passage.

But this "Mousehole," as it quickly came to be called, had shining virtues
as well. It would be cheap, costing about a quarter as much as the three-
tunnel plan. Since it would use regular trains, there would be no need for a
high-speed link to London, nor for sprawling terminals in Folkestone and
Calais. Since it couldn't carry vehicles, the ferry owners were unlikely to object strenuously. It could be built in sixty-four months, even allowing time for
modifying the TBMs.

Careful scheduling could ameliorate the bottleneck characteristics of the
single track: Trains could be sent through in "flights"—ten trains in ninety
minutes, all in the same direction, after which the flow would be reversed.
Even with the tunnel shut six hours a day for maintenance, the Mousehole
could handle sixty trains a day in each direction. CGE's projections of traffic
and revenues indicated an internal rate of return of between 10 percent and
14 percent—sufficient to interest private capital.

If traffic and revenues justified it, the CGE report said, the two larger tunnels could be added later without disturbing the flow of traffic in the Mousehole. "In conclusion, it seems to us that this scaled-down solution merits
deeper study, with the concurrence of the French and British governments,"
the report said in closing.

By February 1977, RTZ and CGE had completed a further study. They
found little to discourage serious thought about the Mousehole, but did
identify some potential difficulties. Hutter laid these out on July 5, when he
called interested parties from both sides of the Channel to a working lunch
at the Maison de l'amérique latin on the boulevard St-Germain in Paris. On
the agenda were four points that the study had raised. Three of these, quite
naturally, had to do with finances: First, there wasn't any more money to take
the studies beyond the very preliminary stage at which they then stood. Second, the costs would almost certainly exceed the means of those assembled,
so money was going to have to come from elsewhere: the governments, perhaps, or from the EEC's Economic Commission, "for whom the CT [Chan-
nel Tunnel] represented a community undertaking of the highest interest."
The third point noted, however, that the governments—Hutter generously

used the plural, although the French had had no role in the shameful act—had cited their financial liabilities as a reason for canceling the earlier project. Therefore, it would be realistic to look to some other form of financing to avoid this peril.

The last point had nothing to do with cost but everything to do with the core problem that faced the venture: "Whatever the plan envisaged, reviving . . . a project so spectacularly abandoned, will require a delicate preparation of public opinion," the report said. "Bringing in a public relations specialist was therefore something worthy of consideration."

In fact, larger events would do a great deal, over the next several years, to prepare public opinion in certain very important quarters. Banks, for instance, became hungry for interesting ventures to which they might lend money. "There was a probability that [mining and oil] was going to run out as a main source of business, or at least was going to slow down," said Colin Stannard, who headed National Westminster Bank's project unit. "I then had about one hundred and twenty staff who needed to be kept employed, and I was quite keen on being employed, too."

Stannard's thoughts turned to Europe, and he ordered some studies to examine the Continent as a possible market. These suggested a number of projects in Europe, mostly involving infrastructure, that might be done with private-sector funding.

One was the Channel fixed link, but Stannard foresaw a problem. "It seemed to me there was going to be a clash of culture," he said. "The British would almost certainly want a heavy involvement of the private sector, whereas the French would almost certainly want it to be a public-financed project." He concluded that the project probably could be put together with private-sector financing taking the lead, though government funds might be needed as well. Stannard forwarded the finished reports to his superiors and turned his attention to other things.

Construction companies, too, were looking for new projects. Costain Civil Engineering was one such interested company. It had proposed an immersed-tube project to the Study Group in the 1960s, and the Davidsons had known the Costain family for years; Al Davidson and Richard Costain played tennis together from time to time.

The company was then finishing the Thames Barrier, a huge publicly funded dam designed to protect London from floods. A lot of other projects were winding down, too, so the idea of a Channel tunnel—a big project that would keep the company busy for much of the decade ahead—had powerful appeal.

The man in charge of the Thames Barrier for Costain was John Reeve, a burly man whose jovial manner tended to conceal an intense and shrewd mind. Costain assigned him to the tunnel project—"seconded" him, as the trade liked to say—and thus gave the project a leader who would carry it forward for more than a decade.

For twenty years, since his first days in the construction industry, Reeve had been telling people that he wanted to build a tunnel across the Channel. He was a chartered quantity surveyor, which meant that his expertise was in commercial and legal aspects of heavy construction rather than engineering.

Big projects required optimists, Reeve was fond of saying. Pessimists would see the risks too clearly and could accomplish nothing. "Optimists and enthusiasts," he said. "They will always look on the bright side, minimize the risks and concerns and go on, because that's what makes the world go round." He paused for a reflective smile. "And then, of course, they have to face the realities of the facts when they happen."

The governments, too, were inclined to look with favor upon a tunnel. The French were cautious, of course, not wishing to suffer another costly humiliation. But Hutter's enthusiasm meant that SNCF favored the project, and government-owned SNCF surely reflected the official French view.

For its part, British Rail was interested—more interested, perhaps, than even SNCF—in building and operating the Mousehole. British Rail now had a leader, Sir Peter Parker, who was unquestionably in favor of a tunnel such as this. Parker noted that you could build the Mousehole for "roughly the price of a score of jumbo jet aircraft. Jumbos last about a decade and a half. Tunnels are more or less forever." He also pointed out that Britain was already spending £800 million annually on rail transport.

Further, British Rail was government-owned. " 'Using the public sector as an engine of growth' was one of the phrases that tripped off the tongue quite freely in the mid-70s," recalled John Noulton, a career civil servant who had been called in to help shut down the tunnel project in 1975. In consequence, the Mousehole "had a fair wind in Paris and a reasonable wind in London."

That wind shifted, of course, when Margaret Thatcher became prime minister in 1979, but not in a way that seriously impeded the slow but steady progress of the tunnel idea. Thatcher was perfectly willing to see a tunnel— or a bridge, or a combination of the two—built across the Channel, as long as the government did not have to pay any part of its cost.

The wind shifted again in May 1981, when France elected François Mitterand its president. But this shift was favorable: Mitterand had amassed considerable political debts, and one of his principal creditors was the Nord-Pas de Calais region, whose Communists and Socialists had gladly given their votes to the socialist Mitterand and now expected to receive.

Nord-Pas de Calais was an economic disaster zone in which agriculture *and* industry *and* mining were all withering. Unemployment for the region as a whole approached 15 percent; in Calais the figure exceeded 20 percent. A Channel link would supply construction jobs from the start, operating jobs when the link was complete. Further, the link would put Nord-Pas de Calais at the hub of a rail network, with more than one hundred million people living within five hundred kilometers of the tunnel's French portal.

Thatcher and Mitterand found common ground in the tunnel: It was something upon which a British Tory and a French Socialist could agree. In late 1981, at their annual summit meeting, they decreed that an Anglo-French commission should study the idea. The task fell to John Noulton in Britain; the report said that a link was a good idea and that a bored tunnel was probably the best way to forge it.

Stannard had played a significant if not entirely voluntary role in bringing matters to this point. He had been approached by a government representative weeks after the Mitterand-Thatcher summit and asked to assess several Channel link proposals that had been submitted by their would-be builders. He demurred at first—it was quite a lot of labor, and the government wanted it done gratis—but his superiors at NatWest told him to do the work.

Now the link came back again to Stannard's desk. This time he was told, by the government via his superiors at NatWest, to examine the prospects and problems of finding money for a fixed Channel link. Stannard felt that any plan for financing such a project would need French participation. He therefore called Marcel Sarmet, who was his opposite number, more or less, at Crédit lyonnais.

Sarmet's response surprised Stannard. Crédit lyonnais had begun work already in just this area and was bound to another partner: Midland Bank, one of the world's largest banks and soon to be one of the most troubled. Stannard quickly realized that Midland had approached the British Ministry of Transport with a proposal to undertake a fixed link financing plan.

Stannard had no objection to having Midland aboard, but the French government did: It insisted that two other French banks, Banque nationale de Paris and Banque indosuez, be added to the panel. The reason for this insistence was that this study wasn't to be an empty exercise: This time, the banks were looking to participate in a real project.

The Five-Bank Report, as it came to be called, was begun in August 1982 and took twenty-one months to complete. It was of a fairly standard type, much used to evaluate "extractive" projects by mining companies. It ran more than five hundred pages, but most of these were filled with computer-generated numbers that predicted the finances of bridges and tunnels (or combinations thereof) under various worst-to-best-case scenarios, in each year from 1983 on through to 2027.

Like the Anglo-French study, this examination concluded that the Dunn model—three bored tunnels—seemed best. The banks also concluded that it might be impossible to finance such a venture with only funds from the private sector: Some government's money, or at least guarantees, would be needed.

"The moment the British government got it they effectively rejected it, by saying straightaway that if it can't be totally privately financed it will not happen," Stannard recalled. "They made it clear that they wanted the totality of the link to be financed by the private sector." After some further discussions with the government—and under some pressure from contracting companies who hoped to build the link—Stannard again got in touch with Sarmet. "I spoke to Marcel and I said, 'Look, what I'm going to do is write to the government and say I believe it can be financed in the private sector, totally. If the government then says OK, do it, are you still in?' " Stannard said. "And he said yes, sure . . . and he got the other banks to say the same."

The drafters of the Five-Bank Report did their best to conceal their unease about the absence from the scene of a strong owner-operator. The report's "Summary and Conclusions" ran nineteen pages and covered ninety-eight points, many in considerable detail. Number 97 read, in full: "The project has no natural sponsoring investment group and an owner will not emerge without adequate encouragement and backing from Governments." But such caveats were all but smothered by the overall tone of the Five-Bank Report, which was hopeful and positive. Yes, it said in effect, there were problems. But they could be solved.

Others weren't nearly so sure. In gathering information, the banks had asked an insurance expert, Allen Sykes, to review the tunnel proposal and comment on its insurability. Sykes summed up his findings in a confidential March 1984 paper, two months before the Five-Bank Report was released. Sykes knew quite a lot about the Channel Tunnel; he had been involved with it in the 1970s and had written several papers for the Major Projects Association, an important trade organization, in the years since.

Sykes noted that the tunnel would be a "giant project," a class of undertakings he defined as having a capital cost of more than $2 billion. The other distinguishing feature of giant projects was an "almost unbelievably high" failure rate. "No projects are harder to achieve," Sykes wrote. "To work on giant projects is always exhausting and often demoralising."

A giant project that went wrong could be lethal to the companies involved: Just carrying tunnel planning to a go–no go decision could cost close to £150 million. After that, the project would demand so much money and so great a commitment of resources that companies would be unable to dilute the risk by taking other, less chancy, work.

Sykes saw that the tunnel faced special problems. It required two governments to remain in agreement for at least seven years, until the project reached a point of no return. "At no time in the last 25 years have the policies of the two governments remained identical for this critical seven-year period," Sykes wrote, noting that France and Britain were already arguing over how to finance a Channel link.

Far worse to Sykes, though, was the lack of what he called a "robust sponsor." The promoters were proposing not simply to dig a tunnel, but also to create "a very major firm" that would finance, own and operate it. "It will easily be in the top 20 businesses existing in either the UK or France," Sykes noted. He was in much doubt about whether it could be done. "The most glaring omission from the present attempt on the Channel Tunnel is the absence of suitable sponsors," he concluded. "If the government is not to be the sponsor, who is? . . . Who will be the owner/promoter, the source of all decisions, the promoter of equity funds, the appointer of the Project directorate, etc? Until this question is satisfactorily resolved it is difficult to see both how and why the project should go forward."

Yet go forward it did. Indeed, Stannard already had been working for more than a year toward the "emergence, structure and capitalization" of an owner. This entity was to be taken and built from the ribs of six contracting companies, five British and one French, that had proposed variations on the Dunn design. The six had straggled in in three different groups after the governments had expressed interest in a Channel link, but the banks had already molded them into a single functioning organism, the English Channel Tunnel Group.

But not everyone was set on a single tunnel. A powerful combine of companies, headed by British Steel, was drawing plans for a huge bridge-and-tunnel, road-and-rail link. This proposal, grandiose even by French standards, came to be called EuroRoute. Great six-lane bridges were to carry road traffic from both sides of the Channel out to artificial islands, one 7 kilometers off the Kent Coast and another 8.5 kilometers off the French coast. The islands would have huge spiral ramps, 250 meters in diameter, to carry road traffic down to and up from a 19-kilometer-long immersed tube tunnel in the seabed. Another immersed tube tunnel would run from shore to shore and would carry all rail traffic. It would take ten years to build, consume a million tons of steel, carry up to a hundred thousand vehicles a day, plus thousands of passengers in trains. Its sponsors said that all of the £5.9 billion needed to build it would come from the private sector without any government guarantee or assistance, and all of it would be paid back to investors in twenty-five years.

EuroRoute was daring and grand, but it wasn't a pipe dream. The consortium had strong companies and banks to design, build and finance it; its backers had the good sense to line up French participants as well as British. And EuroRoute had, at its head, a resource of exceptional value: Ian MacGregor, an industrialist in whom Thatcher's free-market faith was made flesh.

MacGregor had a lot of experience in a lot of areas: He was a partner at Lazard Frères, he was on the board at British Leyland (brought there for the same reason he was recruited for British Steel, to solve its problems). His advice was much sought, and his advice was invariably in support of free enterprise.

He tried to interest Frank Davidson in joining the team, comparing the EuroRoute plan to the Chesapeake Bay Bridge and Tunnel in the United States, which it resembled in outline if not detail. Davidson demurred, convinced that neither a bridge nor a bridge-tunnel combination was economically viable.

Margaret Thatcher had fewer reservations about EuroRoute's bridge-and-tunnel idea. "She loved Ian MacGregor," Davidson recalled, "and when he told her about this thing in the Chesapeake Bay, and said: 'We could do the same, we need great public works to get the economy started,' she took it." EuroRoute also appealed to one of Thatcher's deepest prejudices: She loathed trains. British Rail embodied everything her Tory heart detested: It was an inefficient, expensive, profitless socialist failure, ruined by bureaucrats and ruled by labor unions. She strongly preferred a link through or over which people might drive themselves.

Yet the Channel link project was still merely an idea; none of the contractors or financiers would spend much on further planning until the governments did something decisive. This long-awaited move came in November 1984, at the annual Anglo-French summit between Mitterand and Thatcher. "A fixed cross-Channel link," their joint statement said, "would be in the mutual interests of both countries." A binational working party was authorized to start the process by which would-be builders could formally apply to link Britain and the Continent.

The English Channel Tunnel Group came to the contest with EuroRoute (and several other consortia whose prospects were less bright) with some considerable strengths and several glaring weaknesses. It had enlisted Sir Nicholas Henderson, the former British ambassador to both France and the United States, to serve as its chairman. Its member companies were strong and experienced: In addition to Costain, the group included Balfour Beatty and Taylor Woodrow Construction, both of which had actually worked on the

1974 tunnel as part of Cross Channel Contractors. Tarmac and George Wimpey, both well-known British construction firms, filled out the British ranks.

The French company was Spie Batignolles, which had both reputation and experience to recommend it as a partner. Spie's specialties included electrical installations (particularly nuclear power plants) and heavy construction on land and sea; it was an experienced builder of oil platforms. Spie also had done recent work in the Paris Metro, one of the few tunneling jobs of any consequence in Europe in many years, and had worked on the French TGV lines.

The company had good corporate genes for the Channel Tunnel job: It was a descendant of the Société de construction des batignolles, founded in 1846, which in 1882 had built the Beaumont-design tunnel-boring machine for the French section of the tunnel.

Spie Batignolles also had an interesting corporate culture. Where other French companies tended to be patriarchal and hierarchical, Spie tended toward collegiality. There was an intellectual interest in how companies and projects functioned. At the same time, Spie shared the French managerial passion for synthesis. "Spie was involved in industrial projects in which they needed to mix cultures and different activities," said one of its engineers of this period. "They would put together people for the civil engineering, the pipe work, electrical, everything—and integrate them in the one project. Spie was oriented toward large industrial plants, turnkey contracts, overseas work that was multidiscipline and multicultural. It was quite a pluralistic culture." Spie also had an executive of great value to the project: Pierre Billecocq, the former French transport minister, a man with excellent political contacts.

The companies formed a good pool of executive talent. Among the secondees was Andrew McDowall, a construction engineer who bore a faint but clear resemblance to his distant cousin, the actor Roddy McDowall. The engineer McDowall was then in his early fifties, a director of Wimpey. To meet McDowall was to know a great deal about him. He was tall and rawboned. The resemblance to Roddy was in the square jaw; to this, Andrew McDowall added features that were craggy rather than handsome. He looked hard and stubborn, and he was. He tended to make up his mind quickly: One colleague described him as "a hip-shooter."

Engineering ran in his family; his father had been a structural engineer who served as district building surveyor for Westminster. The younger McDowall went to work at age eighteen for Redpath Dorman Long, a British Steel subsidiary. At the same time, he attended Westminster Technical College one day a week, working toward a bachelor of science degree. "A hard flog," he recalled. It took him seven years to get his degree.

He thus joined his profession via a very well worn British path, one that led the novice engineer through real-world problems as well as classroom exercises. It was an apprentice system in which the company replaced the master, and it was the very antithesis of France's cult of the *polytechnique*. The British engineer was an acknowledged master of finding practical solutions to most any problem—except how to hoist himself to the social plane that his skills merited. English industrialists were admitted to the governing class only if they adopted its views, which were roundly technophobic, driven by a profound nostalgia for a bucolic Britain that had disappeared from the earth but lived on, worshiped, in the nation's imagination. Several of the great Victorian engineers saw this clearly; they did not ask their sons to follow them into what the nation considered a low trade rather than a noble profession.

Britain was even now further reducing the stature of engineers by turning over control of their ventures to managers. "Management has become a cult, with the idea that a good manager can manage anything, which simply isn't true," said Sir Jack Zunz, the head of the British engineering firm Ove Arup, which built (among much else) the Sydney Opera House. In Germany, more than 60 percent of the directors of major construction companies are engineers, Zunz noted. In Britain, the figure was about 10 percent. Akio Morita, the chairman of Sony, remarked in a 1991 lecture in Britain: "In Japan, you will notice that almost every major manufacturer is run by an engineer or technologist. Here in the United Kingdom I am told some manufacturers are led by chief executive officers who do not understand the engineering that goes into their own products. Someone once mentioned to me that many UK corporations are headed by chartered accountants. That strikes me as very curious."

In France, British-style training would condemn an engineer to an eternity in the purgatory through which *polytechniciens* pass in a few years. Yet British engineers were merely different from, not inferior to, their French colleagues. French engineers relied on planning; British engineers relied on their wits.

McDowall differed from the run-of-the-mill British engineer in the height to which he rose. He built a good reputation building some of the skyscrapers that began to dot the London skyline in the early 1960s. One of these jobs gave McDowall his first experience in tunnel work, albeit from an unusual angle. The building had a deep, two-level basement that came very close to one of the London Underground tubes that snaked through St. Giles Circus. The excavation lessened the pressure on one side of one tunnel; McDowall said, "As we went down, the bloody tube moved toward us."

All his experience gave him a deep distrust of joint ventures. "Companies decamp people they don't want and shovel them into joint ventures," he said.

"They never put the best people in, ever. *Ever.* A joint venture starts up and the parent companies say, 'Who have we got to spare?'—not, 'Who do we need?' So they go around to all the departments of the company, and the names that come down are the names of people the regional managers don't want. And *they're* the ones that go into the joint venture."

McDowall's company also detached a young civil engineer, Tony Gueterbock, to work on the project. He was not from the usual English-engineer mold. "He's an old Etonian," McDowall said of his colleague. "A rare animal in Wimpey's, I might tell you. He had superb confidence for a young man. He used to cycle to work—that type. Long hair, but a superb thinker, excellent speaker and superb writer." Gueterbock also, unlike McDowall and most of the top people in the British construction firms, spoke French. Gueterbock wasn't a favorite with some high-level executives in Wimpey, but neither was the Channel Tunnel, a fact that probably accounted for his assignment.

Everyone recognized that the English Channel Tunnel Group—which was soon to become simply the Channel Tunnel Group—needed more French companies, and Spie's representative, Jean Renault, agreed to try to recruit other partners. The first companies Spie approached were Dumez S.A. and Bouygues S.A. Dumez was a civil engineering subsidiary of the Lyonnaise des eaux-dumez group. The group had more than 100,000 employees and business in every continent. Dumez had built most everything: dams, tunnels, housing, seawalls and docks, hydro and nuclear power stations, factories, water treatment plants and hospitals. Dumez's work around Paris indicates the quality of its connections; the projects include I. M. Pei's glass-pyramid entrance to the Louvre and two modules of Terminal 2 at Charles de Gaulle Airport.

Bouygues was something else entirely.

Bouygues was the creation of one man, Francis Bouygues, who had begun his career as an ordinary engineer, a graduate of l'École centrale in Paris, a *grande École* that ranked below the Polytechnique in prestige. In 1952, at the age of thirty, he set up a contracting firm, l'Enterprise Francis Bouygues, to do construction work around Paris. Four years later, he became a builder in his own right. By the time his representatives sat down to talk to Reeve and Gueterbock, Bouygues was far and away the largest construction company in the world, with annual revenues approaching eighty billion francs.

Francis Bouygues had more in common with the founder of the École polytechnique than with its graduates. He led his grand army of workers with a Napoleonic blend of discipline and encouragement; he was by turns the sternest of authoritarians and the most brotherly of companions. He could be delicate or brutal; he could use finesse or force with equal dexterity. He was crafty, cunning, charming or cruel, as the situation demanded. His employees, low and high, loved and feared him in equal measure; they gloried in his successes, basked in the heat of his personality, dreaded his wrath. At a time when all French workers labored every day but Sunday, Bouygues gave them one Saturday a month off so that they could attend to their household business. When he visited his work sites, he always stopped to shake the hands and chat with the *compagnons*—addressing them with the *tu* and *toi* reserved for family, the closest of friends and children.

Bouygues put his hand to everything in his company. In the executive dining room, he chose the wine, decreed which of the staff got what raises. He decided how the tables would be arranged, how many settings each would have and what should be on the menus. He banned cheese, one dining room worker remembered, "because he thought that lunches shouldn't drag on interminably, and that passing over the cheese course would save some time." His behavior sometimes bordered on the bizarre. One of his executives recalled Bouygues inspecting replacement office furniture. "He came to one desk that clearly didn't please him," the executive recalled. "He bent and opened the bottom drawer, where you usually hang the files. He pulled it open to test the rollers. Then, instead of closing the drawer, he climbed into it. It collapsed, of course. 'You can see it's not of good quality,' he said. The manufacturer's rep went white."

His methods created a unique corporate culture, governed by engineers who had been trained—as one said—to "a terrible efficiency." It was less formal than a traditional French corporation—which made Bouygues engineers easier to get along with, outsiders often said—but far more demanding.

"He taught us to present our ideas in a perfect synthesis: One page maximum, encapsulating as complex a problem as you could imagine," said Philippe Montagner, who was to lead Bouygues's examination of the Channel Tunnel project. He was also very attuned to certain exterior signs that revealed much about personality. Bouygues told one subordinate, "I'm not going to visit your work site. I've seen the state in which you keep your automobile."

Bouygues's political clout was such that he could afford to sometimes treat it carelessly. One retired *compagnon* recalled visiting Bouygues's country retreat in the Sologne, the vast lake-studded forest south of Orléans, where he kept a game preserve. Bouygues liked to get up before dawn and repair to a tree perch with a thermos of coffee and a crust of bread, to watch the animals. He and his *compagnon* were thus engaged one morning when a servant came to say that the prime minister, Laurent Fabius, was calling. Bouygues waited an hour before descending.

As might have been expected, when it came to a Channel link, Francis Bouygues was already well along a path of his own choosing. The trouble, from the Channel Tunnel Group's point of view, was that Bouygues wasn't interested in a tunnel. A tunnel was a hole in the ground—not a fit monument for France, nor for one of its most notable citizens. Francis Bouygues wanted to build a bridge across the Strait—a great bridge, a strand of graceful two-kilometer spans stretched between towering pylons.

True, technology was not quite able, just yet, to build such a bridge. No matter. Bouygues had already shown, and would demonstrate again, that technology could achieve prodigies under pressure. You just had to keep your nerve.

If Mrs. Thatcher's sudden enthusiasm for a Channel fixed link came as a pleasant but mild surprise to the contractors, it came as a rude shock to her closest advisers, to whom she had revealed her decision about two months earlier, during the strategy meetings ahead of the Anglo-French summit.

"There isn't really a satisfactory explanation of why she did it," said John Noulton, who took part in the preparatory meetings. "For some reason the Prime Minister said, on one of these purely UK meetings, that the Fixed Link may not be such a bad idea—a nice symbol of our relationship with Europe, and a nice symbol of the newfound strength of the private sector, following, you know, five years of Thatcher government. And there was little short of consternation on the part of some of the other ministers there. . . . It was against all their instincts. Nicholas Ridley was flabbergasted, and he was the Minister that was going to have to carry it forward. . . . And so we were all put to work with the French government to draw up guidelines for Invitations to Promoters."

Ridley was a hard man who liked to say that he had been a Thatcherite before Margaret Thatcher, and no one disputed his claim. His faith in the wisdom and benevolence of market forces was absolute: His 1993 obituary in the *Times* observed that "In the considerable Ridley vocabulary of invective there was no word worse than paternalism." He was a civil engineer until he established himself in politics. His recreation was watercolor painting; his skill was such that he might have made a living from it.

For Reeve and the rest of the tunnel group, Ridley was a thoroughly mixed blessing. On one hand, his devotion to Thatcher and Thatcherism fell in nicely with their private-sector initiative. On the other hand, Ridley quickly revealed a strong preference for a drive-through link. Nicholas Henderson, who knew him well enough to address him in correspondence as "Nicky," summed up Ridley as "difficult to interpret, embodying as he does the instincts of an artist, the training of an engineer and the profession of a politician."

Henderson used his contacts in France to further the project. In the week before Christmas, he and Tony Gueterbock made a crucial swing through France, singing the praises of the Channel Tunnel Group's proposal to politicians and possible partners. It produced the usual blend of encouragement and disappointment. Six days after returning from France, Henderson was able to approach Thatcher when he and his wife attended the prime minister's Boxing Day lunch party at Chequers. Henderson came away with a sense that Thatcher was firm in her support of some sort of link, but enthusiastic only about a drive-through project. This was encouraging only because most of her advisers were either hostile or indifferent to the whole idea of a link.

Henderson summed up his various meetings and conversations at a CTG board meeting on January 7, 1985. He told the assembly—which included Lord Shackleton, who had stayed on as a sort of volunteer pilot—that it would do no harm to remind Thatcher of the financial and technical problems that confronted EuroRoute. The group agreed, and further agreed that use should be made of recent bad weather in the Channel "for publicising the merits of our tunnel" and for "knocking the opposition on the grounds of safety, ventilation, and the construction of islands and bridges as a danger to shipping."

CTG's engineers thought that EuroRoute's plan would founder on the opposition of marine interests to cluttering the Channel with bridge pilings. Permission to build anything in the Channel would have to come from the International Maritime Organization, which would mean getting the approval of more than a hundred maritime nations. Henderson, however, found a very different interpretation of the law when he consulted the United Kingdom's Department of Transport. EuroRoute's plan did not require IMO approval, because its structures would be in inshore waters, not in the shipping lanes. "The truth is," a senior Transport officer told Henderson, "that Euro-Route is very much a runner."

Much of CTG's attention, however, focused on serious questions of need: need for a French partner, need for an owner-operator, need for assurance that there would be money to back their ideas. There had been little progress on these, and the governments' formal request for proposals was imminent.

The French, who still had doubts about the depth of British commitment to the project, had hardly begun to prepare for the effort; Dumez, Spie Batignolles and Bouygues were—at best—merely acting in concert in an ill-defined organization they called "Francemanche." The French Transport Ministry was keeping up strong pressure to expand the group to five. In part, this reflected a simple wish to balance the consortium, to match the five British members. But it happened that the two companies suggested by the government—Société auxiliare d'enterprises, which was immediately stripped down to the acronym SAE, and Société generale d'enterprises, or SGE—were nationalized and would thus give the French government a seat at the table.

On April 2, 1985, the governments issued a formal sixty-four-page "Invitation to Promoters" to anyone who might be interested in building a Channel link that would last at least 120 years, be resistant to terrorist attack, be exceptionally safe for humans and impassible or fatal to rabid animals. Promoters were expected to be financially robust, able to show that they could raise an immense sum of money, and experienced enough to build the link in timely fashion. Each was to put up a deposit of 300,000 ECUs—a genuflection to Europeanness that worked out to about £190,000—that would be refunded if the proposal were rejected. The usual caveat about no government money was restated.

For the contractors, the invitation contained no surprises but little comfort. The deadline for submissions was October 31, which gave them a little less than seven months to draw up a detailed proposal for one of the biggest construction projects that the century would see. The risk was absolute: If they failed to convince the governments that they had the best proposal, all that they'd spent in planning would have been wasted.

When accounts of the invitation appeared in the press the following day, they included the bald statement that Mrs. Thatcher and her closest advisers were pushing for a drive-through option. CTG was alarmed to learn that a representative of EuroRoute had been granted a private audience with Thatcher at 10 Downing Street. This had apparently been arranged by Ian MacGregor and prompted a panicky letter from Henderson to Thatcher, asking for a meeting.

"Perhaps I could clarify one point: The Channel Tunnel Group are examining the possibilities of a drive-through tunnel," Henderson added in his note. "So, the idea of driving should not be seen as the monopoly of Euro-Route."

EuroRoute seemed to be the only serious opponent in the field. Henderson had talked to EuroRoute's chairman, Sir Nigel Broakes, and found him "confident that his scheme is both technically viable and financially feasible." Broakes was chairman of Trafalgar House, a corporate group that had major building, shipping and hotel interests. (Among its holdings were Cunard and London's Ritz Hotel.) He had taken over the chairmanship of EuroRoute in late 1984, when MacGregor had been named to head Britain's National Coal Board. There was no hostility in the relations between Broakes and CTG—in fact, CTG had tried to enlist Broakes in November, just before he took the

EuroRoute post. Then, a month after he joined the competition, Broakes approached CTG with a merger proposal: EuroRoute would build the road link; CTG would build a pure rail tunnel with no provision for a vehicle shuttle. Nothing came of this, but Broakes and Henderson met from time to time to exchange views—often in the splendid Trafalgar Suite in the Ritz.

EuroRoute did not have a ready set of plans for its proposal, as CTG did. Furthermore, EuroRoute, with its far more ambitious proposal, was going to have to raise twice as much money as CTG. But EuroRoute did have two things that CTG conspicuously lacked: French partners, and a consortium that was not simply a group of contractors backed by some banks.

EuroRoute had fifteen member companies: six French, nine British. It comprised three major banks—Banque paribas, Société général and Barclays—the investment bank Kleinwort Benson and several of the most important nationalized British companies—including British Telecom, British Steel and Associated British Ports, all soon to be sold off as part of the Tories' drive to privatize. Eight of the members were major construction companies, including the French giants Usinor, Alsthom and GTM. Anchoring the consortium was Broakes's Trafalgar House, whose depth of management and breadth of experience would shine out in the proposal: Trafalgar House was big enough to build EuroRoute's ambitious bridge-and-tunnel link and savvy enough to operate it.

In contrast, CTG—the freestanding CTG that was envisioned as the Channel Tunnel's owner-operator—still didn't even exist. If the five British companies thought they might somehow finesse this weakness, they were soon disabused of the notion: The word on the street was that some senior member of the government, perhaps Ridley, had been heard to say that "we won't let this tunnel go to a bunch of contractors." A bunch of contractors was, at the moment, an uncomfortably precise description of CTG.

So while seconded engineers and bankers struggled to craft a proposal, Reeve and his colleagues set forth to find a credible owner-operator for their Channel Tunnel. "As I recall, we talked to just about everybody who was large and experienced in the transportation business, whether it be passenger or freight," said Reeve. "We used to brainstorm at our committee meetings: 'Who on earth can we actually identify who has the capability of running this kind of operation?' " The reaction was everywhere the same: a decided lack of enthusiasm. Al Davidson was among those approached, but he turned them down on behalf of Technical Services, troubled by the conflicts of interest that had been built into CTG.

The tunnel group soon had another problem to deal with: organized, sophisticated, vocal, well-funded, ruthless opposition. This came from Flexilink, an organization representing Channel port and maritime interests.

Besides claiming that a modern fleet of ferries could handle all of the cross-Channel traffic more cheaply and efficiently than any bridge or tunnel, Flexilink commenced a brutal public attack on the idea of a fixed link. The propaganda campaign quickly descended to scare tactics and all-but-racist Francophobia. The campaign, noted *The Economist,* "gave off a nasty smell."

The guiding hand behind the campaign was James Sherwood, a colorful Texan who owned a major Bermuda-based shipping company, Sea Containers. Sherwood was a corporate collector who had shown an uncommon ability to preserve (or in some cases resurrect) the useful glories of such institutions as the fabled Orient Express and Venice's Hotel Cipriani. He had bought the SeaLink ferry line, which operated in the Channel, when it was privatized in 1984. The prospectus for Sealink had assured prospective buyers that the government did not expect a fixed Channel link to be in operation within a decade of the sale. Now it seemed that the promise would either be broken or just barely honored and Sherwood felt aggrieved.

Sherwood was not a man who could easily be ignored. He was an important presence in Britain—Sea Container's handsome and imposing London headquarters, on the south bank of the Thames, looked across Blackfriars Bridge into the heart of London. He was on excellent social terms with a great many important Britons, including Thatcher and almost all of her closest advisers.

Flexilink showed a terrier's appetite for the throats of its opponents. The slogans that appeared on billboards and posters in Britain ranged from clever ("The Channel Tunnel—The Black Hole that will put Britain in the Red") to ugly ("There's something about the Channel Tunnel that smells . . . and it isn't garlic"). Lurid visions were summoned of rabid rats and foxes, slinking through the dark passage from France.

On May 7, Henderson went to Bouygues's headquarters in Clamart, a commercial suburb southwest of Paris. He knew that the meeting would be the hinge upon which the entire project swung. If he could not get any movement, the gate was going to stay closed in CTG's face. Bouygues came with two of his own executives and one from Dumez, but what played out was strictly a two-handed game for very high stakes.

Henderson opened by admitting CTG's urgent need for a French partner. Bouygues said he might agree to tentative merger talks in June, but that he would want to wait some months before deciding which project to join. Henderson asked what Bouygues saw in EuroRoute that attracted him.

Bouygues replied that he had no particular interest in joining EuroRoute, whose plans he had examined, but he did wish to thoroughly examine the possibility of building a bridge.

Impossible, Henderson bluffed. Her Majesty's Government would never permit a bridge, nor would the International Maritime Organization. It would take a great deal of time to even ask the authorities for permission to build a bridge, and the answer would inevitably be no.

"Bouygues asked me what the hurry was," Henderson reported back to his board. "Why could we not all wait a few years before coming to a decision?"

Henderson laid out the arguments concerning the political window of opportunity. Then he played a trump: If this opportunity was lost, he said, there would be no fixed link built in this century. If that happened, history would blame him, Henderson. And history would also blame Francis Bouygues. EuroRoute alone could argue with some logic for delay; Broakes's group needed more time to complete the enormous task of planning and estimating the cost of its huge project.

Bouygues pressed for assurance that the project could be financed; Henderson replied that he was confident that money could be found for a rail tunnel, but added that he had doubts about a drive-through tunnel. Bouygues agreed; he didn't think drivers could cope with a fifty-kilometer drive through a tube. He then proceeded to discuss the tunnel project and its finances in detail that suggested a thorough knowledge of the subject.

Henderson pressed on: A partnership agreement was an immediate need; June would be too late, since it fell too near the July and August doldrums, when both nations would be on vacation. "I added that I would be seeing the Prime Minister on 13th May and I would be ashamed if I had to confess that we were still nowhere with the French," Henderson cabled back to the British companies. "Particularly given that Mitterrand himself was so keen." Bouygues said he understood the need for haste and would consider Henderson's arguments.

One week later, CTG received a telex from Bouygues's office in Clamart that began, "We are pleased to inform you that an agreement between the five companies: Bouygues—Dumez—Spie Batignolles—SAE—SGE has been signed yesterday Monday 13th May. The Group's name is: France Manche. . . . Are ready to meet you as soon as possible. Best Regards." It was signed by Philippe Montagner of Bouygues.

Montagner had been appointed France Manche's general manager. Bouygues had put him to work on the project a few weeks earlier, in late April. Montagner, a handsome man whose confidence permitted him a wry sense of humor and a quite un-French loud and frequent laugh, had been with Bouygues since the mid-1960s and had been given major responsibilities on the company's first overseas project, the Teheran Olympic complex in Iran, in 1971. As was often the case in Bouygues, the job came as a bolt from the blue: Montagner, then twenty-nine years old, was summoned by a telephone call one morning from his work on a factory in Dunkirk. He was unusual, in France and in his company, because he afterward continued to accept overseas jobs. Many French engineers found separation from their homeland painful.

This time, Montagner was in no doubt about his boss's preference. He had already seen the lovingly drawn plans for the huge Channel bridge that Bouygues wanted as his monument. However, Bouygues did not try to restrict or steer the study; everything was given the same serious consideration. "All we were given was a line from this area in France to this area in Britain," Montagner recalled. "We formed teams on the French side and said to our engineers, design whatever you want for two months. We could design bridges, tunnels, islands."

Design them they did: One team examined the pros and cons of a bridge, another looked at a bored rail tunnel. There was a team studying an immersed tube tunnel, another looking into a drive-through tunnel. "At that time we met every fifteen days with the British," Montagner said. "Two months later we had a big meeting with the British where it was decided that, between cost and time and capability, the best project was the one we had chosen, the bored tunnel, basically the 1973 design."

There was nothing cursory about the look Montagner's team took at his boss's pet idea. "I was forced to make a real study of a bridge," he said. "Francis Bouygues was convinced it was practical. I convinced him, not with the technical side, mainly on the cost. The cost was twice that of a tunnel. The income was twice as much also, but financing was difficult."

There was some thought given to going ahead on a bridge with only part of the financing in place, with the intention of coming back to the market when the project was under way. This was rejected as too dangerous. It fell to Montagner to break the bad news to Bouygues, who took it well but never let go of the idea. Years later he would say to Montagner, "When the tunnel is crowded in two years I hope you will build the bridge." The tunnel could then be left to trains.

As Montagner's teams went to work, the CTG was trying to deal with the loss of a limb: Midland Bank, crippled by mounting losses from Crocker National Bank, which it had acquired in 1981, had withdrawn from the consortium.

Henderson at least had the comfort of mild encouragement offered by Thatcher at the May 13 meeting. The two had sat down to coffee in the prime minister's second-floor sitting room, overlooking the garden and the Horse Guards Parade Ground. They sat at a low table in front of the fireplace, as a mass of red-coated soldiers and a military band drilled outside.

It was an unhurried meeting, and Henderson was able to lay out his case at full length. He explained the efficiency and safety of CTG's "rolling road"—brightly lighted, air-conditioned shuttle cars whisked along by electric locomotives—and painted a darker picture of a fume-filled drive-through tunnel. He assured Thatcher that the CTG tunnel could make a nice profit without driving the ferries out of business; this meant that neither she nor the Tory MPs of Kent would have to face too mutinous a constituency. At the same time, Henderson noted, healthy competition would bring down the trade-damaging fares—trucks that could move freely between France and Germany were paying, on average, £260 to cross the Channel. Thatcher assured Henderson that she was not backing any one proposal; she merely wanted something to link Britain to Europe.

When the British and French companies gathered in London on July 1 to formally join hands, a serious legal snag appeared: The French wanted the agreement to state that the two groups would work together on an "exclusive basis" to prepare and offer a proposal to the two governments. Lawyers for some of the British contractors argued that this exclusivity might violate European Community law. "Throughout July 1," Henderson recalled, "I was bombarded by telexes forbidding me to sign on the basis that was alone acceptable to the French." His sources in government didn't see the problem, but the lawyers were insistent. "As I probed more deeply into what lay behind the contractors' objections," Henderson concluded, "I gained the impression that they may have been seeking to leave their options open should things not work out as planned."

In the end, Henderson called Reeve, who was the contractors' representative on CTG's executive committee. Reeve did the brave and optimistic thing: He told Henderson to sign and agreed to take all responsibility for any "adverse consequences." The signing took place as scheduled, accompanied by glasses of Pol Roger, under portraits of the queen and President Mitterand.

Having thus come together, the Anglo-French combine instantly had to pull itself apart, at the insistence of the banks, to form an owner and a builder. This was a complex process that involved several stages. The British contracting companies withdrew to form Translink, a joint venture in which each of the five companies held an equal share. The French contractors withdrew to create Transmanche g.i.e. (Groupement d'intérêt économique, a partnership).

These two bodies then agreed to form a joint venture called Transmanche-Link. The British companies each held a 10 percent share in TML, as it quickly came to be called. On the French side, Spie, Dumez and Bouygues each had 11 percent; SGE and SAE split the remaining 17 percent.

This left ownership in the hands of CTG/FM, the entity formed by the signatures that Henderson had been at such pains to collect on July 1. The entity—which would become Eurotunnel—henceforth might glory in the title of "promoter," but in fact it was a curious and frail vessel, its crew a gaggle of people seconded from the ten contracting companies. Henderson was still aboard, as were Jean-Paul Parayre of Dumez, Stannard and Gueterbock. Marcel Sarmet of Crédit lyonnais was there, as was Renault of Spie Batignolles. But Reeve was gone to join TML, along with McDowall and Montagner.

On paper, the respective roles of TML and CTG/FM had been divided and decided weeks before the July 1 signing. In fact, the two were hardly different—Reeve acknowledged that "a number of staff oscillated between the two" for several months—and badly balanced. TML was a combine of ten strong contracting companies, each accustomed to working in joint ventures. CTG/FM was hardly more than a roomful of strangers, dominated by bankers who would never have considered, in normal times or circumstances, ever hazarding a loan to so feeble an entity. CTG/FM by this time had hired a managing director, a finance director and other executives to work on finances and organization, but the contractors on Henderson's board distrusted them.

Further, it was CTG/FM that was supposed to offer by October 31—a scant three months after its hurried formation—a considered and complete plan to finance, to contract for and to oversee construction of the largest privately funded construction project of the twentieth century. There was no way that CTG/FM could prepare such a proposal without help. But the only ones who could help were paid consultants—or the contracting companies who had created CTG/FM, whose executives still sat on and controlled its board. CTG/FM did employ engineering consultants to work on tunnel and terminal designs, but the contractors loomed large in CTG/FM's affairs. In France, the design work was done in-house by the French contracting companies, assisted by Aeroports de Paris, the airport authority.

By any rule of commerce, this was absurd. It meant that CTG/FM would be depending on the assistance of TML to prepare its proposal, while it was simultaneously negotiating a construction contract with TML. It meant that the banks would be considering loans to an entity in which they were shareholders; it meant that the contractors would be signing contracts with an entity they had created and still dominated.

The cooperative spirit that had carried the venture forward gave out, and Henderson had to face a board that was governed by the discord between its factions rather than the commonality of interests. Everyone wanted to win the government concession, but none could agree on how to achieve this. "Our Board meetings at this stage were untidy and unconstructive," Henderson recalled. "There were running battles between the contractors and banks and between the directors and the management." He found it practical to avoid submitting anything to a vote of the directors.

The contractors did not surrender their control of CTG/FM gladly or quickly. Some few companies had expressed an interest in joining the venture—Vickers and Hawker Siddeley were interested; Canadian National Railways wished to consult rather than join—but the contractors saw no reason to dilute their eventual profits. Interested parties who wanted to invest without expecting a role in the tunnel's construction or operation would be welcome, but these proved hard to find. In the end, only Mobil took a small equity holding in the venture.

Design problems in time began to yield. Political problems remained worrisome but as yet hypothetical. Problems with financing the tunnel and with the construction contract, however, remained intractable.

Reeve presented a draft contract at a meeting of CTG/FM and TML on July 9, just days after the group divided officially into owner and contractor. The draft was the product of months of work, all of it by the contractors. There was still considerable question about just what was to be proposed, so the contract was drawn to serve both a rail or a drive-through tunnel, in case the latter should be required. Because of such uncertainties, the contractors proposed that the entire agreement be done on a target-cost basis, under which both sides would share the risks of overruns and the benefits of success.

By the time Reeve presented the draft, of course, it had been scrutinized and altered by the legal departments of ten hard-nosed contracting companies. It was, he would later note, "very obviously heavily weighted in the Contractors' favour." He was thus saddened but unsurprised when the draft met with a reception that was enthusiastic only in its vehemence. It was, he noted, "vociferously objected to by the banks' representatives" and by CTG/FM's consulting engineers.

There was a problem with the price, which TML had estimated, in mid-July, at £2.77 billion, excluding taxes, inflation and interest costs. The banks advised everyone on both sides of the discussion that the project couldn't be financed unless the price were brought down to £2.33 billion. TML and CTG/FM resorted to some fiddling in trying to achieve this first-of-many lower-cost goals. The most glaring example was the removal of all provision for a cooling system in the tunnel—even though, as McDowall said, "we all knew it was required."

While the disagreements ranged over the entire document, most of them sprang from a single root: time. There was a reigning fear that something might slow or delay the project. Perhaps the ground beneath the Channel might not be as ideal for TBMs as was imagined. Perhaps there were fractures through which the Channel waters might enter. Perhaps the layer of good chalk marl might thin to a sliver, leaving the machines to toil through unstable strata and inundations. It was simple enough to imagine the results of such a catastrophe: Bad ground meant lost time, and lost time meant wasted money. A month lost in tunneling meant that the tunnel's revenue stream would begin a month later than predicted and that interest costs would continue to mount throughout that added month. Interest on the huge borrowed sums would devour the project.

The contractors had concluded, after much study, that they needed eight years to design and build the tunnel. The banks, after much study, concluded that the project could not be made fiscally viable unless the tunnel were done in seven. The contractors proposed seven and a half years; the banks insisted it had to be less.

Fear inevitably created suspicion. In the eyes of CTG/FM, time was a weapon that the contractors could easily pick up and use against it. The banks were particularly sensitive to this possible threat; they believed that TML could prolong the job until it went bust—then buy up the works at a distress price and continue with another even weaker and more pliant owner. The bankers therefore insisted on a rigid time frame, with harsh financial penalties for the contractors if they failed to meet the deadline for completion.

The banks faced another dilemma: They knew, of course, that they could not alone supply the loan money that the project was going to require—indeed, it was clear that the sum would be so large that it would require a great many banks, all of them very large, all able to advance a great deal of money for an unusually long term, with very few assurances and an enormous amount of risk. Persuading a huge syndicate of banks to do this would be a formidable task, one that would be rendered more difficult if the contractors maintained their founders' grip on CTG/FM. The banks therefore wanted TML's member companies to become minority shareholders in CTG/FM, and to relinquish control of its board.

But cutting TML out of GTG/FM would replace the contractors' interest in the commercial success of the tunnel with a financial interest in its construction. Higher construction costs would mean more revenue to the contracting companies. The banks therefore rejected the idea of a target-cost contract with its shared risks. They insisted that part of the contract be on a lump-sum basis, meaning that any cost overruns would be borne by the contractors.

This, however, made the contractors fearful. A lump-sum contract was a noose around their necks: If the tunneling was more difficult than scant data and abundant theorizing predicted, the contact would strangle them quite literally to death. They also came to fear that CTG/FM, though weak and dependent, might run off with another suitor, taking the plans, once it had won the concession.

The negotiations ran hard onto these rocks, and floating them clear required a lot of effort. McDowall recalled terrible negotiating sessions: "They kept saying it would never be funded; we said that technically it wasn't on. Then a chairman would stomp out. This would be at midnight, with forty people around the board table, all arguing and screaming. The banks were with us, but they were telling us seven and a half years was too long, that it had to be seven years, that the price was too high. We cut £150 million, which included the cooling system, which we all knew was required. We said there was no way we could finish the tunnels in [seven years]; you'd be cutting six months off the commissioning time, which is suicide."

In fact, CTG/FM had been strengthened, on August 13, when Midland Bank rejoined the group. Midland's change of heart had come at a high level and was caused by pressure from a higher level still: the British government. A consultant who dealt with many second-tier Midland executives said that "they told me that Midland had had the screws put to them by Downing Street directly."

Negotiation eventually produced a contract that was broken into three sections: The tunneling was to be done on a target-cost basis, the rolling stock was to be on a procurement basis (TML would contract to have the stock built; CTG/FM would pay for it), and the "fixed equipment"—basically everything else, from the terminals and all of the gear that would fill the tunnels—was put on a lump-sum basis. The two sides eventually agreed to add £60 million, part to the target costs and part to the lump sum, to cover TML's risks.

Underlying the whole process, however, was a dangerous set of rules that governed prices in the contract. As Reeve explained it, the banks, acting through Stannard and Renault, effectively fixed the cost. TML submitted prices, which were then adjusted by agreement "to ensure that they were below the CTG/FM bank-imposed ceiling," Reeve recalled. The ceiling was determined by the bank's assessment of what was needed to make the project financeable. It was classic fudging, starting at the bottom line and working upward, changing numbers as needed to keep the project viable on paper.

Bechtel, the big American big-project manager, was keenly interested in getting involved in the effort to link Britain and France. Bechtel did not care, particularly, who got the contract; it applied to all of the major players. Nor did the company want full standing as an equity shareholder; it only wanted to manage the project for a fee.

Bechtel had excellent credentials; it had managed giant projects around the world and was quite well known in France. Nonetheless, the reception from the tunnel group was frosty. Bechtel was treated, with some justification, as a brash American upstart. It pushed hard for admission. It did not hesitate to suggest that the project needed Bechtel, and needed it badly. It did not fail to mention its qualifications, to reel off the marvels its had helped create.

This did not go down well on either side of the Channel. Like a squabbling couple interrupted by a peacemaker, Britain and France turned on the intruder. One incident captured the feeling nicely: A Bechtel representative had come to London to present his company's credentials to an assembly of CTG/FM's leaders. He stressed Bechtel's experience, explaining how the company had worked with local firms, many in developing countries, to build major projects.

Jean-Jacques Hessig, who was Crédit lyonnais's representative with CTG/FM, stopped the presentation and buried Bechtel's hopes with a single phrase. "La France n'est pas Gabon," he said.

But Bechtel was a tough competitor and was neither offended nor discouraged by this French dismissal, which the British heartily seconded. Bechtel withdrew to regroup.

More and more, EuroRoute was shaping up as CTG/FM's only serious competitor. The British government's clear and active interest in keeping Midland Bank in the consortium suggested that at some level of its institutional consciousness, the government recognized that the tunnel group had the best and perhaps the only practical plan for a fixed Channel link. Even the rumors that put other projects in the lead agreed in one element: The Channel Tunnel plan might not top anyone's list, but it was everyone's second choice. Support for the other plans might therefore cancel out, leaving CTG/FM the winner by default.

By September, the price had been trimmed to £2.446 billion. CTG/FM then notified TML that an additional £150 million would have to be cut, to bring the price to £2,296 million. This set off the rancorous sessions that McDowall recalled, when the cooling system was removed from the plans. Other costs were cut by simply deferring them until later in the project.

In these final weeks before the October 31 deadline, the Ministry of Transport began receiving mysterious telephone calls. The callers were consulting engineers, and they wanted to know what was required in a Submission to Government. They did not wish, however, to identify their client.

For the tunnel venturers, October was a blur, with the construction contract and the Submission to Governments being drafted and redrafted under the intense and increasing pressure of the October 31 deadline. On October 24, as a fifth revised version of the Submission neared completion, the French contractors gave notice that they would not participate unless a contract were agreed and signed beforehand.

On October 30, with the deadline just hours away, a British contingent led by Henderson and Reeve went out to Stansted Airport, northeast of London, to meet a delegation led by Parayre and Montagner. The purpose was to sign the French version of the Submission, which would then be taken back to Paris and handed in the following day. The Submission by this time had run to fifteen revisions, and its 2,500 pages filled eleven bulky volumes. Ten thousand amendments had been tacked on in October alone.

They met on the tarmac, as in some *noir* film, as the day's shadows grew long. It was to be a routine signing of the Submission documents, but Parayre was grave when he stepped from the plane: There could be no signature, he told Henderson, until certain problems were solved. He suggested they sit down somewhere and talk. They repaired to an employees' lounge in a hangar, "with broken-down chairs and a coffee machine and one or two airport employees sitting around disconsolately," Henderson recalled.

It would not do, Parayre said: This meeting was going to take some time, and it couldn't be conducted in front of the lounging airport workers. Henderson loaded the parties into a fleet of cars and headed for the distant restaurant in the airport terminal. It turned out to be a hot-table cafeteria with a dining area all but filled with small tables, each surrounded by four chairs. The chairs were bolted to the floor.

There was one larger table and a few unbolted chairs, and here the group settled down to negotiations. It became clear that the insistence of the French contractors on a written, signed, governing document was not a pose or a negotiating position: If no agreement emerged at Stansted Airport, the contractors would not participate in the following day's Submission to Governments.

"In order to ease our work in the unpromising setting of the self-service restaurant I went to the bar to order some wine," Henderson recalled. " 'Not till six o'clock,' the barmaid told me with that look of pleasurable rejection that makes me wonder why Napoleon ever called us a nation of shopkeepers. So we started with tea." The wine, when it arrived, was a muscadet that did not even impress the English.

The session dragged on through the evening, punctuated by dozens of calls to Paris and London, to the banks and the companies and the executives of CTG and France Manche. Henderson sought guidance from Stannard, who was not at the meeting.

"The contractors attempted at the last moment to in effect put in a construction contract, which they wanted signed before anything went forward," Stannard said. "To all intents and purposes, it was, 'We do it and you pay for it.' "

Stannard nonetheless told Henderson to go ahead and sign the document, which came to be called the Stansted Protocol. In his view, the protocol was irrelevant: If CTG/FM won the concession, there would have to be a real contract, one that would satisfy the lending banks. No bank would lend any money on a document like the Stansted Protocol.

The contractors, Stannard admitted, probably believed that they had, and would keep, enough power to make the protocol stand. "I think that they believed that they were totally in charge," he said. "And as far as CTG was concerned, they were. I mean, they wouldn't even allow Sir Nicholas Henderson to have a vote, even though he was chairman."

What the contractors got in the Stansted Protocol was a six-page document that guaranteed good profits, limited liability for damages, and promised bonuses if the work was finished within seven years. It incorporated a ninety-seven-page draft contract that gave the contractors a 12.36 percent fee on actual costs up to the target cost, 6 percent on any overrun costs. If there were savings on the target-cost works, the contractors would get half; if there were extra costs, they would be responsible for just 30 percent. The contractors' fee on the lump-sum works was 16 percent; they could be assessed £328,000 per day in damages if the tunnel wasn't completed on time, up to a maximum of £120 million. The daily damages could be adjusted for inflation, but the maximum could not.

History would come to treat the protocol derisively, as an example of the contractors' greed. This was not entirely just. The margins were reasonable, given the risks. The protocol was surely tender in its concern for the contractors' worries, but many of the worries were genuine. A seven-year contract meant that actual construction would be crammed into little more than five years; planning the tunnel's details, getting the tunnel-boring machines and securing parliamentary approval would devour most of two years. A cap on damages simply guaranteed that the companies would not be ruined if the tunneling ran into grave problems. Henderson and Parayre, Reeve and Montagner signed the protocol before midnight, and the French went home with their signed and agreed copy of the Submission. The next morning, Henderson and the weighty document were loaded into a special van and sent off to the Department of Transport's headquarters.

When the meeting convened in the minister's office, there were some familiar faces: Ridley, of course, and Henderson and Broakes, and Lord Layton, chairman of Eurobridge. Another face was familiar but quite unexpected in the circumstances: James Sherwood, the American ferry owner, the gray eminence behind the dirty public-relations war against the fixed link—and, it now appeared, the man behind those mysterious telephone calls requesting information about rules governing Submissions to Governments.

Sherwood, it turned out, had brought in a plan of his own for a fixed link. He was no longer simply an opponent. He was a competitor.

6

The ten proposals submitted to the governments ranged from the ridiculous to the barely possible.

There was a proposal from a Mr. M. L. McCullouch for a Hoover-style dam across the Channel, with a road on top and a Panama-style canal lock in the middle through which shipping might pass. The Boothroyd Airship Company of Bournemouth suggested a bridge whose sections would be hoisted by gasbags. There were proposals for bridges whose decks would swing from fibers not yet invented, a rail-only tunnel whose projected cost was a dizzying £115 billion, a dam-and-tunnel that would use the Channel's tides (its designer said) to generate enough electricity to help pay off the estimated £12 billion construction cost.

Sherwood's plan, which he had dubbed Channel Expressway, seemed to belong in this pipe-dream category. Indeed, it was easy enough to believe that it was intended as satire, a not-so-modest proposal meant to expose the absurdity of ideas that had been put forward in earnest. Sherwood promised two colossal bored tunnels, each 11.3 meters in inner diameter, each carrying rail *and* road traffic, at a cost of £2.1 billion—cheaper than CTG/FM's £2.6 billion and a pittance next to EuroRoute's £5 billion projected cost. SeaLink's ferry employees would operate the tunnel, so there would be no layoffs in Kent. Channel Expressway would be entirely privately financed through the sale of common stock, half of which would be issued in Britain and half in France.

"Harnessing advanced technology developed and successfully operating in the North Sea and Japan, Channel Expressway has solved the crucial problem of ventilation," Sherwood's brochure said. The solution involved putting electrostatic scrubbers in side tunnels to remove particulate matter from the air, and pumping in fresh air from two offshore ventilation shafts.

The air would be further cleansed by the unique arrangements Channel Expressway envisioned for traffic. Automobiles and trucks would drive through the tunnels along two same-direction lanes in each tunnel, at one hundred kilometers an hour. Once each hour, motor traffic would be halted and a train would run through, on tracks embedded in the roadway. The locomotive's speed would be controlled from a scout vehicle that would range ahead to make sure no stray cars were still in the tunnel. The train's pistonlike passage would help freshen the air. Sherwood said that 3,200 automobiles and 600 trucks could pass through the tunnel each hour with this system.

Competitors set upon Sherwood's proposal like hounds on a hare. It was illegal, they said, since it had not been submitted to the French government. It was technically impossible, because the chalk marl layer wasn't thick enough to accommodate Channel Expressway's tunnels, which would require a bored passage with a diameter of 12.25 meters. If attempted, it would cost far more than £2.1 billion and could not be finished in the promised five years. If built, it would be impractical and unsafe to have trains and cars sharing the same passageway. If they did run, it was far from certain that the scrubbers and pumps could render the air fit for human lungs.

The doubts did not come only from competitors. "Completely crazy," was the verdict of Philippe Essig, the chairman of SNCF. Another French expert called the ventilation system "irréaliste et dangereuse."

Assessing the proposals fell to an Anglo-French group that was an outgrowth of the unit that had prepared the invitation to promoters, and it was, as before, headed in Britain by John Noulton. Even though only four proposals had to be examined—only CTG/FM, EuroRoute, Channel Expressway and Eurobridge, a high-tech, high-cost bridge proposal, had put up the required cash deposit in both France and Britain—it was still a daunting task. The governments had said they would decide who got the concession within ninety days, so the promoters were only bound to stand by their submissions for a hundred days. There was also not a moment to be lost in getting a fixed-link bill before Parliament. If the process dragged on too long, the whole effort might again come off the rails.

As this was going on, France Manche and the Channel Tunnel Group set up matching French and British entities that shared the name by which the venture would henceforth be known: Eurotunnel, often shortened to ET. And TML took the first steps toward actually planning and building the tunnel. David Brown was one of the first to be called to start up the great project. The call came on a dance floor, at one of the dances that Balfour Beatty used to sponsor for its employees.

"Fairfield Hall in Croyden," he recalled. "There were about four hundred people there. Recession later claimed those traditional dances. They were gatherings where you got to know your colleagues, where the clashes of personalities that have developed over the years are mellowed."

Brown was a tall, soft-spoken man whose thinning hair and mild look gave him something of the appearance of a country parson. He was a carpenter's son who had entered engineering as an apprentice. He owed his advancement (he was then Balfour Beatty Engineering's director of operations) to education, and he owed that to a combination of intellect and brawn. The former had pulled him out of the ranks and sent him to university; the latter had paid the bills: Brown stood well over six feet tall, and his skill as an oarsman won him scholarships.

He had spent a lot of time overseas for Balfour Beatty, mostly in short stretches. "I went out purely on a bachelor basis. As operations director, I was moving around the world—Venezuela, Nigeria, South America. Most of my career has been one month out, back for two weeks, then another month out in another location," he said. His most recent tour had been in Nigeria, where Balfour Beatty was doing a group of projects for the government. "Primarily dams, water systems, hospitals, clinics, agricultural equipment," he said. "About £300 million worth of projects, mainly in the Plateau State there." He had gone there expecting to stay a week; the work held him for three months.

There had been hints, before he left Nigeria to be home for Christmas, that his bosses wanted to talk to him about the Channel Tunnel. He remembered these hints as he circled the dance floor at Fairfield Hall, and the music carried him toward a table occupied by Don Holland, the chairman of Balfour Beatty.

After an exchange of pleasantries, Holland got down to business. "I want you to get involved with this Channel Tunnel project," he said. "We've put this proposal together; we want you to have a look at it. Between now and the end of December, you'll go to see the director-general of UK works, which is John Reeve. Your name is being put forward as the engineering director of UK works."

All Brown knew of Reeve was that he had been responsible for the Thames Barrier job. The meeting took place in Costain's headquarters office. Brown found Reeve "a very jolly, jovial character."

"I've been looking at your CV," Reeve said. "Your background is engineering, you've worked on multi-discipline projects, major projects. I know you're operations director at Balfour Beatty now, but we're interested in you as engineering director. Would you be interested in changing, going back to what you were doing previously?"

"It sounds like an interesting project," Brown said. In the back of his mind, he imagined a close-to-home job without the political headaches he had dealt with overseas.

"I thought, well, this is a straight engineering job," Brown recalled. "Go in, get the project going. Reeve told me there was nothing, no plan. It was going to be, go in and build the Channel Tunnel from scratch. A great challenge. So I said yes, I would take the assignment."

"Right, it's your job," Reeve said. The meeting had taken fifteen minutes.

Noulton's joint study group sorted through the proposals and rather easily decided to recommend Eurotunnel's. This was dictated more by the deficiencies of the competition than by Eurotunnel's excellence.

"I'm probably being unfair to the Eurotunnel project, but it did seem to me that the bored tunnel was everyone's second choice," Noulton said. "There was a great deal of support for a drive-across scheme, and we had three of those. One, the Eurobridge thing, I think we discounted because it didn't stand up as well as the others, technically or financially. It would have been the first multispan suspension bridge anywhere; each span was longer than any existing suspension bridge, and it used a special lightweight plastic rope for the suspension cables that was a little bit iffy. It was theoretically possible, but it was such a technological leap that it didn't stand up. The financial markets felt similarly."

EuroRoute had built up solid support, but it had a number of important drawbacks. Noulton's group felt that the combination of high bridge, spiral ramp and long underwater tunnel would challenge and perhaps unnerve drivers. It would put a large number of bridge towers in the inshore waters on both sides of the Channel, plus two major islands to accommodate the ramps. And, finally, EuroRoute's higher cost made private financing more problematical.

The deficiencies that opponents gleefully pointed out in Sherwood's Channel Expressway were equally evident to Noulton's group. It was nonetheless difficult to dismiss. "Remember, this was a businessman, in the transport business," Noulton said. "This singled him out from the others, who were basically contractors and bankers, who wanted to make money out of it. This was a chap who was ready to run a transport operation, and the way he served up his proposal was extremely slick. There wasn't a whiff of doubt about it. It was confident, slick, brisk, well-packaged. But it was an empty box."

Nevertheless, it proved difficult to knock down Channel Expressway, despite what the joint assessment group saw as "fundamental flaws" in the plan. "Every time an objection was raised, he [Sherwood] would say that it was solvable, and he'd produce an expert," Noulton said. "When railway inspectors said you can't have rails in a road tunnel, because if there was a derailment the train would slide all around, Sherwood said he'd have a separate bored tunnel for the railroad. Just like that: No problem. If you want it, you can have it. It made it difficult for the experts to take him seriously." Noulton paused. "But the politicians swallowed his medicine wholesale."

Sherwood's competitors were furious when he was permitted, against all of the rules, to change his plan to four tunnels rather than two. Their fear was justified, because such permission was a signal that the unthinkable was about to happen: The British government was about to make James Sherwood's cockamamy scheme a front-runner in this long and exhausting race.

Noulton's group handed its final report to the governments on December 20, 1985. It recommended that the concession go to Eurotunnel. This did not please some very important people in France. The contest at that point had one month to run; Mitterand and Thatcher were to meet January 20 in Lille to announce their governments' decision. Henderson could hardly have imagined how frantic those intervening weeks would be.

It was a crowded canvas, with two cultures, two governments and four promoters in the picture. The broad strokes were these. The British government, and particularly Ridley, wanted two elements in the composition: James Sherwood and a drive-through link. France was flexible, but there was influential backing for a bridge.

Ridley's convictions, it seemed, had heightened the fever pitch of the debate: He believed that Sherwood deserved a chance, believed that the Transmanche contractors should not get a free shot at enormous profits, believed that he could force an amalgamation that would give Sherwood a share, believed he could get a drive-through link, believed he could get the French to accept a solution that he proposed.

But there is interesting evidence that Ridley deliberately created all the confusion and bitter infighting among the contestants, as part of a negotiating strategy that had for him become habitual. An important part of Ridley's negotiating, the *Financial Times* later reported, "is based on the deliberate creation of doubt. If you are in a complex negotiation, Mr. Ridley says, you must first persuade all of the protagonists that it is likely to fail. It means suggesting confusion in your own mind as well.

"You tell everyone that they have lost, and then you ask whether it might be possible to rescue something from the wreck. In that way you can establish the bottom line of all the parties involved. Then you can start negotiating again, this time seriously."

Certainly the events of those times support the theory that Ridley was practicing what he would shortly preach. He introduced a sense of confusion and deadlock on January 7, 1986, when he met with Jean Auroux, the French minister of transport. The purpose of the meeting was to thin the field from the four. The Anglo-French assessment that Noulton had helped prepare was in hand, and its conclusions were clear: Channel Expressway was sketchy, Eurobridge was technologically and financially uncertain, EuroRoute's virtues were in substantial measure offset by its high cost, Eurotunnel was banal and lacked a drive-through element but involved the fewest and smallest risks.

Indeed, Auroux and Ridley did agree quickly to eliminate Eurobridge. But when Auroux suggested that Channel Expressway be similarly rejected, Ridley balked. There was much to recommend Sherwood's plan, he said, particularly the drive-through capability it offered. Ridley instead suggested that EuroRoute be dropped.

This was clearly an impossible request at that time. As Noulton had discovered, there was still powerful support in France for EuroRoute. Henderson, playing his sources, had traced this support to its roots in the Élysée Palace and in the top ranks of the French banking system. This was not nominal support, not a bargaining position, but a deeply held belief. It was—as Ridley must have realized—impolitic to suggest so abruptly and summarily that EuroRoute should be tossed aside. The meeting went nowhere; another was scheduled for the following week, the last before the scheduled announcement of a winner. Eurotunnel was hardly mentioned.

The French banks now urged Auroux to stand firm behind EuroRoute; newspaper stories in Britain began to suggest that Broakes and Sherwood might join forces. On January 13, a message arrived at Eurotunnel's headquarters from Bouygues' London representative, saying that Broakes had invited Henderson and Parayre to lunch that day. The lunch was in the Trafalgar Suite at the Ritz, and Trafalgar House's entire board was there. Broakes again lofted a proposal that had been in the air before, that he build the road bridge and tunnel and Eurotunnel build the rail tunnel.

Broakes's people could see that they had only to sell their plan in Britain to win the competition—French support was firm. In Britain, the offshore island, with its spiral ramp linking bridge to tunnel, was a magnet for criticism from the authorities and the opposition. EuroRoute was now offering to eliminate the ramp island and substitute a tunnel for the bridge section on the British side.

But Eurotunnel was not interested in joining anyone; its board rejected any sort of combination. Though the issue was still very much in doubt, Eurotunnel had acquired composure if not confidence. The board "did not

One of EuroRoute's proposed offshore islands, with its tunnel-to-bridge ramp.

think that we could compromise on the project; there was no need to bring in either of the other contestants," Henderson noted. "And they saw no reason to panic about our prospects."

The banks were more agitated, and wanted Eurotunnel to sink a quick £70,000 into last-minute advertising to try to sway the Cabinet when it met the next day, Thursday, to decide (if it could) to whom it would award the concession.

On Thursday, as the ministers mulled the question, Henderson met Sherwood—alone—for lunch in the latter's office near Blackfriars Bridge. Sherwood said he had proposed to Bouygues that the two groups get together and build the Mousehole—a single, rail-only tunnel, seven meters in diameter. If that project went well, the coventurers could then build either the Channel Expressway drive-through tunnels or the Eurotunnel rail-shuttle project.

Both men knew that they were playing the last hand in a high-stakes game. Sherwood knew more: He knew that Henderson held all the cards. Like a good poker player, he kept this information to himself during the lunch. But he knew that unless he could convince Eurotunnel to agree to a joint venture, he had lost.

Sherwood had been stymied by the French, who insisted that half the project had to be owned by French companies. Sherwood protested that the tender documents said nothing about the project having to be half French-owned.

"And they said, 'Well, the British are so naive, they would produce a document like that. But this is France, and we would never permit the project to be developed by a group that wasn't at least fifty per cent French,' " Sherwood recalled.

By then, he said, "it was getting very late in the day, and to line up suitable

French partners was extremely difficult." The problem was that every French company he contacted first called for government approval to join, and the government in every case refused.

"They checked with the palace, and were told no, they were not to participate in our consortium," Sherwood said. "So we effectively were blocked from the deal."

Ridley, meanwhile, told Sherwood that environmental and cost concerns made EuroRoute unacceptable to the British government. Sherwood tried to get Broakes to join forces with him, but Broakes—encouraged by assurances from France that he would win the concession—refused. "I know from President Mitterand that EuroRoute is going to win this bid," Broakes told Sherwood. "Therefore, I will not contemplate handing over or joining forces with you."

So when Sherwood and Henderson sat down to lunch, they sat down to decide the contest. Henderson did not know this, but his board had decided to play the cards it had. The two men swapped offers and observations. The meeting ended where it had begun: Henderson and Sherwood were still competitors, would never be partners. At that moment, Sherwood knew he had lost. He also knew, as Henderson did not, that Eurotunnel had won. The one item on which both governments agreed—that a drive-through link was the best possible solution—had created the deadlock that doomed both drive-through proposals. "Since they couldn't reach any agreement, they chose the compromise, and the compromise was Eurotunnel," Sherwood said. "Which in my opinion was the worst of all worlds, because it was neither fish nor fowl: It didn't offer the drive-through facilty, which it seems to me is what everybody wants. That's what transportation is all about today: The motor vehicle."

Sherwood did not retire quietly to lick his wounds. With hope gone of his ever building a fixed link, he turned his considerable energy and resources to trying to ensure that no one else built one.

Sherwood wanted to defeat the fixed link utterly, and he (and the other members of Flexilink) chose to do this by questioning the safety of the tunnel both as an investment and as a means of transportation. Investors were cautioned that their investment would go up in smoke; travelers were encouraged to think about themselves doing the same in some submarine holocaust. This latter was an argument of wonderful persuasiveness, awakening the claustrophobe in everyone and stimulating the peculiarly British mania for safety. The belief that perfect safety is an achievable goal is writ in every British soul, as is the belief that the pursuit and assurance of a risk-free environment is a proper goal of government. Thus Sherwood's warnings did not fall on deaf ears.

. . .

Not knowing that Eurotunnel was sure to win, Henderson was still responsive to pressures that he might have felt less keenly if he had shared Sherwood's knowledge. The governments were insisting that the promoters reach agreement with British Rail and SNCF concerning the railways' usage of the tunnel. Without such an agreement, all were told, there could be no grant of concession.

So Henderson and his colleagues at Eurotunnel spent the next few days in a fevered effort to agree. It was an unequal and unfair struggle, and the results were predictable.

"We had to reach agreement with British Rail and SNCF on usage," Stannard said. "That was the government requirement, and it gave BR and SNCF—mainly SNCF—an *immensely* powerful position [in deciding] who was going to win. Bear in mind that the railways had their own scheme that had been rejected 'way back, they were not exactly pleased they were talking to other competitors, as it were.

"The first meeting we had was in France, with French railway and BR people there as well. It was in Paris, in the SNCF offices, in their great big boardroom, with the map on the wall showing Paris as the center of the universe and all the trains going to it. SNCF's attitude was that we were taking over a project that should have been financed by them, as a French government entity. . . . Effectively they were saying, 'You shouldn't even be here. This is supposed to be our project, and quite frankly, we're not going to pay more than what it would cost us if we'd built our own thing and were running it.'

"The difficulty was that they also had been given—by the governments— *all* of the financial analyses that had been prepared, so they knew the whole of our pricing. They knew *everything* that we were relying on from the point of view of income from the railways, from everywhere. It became an impossible negotiation."

On Saturday, forty-eight hours before Mitterand and Thatcher were to meet in Lille to announce their choice, Henderson was tipped that Eurotunnel was the likely winner.

By Sunday morning, the same information was in the British press; newspapers said an award to Eurotunnel was a certainty, although Henderson himself was certain that it was not. As night fell, the railway negotiations stalled in Paris; Parayre called Henderson in despair. Auroux, said Parayre, was both despairing and angry: in despair thinking the negotiations were doomed, in a fury at the British press's assertion that the concession would fall to Eurotunnel. Nothing was certain, Auroux told Parayre.

"In the end, we got to a silly situation where we had to stop the clock,"

Stannard said. "At midnight we were supposed to stop negotiating and tell the government that we'd reached a conclusion. And we couldn't. So we went on into the small hours of the morning, with myself being adamant that we were not going to drop our price."

In the end, the railways basically received the right to use half of the tunnel's capacity for fees that were forty percent of the total revenue. "That went in to the governments," said Stannard, "with SNCF saying in effect they couldn't recommend this, but, well, we'd run out of time so we all ought to go home." Both sides agreed to send the fifty-forty plan to the governments. After that, Stannard said, "we all just sat and waited."

Jean Renault led the Eurotunnel contingent that attended the award ceremony the next day, and he entered Lille's Hotel de Ville feeling that the governments' decision was still very much in doubt. Thatcher and Mitterand quickly put his fears to rest; Eurotunnel was the winner. The leaders of the respective nations made the appropriate noises, pronouncing the link a good thing, the project a historic undertaking, the moment a symbol of amity and understanding between neighbors.

There was, it must be said, more than a bit of anticlimax in the event. Henderson later wrote, "What was interesting to me was the lack of enthusiasm for the project on both sides of the House." Only the dedicated anti-European members—who wanted the project scrapped—could summon any real feeling about it, he thought. The best that anyone seemed to be able to say was that the Channel Tunnel wasn't the worst proposal; that it had fewer glaring political or technical or financial flaws than its competitors. Any doubt that it was everyone's second choice was swept away by a scrap of information that later came to Henderson: In the last stages of the competition, the French government had sent an emissary to Britain to say that Mitterand would drop his insistence on EuroRoute if the British dropped their preference for Sherwood's Channel Expressway. The two sides would then compromise on the Channel Tunnel. It was, Henderson wrote, "the ultimate in the process of eliminations."

Eurotunnel now faced several hurdles: It had to create itself, making a functioning organization from an unformed lump of secondees from the banks and contractors. This organization had to shepherd legislation through the governments of two nations. It had to negotiate a contract for more than £2 billion with some of the biggest and most experienced contracting companies on the globe. And it had to raise money.

The political task seemed easiest. "There was never a big problem" with the political end of things, Stannard said. "It went through all of those things in apple-pie order." The other hurdles were far more difficult.

Eurotunnel's great triumph—winning the concession—had perversely weakened the company badly. The contractors immediately turned to the business of Transmanche-Link, stripping Eurotunnel of much expert assistance, including Reeve and McDowall. Stannard and Jean Renault of Spie Batignolles stayed on as managing directors of Eurotunnel, but the concession emptied many slots in the organization.

Stannard had seen this coming when everyone was still working on the bid. "I time and again tried to drive it home that you've got to build a company," he said. "But I was a voice in the wilderness." Everything had been geared to the bid; no one had thought to look beyond that horizon. "The moment we won, we still had temporary people. I was there temporarily, Jean Renault was there temporarily. They were going out and trying to find people to take these jobs.

"And let's be honest with this: *Nobody wanted them.* Bear in mind what the situation was at that time: Would *you* join a company that is negotiating a concession and a treaty, a construction contract, that has still got to raise its money, and has got to go through two years of Parliamentary process, which *may* actually throw the whole thing out, if you'd got a good job paying you a lot of money now? And the answer is that most of the people we spoke to just said no, don't be silly.

"What happened is that the people—being as nice to them as you possibly can—the people who actually took the jobs were ones that *needed a job!* And I don't think they got the best people at *all.*"

It was true that not many senior executives answered Eurotunnel's desperate calls for help. The banks found few volunteers to take on the immense task of finding the £5 billion in loans needed to build the tunnel, and as a consequence a large number of very young bankers found themselves drafted.

The architect of the financing was one of the few professionals that Eurotunnel possessed: Quentin Morris, a former senior executive of British Petroleum whom Henderson had recruited in mid-1985. Morris, who was called "Q" by everyone with whom he worked, had done excellent work in financing the exploitation of the North Sea oil fields.

For staff, Morris had secondees from the banks. One such was Ian Callaghan, a calm young man whose qualifications for the job tell a great deal about how the Channel Tunnel project stood. "I was born in Africa," he said.

"Educated in English boarding schools. I went to London University and read English." He went to the United States, on an exchange program, and wound up studying the Vietnam War for two years.

"Then my wife said it would be nice to earn some money," he said. "So being a banker seemed like as good an idea as any." He sent an application to NatWest in early 1983; he was twenty-five years old. "I literally had just come off the graduate training program when the Eurotunnel thing came along," he said. "I'd never done a lending deal in my life. I'd never lent anyone any money to do anything. It was one of those fateful things: I just happened to finish one thing, and this came along."

The questions that faced Callaghan and Morris were very basic. "We just started with a blank sheet of paper and a cost that had to be financed," Callaghan said. "It was a question of working from there. Q and I were at the center of that whole thing. And we just had endless meetings with the banks.

"There were many possibilities and ways of doing things: liens and instruments, bonds which would turn into equity in due course—all these weird and wonderful instruments that were kind of beginning to be around just about the time that this issue was really taking off. There were all sorts of leveraged buyouts going on in the States, all these things that people were dreaming up and going to jail for. . . . But in the end we just brought it right back down to basics, and made it straight equity and straight debt."

Basic it might be; simple it was not. Financing the tunnel was going to require a long and elaborate series of successes. The promoters of the Channel Tunnel had taken several leaps of faith to conclude that the project would be financially sound. Now banks and investors great and small were going to be asked to make those same leaps.

The departure of the contractors' staffs to Transmanche-Link left the banks in charge of Eurotunnel. The banks no longer spoke with one voice, however. NatWest, which had staked its reputation on getting the tunnel financed, had not forgiven Midland for its defection during the Crocker crisis. Now NatWest and Crédit lyonnais dictated a division of responsibilities: They would take care of structuring the financing. Midland and BNP were given the task of dealing with technical questions about the project.

In any normal project, the financial work would be by far the more important responsibility. The technical banks would be doing scut work, checking contracts and counting beans. The financing banks would be doing the more glamorous work of gathering a mighty group of powerful banks to fund one of the century's great projects. Midland would be peeling potatoes and washing pots while NatWest led a cavalry charge.

Such a situation produced the expected hard feelings. Chris Deacon, a young Midland executive, found this when he was assigned to the Channel Tunnel in December 1985. When Midland returned to the project, Deacon said, it was "clearly not leading events. . . . It had allowed the pole position to move to NatWest and CL."

Deacon was typical of the troops who were thrown into this great campaign. He was then thirty-seven years old, with enough promise to get the attention of his superiors, and enough experience and education to handle complex banking work. He had little enough seniority at Midland to be expendable—if the campaign failed, his career would be over—but enough ambition and confidence to take the risk. If he collapsed under pressure, well, it would be a shame, but Midland could survive the loss.

"All of the banks had people [in the project] of about the same age," he recalled. "Natwest had some rather older people, but the Frenchmen were about my age. I mean, there were people more senior than us who were controlling us. But the day-to-day was done by us. And you know, when the going got rough, one felt that all of the debt was on our shoulders, and people were running for cover up there."

The construction contract, Deacon noted, "had been put together at that earlier stage when conflicts of interests weren't recognized. It was put together by contractors and banks working as one team, and one of the things that upset the contractors was that when we split, they saw the bank as going back on a contract that they had helped write. The banks, of course, saw it slightly differently. The banks still saw Eurotunnel as a creature of the contractors, who indeed held a majority of its stock."

When Deacon joined the effort, the banking syndicate comprised about two dozen banks, each of which had signed a letter of intent. The letters had little legal standing, and also, as Deacon noted, "basically gave the banks all the let-outs in the world." The depth of commitment varied greatly; many of the banks had been sweet-talked into signing up; others, such as Deutsche Bank, were so intent on being part of the fixed-link project that they had signed on with several of the consortia.

The banking syndicate resembled a three-tiered wedding cake. The Arranging Banks—NatWest, Midland, Crédit lyonnais, Banque nationale de Paris and Banque indosuez—were the top tier. The second tier was the Agent Banks—major banks who acted as intermediaries between the Arranging Banks and the third and lowest tier: the Underwriting Banks, drawn from every part of the globe with the almost total exception of the United States. In time, the ranks of this bank syndicate would swell to more than 220.

This was far more than had been envisioned. "It was put together on the basis that you'd have about eighty top-quality banks in the deal, banks who understood project financing and were sizeable in terms of capital," Deacon said. "We ended up with more than two hundred and twenty banks, with some that should never have been in the deal—some of whom we'd never heard of."

The Agent Banks were divided along the same lines as the Arranging Banks, into a technical group and a financial group. Deacon came to feel that NatWest and Crédit lyonnais had used their leverage to make life a little easier for themselves. "It always seemed to me that my dear friends in CL—who *are* my dear friends—chose to stuff Midwest and BNP with the difficult banks," he said. "A lot of the problems were as a result of that particular structure."

The technical Agent Banks were Deutsche Bank, Union Bank of Switzerland, Amsterdam-Rotterdam Bank (usually abbreviated AmRo) and the Industrial Bank of Japan. They were acutely aware of the conflicts of interest in Eurotunnel, and they were not about to tolerate them.

"Nobody in the banks at that stage trusted the Arranging Banks," Deacon said. "They said, 'You are a shareholder and you are a lender. You have a conflict of interest.' . . . Certain of the banks—Deutsche in particular—were playing a very, very aggressive and tough line at this stage."

But in general these currents of suspicion and doubt were deep and hidden. On the surface, events seemed to be flowing smoothly. On February 7, less than three weeks after the announcement of the government's selection of the Channel Tunnel project, Noulton completed negotiations with Eurotunnel on a draft of the official concession agreement. The Monday after, February 10, Eurotunnel opened a public information center in Tontine House, Folkestone, that was to draw fourteen thousand visitors in its first three months of operation.

On Wednesday, February 12, representatives of Her Majesty, the Queen of the United Kingdom of Great Britain and Northern Ireland and of Her Other Realms and Territories, Head of the Commonwealth, and the president of the French Republic, met in Canterbury Cathedral to sign a treaty "Concerning the Construction and Operation By Private Concessionaires of a Channel Fixed Link."

It was a lovely document, majestic in its simplicity, entirely symbolic until ratified by the signatory nations. Its sole power at that moment was the ability to stimulate opponents of the tunnel to action. As Mitterand and Thatcher watched their foreign secretaries sign the treaty, protesters stood behind police lines in the cathedral grounds and shouted their disapproval. Their nationality and the source of their feelings could be deduced from their chant: "Froggy, froggy, froggy—Out, out, out."

The treaty directed that two bodies be organized to oversee the project: the Intergovernmental Commission and the Safety Authority. The former was to have up to sixteen members, half from each nation, at least two drawn from the Safety Authority. The IGC's charter was to "supervise, in the name and on behalf of the two Governments, all matters concerning the construction and operation of the Fixed Link." Its functions were broad and stated in general terms: It was to monitor the construction and operation of the link, consult with the concessionaires, approve proposals of the Safety Authority, advise the governments and the concessionaire. It was charged with "drawing up, or participating in the preparation of, regulations applicable to the Fixed Link," and "considering any matter referred to it by the Governments or the Safety Authority or any other matter which appears to it to be necessary to consider." It could draw up its own rules or procedure and could draw upon the authority of the sovereign nations for help in carrying out its functions.

The Safety Authority was almost identically constituted and empowered. Its function was to "advise and assist the Intergovernmental Commission on all matters concerning safety in the construction and operation of the Fixed Link." It was to participate in drawing up regulations governing safety and, after making sure that they complied with the the laws of both nations, it was to enforce them.

Eurotunnel was responsible for the expenses of both these bodies, and it naturally had to bear the cost of anything they might require in the construction and operation of the Channel Tunnel. The Intergovernmental Commission and the Safety Authority, on the other hand, did not have to worry about any costs at all. Nothing in their charters required them to consider the costs of anything they might decree. The predictable effects of this arrangement on the tunnel's cost were not long in appearing.

At the time, many believed that the contractors had deliberately overstated the cost of the tunnel to assure themselves a fat profit on the work. SNCF, for instance, concluded that the stated £2.7 billion cost had been inflated by 10 to 15 percent.

The contractors themselves did little to dispel this impression. Deacon recalled a January meeting at Wimpey's headquarters, "when the British chairmen sat down and congratulated themselves around the table at what a wonderful contract they had negotiated with Eurotunnel. . . . And I had to say 'Well, of course, you know the banks haven't reviewed it, so please don't join us in your congratulations.' "

This belief that the contract favored the contractors, said SNCF's Philippe Essig, gave everyone on the other side of the bargain—the banks, the governments and Eurotunnel—"a general view . . . that it was possible to obtain a better project, to increase the requirements of the technical specifications, inside the budget. . . . I was a witness to that. *Everybody* believed the costs were too high, and there was a float, a margin."

It created "suspicion between each and everyone," Essig said. "Everyone. Between the banks and the owner; between the owner and the contractors, between the contractors and the *maître d'oeuvre*. Suspicion generally spread all over the project."

This suspicion caused the banks and Eurotunnel to think that they could have—indeed, that they deserved—the best tunnel that technology could offer. This view was seriously at odds with the contractors' view, which was that they were required simply to supply a tunnel that was able to carry a certain number of trains and shuttles per day at certain speeds—in other words, a performance contract in which the contractors got to decide how to meet the operating specifications.

David Brown summed up the contractors' understanding in a simplified fashion: "You (Eurotunnel) go away, and come back in seven years; I'll be responsible for constructing [the tunnel], and it will operate to enable you to get these numbers of vehicles through. But *don't dabble with me* from now onward, because it is a performance contract."

This view mimicked the concession, which was itself based on performance rather than specifics of design. The banking syndicate, however, was horrified by the thought of letting the contractors go off on their own, unsupervised, to build a tunnel with the banks' money. The technical Agent Banks were keenly aware of their ignorance of engineering matters, and they demanded oversight.

Technically speaking, the banks did have a technical adviser, in the form of the *maître d'oeuvre,* a joint venture by the British consulting engineers W. S. Atkins and SETEC, the French firm that had been involved in Channel Tunnel work since the early Davidson days. Although an MdO was supposed to have an Olympian view of a project, and to oversee the project for the owner, Atkins/SETEC had been chosen by the contractors.

Deacon and the few people he had working with him "identified a list of eminent British and French [consulting] firms, and we invited the technical banks to join us in making a decision." They held an audition for these firms on February 18, 1986, in the *sous-sol* of BNP's ornate Beaux-Arts headquarters on boulevard des Italiens, near the Paris Opera; a half-dozen well-known consulting engineers sent their best people to make presentations.

The Agent Banks' response, said Deacon, was: "Well, these firms are all very well. But they, too, have a conflict of interest because they are both British and French, and they will want this project to succeed. We are an international consortium; there must be an international group of consultants." Deacon duly arranged to hold another audition on February 27 in Zurich, with consultants from other nations.

What followed from all this was the sole instance that Deacon could recall in which national interests dictated the course of events. The French banks decided that they wanted an American-based firm, Louis Berger Associates, installed as a consultant to the technical banks.

"The French banks put forward Berger's name because they had an office in Paris," Deacon said. "I remember getting a phone call from the guy who ran their office, François Fahri, who's a very elegant, sophisticated international French businessman. And he said, 'Well, of course, Chris, if you back our bid we'll open an office in London.' And I thought, Oh, Christ, they haven't even got a bloody office in London yet, what's that for being an international firm of consultants."

Appearances here were somewhat misleading; Berger was a bona fide international consulting company, with operations in more than sixty countries. The Paris office in truth was nothing much, but it *was* in Paris, and the French—who always pronounced the name of the company in French fashion, with a soft *g*—insisted on having Berger. For the first and last time, the French insistence on having three of its banks in the five-bank group paid off; Banque indosuez's vote tipped the scale and Berger was hired. The British, consoled by the fact that Berger at least had its headquarters in a former colony, acceded to the French demand.

A few other technical consultants were added to satisfy other national interests—Lahmeyer International of Frankfurt, in which Deutsche Bank had a financial interest, and Dr. Yutaka Mochida, who had spent twenty-five difficult years carving the Seikan Tunnel through the granite under the deep strait between Honshu and Hokkaido. This job—in the heart of an earthquake belt, within sight of steaming volcanoes—made the English Channel project look like a classroom exercise. Mochida was never to see, or be, a problem.

Naming Mochida required a further compromise: Some of the Japanese banks wanted him as their adviser; another group wanted a consultant from the Japanese railway system. "In a rather elegant way, they arranged for Dr. Mochida to carry a Japan Railways consultant's card," Deacon recalled. "Honor was satisfied all around."

What remained, then, was to satisy Berger and Lahmeyer and Dr. Mochida that the project was possible and that the construction contract was a proper and trusty instrument.

As events were shortly to prove, this would not be easy. Deacon and his colleagues were soon to discover that they had created a monster.

7

Once Henderson had signed the concession documents, he began edging toward the exit, knowing that if he didn't walk out he would be pushed. "I think it was generally agreed that Nicko had served his purpose," Alan Osborne, Tarmac's representative on the CTG board, told an interviewer. "To put it crudely."

Replacing Henderson wasn't easy; Eurotunnel was still so chancy an operation that it held little appeal for executives who cared for their careers. In March, the board settled finally on Lord Pennock, a distinguished executive who had been chairman of Balfour Beatty's parent company, BICC, until 1984. He had begun, by then, to rest on his laurels in various employers' associations and in various boardrooms.

Osborne recalled the meeting, on a Saturday morning in Wimpey's offices, when Pennock was offered the chairman's job. Pennock had been called back from a business trip to Japan and complained at some length about all of the demands on his time.

"The more I heard, the less I liked," Osborne said. "I passed a note to Frank Gibb (Taylor Woodrow's chairman) saying, 'Look, if he doesn't want the job, let's forget it.' Frank said, 'Who else have we got?' That was an awful reason for making the appointment, but we had to move on because Henderson was starting to become disenchanted."

Osborne noted that Eurotunnel was unable to offer Pennock the organizational support to which he was accustomed. This was understating things greatly: Eurotunnel was riven by rivalries among the contracting companies that still largely owned and governed the venture. The contractors were, in turn, under intense pressure from the banks to clear out and terminate their conflicted interests in the company. Company business, Osborne said, was often a matter of "kicking and shouting."

The situation needed an autocrat to bring order and purpose to the company. In Pennock, it got a statesman who could summon an air of authority. He had excellent political contacts, and access to Thatcher, but Eurotunnel was not then occupied with stately questions. Pennock later told an associate that he found Eurotunnel so consumed by trivial passions about perquisites—who would have a personal assistant, a car, a desirable office—that it couldn't hope to deal with the critical issues of the construction contract. "This was more important to some people than the job," Pennock told the associate. "I've been director of ICI for many years. I never had to deal with such chaos." But the job, unfortunately for Pennock, was all about chaos.

The contractors had their organization, Transmanche-Link, in better order. However, they did not appreciate the intensity of the storm that was gathering over the contract.

On March 6, John Reeve submitted a written summary of the contract history and its then-current status to the chairmen of the British partner companies. He correctly identified one serious difference of opinion: The contractors believed that all responsibility for the design of the project would pass from the owner to the contractors at the moment the contract was signed. Thereafter, the contractors would be bound only by the performance standards—the train speeds, passage times and passenger capacities—in the Submission to Government. Eurotunnel, on the other hand, said that any decisions by the contractors regarding "the whole system design" should be discussed with the owners. Eurotunnel wanted everything be to be left open for improvement—that is, it wanted a continuing review to ensure that it was getting the best possible project for the price.

There was a word for what Eurotunnel wanted: optimization. A simple (and, as events were to show, particularly relevant) example was the signaling system. The 1974 plan called for conventional trackside signal lights. TML's view was that if it could find a cheaper way to provide signaling, it could do so. Eurotunnel's view was that if a better signaling system now existed, it could demand that it be installed.

Optimization was a pit into which Reeve did not wish to fall. Yet there was a risk in taking too hard a line in negotiating with Eurotunnel. That, he told his chairmen, could open the door for an increased role for consultants that might "result in the drastic erosion of the benefits of the present contract. It is also possible that the Banks and/or future investors would like to see this, in order to try to reopen the whole subject of the present contract, and to introduce additional external consultants."

Reeve was entirely correct, but it was already too late. The next day—March 7, 1986—before Reeve's summation even reached the chairmen, a fateful presence was summoned to the project.

His name was Howard Heydon. He was an engineer who had just moved to semiretirement on the west coast of Florida when he received a telephone call from Derish Wolf, the president of Louis Berger International.

Wolf explained that Berger was in the running for a consulting job on the Channel Tunnel and was hoping to enlist Heydon for about five weeks of work if the contract came through. His job would be to review the construction contract for the Channel Tunnel on behalf of the technical banks. "Sure," Heydon said. "It sounds interesting."

"I'll let you know if we get the job," Wolf said.

Wolf called back six days later, on a Thursday evening. He asked if Heydon could be in Paris at eight o'clock Monday morning.

"Maybe Tuesday," Heydon said, a little bit stunned.

Heydon would leave an indelible impression on everyone he met, and on the project itself. Ian McMillan, a young Midland executive who was working with Deacon, remembered Heydon as "a very affable chap, ex-US Air Force, Bomber Command . . . very bombastic, quite short, rotund figure, very aggressive, very American in the nicest sense.

"Heydon didn't like the Japs in the syndicate as a result of the war," McMillan added. "Didn't like anyone, really. Didn't trust the French."

This was both too harsh (Heydon liked a good number of people he encountered on the project) and too mild (he trusted the English less than he trusted the French). He was, in fact, a confirmed skeptic, a man whose opinions of human nature had been shaped by bitter experience in both war and peace.

He was then sixty-two years old. He had retired two years before as chief engineer of the New Jersey Turnpike, a road that he knew as intimately as a farmer knows his fields. He had gone to work there on his thirtieth birthday, February 23, 1953, already a disillusioned man.

Heydon had interrupted his college education in 1943 to get into the war. He married before going overseas, the next year, in the first group of B-29s that went out to the Pacific war. He flew twenty-six missions over Japan and came through the experience unscathed but changed. "I still had feelings about the Japs that were," he admitted, frowning while he searched for the right word, "*difficult.*"

He went back to Stevens Institute of Technology in New Jersey after the war, into a tough, intense program that trained mechanical engineers. "School was eight hours a day, six days a week," he recalled. "Ran out of money, saved by the GI Bill and my wife. . . . Got out of school in forty-eight; by that time I had two kids."

His first job was with the Port of New York Authority, a quasi-public organization that built and operates much of the New York City region's transportation infrastructure—bridges, tunnels, bus terminals and the major airports.

"I enjoyed that very much," Heydon said. "The engineering department
there, from the late nineteen-twenties until the fifties, was one of the best in
the world. It was an unbelievable experience." He might have lived out his
career there had it not been for a dispute in 1950. Heydon was asked to review some claims for extra payment from companies that were building a big
bus terminal. "We had a major disagreement about whether the contractor
was entitled to money," Heydon said. "I said no, and they said yes." Higher-
ups at the authority agreed to pay the claims. Heydon quit.

Heydon's first brush with sinners changed him; it left him deeply suspi-
cious of contractors and their methods. "It was the beginning," he said more
than forty years later. "Greed, I think, is the primary driving force. And I've
been disappointed by that." His experience at the Turnpike had been better,
but also clouded by the presence of graft and inefficiencies, and when the
time came to retire, Heydon left to spend time with his wife and *Fascination,*
his thirty-six-foot trawler. He had just brought the boat south to Florida when
Derish Wolf called.

When Heydon looked over the draft construction contract for the tunnel, he
recalled, "My immediate impression was that there was no significant separation between the people who were writing the contract and the people who
were going to execute the contract. They were the same people, or in the
same employ, or they had been so close for so long that they couldn't tell the
difference."

Heydon pulled in a team to examine the contract in detail. Lahmeyer appointed a tough but charming engineer named Peter Keitel to work with
Heydon; the two men got along well. In time, the team grew to comprise
more than fifteen members. It had a decidedly international flavor, with
Swedes, French, Germans, Britons and Americans all laboring together.
They faced a dauntingly large task; the draft construction contract had grown
into a four-volume document that included twenty-seven schedules in addition to a book-length "Contract Agreement and General Conditions" section.
There were nine volumes of documents that had been submitted to the governments, as well as the Stansted Protocol. Heydon was handed nearly a
dozen other documents, including earlier technical audits of the project,
comments on the cost estimates and technical papers relating to the science
and dangers of tunneling under water. About half of these were French studies, in French.

The technical banks, said Heydon, "wanted us to say whether this was a technically feasible project, and whether this contract provided for protection of the banks." The banks needed answers soon: They wanted a detailed oral report in six weeks, a full written evaluation in seven.

Heydon's group was not the only one straining to achieve a difficult goal against a hard deadline. David Brown had begun the monumental work of design—which meant first designing and creating the organization that would, when complete, oversee design of the tunnel itself by a group of engineering consultants. On March 3, he moved into Transmanche-Link's first office, a gloomy, abandoned building that Taylor Woodrow owned in Hayes, near Heathrow Airport in Middlesex. "A warehouse which was piled high with any old rubbish that Taylor Woodrow wanted to deposit," he recalled. The building had one saving grace for the French engineers: Heathrow's proximity made their commuting easier.

"The first thing we had to do was to get an engineering group together, to create a tunnels organisation, a terminals organisation, one for fixed equipment, for rolling stock, for operations and safety . . . and to pull in key engineers who were competent in those areas," Brown said.

Speed was essential. TML was going to have to order the tunnel-boring machines soon, because they would take more than a year to manufacture and deliver to the site. The work sites themselves were going to need quick attention, so that construction work could start on the tunnel and terminals.

There was an even more fundamental need facing Brown: money. "There was no money available, because there was no contract between Eurotunnel and TML," Brown said. When it came to money, TML was diligent in supporting the independence of Eurotunnel. It had no contract yet with Eurotunnel; therefore, it had no responsibility to fund anything to do with the tunnel. Reeve later estimated that each of the five British companies had spent about £1 million to carry the project this far; this was about as much as they wished to risk without a contract.

"We had to go round cap-in-hand at the very beginning," Brown said. "John Reeve, the Director-General on the UK side, went round the contractors to attempt to get £250,000 to enable key design work to start."

The maddening fact, for Brown, was that this design work had already been done for the 1974 effort, but he could not get his hands on it. Those plans were now government property, acquired when the project collapsed and the governments had to buy it up from RTZ. When he first became involved with designing the project, he had asked Reeve what information was available, what work had already been done. He was given a sheet of paper.

"Blank, virtually," Brown remembered. "I said, 'Is that all we've got?' And he said, 'Yes, well, there's a pack of drawings which show the layout of the terminal, very broad-brush.' " Brown also was given sketches of the tunnel in cross section and drawings of some of the mechanical and electrical systems. "Very crude, single-line diagrams," he said.

When he moved into the building at Hayes, Brown approached Eurotunnel and asked them to help get the 1974 documents. Eurotunnel returned with word that the government would sell the plans—for £12 million. "I have no idea as to how they came to that number," Brown said. "I think it was just a question of the scrap value of paper, mainly. Well, we hadn't got the money to pay that. We were struggling to get a sum—not anywhere near that kind of money—to put the orders out for the TBMs. Time was running out, so I said enough is enough: We are going to do it our way. Do it from scratch. From a blank sheet of paper, to all intents and purposes."

"A blank sheet of paper" was not an empty phrase. Brown began with about two dozen engineers and ended with more than sixty. He knew that his job was "to blend the French and UK methods of doing the works into one harmonious institution . . . to sit on the top and orchestrate these engineers."

That much he knew. There was far more that he did not know. For instance, he did not know what the diameter of the tunnels was to be. That—and much else—had not yet been decided.

Thus the Channel Tunnel project began a sort of steeplechase, with hurdles and hazards scattered over the next several months. The prize, as with a horse race, was money: If the project completed the course, it would have funds and the great work could commence.

The trouble was that the obstacles were awkwardly placed. They were too close together; a misstep at one would mean disaster at the next. The Channel Tunnel Bill had to begin its course through Parliament (French investors were pessimistic enough to insist that the project be insured against non-ratification of the treaty), the banks had to be satisfied that the construction contract was proper and might be signed and all this needed to be done quickly, so that everything would be ready for Equity 2.

Equity 2 was the second of three scheduled sales of shares in Eurotunnel. Equity 1 was about £46 million in seed money to be put in by the founding shareholders—the banks and the contracting companies—to pay for design work. Equity 2 was to be a private offering to institutions of about £206 million, to pay for the tunnel-boring machines and some essential preparatory work. Equity 3 would be the sale of about £770 million worth of shares to individual investors.

Equity 2 had a more than monetary significance. It was also a call to the financial community for a vote of confidence. Further, and more important to the bankers, it was the mechanism by which the contractors and arranging banks would be reduced to minority shareholders in the venture. Until the Equity 2 shares were distributed among institutional investors, Eurotunnel would remain a creature of the companies it was supposed to govern.

The timing was exceptionally tight: The draft prospectus for Equity 2 would have to be ready by June 30. This meant that the banking syndicate had to agree to the underwriting—a necessary assurance for the Equity 2 investors—no later than June 16. Deacon expected to get Heydon's report no sooner than May 12. There was already evidence that the report might be a serious obstacle on this steeplechase course. On April 7, Heydon gave the banks a thumbnail report at a big meeting in London. He was brief and brutal: "I said that this was the worst contract I ever saw in my life, and nobody should sign it," he recalled.

Chris Deacon was at the meeting, and his diary suggests the depth and detail of Heydon's displeasure. The laundry list of problems, as reflected by Deacon's scribbled notes, included: "Admission of actual cost, fees and gross negligence . . . the description of the lump sum and the reimbursement contract . . . incentives, penalties, key dates, question of design responsibility, fitness for purpose, role of the MdO, liability of subcontractors on procurement items, question of warranties and assignment of them, questions of prices and price fluctuations, payments and control of payments, insurance, assignments, employers brief, delay by subcontractors . . . joint and several liability, completion tests, retentions and bonding."

These criticisms reached Reeve and his fellows in TML in an April 14 letter from the banks, just three days after the Channel Tunnel Bill went to Parliament. The contractors were peeved by this letter, but they viewed it as a bargaining tactic to wring some concessions from them in the contract.

On May 9, Heydon forwarded his formal written report to Midland Bank and Banque nationale de Paris. It was fat, 193 pages, and its opening section had a mild, encouraging tone. But the mildness of these prefatory remarks was misleading. While the tone remained professionally polite throughout the report, the substance was sharply critical. Heydon's engineers concluded that two of the contract's three major parts were overpriced, that the third part was underpriced and that the result in all cases was likely to be bad for Eurotunnel. The £1.1 billion in the contract for the target costs, which was to pay for the tunnels themselves, was about 20 percent high, Heydon wrote. Keitel's people had compared the actual costs of other recent tunnel projects—including about fifty German railroad tunnels, ranging in length from four hundred meters to eleven kilometers—to the projected Channel Tunnel cost. European tunnels ranged from £55 to £140 per cubic meter of open tunnel; the Channel Tunnel target cost was £181 per cubic meter on the British side and £203 per cubic meter on the French side, because of the more difficult conditions expected there.

The contract's £1.02 billion for the lump sum, which was to pay for the terminals and for the fixed equipment in the tunnels, was 10 to 15 percent too high, Heydon said. As with the target cost, this conclusion emerged from a study of other projects and industry standards.

The £233 million for procurement items, to purchase the rolling stock— all of the locomotives and cars that would make up the tunnel trains— seemed "low by a factor of 20% to 30%," the report said, after dwelling on the many special problems—such as ventilation, heating and cooling, aerodynamic drag and soundproofing—that train design would have to anticipate.

Yet Heydon's deepest concerns lay elsewhere, in structural weaknesses in the contract that he thought encouraged TML to let costs increase, to stint on quality and to ignore the tight construction timetable that was critical to Eurotunnel's commercial success. It wasn't simply that costs were high, but that there was no incentive to contain them; not simply that specifications were lacking, but that the contract had no mechanisms to ensure a first-rate product.

Heydon believed that the contractors deserved a profit—even fat profits could be justified if the risks were great and if there were guarantees that the product would be of superior quality—but in this case neither the risks nor the guarantees were enough to justify the projected cost.

There was little in the contract to stimulate the contractors to work with all proper speed. In fact, Heydon's engineers found, there were incentives to delay, to let costs rise, to cheapen the job. If the tunneling costs ran high, for instance, TML was responsible for just 30 percent of the cost, and that only to 6 percent of the total. Once the cost exceeded 6 percent, TML was off the hook. Perhaps even more astonishing, the contractors were guaranteed an early completion bonus, no matter when they finished the work. This bonus was about equal to the sum of all liquidated damages that the contractors would have to pay if construction lagged. The report went on for page after page, chanting a litany about cheapness, delay, costliness. For example, there was no provision in the contract for finishing the cinder-block exterior of the terminal buildings. The contract did not always agree with the Submission to Government—a significant problem, since the Proposal was a promise that sovereign nations might insist be honored. Such vagueness begged elucidation, and a strong Eurotunnel could use this to its advantage. It could, Heydon said, require optimization.

To Heydon, optimization was not the dirty word it was to Reeve or the curse it would become to TML. For Heydon, it meant simply holding the contractors to promises they had made in their proposal to the governments. As things then stood, the contract's flaws posed "major risks," the report said. "Unless these are satisfactorily resolved we do not believe the Contract should be approved by the Lending Banks." Further, it "recommended that the Lending Banks maintain a technical presence on the project during the Construction phase and throughout the operational phase to attend to their interests."

In summing up, Heydon noted that not every problem need be corrected for the balance of risk to be restored, but that Eurotunnel badly needed strengthening for the hard negotiation that lay ahead. In private, however, Heydon spoke of the contract—and the cast of characters engaged in the negotiations—in far harsher terms than he used in the report. He summed up the draft contract in two words: "Really horrible." He believed that Eurotunnel was badly overmatched and likely to remain so in the oncoming struggles over the contract, the financing and the start of construction. "They had no management," he said privately, and Atkins and SETEC, working together as the *maître d'oeuvre*, were too much the creature of the contractors to play this role. "With the MdO it was totally, 'Whatever the contractor says is right,'" Heydon said. "They'd been working with the contractor for years. The contractor was paying them. How the hell can you have an independent consultant who won't get any more of the job if he doesn't behave himself?"

The Berger report therefore "strongly recommended that the Owner employ an independent Engineer to supervise the technical work. . . . The present contractual conditions obviously do not define such an independent role for the Maître d'Oeuvre."

This fell in line wonderfully well with the thinking at Bechtel, whose contact with the project now lay with a senior vice president named Pete Behr.

Like several others who ended up involved with the Chunnel, Behr had been close to retirement when he was called, in January 1986, to look at the Channel Tunnel project. The call was from John Neerhout, Bechtel's executive vice president, who told him the company had been trying to get involved with the tunnel "but were getting kind of a cold shoulder." Neerhout asked Behr to postpone retirement and see what he could do.

Behr was a natural choice. He had been in charge of Bechtel's involvement at the French steel mill at Fos between 1971 and 1974. He was a thorough professional who had studied French at night to prepare himself for the job; he had achieved fluency. When Neerhout called him, he was working in the Bechtel Tower in Houston, looking forward, like many big-company engineers, to retiring to a life of private consulting.

He dutifully made his way to Europe and talked to the people in and around the Channel Tunnel project. He was not encouraged by what he found; Atkins/SETEC, the *maître-d'oeuvre,* was entrenched. Still, Behr went to work to see what he could do. "By early February, I had an idea of the structure, and I was trying to decide what we could offer," he said. By the end of the month, he was in contact with Colin Stannard and other NatWest representatives on the project.*

Behr continued his rounds of the project's participants. "We met John Reeve early on, in his office," Behr recalled. "He had a lot of people working for him on design. He told me he had fifty people, twenty-five French and twenty-five British, all working in London. I asked him how bilingual the staff was. He said, 'It's fifty per cent bilingual. The French all speak English, and none of the British speak French.' "

In early April a BNP executive, Jean Gabriel, told Behr that Bechtel had made a bad impression with its earlier presentations. "He said Bechtel had seemed arrogant in the Fall 1985 meeting," Behr said. "That was when Hessig made his France-is-not-Gabon remark. He told me about the Berger contract." Gabriel said there might be a role for Bechtel in the project someday; he counseled patience in the meantime. "Gabriel told me to see the technical banks," Behr recalled. "Which we did. He felt that the deal wouldn't go unless those guys were convinced."

Behr thereby stepped on some toes. "When we were trying to raise the money, Bechtel went to see an awful lot of the banks we were going to see," Colin Stannard recalled years later, with hardly diminished anger. "And they said that this project couldn't possibly be done without their involvement— to the extent that the senior executives in the banks had to write to the chief executive of Bechtel saying, 'Stop this, or we're in fact going to report this to the American government. It is unacceptable for you to go around the world saying the British and French are incapable of doing this on their own, which is what you are actually saying.' "

The letter of protest to Bechtel's headquarters was penned by Lord Pennock and John Franklin, a young Morgan Grenfell executive who had been

---

* At about the same time, Behr said, Al Davidson contacted him. Behr had already heard talk that Frank Davidson was talking about bringing Merrill Lynch into the project as a source of funds. Behr thought that this was unlikely to happen. So, it turned out, did Al Davidson.

Davidson had already spoken to the same NatWest people as had Behr. "NatWest was the lead bank in this; they wanted me very badly," Al Davidson said. "I had many conversations with them, with John Bennett and Denis Child (both NatWest executives). I wouldn't accept unless they put a controlling body over the contractors. They were in a position to do it—they had the money—but my conception of how to do it didn't agree with theirs. . . . I recommended against Technical Services getting involved with this new setup." Davidson also discouraged American bankers from getting involved as well. "I met with the whole British group of contractors. I talked to them, I told them what I was telling Bennett—that I couldn't recommend that anyone put money into it."

(Within a few months, Technical Services would go to court in an unsuccessful try to recover the money promised to Technical Services as part of the 1974 attempt. This would end the Davidson brothers' long involvement with the Channel Tunnel.)

working for more than a year on the tunnel's financing. Franklin and Pennock were furious; Steve Bechtel Jr. answered them in honeyed, conciliatory tones, saying that Bechtel wasn't trying to damage the project, as Franklin suggested, but was merely trying to offer help that was certain to be needed.

Until Heydon made his report, the inner circle of Arranging Banks had—at best—a hazy sense that something might be wrong with the contract. What unease there was in the central group of banks was mostly in France, where the government had begun to sense some deep and serious problems. An official of Banque indosuez told Behr that the Caisse des dépôts was worried enough to have sent "deux X"—two *polytechniciens*—to examine the contract in April 1986. The Caisse des dépôts et consignations is another peculiarly French institution, with enormous power in French economic affairs. This power comes from wealth: It is the repository for fees collected by notaries, which means that money from each real estate transaction goes into its purse. It also administers the money that French citizens consign to their *caisses d'épargne,* the national savings banks. As one French executive put it, "You can't really build a very large project in France without having recourse to the Caisse des dépôts."

Similar unease gripped the hard-line agent banks, led by Deutsche Bank. The gloom here was deep; a German banker told Behr he was already too late. "He said to me it was a good idea to reinforce the management of Eurotunnel, 'But the problem is, there's no management to reinforce,' " Behr said.

Behr visited the banks, selling them on the idea of bringing in Bechtel. "Franklin tried to dissuade us from going to Japan," Behr said. "I told him, 'Bechtel should not be made a whipping boy for pointing out a flaw in the concept that is evident to many banks.' " Behr believed that with so many consultants looking for a piece of the action, Bechtel couldn't afford to ignore the Japanese. The Japanese banks "knew Bechtel better than they knew some of the European banks," Behr added. "And a couple of the banks were disappointed at the lack of participation by US banks, and thought that Bechtel might have enough influence to bring the American banks in."

This was a vain hope; the American banks were at best cool to the project. Different participants in the venture judged this diffidence differently. Some saw it as a simple business decision that reflected a national attitude: The tunnel was a long-term project, requiring long-term loans. "The story was that American banks didn't like long-term investments. They wanted to get their money out," said Behr. The loans were to run eighteen years and, as Deacon noted, "American banks have a problem with debt over ten years."

Jean Renault saw business and politics in the American banks' reticence. They had been through some then-recent hard times, he noted, with bad loans in Latin America. They were surely conscious that France had done a lot of nationalization when Mitterand and the Socialists came to power. But also, Renault said, "I think somewhere, someone in the U.S. thought that a fixed link would allow a *rapprochement* that was not in the strategic interest of the U.S."

Ignorance, too, played a role in keeping dollars out of the tunnel. In the world of American finance, the English Channel was a faraway place and European concerns were foggy and foreign. Ian Callaghan recalled a conversation—preliminary to a sales visit—with one of the largest and oldest American investment banks. "We said, 'We're coming next week, what shall we bring?' 'First thing is, maps,' they said. I said, 'What, showing where the tunnel is?' No, they said, 'Maps showing where *England* is.'"

Heydon's report had given the technical banks an almost inexhaustible supply of ammunition with which to attack the contract, and the hard-core banks were not at all loath to do so. When the banks spoke with one voice—as they most often did after this point—the voice usually was that of Till Pahl of Deutsche Bank.

"An outstanding, outstanding guy, whose office in Deutsche Bank was just shelves of books," Deacon said of Pahl. "The only German—the only *foreigner* I know who's got Sir John Clapham's *History of the Bank of England* in three volumes—in English—on his bookshelf. And he would remark that Proust read so much better, of course, in French than in English. He was a polymath, a wonderful chap, but hard as nails at that time."

Pahl was not the only hard man. Union Bank of Switzerland had assigned people who were "like dogs with bones," Deacon recalled. "Wouldn't budge . . . very hardline, straight up-and-down, black and white, dot the I's, cross the T's." This hard-line group had the covert and overt support of Banque indosuez, Deacon said, "because that would make their life easier as equity was raised later on."

Pahl's response to Heydon's report, Deacon said, was: "Yes, well, it's a very good report. There are one or two things. We will support it if every one of the amendments in this commentary on the contract are accepted. Every one." He handed Deacon a list of more than four hundred points, culled from the long list of objections that Heydon's team had found.

Deacon was not immediately concerned. "We took him to mean, well, take the main principles. Because you can't do more than that, can you? You don't set your negotiator to get every point." Telling the story years later, Deacon's voice dropped to almost a whisper. "But he meant it."

The contractors were infuriated. Deacon's group had already given them a list of lawyers' objections to the contract, and, as Deacon put it, "they said we were having two bites of the cherry." Nor were the contractors the only ones angered; NatWest and Crédit lyonnais also were furious. "All this resistance to the contract was entirely unexpected," Deacon said. "It came as a total shock. Nobody could understand it. . . . I attended a meeting called by NatWest when this matter first blew up, and they made very clear—at this public meeting with the chairmen of the British contractors, in the NatWest tower—that NatWest were pointing the finger of blame at Midland."

This rift between the banks would never close. It became clear that NatWest and Crédit lyonnais had made a serious error in dumping the difficult banks on Midland and BNP. "The mistake they made was lining up on the same side, leaving the two doubters to work together," said Ian McMillan, one of Deacon's Midland associates.

Why did any of the banks stay, with so many voices urging caution? "High fees," said Behr. "They wanted to keep it going for business reasons. But they didn't want to be involved in a folly."

Politics, as well as finances, were troubling Lord Pennock at this hour. The Channel Tunnel Bill had been given its first reading in the House of Commons on April 11 and was to have its second reading, when members would vote on it, in early May. Passage at the second reading would constitute government approval of the public aspects of the hybrid bill. Hearings on the private aspects would follow, but any citizen who wished to attack the project would first have to show that he or she would be personally affected by it. There could be no appeal—officially, at least—to esthetics, to islandhood, or to the cause of endangered species once the bill had its second reading.

Opponents of the tunnel unsurprisingly ambushed the bill as it made its way through committee toward the second reading. The leader was Jonathan Aitken, member for Thanet, a longtime dedicated foe of the project. The attack charged that the bill had been submitted "out of time"—that is, contrary to the procedural rules of Parliament.

It was a niggling point, but it was sufficient to stall the bill. The Commons' Standing Orders Committee agreed to halt the bill's progress while it considered a petition from the Dover Harbor Board and SeaLink Ferries.

Delay, everyone recognized, was an effective tactic to use against the tunnel. If any unit stopped slogging forward, the entire parade came to a halt. A stalled bill stanched the flow of cash, which stopped David Brown from going on with his design, which meant that the start of construction might be delayed, perhaps fatally.

But delay in Parliament hardly mattered: The truly critical problem lay with the construction contract. Until the hawkish technical banks could be satisfied that it was a good and proper document, there would be no loan agreement and—more critical still—no possibility of raising the Equity 2 money for design.

So it was that in mid-May, Chris Deacon and his colleagues set about trying to resolve the more than four hundred objections that the technical banks had to the draft contract. *His* deadline had not changed: He had to have the technical Agent Banks' *nihil obstat—imprimatur* by June 16, so that Equity 2 could proceed, as scheduled, on July 10.

For company and assistance in his travails, Deacon now had Pierre Coindreau, a man of his age and, lately, his calling. Coindreau had been assigned to the project in April by his employer, Banque nationale de Paris. The two men were different in more ways than mere nationality: Deacon was tall and lank and languid in the English manner; Coindreau was dark, intense, compact, with hard Bogart looks softened by better, finer features. His five-o'clock shadow was unfailingly punctual, his English fluent and near perfect, a useful rather than clumsy tool. Coindreau's grasp of the language was better than that of many of his French colleagues on the mission, who were sometimes trampled in the stampede of English when feelings grew hot in the many meetings.

Coindreau and Deacon did share a deeply ironic view of the world of commerce. The events of the next two years would further unite them; they would emerge from the project fused and bonded by their shared experiences. It was common on this project, which had scores of such French-and-British pairs assigned to work together on a single problem. These pairs were like port-and-starboard slaves on the same galley: Only one's counterpart could fully appreciate the brutal demands of the work. The job demanded; the partner alone understood and commiserated. Deacon and Coindreau, like many others, came in time to feel that they alone were sane, well-meaning and dedicated to the honest success of the project; all of the others were fools or knaves or villains.

The two men differed in the experience they brought to the work. Deacon was a banker—a junior one, it is true, but a banker nonetheless. Coindreau, astonishingly, was not; he was a civil engineer who was as new to banking as he was to the project. The same slowdown that had set the banks looking for new undertakings had sent Coindreau in search of a new career.

"I had worked in a civil engineering firm for twelve years," Coindreau said. "I went to business school, and changed completely my career, because at that time, in Eighty-four and Eighty-five, there was a very deep crisis for the construction industry. I decided to find something else. I wasn't aiming at banking specifically; I really ended up in the bank by pure chance, I would say." He was looking for a job when Eurotunnel won the concession; he was still looking when the concession agreement was signed in March, still looking when Howard Heydon began examining the the contract.

"BNP suddenly realized they had a big job on their shoulders, and they needed some additional staff," Coindreau said. "They wanted people with some engineering expertise, because there was a lot of engineering matters to deal with in the early days. So I was hired in a hurry. . . . On Eurotunnel, everything was done in a rush: I entered BNP in a rush, and I entered the project in a rush."

When he was hired at BNP, Coindreau naturally enough asked his soon-to-be boss for a briefing on where matters stood.

"He said, 'Well, we're going to sign the contract in two weeks.' " Coindreau said. "He had told me before, 'We need people like you, engineers, because we have no experience in construction contracts.' "

Two weeks was hardly enough time for one person, even a trained engineer, to read a construction contract, much less comment on it. Nevertheless, Coindreau took a look. He did not like what he saw.

"The document was miles away from being capable of any sort of signature. Full of blanks, no technical backup, just words. You do not sign a construction agreement without mountains of technical stuff—drawings, specifications, all the rest of it. This was not even finished. It was a joke, it was really a joke. And there were people believing that this was a contract that could be signed. . . . A lot of promises had been made and people simply believed them. They didn't realize that a promise, when it's not committed to paper, when lawyers are fighting on both sides of the table for hours, is not worth very much. When you're talking about a project that size, friendship doesn't count, really."

But Coindreau's misgivings faced an avalanche of pro-project momentum. "There was tremendous pressure at that time," Coindreau recalled. "The ball had started rolling and there was no way it could be stopped. And if you were the guy saying, no, don't do this, you must stop, think about it—you were simply pushed aside. The pressure came from everywhere: from the political side, after the concession had been signed. There was also tremendous financial pressure, because a lot of money had been spent, and the promoters didn't want to lose their money. And the contractors were absolutely adamant to have a contract signed as soon as possible.

"The financiers were very naive," he said. "There was a contract with a price of twenty-seven billion French francs, and there was nothing behind it: There was no design, there were hardly any specifications. There were just good intentions—I hope—and that's it." Coindreau was quite correct, and the good intentions led where good intentions usually do.

But at that moment, he and Deacon had their marching orders, and they began the numbing labor of negotiating a contract that pleased (or at least did not offend) all sides. It was like playing a dozen games of chess simultaneously.

Deacon vividly recalled one meeting, on a high floor in an office tower, that broke up at four in the morning. The elevators had long since gone out of service, so he and some others walked down, only to find the staircase doors locked at the bottom. "So we had to climb back twenty floors," he said. "By then they'd got the lift working again." In its own way, this symbolized the negotiating process perfectly.

"There were nervous breakdowns galore. Certainly one of my staff was acting very strangely. I didn't know whether I was coming or going. People were getting paranoid. . . . I attended a board meeting when Eurotunnel actually collapsed. . . . Pennock swore at Paterson [Midland Bank's chairman]. Paterson walked out. The British side of the table started shouting at the French. The French stood up and started shouting at the English—in French. And the Eurotunnel board just collapsed. It just had no future at that stage. It was 10 o'clock at night, and at that moment the project didn't exist."

But the meetings went on, at great cost to the participants, and the banks won some ground against the contractors. The guaranteed £60 million early completion bonus was removed and made part of the regular contract payments, which meant it could be lost to penalties. The six percent profit on target cost overruns was eliminated. Negotiation increased the maximum amount of liquidated damages from £120 million to £150 million and accelerated the rate at which they could be assessed.

On June 16, Eurotunnel briefed the press on events scheduled for the following several weeks. These included "confirmation of loans from world banks" and raising of Equity 2, all before the end of the month. The construction contract would then be signed in late July. The press release contained a mild disclaimer that "some dates are still being finalised."

On that same day, Heydon delivered his second report to the technical banks. It noted that there had been many meetings, including a virtually continuous session that had lasted from May 19 to June 3. The report ran 144 pages, but no one had to read farther than the fifth paragraph of the cover letter to discover the sum of its findings. This sentence said, "Unfortunately the process has not yet yielded sufficient change to warrant our confidence in the Construction Contract."

Deacon of course read every word, but the verdict was everywhere the same: "Insufficient changes have been made to give us confidence that the anticipated high quality, comfort, safety performance and other characteristics promised by the proposal will be furnished on time and at reasonable cost under this construction contract."

Even when telling the story years later, Deacon still sagged at remembrance of the judgment and the recollection of what it caused.

"At that point we were about a fortnight away from Equity 2," he said. "And that was when the postponement occurred. That was when the bomb went off."

8

A few days after Heydon's pessimistic second report turned the Channel Tunnel project into a salvage operation, a retired French executive named André Bénard called on a longtime business friend. Bénard was looking for a charitable contribution. He came away with a mission.

"I went to see a good friend of mine, Alain Chevalier, who was then the head of LVMH—you know, Louis Vuitton-Moët et Chandon," Bénard recalled. "I had retired three years before from Shell, where I was managing director of a group." This fact said a great deal about Bénard's abilities; since the leadership of Royal Dutch Shell was (and had always been) heavily Dutch and British.

Bénard had a home in Paris near the Bois de Boulogne and a *maison secondaire* in the south of France, but he kept an apartment in London, too. "I had kept a foot in London because, having spent thirteen years outside my own country, I was offered all sorts of new activities," he said. "In America— I had become an adviser to Lazards in New York—Belgium, Holland, whatever. So I had stayed in London. I started getting interested in art foundations, things like that, and I went to LVMH to try and extract some money for one of the art foundations I was trying to help."

Chevalier heard Bénard's request, then responded with his own.

"He said, 'You're coming to ask me for something; I'll ask you for something in return,'" Bénard said. "What he asked me in return was, would I be prepared to take the chairmanship of the Channel Tunnel. It had nothing to do with him, but he was part of a small establishment of people in France who were looking for somebody who they thought would be able to do that, and prepared to do that."

Bénard was then sixty-three years old and looked precisely like what he was: a well-educated man who had risen to a very high level in a very large international organization. He wore his sophistication and self-assurance on his well-tailored sleeve. He was French by birth, a thorough cosmopolite by training and habit. But he had been so long in England that he could think like an Englishman as well as speak his language flawlessly.

He made a powerful impression on people, more by manner than appearance. He was of no more than average height, his hair had gone gray and thin. His features were strong rather than handsome. But his carriage was confident and vigorous, and he had a democratic warmth that came from confidence. Bénard did not try to upstage, to one-up, to overawe, to dominate; he had the perfect calm that comes from perfect assurance.

Yet beneath this favorite-uncle surface lay the mental toughness of a *polytechnicien* (which he was, of course) and more than a trace of the autocratic rigor for which the breed was famous. He seemed to have cultivated Roman virtues: the duty of the citizen to leave his plow to work for the common good, the wisdom to understand the role of folly in human endeavor, the disciplined strength of mind and spirit to withstand adversity. He answered difficult questions with the same frankness as easy ones. His view of associates was Olympian: The eye saw the weakness; the intellect forgave it. Bénard had within himself what Eurotunnel and Transmanche both lacked: a *noyau dur.*

People who encountered this hard core tended to have quite a different opinion about Bénard than those who saw only the urbane exterior. If one happened to be sitting on the same side of the table, Bénard seemed admirably tough, a formidable resource. If one were on the other side, however, Bénard might seem—as Andrew McDowall said from experience—"a very smooth guy . . . but a very, very difficult, devious, nasty bit of work." A less harsh but more common view of Bénard was that his courtesy was both genuine (no gentleman would stoop to less) and utilitarian: It was the best way to do business.

Bénard's name had been put forward by Jean-Paul Parayre, the French chairman of Eurotunnel. It was not the first and certainly not the only name suggested. "They had been looking all over the place and they hadn't really found anybody," Bénard said. "The selection of a chairman is not really a rational thing: You look around, you think about the people you know, and in the end, you have to form your own judgement. [At first] I was not on the list at all, because I had spent thirteen years outside France."

Parayre's involvement was eloquent testimony to the confusion of roles that existed inside Eurotunnel. Parayre was, at the time, in the process of leaving Eurotunnel to take over the leadership of the French group of contractors within TML. In the meantime, he was leading Eurotunnel as it negotiated the terms of the construction contract.

André Bénard.

Bénard at first believed he was being brought in because Parayre recognized this conflict, in which he would, in effect, negotiate and sign a contract with himself.

"But that was not so," Bénard recalled. "In fact, he [Parayre] said, 'I will only hand over *after* I've signed the construction agreement.' Which demonstrates that the contractors didn't really care about that problem—even though, to a sensible observer, it was quite clear that this was one of the pitfalls. . . . Parayre thought if he didn't stay, the contract would be different from what he wanted." This sorting-out of loyalties was using quite a lot of Eurotunnel's energies at the time; Francis Bouygues had only been induced to resign from the board in April, when it finally became clear to him that the banks would not tolerate his continued presence there.

Of course, if Parayre stayed on, the construction contract would lack an important element: Bénard's signature. It would not be "his" contract; he could never be blamed for its deficiencies. As Philippe Essig put it, "It would not be his baby."

Bénard told the recruiters that he was interested in the proposition but wished to study it. Parayre provided him with the necessary documents, and Bénard retired to Paris, for the weekend of June 21 and 22, to consider them.

The problems were evident. "There were the conflicts of interest, of course," he said. "Another major question was the political support in the

UK. In France it was clear that there was no problem. But it required the re-election of Mrs Thatcher. . . . If she were defeated in the Spring of 1987, Labour would come in, and Labour had decided at that time that they wanted a whole reopening of the issue, with free discussion in Parliament of the project. The one-year interruption that would result—minimum—would kill the whole thing. So it was quite essential that she win."

Bénard held a tolerant Gallic view of the conflicts between the project participants, governed by pragmatism rather than the letter of the contract and the relationship of the persons who signed it. This view—recognize the benefits, live with the consequences—was general in France, rare or absent in Britain, intolerable to Americans who were drawn into the project.

"If you don't like conflicts you should not be in Eurotunnel," was the way Pierre Coindreau of BNP put it. "Eurotunnel is a complete conflict, from everywhere. BNP is a sponsor and a founding shareholder. We have a director on the board. We are a lender and we are an equity holder and an agent. All simultaneously. Crédit lyonnais is in the same situation.

"But I think the notion of conflict of interest in this sort of deal maybe should be seen differently: This is not a normal business. . . . Eurotunnel is a company that was so . . . *strange,* that I think for the bank it was good—and probably necessary—to be represented on the board."

Foreign banks were less sympathetic to that view, of course, because they were not the ones sitting on Eurotunnel's board. Bénard recognized that and, in the course of a long weekend, tried to balance all that was acting for and against the project, to evaluate the Channel Tunnel's chances of surviving.

"You had to ask yourself, at what stage and to what degree is this inbuilt problem—this major problem—going to figure, and will it destroy us or not?" Bénard said. "That was really the essence of what I pondered over during the long weekend. And my conclusion at that time was, yes, there were conflicts of interest, but at the end of the day, the prevailing interest of governments, banks, contractors—everybody—would be so overwhelming that the problems would somehow be surmounted.

"I thought there was perhaps a thirty per cent chance of bringing it off," he said. It was enough; he agreed to take the chairman's seat once the contract was signed.

In Britain, there was angry speculation that Heydon was out to ruin the project with impossible demands.

"There were a lot of people, old-timers on the project, who started to mutter about Berger being in the pay of the opposition—that is, one of the rivals," Deacon said. "Everybody got paranoid. Heydon got paranoid. I got paranoid at various stages."

Whatever anyone believed, the fact was that the hard-core technical banks, particularly Deutsche Bank and Union Bank of Switzerland, were now in control of the process, and they would not commit any money until the contract suited them. On July 5, Morgan Grenfell and Robert Fleming, the two investment banks advising Eurotunnel, notified the board that there was no possibility of going ahead with Equity 2 before autumn, when pension fund trustees and insurance companies' investment committees returned from summer vacations.

"We have already announced that Equity 2 will be undertaken in July," the investment bankers wrote to Eurotunnel. "However, we believe that, provided a leak does not occur beforehand, a suitable press release could be issued later this week which would present the delay in a favourable light . . ."

At this time, another body was commencing a scrutiny of the project: the House of Commons. The Channel Tunnel Bill had struggled free of the procedural swamp in Parliament, winning its second reading on June 5 by a 309-to-44 vote. This was legal ratification of the public part of the project: Britain had decided that it was good public policy. It now remained for the private part of the bill to achieve passage, and this required hearings by the House of Commons Select Committee on the Channel Tunnel Bill.

The Select Committee held its first meeting, to set dates and procedures, on June 24, 1986, a day so sultry that one resolution read, "Resolved, That, because of the exceptionally warm weather, Counsel be invited to appear without wigs and gowns."

The first speaker on that second day was Michael Fitzgerald, Queen's Counsel, who was to present the government's opening statement. He commenced with a promise to be factual and brief. These were, of course, rather contradictory aims. With such a complex project, the number of facts in effect precluded brevity. Fitzgerald, aided by diagrams, settled down for a long explication of the Channel Tunnel.

He explained the purpose of the Channel Tunnel Act. He pointed out the intended route of the tunnel and offered some details about the geography and landforms at the British end. He indicated the location and purpose of the shuttle terminal at Cheriton, the service and maintenance area at the foot of Shakespeare Cliff, the customs facilities at Ashford, the planned improvements to the region's road and rail networks.

He moved on to introduce the various entities that had come together as Eurotunnel. He guided his listeners through the treaty concluded at Canterbury, the concession granted to Eurotunnel, the rights and obligations that Eurotunnel thereby assumed, the absolute absence of any government guarantee.

"I would like, if I may, to pass on now to a description of some of the historical background to the Bill," Fitzgerald then said. "Including the Parliamentary history." He recounted the 1802 French tunnel proposal, the hydrogeologic studies of 1833, the incorporation of the Channel Tunnel Company in 1881. He had carried his narrative as far as June 1982 when the stuffy heat of the room overwhelmed him, and he fainted.

There was considerable public interest in the committee's work—the number of petitioners eventually reached 4,845—and despite the chairman's firm refusal to hear irrelevant testimony, the leaves would be off the trees before the committee finished its work.

A few issues consumed much time: Kent groups were worried about dust, noise, traffic and other disruptions during construction, and the effect on the local economy once the tunnel was open. A parade of witnesses trudged over issues that would become drearily familiar: the unpopular Dollands Moor freight sidings, the entry and exit roads for the shuttle terminal, the disposal of excavated rock, road traffic, construction sites, fire safety.

One petition came from the Ham Street Road Study Group, represented by Dr. Andrew Burnett, one of its members. Dr. Burnett first had to locate Ham Street for his listeners: He handed out copies of a hand-drawn map and explained that Ham Street was a small village near another small village near Ashford. He did not try to impress the committee with the size of his constituency: The group, he said, had four members, all from the village. It had been formed in 1985, after two girls—"one was just twelve and the other almost thirteen"—had been hit by a truck and killed on the A2070, the road that ran north through Ham Street to Ashford.

The A2070, Dr. Burnett noted, was a former "B" road that had been upgraded in 1967 to "A" status. The upgrading was mostly on paper; the main physical improvement had been to widen—by a little—the stretches north and south of Ham Street. Nothing could be done in the village, of course, without removing most of its buildings. "The effect has been to provide two fast stretches with the village acting as a chicane in the middle with increased traffic," Dr. Burnett said.

The new tunnel facilities at Ashford—a main passenger terminal for trains to and from the Continent, plus the main customs clearing point for freight—would act as a magnet, doubling the A2070 traffic through Ham Street to about two thousand cars and two hundred trucks a day. Dr. Burnett said that a two-and-a-half-kilometer bypass would remove three quarters of that traffic, almost all the trucks and most of the danger to residents. It would cost about £2.6 million, and he begged the Kent authorities or Eurotunnel to finance it.

They declined, but in as kindly a fashion as they could. Fitzgerald pointed out that Kent had a broad plan for improving its roads, and while the Ham Street bypass was included, the expected annual benefit from it was only £30,000. Other planned bypasses promised greater benefits. So while he sympathized with Dr. Burnett, Fitzgerald could offer no hope that his request would be granted. Dr. Burnett accepted this with the grace that marked his whole presentation, though he could not help but say, "I would hope that the children in Ham Street are worth a bit more than £30,000."

Though no one in the room could then appreciate it, there was a bitter irony in Dr. Burnett's petition and the reception that it received. There were Ham Streets all over Britain—and France as well—asking every level of government to make their local roads safer. The requests were subjected to the same cost-benefit examination, and almost all were found wanting in merit.

The tunnel, however, would be judged by a different standard. There would be no weighing of costs against benefits. The goal for the tunnel would be absolute safety, an absolute removal of risk, with safety equipment double- and even triple-banked to ensure that no one would ever die by mischance in the Channel Tunnel. This standard would be set and upheld by official bodies—the Intergovernmental Commission and its offshoot, the Safety Authority—that would bear none of the cost of providing this marvelous security, but much of the responsibility if anything were to go wrong. The results of such an arrangement were easy to predict.

The Select Committee was generous in the attention it paid to concerned citizens. The Deal and Walmer Inshore Fishermen's Association was concerned about the plans to dredge fill for the terminal site from the Goodwin Sands, a notorious shoal four miles offshore, ten miles up the coast from Dover. (The boatmen of Deal were particularly skilled in rescue work, one historian wrote in 1911, because "the terrible Goodwins provide them with constant practice.") Two hang-gliding clubs worried that they would be denied use of the airspace over the terminal, a worry shared by the Bloobird Radio Flyers, pilots of model airplanes. Residents of Capel-le-Ferne, a clifftop village between Folkestone and Dover and directly above the tunnel route, were concerned about ground subsidence, even though the tunnel would be a full hundred meters below ground at that point.

The heaviest broadside, of course, came from the ferry owners and port interests. It began on July 22 with a barrage of paper, in the form of suggested amendments to the bill. The companies wanted statutory guarantees of fair competition, the right to form a cartel, compensation for the loss of business to a government-chartered venture, assurances that spoil from the tunnel would not damage the ports, road improvements to ease the passage of vehicles to the ferry docks, guarantees that the government would not assist the tunnel if it failed as a business, freedom to set their own rates without government interference and the like.

Eurotunnel met the attack in the committee hearing by arguing, successfully, that the tunnel's financial viability did not lie within the committee's charter. This effectively gutted the petitions, although the testimony carried on for several days. The committee also stifled a ferry-led attack on tunnel safety, on the grounds that a competitor who had no special expertise in railway matters should not speak on a subject that Eurotunnel intended to address, in detail, in response to a request from the committee itself.

On July 31, the last day before the committee recessed, Major Charles F. Rose, the Department of Transport's chief of railway safety, testified and submitted a memorandum on safety. It was a nice cap for Eurotunnel on what had been a good set of hearings: Rose's memorandum said, in sum, that safety had been much studied in 1974, examined again in 1982 and addressed further in the events preceeding the concession. Most of the conclusions and findings from those studies still held true, including the overall one that a safe tunnel could be built along the lines suggested by Eurotunnel.

Rose's document accepted several very important assumptions: Passengers in the shuttle trains would remain with their vehicles. Shuttle wagons would resist fire for thirty minutes, to allow them to be pulled out of the tunnel while passengers moved through fire-resistant "doors or curtains" to other wagons. In the worst case—the evacuation of a train stopped by a serious fire—passengers would reach the surface, via the service tunnel, within ninety minutes.

"The efficacy of the fire curtains and of the alarm systems," Rose's memo said, still had to be demonstrated; the 1974 project had been canceled just as these systems were about to be tested. But there was no suggestion in his memorandum to suggest that Eurotunnel would have any trouble meeting safety standards set down by the Safety Authority, of which he would be a member. He added that the Authority, whose official existence had to await ratification of the Channel Tunnel treaty, had nonetheless met informally to consider the project.

This was most encouraging for Eurotunnel, which filed its own memorandum on safety with the Select Committee. Eurotunnel's memo seemed to promise a greater commitment to safety than Rose's memo asked. It certainly offered more details: Pamphlets, notices, public address and video-screen messages, all in several languages, would tell passengers how to report a fire. But Eurotunnel's memo said that "the shuttle trains will have fire partitions with a resistance of 30 minutes between each vehicle." The Rose memorandum, in contrast, said that "the wagons would be designed to withstand a serious fire for at least 30 minutes, enabling the train to get out of the Tunnel." Between those two statements lay a great gulf that Eurotunnel, TML and Colonel Rose's Safety Commission would explore in exhaustive detail over the next several years.

With that, the committee stood down until September 16, when it intended to reconvene for further hearings around Folkestone and Dover. All of this would produce a report to the House of Commons. The procedure would then be repeated in the House of Lords. After that, barring mischance or political upheaval, the bill would make its way to the sovereign for her signature. With that, the Channel Tunnel Act would be law, the treaty with France could be ratified and the tunnel could legally be built.

As the committee closed up shop, the project took a huge step forward: On July 31, Deacon and his cohort wrung a letter from Howard Heydon that said that the contract had been improved enough to work in the hands of "a strong and independent owner." Heydon emphatically did not believe that Eurotunnel was either strong or independent, and he certainly didn't believe that Eurotunnel should sign the contract. But it didn't matter: The letter silenced the technical banks long enough to get the construction contract signed.

This was done with appropriate solemnity at Crédit lyonnais on August 13. Nevertheless, everyone was still trying to sort out the four hundred points that Heydon had found wanting in the draft contract, points that the technical banks had insisted be changed before they would agree to lend money to Eurotunnel. "Points were being settled not on the basis of evidence but by horse-trading," Deacon recalled. Working them out had sometimes been a rough-and-ready affair.

"The quality of the debate about the smaller points was low," Deacon said. "The project cost more than it would have *if* time had been available at the outset to create a watertight contract. It was never to be. But we got most of them, and if we hadn't gotten them, Eurotunnel would have been in a lot worse shape."

Deacon and his cohort knew that they would be held responsible if the project collapsed for any reason. As Deacon put it, "We knew rock would be heaped upon us if we failed."

Thus they lived the project; days often simply ran together, without pause or break for sleep. The French were stranded in London for days on end, usually with no idea of when they would get to go home. "I was always astonishing the people at the counter," remembered Coindreau of his passages through London's airports. "When they were asking for my ticket, I would put in front of them a bunch—six or seven tickets—and then ask them to choose one."

Everyone stayed in the Royal Westminster Hotel, next to Eurotunnel's headquarters in Stag Place, near Victoria Station. "It was really Eurotunnel house," said Coindreau. "You had bankers, advisers, staff—everyone was living there, and it was part of the problem, because you could not relax, really, for one hour. You would go for dinner and inevitably there would be three or four tables with Eurotunnel people, and you would start discussing the project. So the project was in your mind from morning to night."

The British saw things differently, of course. "The French lived in the hotel, so there was no rush to get home at 5:00 PM," Deacon said. "Then, being French, they expected us to go to dinner with them. Being English, we did. The French would work any time but August."

Proximity lessened the burden only a little. Ian McMillan, Deacon's colleague on the Midland team, lived a scant five miles from Stag Place and commuted by taxi. "I missed the whole of the 1986 World Cup," he remembered. "The games were at 7:00 PM and 11:00 PM, and the latter was live—the series was played in Mexico. We decided we were never going to see the first game, but we'd be home in time to see the second. And of course I didn't see any of the live games."

Deacon recalled a time when the press of negotiating kept him in London for three straight weeks—even though he lived in Essex, about thirty-five miles and three quarters of an hour by train from London.

"I was living out of a dirty suitcase in hotels," he said. "And then Paterson said I had to go to Tokyo; we had to give a presentation on the project to the underwriters in Japan. I said, I have to go back to get a bag. He said, 'You are not leaving London. I refuse to let you leave to pack a bag.' I said, this is bloody ridiculous. So he actually arranged for his chauffeur in his Jaguar to drive out to my house to pick up a bag for me."

Deacon flew to Paris, met Christian DeFenoyl, a senior BNP executive who was Coindreau's boss, and the two caught a flight to Tokyo. When they reached their hotel, there was a message that DeFenoyl was needed back in London. "There was another crisis on the construction contract," Deacon said. "He took a pill, went to sleep, got on the plane the next day. That was how things were." Deacon paused in the telling, then went on: "You can see why my marriage broke up, can't you?"

Negotiations at Eurotunnel's headquarters in Stag Place were boisterous mob scenes that often shocked newcomers. The pressure—which some had endured for a year and more, from the days of preparing the Submission to Government—told in different ways on different people. There were some who simply cracked and were taken off the project, for a rest or forever, by their superiors. Others began to act in strange ways. McMillan recalled one junior Midland executive who, after a murderously intense stretch of work, "sent up a very contentious report, saying we should pull out of the deal, and saying that 'NatWest couldn't organize a piss-up in a brewery.' Really over the top." So ripe a judgment would have been odd but acceptable, perhaps, in an internal document, but the exasperated executive also brought it to the table at a meeting of all five Arranging Banks. "So now the other four banks were sitting there reading that NatWest couldn't organize a piss-up in a brewery," McMillan said. "It may well be the other banks agreed. But nevertheless, to *table* something like that! He was then removed from the project. . . . He had obviously had a breakdown of sorts."

Odd behavior wasn't restricted to the foot soldiers; it sometimes reached high up to the banks' commanders. McMillan recalled telephoning a report to his superior at Midland, who then discussed it with Roger Byatt, a high-ranking NatWest executive, who had also been present. "Byatt said everything I had told him was a pack of lies," McMillan said. "Which it wasn't. He called me a liar, which was a bit rich, because obviously the gulf between Roger Byatt and me was immense. Byatt apologised a week later. But that's the kind of tension there was, because that was completely out of character for him."

The brawling style of the meetings demanded special skills. Deacon and McMillan admired the way Adrian Montague, the lawyer who was responsible for the legal coherence of the project and the structure of its Anglo-French equity shares, dealt with the clamor. "There would be hundreds of people sitting around the table, with many conversations going on at one time," McMillan said. "And he would speak very softly, so that everyone would have to shut up if they hoped to hear what he was saying."

In the end, after a long campaign waged with faxes and telephone calls, it fell to two lawyers, Montague and Stan Perlowski, who had come with Heydon from Berger, to set the terms of an uneasy truce. "We went round to [Montague's] offices, and he went off quietly into a room at midnight," Deacon said. Montague and Perlowski negotiated by telephone. "And it was only at two o'clock in the morning—it might have been three o'clock—that they actually changed their minds."

Deacon and his legion could then scramble back from their hellish torments to the merely purgatorial sufferings of hard work, long days and impossible deadlines. These, they knew, were at least finite.

The struggle had been more dangerously wearing than anyone could appreciate at the time. "You gear yourself up to work silly hours," McMillan said. "The minute you stop, you start to feel ill. . . . It was almost as if you had stopped taking drugs."

Coindreau felt this, too. "It was a nightmare," he said. "On large projects, the stakes are so high that human beings do not count, really. You are always crushed by the machine. The machine is stronger than you. If you have to meet a deadline, the consequences if you miss it are such that you *can't* miss it—if you have to work days and nights, too bad."

Signing the construction contract broke the logjam—at least for the moment—and a torrent of events surged through the weeks that followed. On August 16, three days after the formal contract signing, Eurotunnel signed the documents necessary for Equity 1.

The bank-loan underwriting agreement was signed before the end of the month, and Transmanche-Link put in the first orders for TBMs. On September 1, Equity 1 went through. On paper, this was a purchase of £46 million worth of equity in the project by its founding members; in reality it was simply a conversion into stock of cash advances that the partners had already made to the venture. Heydon delivered a second report that opened with the statement that negotiations had "materially altered the balance of the Contract towards a more equitable sharing of risks between the Employer and the Contractor." The rest of the report was a litany of cautions, but these were—for the moment—insufficient to stanch the enthusiastic flow.

Most of the Rail Usage Contract with British Rail and SNCF had been haggled out. The railways had agreed to pay somewhat more in the early days of the tunnel's operation, in return for later rate reductions.

Bénard joined Eurotunnel as Lord Pennock's cochairman; Parayre stepped aside but kept his seat on the board. Bénard's role in the project almost ended before it ever began. On September 11, Bechtel's Pete Behr heard that Bénard was out because he was "too Anglo-Saxon." The French side wanted someone from Banque indosuez for the post, Behr was told. Eleven days later, Behr heard that the crisis had passed and that Bénard was once again the choice to take the Eurotunnel chair. Bénard was far from the only new face at Eurotunnel; an entire new cadre arrived to occupy the executive offices. Stannard and Renault were removed as managing directors. They stayed with the project, but only as advisers for "an interim period" before rejoining their original employers. Marcel Sarmet, the Crédit lyonnais executive who had been seconded as Eurotunnel's finance director, was similarly retained as an interim adviser. Sir Alistair Frame, who had championed the 1974 tunnel project for Rio Tinto Zinc, joined the Eurotunnel board. Frame and RTZ agreed to give Eurotunnel the benefit of their bitter experience in building a tunnel to France.

RTZ also contributed a top executive: Jean-Loup Dherse, a fifty-three-year-old *polytechnicien,* RTZ board member and the World Bank's vice president for energy and industry, became Eurotunnel's chief executive. Dherse was a deeply religious man with an honest warmth about him. Asked how investors should think of Eurotunnel shares, he said, "The custom in my part of the world, Normandy, is for parents to plant poplar trees for their baby daughters, and when the daughters marry they sell the trees to raise a dowry. I think people will see Eurotunnel shares in the same way." The fact that Dherse was French balanced the fact that Eurotunnel was going to have its headquarters in London.

Less remarked in this influx was a fifty-six-year-old French engineer named Pierre Durand-Rival, who became deputy chief executive for technical matters. He had the usual (excellent) educational qualifications—the Polytechnique and the École nationale des ponts et chaussées—and the high regard of France's elite. Bénard had brought him aboard, with the assent and recommendation of well-placed friends. Durand-Rival had built his reputation on one enormous project, the huge Solmer steel mill at Fos, a $1.4 billion factory on a landfill site in the port of Marseilles. The site was bigger in area than San Francisco. Fos, built between 1970 and 1974, was the most efficient steel plant in Europe, rivaling Japan in the base cost of the steel it produced. It suffered because the French government, for political reasons, refused to close down the old steel mills in northern France. This policy starved Fos for orders and never permitted the plant to demonstrate its excellence, though it later became profitable.

At Fos, Durand-Rival had hired Bechtel to oversee the construction. The chief of Bechtel's six-hundred-man contingent at Fos was Pete Behr who, naturally enough, got to know Durand-Rival very well.

The reputation that Durand-Rival built at Fos looked quite different to different people. He was, Behr recalled, "certainly very demanding. He had come up in the iron and steel business after being a *fonctionnaire* (a civil servant). . . . He had built successfully, on budget, a big rolling mill in northern France." This was a remarkable achievement for someone coming out of the bureaucracy. He did it by first building a strong management team, drawn mostly from northern France and Alsace.

"Extremely serious people," Behr said. "Strong-willed and determined. The team was almost like a military unit: It ran on loyalty and devotion to duty, hard work and knowledge. The team came with him to Fos. Once I got to know and understand them, I could only admire them."

Behr said he found Durand-Rival "hard, disciplined, but completely ethical. He might have been too tough for some people." At Fos, Behr added, "he did have trouble with unions. There were strikes."

Behr and Bechtel were to benefit mightily from Durand-Rival's ascension: The French establishment that had anointed Durand-Rival was deeply con-

cerned about the Anglo-French balance of power within the project; it also
believed that Eurotunnel was too weak to manage the project. Behr wasn't
French, but he spoke the language and had worked hard and well *à la
française* at Fos. And he was not British.

Lord Pennock had initiated a meeting with Behr on August 19, after conversations with Sir Alistair Frame and Bénard. They discussed a possible role
for Bechtel in the project, but Pennock said any decision would have to await
the arrival, then as yet unannounced, of Durand-Rival as technical director.
Eurotunnel seemed concerned that Bechtel would cost too much and might
take over the project in unwanted ways and to an unacceptable degree, Behr
said. Pennock said he would keep Behr current on developments.

Durand-Rival told Behr that he didn't expect to be in office and functioning before mid-December. For the moment, Eurotunnel asked for some
minor help with contract and cost work. This wasn't the role that Behr
wanted—it was, he said, "body rental" rather than project management—but
he put a few people in as requested, even though they had to work with some
recent Eurotunnel hires of middling quality. Behr busied himself with tend-
ing his contacts and designing a role for Bechtel that he could present when
Durand-Rival was installed.

At this time, Transmanche-Link too suffered from wobbly management. The
problem ran deep; there was a distinct lack of tunneling expertise among the
contractors.

"There had been no tunneling of any consequence done in Europe for
years," said Andrew McDowall. "Spie Batignolles had done the Metro in
France fairly recently, but in this country there had been no tunneling and all
the tunneling engineers and experts had gone overseas. . . . We set up a traveling circus of recruiters who went around the world, and we recruited the
best people we could find." It happened that some major tunneling projects
were winding down in South Africa, as was a large job on Cairo's sewer system. Both yielded engineers for the Channel Tunnel effort. Those engineers,
in turn, knew where others of their profession were to be found.

Transmanche also had to assemble a top management group to cope with
the project's demands. The group shortly wound up with McDowall as chairman of a management board; John Reeve and, initially, Philippe Montagner
took over as directors-general. Montagner stayed only a short time before returning to Bouygues. His replacement was a boyish forty-six-year-old Spie
Batignolles engineer named François Jolivet.

Jolivet was unusual and very difficult to categorize. He was a distinguished
engineer who had overseen the design and construction of projects, such as
the Koeberg nuclear power station in South Africa, that rivaled the Channel

Tunnel in scale and complexity. He had been in charge of single projects and, later, in charge of a company division that was responsible for many such projects—the Koeberg plant, a three-thousand-unit housing development in Uruguay, a military complex in Saudi Arabia, a big hospital in South Africa.

Most of his work on these projects was done from Paris. Jolivet visited the sites, of course, but the day-to-day responsibility was delegated to project directors.

He was not a *polytechnicien*. He had been born in Haute-Marne—between Champagne and Burgundy, he liked to say. He had studied hydraulic, electrical and electromechanical engineering at the University of Toulouse and gone to work as a hydraulic engineer there for a company that Spie later acquired. He became a construction manager for the Autoroutes; he managed a plant that made concrete bridge sections. In all, he built more than a hundred Autoroute bridges.

On first meeting, Jolivet seemed miscast as the leading player on the French side. He did not have the icy, autocratic air that some—perhaps most—expected in a director-general. He did not look the part. "I was disappointed; he didn't look like a top director," said Daniele DeMori Calderon, a Frenchwoman who joined the project later as Jolivet's secretary and personal assistant. "Monsieur Jolivet didn't project that allure. He was relaxed." He was also, she found, monkish, isolated, devoted to modern art (of which he had an excellent collection), direct and simple in speech and habits. He flew economy class. He had no car or driver, preferring to take TML's company bus. His private life remained strictly private.

All of this, Calderon and other intelligent observers discovered, derived from Jolivet's conscious rejection of pomp and his devotion to certain ideals about how a large project should be organized and administered. He excelled, Calderon said, at what the French call "the Exercise of the Simple Man": the reduction of a complex problem to simple and clear elements that could be easily explained to, and grasped by, the meanest intellect.

In Spie, Jolivet had found a pluralistic corporate culture that suited him very well. Spie was oriented toward very large turnkey projects. These required a thorough mixing of disciplines; the fact that the jobs were overseas required an ability to mix cultures as well. In the early 1980s, the company was involved in a dizzying array of projects, most of them fast-track undertakings on a grand scale: hydroelectric plants in Chile, Venezuela, Colombia and Indonesia; a mass transit system in Caracas; an ore-shipping facility in Morocco; a railway across Gabon; the Baghdad airport; nuclear plants in Iran and South Africa; chemical and fertilizer plants in China, Jordan and Indonesia; pipelines in Saudi Arabia and Australia.

Each of these projects held the possibility of breathtaking failure as well as profit, and Spie's executives quite sensibly decided to see if they could avoid the former. They asked Jolivet to see if there were lessons to be learned from other big projects, ones costing more than fifty million dollars.

France, with its crash building programs to create Autoroutes, the TGV high-speed train system and the web of nuclear power stations, had been a testing ground for traditional project organizations in the 1970s and early 1980s. The two commonest forms were *coordination par projet,* which basically forced each project into the existing corporate structure, and the *organisation matricelle,* in which the central corporate structure delegated some decision-making power to a self-contained project management. Both had been found wanting.

Jolivet studied a hundred major projects with an eye toward identifying traits common to those that had been successes. The result of this research was a set of seventeen governing principles that Jolivet called *meta-règles,* which he compared to a nation's constitution—that is, a set of general principles that regulated statutory law. The *meta-règles*—five governing project organization, twelve devoted to administration—were incorporated in an internal Spie pamphlet, *La directive pour la conduite des grands projets.*

Summed up, Jolivet's research found that the delegation of broad powers to a project director was essential. This director could summon corporate resources but retained his independence, needing only to give an accounting of his management from time to time. The project director's power should be distributed freely among *sous-chefs* of self-contained "cells." The cells would have as few workers as practical, but as many responsibilities as possible. Tasks were to be "detaylorized," freed from the rigid mechanical view of Frederick Winslow Taylor, the American whose principles of "scientific management" had governed the operation of factories and mills since the early years of this century. Taylorism was an excellent medium for the growth of a rampant bureaucracy, Jolivet believed.

Flexible administration that kept looking in the rearview mirror worked best, Jolivet's study found. Regular reviews that led to adjustments in the administrative structure were helpful. In general, an evolving and temporary organization built of cells succeeded better than a permanent, pyramidal organization governed by fixed rules.

"My overall philosophy is that no matter how large the project, it must never crush individuals," Jolivet said. But as Coindreau had already observed, that was precisely what the Channel Tunnel project was doing.

In June, Spie's top-level executives asked Jolivet if he was prepared to become the French director-general of Transmanche-Link, the counterpart of John Reeve. There were three candidates on the French side, but after Jolivet had met the chairmen of the other French companies, it was clear that the job was his for the asking, and he accepted.

Ironically, the tunnel would demand something that foreign projects had not: relocation. Even though the Sangatte work site was only two hundred kilometers away, Jolivet knew that the size of the project, and its binational character, would require him to spend long stretches in London. That meant that he would be separated from his family for much of the next several years. He had two daughters preparing to be engineers and a son studying medicine; he didn't wish to disturb their studies.

Still, he was happy to have the challenge. He spent a few weeks defining his role and two objectives: One, to create an organization to construct the French section of the tunnel. Two, to create a Franco-British governing organization with Reeve. He rated these equal in importance.

It was a formidable undertaking, of course. "The French team was only about fifty people at that time," he recalled. "It was about the same on the British side. And the overall objective of TML was to have almost eight thousand people working three and a half years later."

Jolivet presented an admirably complete and clear study of his plans to an August 14 meeting of the top French representatives in TML. He had, by that time, conferred with Reeve about how they would structure the venture. There was "a gentlemen's agreement about what he will do and I will do," Jolivet said. Although each had a charter to create an organization along national lines, they decided instead to divide the work by function. "It was agreed that I will organize and supervise the overall engineering package and the transportation system and the construction in France," Jolivet said. "And John Reeve will supervise contract administration, finance and British construction." This divided the responsibilities along the lines of each man's affinity and training. It was an important step. At the time, Jolivet said, Transmanche-Link was two-headed, with two directors-general and two boards. "There was liaison between the two supervisory boards," he said. "But mainly people were thinking along national lines first."

Everyone's initial impulse had been to set up mirror organizations in each country. The looked-for result was the creation of what would in effect be two separate projects: a British tunnel leading out under the Channel from Folkestone and a French one leading to the same underwater point from Coquelles. They would be compatible, but not identical, independent projects.

Jolivet altered this. Instead of two mirror-image organizations, he designed a triptych. One side panel was Reeve's British organization; the other was Jolivet's French one. Between them was the engineering group, whose director was David Brown. "We were to have French and British engineering managers," Jolivet said. "I decided we would have only one, so I sent back the

French engineering manager to his mother company, Spie Batignolles." On paper, Brown was under the supervision of both Jolivet and Reeve, but the gentlemen's agreement meant that engineering was Jolivet's responsibility. He and Brown got along well; Jolivet considered him a good friend.

For French construction, Jolivet set up three *sous-projets*: the terminal, the tunnels and the manufacture of precast concrete ring segments. The tunneling he broke into four pieces: one for each of the three tubes and one that would be responsible for the access shaft and logistics. "This reduced the magnitude and complexity down to classical size," he said. "It was human size for a *good* project manager. The breakdown was not functional, it was operational—quite a new approach for managing projects."

But the arrangement needed an overall construction manager who would function at David Brown's level; who would oversee all of the *sous-projets* and report to Jolivet and—on paper—to Reeve. This was a critical and difficult job: The men that Jolivet named to run the *sous-projets* came from the top echelons of their mother companies' managements. Here, they would be down at the third level, looking up to the construction director and, beyond him, to Jolivet. So the construction manager would have to lead as well as command. He would have to be able to give and enforce orders, but also be able to earn the loyalty and respect of those who served under him. Fortunately, the French had an excellent candidate: Pierre Matheron.

When the Channel Tunnel project came to Matheron in December 1985, he was fifty-eight years old and, like Alexander the Great, worried that there were no more worlds to conquer. He was just finishing construction of a huge port facility in Damietta, Egypt, for his company, SGE. The horizon was empty of new challenges; it seemed that the era of great civil works was coming to a close. He had already decided to retire if nothing came along to challenge his abilities. Then the president of SGE came to visit him in Egypt. If the Eurotunnel group won the concession, he told Matheron, they wanted him to come and help run the project.

Matheron was not overwhelmed by the idea. He had followed press accounts of the project without much thought. It was a big tunnel, but it was, all the same, a tunnel. "It was, without a doubt, out of the ordinary," he recalled years later. "But it was quite a bit less remarkable than the project we undertook during the Fifties, when we had to rebuild the whole country."

He was a hard driver from principle as well as habit and preference. "I have a passion for the *Deux Chevaux*," he told an interviewer, referring to the Citroën car that had been a beloved symbol of France for decades. "There's only one way to drive it: *pied au plancher*." This pedal-to-the-floor style was his trademark, the way he approached a project: He got things moving and kept them moving until the job was done. He left debate to others.

This he tempered with a deep concern for the morale of his troops. He had learned this second principle the hard way, on another big project: Durand-Rival's steel mill at Fos. He later noted that more than one day in five were lost to strikes at Fos. "It was a lesson to me," he said. "You can't run a project the size of the Channel Tunnel as if you were a caliph." You had to involve the workers, let them know that you expected great things from them, assure them that their efforts would be noticed and rewarded. A secretary who worked under Matheron summed up his management style as, "I'll look after you—but you have to look after me."

An optimist might have concluded that things were falling into place in interesting and encouraging ways: Eurotunnel's strengthened management included André Bénard, a mature and accomplished executive of great diplomatic skill. TML had been strengthened by the addition of Jolivet, a humane and experienced engineer whose skills neatly complemented those of Reeve. Underpinning this top level were Durand-Rival and Matheron—men who were big enough for the job and who had worked successfully together in the past. Both knew and had worked with Pete Behr and Bechtel, whose resources might prove vital. There was a signed contract whose admitted im-

Pierre Matheron.

perfections were being eliminated through slow but continuing negotiations. The governments were in accord, and while opponents of the tunnel might rail against it, there seemed little risk that politics would wreck the project.

Unfortunately, the view of this cheery prospect was entirely blocked by a truly grave problem: The marketplace did not wish to invest in the Channel Tunnel. Equity 2 was failing.

9

On September 26, three months late, the pathfinder prospectus for Equity 2 finally saw print. There had been reasonable hopes that the prospectus would be greeted politely and that the shares would sell. The fund managers to whom the pathfinder was sent had agreed months earlier—informally, of course—to buy into Eurotunnel when it came to market.

The first inkling that all wasn't well reached Sir David Walker within a few weeks. Walker was then one of four executive directors of the Bank of England; his zone of responsibility comprised industrial finance by all of the City's financial institutions except banks. The messengers who brought news of Equity 2's problems were two investment bankers: Charles Rawlinson of Morgan Grenfell and Lawrence Banks of Robert Fleming. "They believed they'd had rather encouraging responses from a large number of institutions, mainly life assurance companies," Walker recalled. "Unfortunately, they said, 'We've now got to the position of issuing a draft prospectus, and we've gone back to the institutions, and they're not responding. And, you know, a few of them are being rather obstructive and slow.' "

The request to the Bank of England had actually originated with John Franklin, who was one of the young men that the financial institutions—in his case, Morgan Grenfell—had thrown into the Channel Tunnel project. He was a veteran, having joined the effort in early 1985 to work in the Channel Tunnel Group's campaign to win the concession—and he had the war stories and emotional scars to prove it.

Franklin also had been involved in negotiating the sketchy, last-minute agreement with the railroads in the days and hours before CTG handed in its proposal to the governments.

"I remember being summoned one morning," he recalled. "A Thursday. I was in the office early, and I was telephoned and told that I had to be on the ten o'clock plane to Paris—a day's meeting with SNCF."

Franklin scrambled through the offices, borrowing any French francs he could find. "I went outside, got into a taxi and told the driver he had thirty-five minutes to get me to London Airport. We arrived there with smoke coming out of the bonnet." The round-trip took longer than expected. "Instead of getting back that night, I got back—eventually—on Tuesday. I had to keep going off to buy myself shirts and underclothes. . . . We were up till three in the morning every night and started out again at daylight, haggling with the railroads. Eventually we signed an agreement that I think was the worst I've ever seen, which said that tariffs will be not more than X, and not less than Y. But the gap was so large that it was rather like saying the price of a picture will be not more than a million pounds, and not less than a thousand. The gap was phenomenal. But we were running out of time."

Negotiations with the railroads to tighten up the agreement continued through all of 1986. "We had a session just before the French election in March," Franklin said. "It was in SNCF's offices and we put together another agreement; it was half in English, half in French, and I remember trying to find photocopying paper and staplers and things like that at about two o'clock in the morning. French elections are on Sunday; we had to get it done by Saturday night, because the minister who was going to sign, or authorize SNCF to sign, could well change the following day.

"I remember searching the director-general's office and finding the only stapler in SNCF in his desk. There were several of us trying to get this photocopier to work. None of us could, and there were no secretaries around, and we had an agreement half-typed in French, with amendments in English and other amendments in French. Complete nonsense. We then flew back to London and had a board meeting of CTG in Wimpey's offices on Sunday morning." Franklin and his British colleagues took up near-residence at the Royal Monceau Hotel, near the Arc de Triomphe, because one could get food there at three in the morning.

He had been among the troops who had gone out, in the spring of 1986, to reconnoiter the City to gauge the strength of its commitment to buy into Eurotunnel when Equity 2 arrived. He had carried financial analyses of the project to the fund directors of insurance companies and pension funds, explaining and asking the crucial question: Would they, when the time came, buy?

"We got letters of intent, non-binding letters of intent," he said. "They would never commit themselves to investing, but they said they would seriously consider investing. There were very strong comfort letters. 'Comfort letter' is a technical term; basically, it's going as near as you can to a guarantee without actually committing yourself."

Now, with the pathfinder in circulation and the Equity 2 sale a scant few weeks in the offing, Eurotunnel's financial people began calling on those who had signed comfort letters. They were dismayed to discover that the commitment had withered. There was little money on offer, and no comfort at all for Franklin's group.

It became a desperate campaign. Franklin and representatives of other investment banks hunkered down in the Catto room at Morgan Grenfell's headquarters. There was dark symbolism in the site: The Lord Catto for whom the room was named, who was then Morgan Grenfell's president (a largely honorary title, conferred in retirement), had denounced the Channel Tunnel and backed a Channel Bridge in the 1970s.

The Catto room came to be called "The Bunker," and the atmosphere was as grim and cheerless as the nickname suggested. It was apparent to its occupants that something extraordinary would be needed to make Equity 2 a success. Government intervention was not a possibility. That left the Bank of England.

"I initiated it, actually, when I heard that things were not going well," Franklin said. "I remember going to [Eurotunnel] and reporting to them that I thought it was not going to go, and we should tell the Bank of England and see whether there was anything they could do to help."

There were good reasons for the problems that Eurotunnel was experiencing. As Walker pointed out, it was "a very go-go era in the London financial markets, [a] time when you could make a lot of money in share trading, and here's this thing that ten years hence might fly." He added that the government hadn't done anything to assist the issue. Further, the effort to win the concession had left Eurotunnel exhausted; there had been a general collapse once the race was won.

This was evident to the government. "All the people we had been dealing with disappeared," said John Noulton. "They had looked to us like quite a strong organisation, but the moment the concession was awarded, the bankers went out one door and formed themselves into the agent banks . . . and the contractors went out the other door and formed TML. And what was left in the middle was a fairly feeble organisation, with one or two worthy people at a fairly junior level. . . . There were a few people around who knew the project, but they weren't go-getters. There was nobody around with the muscle, and for the next six to eight months the organisation lumbered on. But it was very weak. And it was very worrying."

There were also some unusual, if not unique, reasons for Equity 2's problems, Franklin knew. "One has to realize that this was the first *contested* equity placement that I think has ever been done," he said. "The ferry companies had a vested interest in making sure the project did not go ahead, and they therefore produced documents which they sent round to all the institutions, casting enormous doubts on the viability of the project—on the costings that we'd got in our prospectus, on the feasibility of actually completing the project, and on the traffic projections."

When he and his colleagues made the rounds to call in the promised financing, all of the institutions "had on their desks these documents from the ferries saying that it was a lousy project. And a lot of them, who were acting for pensions and things, said, 'Well you know there's an awful lot of doubt about this project. Is it right for us to invest in it?' And if you're investing pensioners' money you will tend to take a cautious view."

And so, Rawlinson and Banks told Walker, there was "a little gap" between what was being asked and what was being offered. "The implication to me," Walker said, "was that if only the Bank of England would use its good offices—you know, there might be a gap of ten or fifteen million—but they'd then be clear and dry."

The Bank of England has a long history of involving itself in private affairs that bear upon the nation's interest. This has been overt, Walker said, since the years between the world wars, and possibly before that.

"The Bank stands ready to call parties who may have reached an impasse to the table to try to resolve matters in a calm way," Walker said. "If a company is in trouble, the Bank of England can, and does, call the creditor banks and ask them to agree to a freeze, to let all stand in abeyance for a month to see if the problems can be sorted out. Or it can take up the cause of a company like Eurotunnel."

Like the English constitution, the Bank's powers are unwritten. Like the constitution, they have the force and power of something far more solid than statute: tradition. Asked why the Bank can do such things, Walker began by saying, "It's three hundred years old." So although intervention may be a casual, clubby affair—"All we can say is look, I'd like to tell you this is an important project, and sometimes you have to do something which extends a little bit beyond your short commercial interest," Walker said—the power is not taken lightly, either by the Bank or by the institutions in whose affairs it intervenes. The Bank does not intervene on whim.

"It's extremely careful not to do it inappropriately," said Walker. "On the whole, it has a fairly good track record. Above all, the Bank is trusted. The Bank carries a brief for nobody. Sometimes it's supportive of the government; sometimes it isn't. . . . I think most major British financial institutions one time or another turn to the Bank of England and say 'Look, we've got ourselves in a hole, or someone else has put us in a hole. We're not asking you to solve the problem, but can you apply a drop of lubrication on this creaking joint?' And very often the Bank can."

Walker "pondered," then took the matter to the governor at the time, Robin Leigh-Pemberton. It was "speedily concluded," said Walker, that the Channel Tunnel was an important project and that the Bank should help with Equity 2. Walker told Rawlinson and Banks that he would see what he could do.

The crisis was in fact far deeper than Walker knew; Rawlinson and Banks had understated the gravity of the situation. Equity 2 was not a few million pounds short of its goal, it was almost one hundred million pounds short. In all, Walker found a scant five million pounds committed. Thirty-eight institutions had reneged on their promises.

Walker quickly decided against calling a general meeting of all of the fund managers. "I judged that would not be a good approach," he said. "You have a big meeting, and if one of them comes out hawkishly negative, the group dynamics are such that all the rest will follow." He spoke to each of the thirty-eight companies individually. Each replied to his questions with a denial and a complaint: They had never truly committed themselves to invest, and Eurotunnel had since given them ample reason to never invest. It was weak, wounded, unable even to respond effectively to the ferries' attacks.

"There were other, more attractive offerings around," Walker said. "And in the past six months, the degree of confidence about the management—the purposefulness of Eurotunnel—had taken a bad knock. It seemed to be drifting."

The Thatcher government's aggressive sell-off of government-owned industries had made Eurotunnel's task more difficult. By that time, the Thatcher years had seen the privatization of all or part of British Petroleum, British Aerospace, British Sugar, Cable & Wireless, the National Freight Consortium, Britoil, Associated British Ports, British Telecom and Jaguar, among other companies. As Eurotunnel struggled to sell itself, British Gas was on the block; British Airways and a remaining huge chunk of British Petroleum would come to market in 1987. "I think the Americans and Canadians—and the Japanese—saw those as attractive things to underwrite," Walker said. "But this hole under the North Sea? Might not happen. The others were corporations. This was only a project."

Various gimmicks common in privatizations, such as discount vouchers and special deals, also were pernicious. As one investment adviser noted, "the long-term effect of these incentives was to lead the retail investor in England to expect give-aways, bonus shares, hot deals and the prize-from-the-box. If incentives were not offered, the retail investor didn't understand why he should invest, and didn't." Privatization was thus raising expectations among private small investors—to whom Eurotunnel would be trying to sell shares the next year, in Equity 3—at the same time it was luring big institutional investors away from Equity 2.

Walker found that a word to the fund managers was usually sufficient, but the agreements came with reservations. Walker said: "The message that came from a lot of these institutions [was], 'Well, we're doing it, the Bank of

England has asked it. . . . But really, old Bank of England, you have to give us an assurance that you will use your muscle the other way round, and get some decent direction and strengthen the board.' And I gave my undertaking that we would do it."

The Bank's first move to strengthen management was to convince all parties that Sir Nigel Broakes of Trafalgar House should join the Eurotunnel board, which he did in late October. If all went well, he would step forward to lead when Pennock could with good grace step aside. Trafalgar House wasn't pleased to see its chairman off helping a recent competitor, and Eurotunnel was equally cool to someone who, until just a few months earlier, had been a harsh and effective critic of its plans, personnel and outlook. But it was a start.

Heroic sales efforts by Walker and others brought two major overseas underwriters to the effort; Nomura Securities took 10 percent of the issue for Japan and Salomon Brothers took the same amount for the United States market. But other overseas efforts bore little fruit.

The French could not resist a little nationalistic gloating. "The French publicly were rubbing their hands and saying, 'Well, it's all done on our side," Ian Callaghan said. "This nationalism took over." One reason for the French success, Walker pointed out, was the fact that the French banks were government-owned, so "the Treasury pull the lever and they all go in; they *call* it private sector. We don't have that." Another reason things moved more smoothly across the Channel was the assistance of the Caisse des dépôts, which Walker described simply and accurately as "a huge bucket of money."

Much later, it would become apparent that the French, too, had had severe troubles selling Equity 2. Deacon heard that French banking authorities were twisting arms almost as strenuously as the Bank of England, and that the Élysée Palace had applied pressure as well.

"They'd always told us that as far as they were concerned it was a government project," Callaghan said of the French. "And since Crédit lyonnais and so on were nationalized banks anyway, it was just government money by another route. But as it turned out there were obviously people who were actually having to make the decisions high up in these banks, who were less than convinced by the whole thing. So it was quite touch-and-go on their side as well."

In the end, Equity 2 was proclaimed a success. It was not; it was a substantial failure. Walker estimated that £75 million to £80 million of Britain's £103 million were sold. The would-be sellers had to mop up the huge pools of stock for which they failed to find buyers. Morgan Grenfell and Fleming "took quite a large investment" of such unwanted stock, Franklin said. Midland and NatWest also helped clean up. "I know that pressure was put on Midland and NatWest, and at very high levels," Chris Deacon said. "We took

Equity 2 and the [Midland] pension fund took Equity 2 as well, thank you very much." Banque nationale de Paris was stuck, too, with a large chunk of Eurotunnel stock that couldn't be sold.

Such failure required a scapegoat, of course. The blame fell on Franklin, who was removed from the project. The blame was heaped on him by people who were so far removed that their understanding of the events was deficient, and by the people who now streamed into Eurotunnel as a result of the money that Equity 2 provided.

Franklin—who swallowed whatever bitterness he might have felt at such treatment—recalled a conversation with one of this latter group. "He said, 'Well, it's quite ridiculous, you should have had a chief executive, you should have had independent people doing this, that and the other.' Which was absolutely true. But who was going to pay for it?"

Equity 2 dramatically changed the dynamics of the venture, although this wasn't noted at the time. The sale of equity had reduced the founding companies and banks to minority shareholders in Eurotunnel. In business as in nature, energy is conserved, and the power that was stripped away from the founders didn't simply disappear. It shifted to the banking syndicate—which, as the source-to-be of 80 percent of the estimated £5 billion needed to build the tunnel, could enforce any demand it wished. And as things stood at that moment, the banking syndicate was not governed by the five Agent Banks that had put it together, but by the toughest and most demanding of the arranging banks: Deutsche Bank, Union Bank of Switzerland (UBS) and AmRo.

This did not augur well for people like Deacon and Callaghan, who now faced the task of getting the more than two hundred banks in the syndicate to sign off on the loan agreement. And Equity 2's difficulties did not augur well for Equity 3, the sale of £770 million of Eurotunnel shares to the public. Equity 3 was to take place in July, after which the banks' loan agreement could be made official and binding.

The drama surrounding Equity 2 obscured an event of great importance that followed on its heels: the actual start of construction on the tunnel.

The obscurity was intended. On October 30, 1986, the day after Equity 2 was declared a success, Matheron set crews to excavating at Sangatte. Over the several months that followed, the excavations would create a huge circular shaft surrounded by a titanic cofferdam: *le puits de Sangatte*—the Well of Sangatte, itself a wonder of the engineering world.

French engineers remembered the painful lessons of The Descenderie. This time, there would be no slogging downward through the fractured chalk and cascades of water. Jolivet and the others in charge had decided to create this huge cylindrical access shaft, an extraordinary fifty-five meters in diameter and sixty-five meters deep—big enough to easily swallow the Arc de Triomphe. Surrounding it was a cofferdam which enclosed an ellipse ninety-seven meters wide and almost two hundred meters long. The cofferdam's wall ran sixty meters down into the ground, down to the impermeable chalk marl that lay below the silt and sand and fractured chalk nearer the surface. The cofferdam would hold back the groundwater to permit construction of six marshaling chambers, three on each side of the shaft, where the tunnel-boring machines would be assembled to begin their underground journeys.

The great shaft would be the passage through which the sections of concrete tunnel liner would be brought in and through which the tunnel spoil would be evacuated. The French had decided to slurry the spoil—that is, crush it and mix it with water to form a soup—and pump it up into the Fond Pignon, a 50-hectare basin (125 acres) in a depression atop Mont-Saint-Hubert, about two kilometers from the shaft. There, behind sloping walls of excavated chalk that resembled a Vauban fortress, the water would drain out and the crushed rock would remain. Six slurry pumps (each able to pump 90 cubic meters of slurry per hour, enough to cover a baseball diamond to a depth of 12 meters) and five huge slurry crushers and mixers would sit in the very bottom of the Sangatte shaft, 17.5 meters below the marshaling chambers. The lowest level would also house two sumps—drainage pits—with a combined capacity of 3,500 cubic meters of water. Any water that wasn't used to make slurry could be pumped into the sea via a buried pipe. The shaft would have five elevators: two small ones, each capable of carrying a dozen men, and three large ones, each able to lift or lower 7.5 tons—eighty men, or one of the small "manrider" service trains used to transport workers in the tunnel. The shaft would be roofed over by two huge sheds which were called—appropriately enough, given the cathedral-scale grandeur of the undertaking—naves. The north-south nave would have a gantry crane, designed to lower the TBM components, that could handle 430 tons; it would also have two 60-ton cranes for lowering segments for the running tunnels. Another nave on the landward side of the shaft would have a 30-ton lift for the service-tunnel segments.

Just as the digging began at Sangatte, an official from Calais toured the site and noted the work in progress. It was, Matheron explained, a mere bit of "exploratory work." The official went away satisfied, and Matheron's crews kept working at their Herculean task. Matheron could not afford to lose any time, and time was the likely cost of observing bureaucratic niceties. And thus did work commence on one of the millennium's great projects—without a construction permit, without even a nod to, or a nod from, the authorities.

Eurotunnel, however, was still limping along. One of its worst problems was that all of its business was conducted in a fishbowl. Meetings were mob scenes, with bankers, contractors, merchant bankers, lawyers and consultants thronged around huge tables. There were no secrets and, as usual in such circumstances, bad news leaked out fastest. The predatory British press distilled this; there was never a lack of critics to put the most negative interpretation on events.

Heydon was both a victim and an exacerbator of this phenomenon. He was trying to supply the banks and Eurotunnel with advice about how to protect themselves. To effect this, he peppered the project with strong, frequent, pointed criticism. This was intended to help the project, but the criticisms he brought to one meeting would appear in the next edition of the newspapers, giving tunnel opponents yet more ammunition.

Heavy construction equipment in Le Puits de Sangatte.

But Heydon was more worried by the fact that everything he said was quickly reported to the contractors. "There was no accounting for copies of my reports," he said. "I was sure that at least one copy of everything went directly to the contractor. We were giving him his plan of battle. . . . I kept trying to say, 'We have to keep this secret, this is confidential.' But I couldn't get them to do it."

Bénard saw it as a question of loyalty. Eurotunnel was in such turmoil that no one could be sure if he, or indeed the company, would be there the next week. The ranks were filled with secondees and recruits, often men of indifferent quality, who believed that they might soon be looking for other employment. The parent contracting companies thus became repositories for the hopes and loyalties of many of Eurotunnel's staff.

Eurotunnel was buoyed, however, by the report that the House of Commons Select Committee published in November, following a second set of hearings in London and in various Kentish towns near the tunnel's mouth. Initially, the resumed hearings had produced testimony from people whose chief concern was possible damage to the environment.

Some of these witnesses showed much charm and wit. One such was Mr. Donald Ivor Litten, who asked leave to introduce the testimony of six experts. "You will, however, be pleased to know that they are all wild flowers and that they are forbidden to appear in person under the provisions of the Wildlife and Countryside Act of 1981," he said. "First, I call the crimson grass vetchling, known to botanists as *Lathyrus nissola*. At the beginning of this century it was officially described as rare. . . ."

Litten went on to say that he had nonetheless found *L. nissola* growing on the terminal site. He had also found a fairy flax plant growing where Eurotunnel wanted to build a viewing platform "so that trippers can gawp at the shuttle loopline, where our green valley used to be." He recounted his joy at kneeling to view the fairy flax—a tiny plant four or five inches tall—through a magnifying glass: "It was a delight to behold the salven-shaped corolla had five creamy white petals delicately veined in rose pink." He also called the evergreen alkanet (*Anchusa sempervivens*), the Nottingham catchfly, the restharrow (*Ononis anvennis*) and the early spider orchis, which he found on the site of a proposed Eurotunnel work site at Holywell Coombe. "In these days of leapfrogging materialism, we need to recognize and protect those beautiful things which refresh the mind, feed the soul and uplift the human spirit," Litten said. He emphasized that his only concern was with possible environmental damage to the terminal site; the tunnel itself didn't trouble him. He suggested the spoil be sold to the Dutch, who "could fill the Zuider Zee and grow tomatoes on it."

Nina Assheton, who lived in the village of Acrise, about three miles north of the tunnel entrance, was one of many witnesses who voiced the peculiarly British dread of rabies. Assheton, who described herself as a "country-lover and a keen dog-walker," admitted that there was an existing national threat of the disease from smuggled pets, "but if infected foxes or stray dogs or cats or other wild animals got into the tunnel, this threat would be specific to this corner of the country and it would be very likely to result in an epidemic because it would be less easily spotted," she said. If that happened, seeing a wild animal would be "tinged with fear."

Nevertheless, the report did no real damage to the tunnel effort. The committees suggested seventy revisions to the Channel Tunnel Bill, but the only major ones had to do with rerouting access roads to the terminal. One member filed a minority report that suggested a full review of passenger segregation because of the "horrendous potential consequences of a serious fire in the tunnel." Had this been the majority view, it would have been quite serious—it could have delayed the bill until after the next elections, in 1987. If Mrs. Thatcher lost and Labour took over, the project could be in mortal peril.

But the minority report remained just a footnote. It now remained for the House of Lords' Select Committee on the Channel Tunnel to essentially repeat the process. The greatest loss in the Lords' Select Committee had been time; Eurotunnel had hoped to see the bill much farther on in the parliamentary process by the end of the year.

On Christmas Eve, Reeve and Jolivet met Durand-Rival in Paris and agreed to changes to the construction contract. The document that emerged contained two serious pitfalls for TML.

The first was Clause 1.(2), a broadly written section about who should be responsible for extra costs under various circumstances. A TML attorney later summed it up by saying that "it permits the client (Eurotunnel) to shift extra cost to the contractors by asserting that they have been stupid, negligent, careless, whatever." It was, he said, "an invitation to Eurotunnel to make life difficult for TML."

Deeper within the new contract was another pitfall: Clause 7.(2), which introduced optimization. It said, in an oddly redundant and unpunctuated summation, that both sides recognized that "the process of producing optimising developing and finalising the design of the Works will require the closest consultation co-operation communication and co-ordination between them." Both sides should work on "optimising safety, comfort, speed and commercial viability of the Fixed Link without increasing the Lump Sum Price or the Target Cost."

According to Reeve, TML's view was that the optimizing would be done on the original Proposal to Governments and that it would be accomplished—

as another section of the contract made clear—"without increasing prices, costs or the time schedule."

Optimization of this sort was already driving David Brown's design work, which he had begun in March. He had to meet the operating standards promised in the Channel Tunnel Group's original submission to the governments, and to do this as economically as possible. The best possible solution for moving trains between two points is a straight, level line. Since that wasn't an option for crossing the English Channel, Brown's engineers had to find the optimal path between Coquelles and Folkestone.

Brown's group had spent six months doing space coordination work, sizing all elements of the system—tunnels, trains, tracks, ties, locomotives, the overhead catenary wire that would supply power—to minimize drag and thus reduce energy consumption. They had studied and optimized the slopes in the tunnel and the number and size of pumping stations to remove water that leaked in, and had calculated the optimum diameter of the tunnels themselves.

Brown's task was numbingly complex, but it all came down to a single coherent goal: to move loaded shuttle trains platform to platform between France and England within thirty-five minutes. This was the core performance criterion, set forth in the construction contract: Transit time was to be thirty-three minutes, with a two-minute tolerance. If Brown couldn't provide that performance at the first test, it would cost TML about £1 million—"inconvenience money," Brown called it. But if he couldn't correct things—if it proved impossible to keep the transit time to less than thirty-five minutes—the contract required TML to pay liquidated damages, and these would be much more than an inconvenience. If the shuttle could not break the thirty-five-minute mark, it would cost £10 million. If the time were thirty-nine minutes, the damages would exceed £40 million.

There was a part of the problem that Brown could not control: the use of the tunnel by SNCF and British Rail. The tunnel was supposed to operate on three-minute headways—that is, trains could pass through within three minutes of each other. That meant that there were twenty "paths" in each hour and that ten of these were allotted to SNCF and British Rail. The national railroads wanted to run trains through the tunnel at whatever speed suited their schedules: They wanted freight trains to lumber along and passenger trains to sweep through swiftly. The agreement also gave SNCF and BR a great deal of power in deciding when to use their paths—they could, for instance, decide to cluster their allotted paths in a peak hour, monopolizing the tunnel.

Brown's group thus had to tailor its optimization, which was all about the shuttles' thirty-five minute passage, to accommodate these interlopers. A through train traveling from London to Paris would disrupt the flow of

Folkestone-to-Dover shuttles, so Eurotunnel wanted the shuttles to be able to make up time—to accelerate faster away from the platforms, to power up the incline to the other terminal at high speed. But Brown's view was that Eurotunnel was asking for enhancements rather than optimization and that it should pay for them. All that TML had contracted to build, at the given price, was a tunnel and transportation system that would move shuttles from one platform to another within thirty-five minutes.

Eurotunnel held that it could require such changes, at no cost to itself, under optimization. If the solution was to put in heavier locomotives or a more sophisticated signaling system, the contract required TML to provide it.

As summer turned to autumn, Brown faced a different problem: He had to optimize the path of the tunnel—that is, he had to find a route in which the slopes were steep enough to allow seepage water to drain away into sumps, but gentle enough to allow locomotives to pull trains up them at good speed. The tunnel path had to fit into the thin, rumpled layer of chalk marl that ran from the tunnel portal in Folkestone to the bottom of the Sangatte shaft. It was essential that Brown's design group know very precisely where and how thick this layer was, at every point along the tunnel's projected path.

There was already a good deal of information available about the path of the chalk marl. The failed 1882 attempt had left sections of tunnel on both sides of the Channel. The French part had been pumped clear and examined in 1958 and 1959, when Frank and Al Davidson commenced their campaign. That same campaign had drilled a total of seventy boreholes in the Channel bed, along with others on land. The 1974 project had drilled eight marine and seven land boreholes. Each of these borehole campaigns was accompanied by seismic surveying.

Ironically, those boreholes were now hazards that Brown's engineers had to avoid, since they were essentially pipes that would allow the English Channel to drain into the tunnel if their paths crossed. Some were supposed to have been capped, but no one wanted to depend on old and questionable information. Worse, some of the boreholes from the 1960s had not even been charted.

Brown's group considered man-made hazards as well. "During the war there were a lot of bombs dropped, or deposited, by the German Luftwaffe in the Channel before they returned," he said. There was concern that "dam-buster" bombs could have penetrated far enough to be in the path of a TBM. "We had a lot of discussions with the military as to the potential depth of penetration, and we came to the conclusion that the risk was very, very low indeed."

Faults—cracks in the rock under the Channel—did penetrate to great depths and posed considerable risk. Past borehole and seismic campaigns had identified a number of these cracks. Six substantial faults lay in the tunnel's

An engine from a World War II bomber, found during construction of the Shakespeare Cliff seawall.

path within three kilometers of the French coast; these had "throws"—movement of one side in relation to the other—of two meters to twenty meters. Two other good-sized faults lay nearby. "We had to then angle the alignment to cut across them, rather than run with them," Brown said of the faults.

For all these reasons, Brown needed more information; he needed more boreholes to tell him more about the geology under the Channel and also along the tunnel route between Dover and the terminal. This latter was an old coal-mining region, and there was reason to worry about methane, the explosive gas that canaries were carried into coal mines to detect.

Brown knew soon after starting work in March 1986 that he needed more information. But boreholes—particularly ones drilled through the seabed under one of the busiest and least predictable bodies of water on the planet—do not come cheap. "Ideally, we should have gone in the summer period," Brown said. "But we had no money." The contractor's group put up £100,000 in mid-April for design work, but it wasn't until the £42 million from Equity 1 arrived, months later, that Brown got the money he needed. By then, of course, most of the calm summer months had slipped away.

At first, TML tried drilling in sixty meters of water from a ship, with poor success; the currents in the Channel were too strong and pulled the drill bit out of plumb. The first borehole was so delayed and so expensive that the designers thought it would be impossible to complete the borehole campaign. Each hole would require extra vessels to steady the drill ship, and Brown could only get permits to work in the Channel for short periods of time. If bad weather forced the ships to seek shelter—and it was by this time October, when gales were common—the permits might expire.

As the weather worsened (there were several heavy gales that October), Brown's luck changed for the better. It occurred to him that a fixed drilling platform might be faster, cheaper and more dependable for the job, even if it had to come from the Gulf of Mexico. As it happened, Brown found a rig much nearer to home: The Nova Zapatana, a rig that had finished its work in the North Sea and was, at the moment, heading for Felixstowe. "We were able to negotiate a very attractive rate, because there was no work for it," Brown said. "It had a crew on board, and we were able to divert it immediately and drop it straight on station."

The Nova Zapatana gave TML a dozen reliable boreholes at the bargain price of £80,000 apiece. The cores went three hundred meters into the seabed, into the Greensand that lay beneath the tunnel route. They examined the northern end of the Fosse Dangeard, the dangerous infilled valley in the Channel's bed, to make sure that it would not affect the tunnel.

The cores mostly confirmed what was known or had been deduced about the seabed and the precious layer of chalk marl. They did dictate some changes: The tunnel alignment was shifted a little here and there, and the British crossover cavern was moved two hundred meters closer to France to better fit it into the good digging ground.

Crighton and Laurent Leblond later described the path that resulted from all these calculations in a scientific paper that was a model of clarity and style. On the British side, they wrote, the tunnel ". . . leaves the Kent Coast at a depth of 45 m approximately below seabed, following a slight eastward dip of the Chalk Marl stratum. The tunnels reach their lower point 115 m below sea level approximately 13 km offshore, at a point where the rock cover above the tunnels is at its greatest, approximately 75 m. Over this section the geological conditions are sensibly uniform, the strata are gently warped and the tunnel passes through the central axis of two minor folds. There is evidence of minor faulting associated with these folds which may result in the ground being fractured to a greater degree along their crests, particularly in the more brittle chalks overlying the Chalk Marl; these are, however, well above the tunnel horizon.

"From the low point in the UK section, the tunnels continue in the Chalk Marl and rise gently toward the mid-Channel position. Over this central section, the tunnels run parallel with, but at least a half kilometer away from, the Fosse Dangeard, a major buried valley. . . .

"The French seaward tunnel drives leave the coast at a depth of 35 m below seabed and remain within the Chalk Marl stratum wherever possible. However, geological folding, relatively high strata dip and minor flexures in the French section required careful alignment of the tunnel to maintain an optimum position. . . .

"Several geological faults and one substantial fault were identified within the French section. The latter crosses the tunnel alignment obliquely and the fault is subject to deep penetrative weathering within the Grey Chalk, although current evidence indicates that this does not affect the Chalk Marl and is not expected to extend down to tunnel level."

As TML grew more certain about the path it was to take, Sir David Walker set about fulfilling his promise to Equity 2's subscribers: providing Euro-

The drill rig Nova Zapatana *doing test borings off Shakespeare Cliff in December 1986.*

tunnel with strong management. Time had shown that Sir Nigel Broakes of Trafalgar House was not the man for the job. Nor was Ray Pennock, who was considered too old for the task. Walker cast about for other candidates for the British cochairmanship. He warned off the contractors. "To be fair, it wasn't hard to convince them that they were agents and should keep their distance," he said. "We said to them, 'Our task is to find a strong chairman.' "

This was a difficult problem even for the Bank of England. "I don't want to talk about the names we talked to and rejected," Walker said. "We talked to people like the former chairman of Shell, people of that weight, with major big experience in big projects. The people we talked to I think were interested without exception, but none was able to take it on."

Walker sensed a reluctance among those he approached—"the strong sense that the things they'd taken on were not necessarily as big as this, but they *were certain*. They were companies, with boards. They were not projects with no equity."

This beating of corporate bushes was conducted as discreetly as possible, but word of it seeped out to further damage Eurotunnel's standing. Several well-qualified executives, including John Harvey-Jones of ICI, Sir Jeffrey Sterling of P&O and Sir Ian MacGregor, had declined the honor. The Bank had even considered a top executive of one of the contracting companies for the post, a bad idea born of desperation. Then, on a Friday afternoon in mid-February, Alastair Morton walked into Walker's office and solved the problem.

Walker knew Morton and respected his abilities. He had been one of a very select group of young executives—fewer than a dozen—who had been chosen by the British government in 1967 to save British industry. The instrument of this attempted salvation was the Industrial Reorganisation Corporation. The effort was a failure, but the young men it had recruited went on to become successes.

"The main distinction of the IRC is not what it did, but the extraordinary group of bright young people that it brought together," Walker said. Most of the IRC recruits ended up in the top slots of big companies; Morton rose, too, but his résumé suggested both talent and trouble. He had many talents, but few so well developed as that for confrontation. This he relished, the way some athletes relish the raw clash of a contact sport. He did not shrink from confrontation, he sought it and rejoiced in it. As with a sport, he won some contests and lost others.

He was what Britain once called a colonial, born elsewhere in the Empire—in this case, South Africa. The belief persists that colonials are a breed that, rather like horses, have been altered by the admixture of some wilder blood. As one London writer observed, in referring to Morton, "brash lads from former colonies regularly cut swathes today through the more urbane and relaxed corners of the City and British industry. They bring a freshness and ruthlessness to solving problems which everybody else had settled for living with."

He was born in Johannesburg, the son of a Scottish oil executive who had emigrated after the First World War and married into an old and powerful Afrikaner family. He won the first DeBeers Scholarship to Oxford, went on to study at MIT and in 1959, at the age of 21, went to work financing infrastructure projects in Central Africa for the big Anglo American Corporation.

In 1964, as the political situation in Africa deteriorated, Morton took a position with the World Bank in Washington. It was stodgy, but it was a good place to improve his résumé and watch for an opening that might hold the promise of rapid advancement. The IRC provided that chance and brought him to London, where he cut quite a figure: very tall, lean and tough; bearded in a clean-shaven City. He liked potting around in sailboats, but a growing addiction to work gradually eliminated that pastime. Most all of the South African accent went, too, and what remained was concealed under a gravelly roughness of speech. When the beard, too, disappeared, Morton might have passed for just another well-dressed London workaholic.

But he had not lost his appetite for conflict, which gained him some admirers (like Walker) and at least as many enemies and detractors. Neither admiration nor opprobrium softened him.

Walker thought that Morton might be a good candidate. He considered the question over the weekend and consulted Leigh-Pemberton, who agreed. Walker called Morton at home and asked him to come to his office on Monday morning.

"I said, 'I can't offer this to you, but if you *were* offered it by those in whose power it lies, would you be interested?' His answer was yes.

"I talked to Ray Pennock, [who] told me later that day or early the following day that if Alastair were ready to take it *and* if he were acceptable to the French co-chairman, André Bénard—which was very important—then he would be quite ready to stand down. So I talked to André Bénard, whom I knew slightly. I rang him in Paris."

Bénard said he would be in London the next day, for the Eurotunnel board meeting on Wednesday. Bénard kept an office in the Shell Centre, next to Waterloo Station, and Walker took Morton there to meet him.

"I introduced them and they talked," Walker recalled. "I said, look, I don't think I have a part to play; you must talk to each other. André took Alastair to Paris with him that evening, if I recollect; they had dinner together and he introduced him to several French people. Alastair spoke some French, and they got along well together.

"In the meantime I consulted as many people as I could domestically. Basically, people didn't know Alastair very well, and they really, I think, backed the Bank of England's judgment. I said, 'Well, the governor and I believe he has the strength, the masterly intellect and all, to do it.' And they said right, we'll back him.

"And on the Wednesday evening, there was a red-hot meeting of Eurotunnel's board, and Alastair was elected joint chairman. He was in post by Wednesday evening."

10

Alastair Morton arrived at Eurotunnel to mixed reviews.

He was, people noted, the seventh person—or eighth, or fifth, or tenth, depending on the source—that the Bank of England had approached to take the job, and the first (and only) to accept. "It would be unkind to groan too loudly about the appointment of Alastair Morton as the man to dig Eurotunnel out of its public relations hole," the *Telegraph* said by way of greeting. "He is not, on his record, an appointment which will put its success beyond doubt."

The *Telegraph* editorial, which was echoed by other papers that had been dogging the tunnel project, was unkind enough to point out that Guinness Peat—the investment banking house that Morton had led for several years until mid-1986—"also turned down the chance to put up cash last summer when the last fundraising operation for the tunnel so nearly failed."

Morton's reputation for combativeness preceded him. A *Sunday Times* story noted, "One point that critics feel he will have to curb is the boardroom rows that have punctuated his career. . . . In the space of a year, six leading Peat executives left. It is not the sort of feuding that Eurotunnel can afford." The piece went on to quote an unnamed observer who said that Morton "can be a bit of a City thug, but he's just what the project needs."

Prominence and personalities aside, there were serious questions about the sort of people who were now running Eurotunnel in an uneasy and sometimes incestuous partnership with the banks. The removal of the contractors had excised most of the company's technical expertise. Morton, for his part, was not impressed with what he found at Eurotunnel. He used Disraeli's famous remark about Gladstone's ministers to describe the existing board to Walker: They were, he said, like a range of exhausted volcanoes. And no matter what any newspaper might say, many people close to the project saw Morton's accession as auspicious. John Noulton noted that Morton's expertise was raising money, which was precisely what Eurotunnel needed. Morton also had a brilliant flair for marketing and public relations, and his speech was as aggressive as his personality. If the marketplace sought reassurance, Morton was ready to give it in generous measure. One of his early pronouncements was that Eurotunnel was already working on plans for a *second* Channel Tunnel, a drive-through, so certain were its executives that the first would be quickly overwhelmed by demand for its services.

The ferries, however, were still hammering away, blaring that the tunnel was safe neither as an investment nor as a means of transportation; that both investors and travelers ran the risk of being burned.

People like Deacon and Callaghan still were ruining their health and risking their careers through long hours, long days, long weeks, crafting the Credit Agreement and the Equity 3 prospectus. For Callaghan, it was the third year of six- and often seven-day weeks filled with the most numbing detail work imaginable on documents in two languages.

"We would work on the text all week and print on Friday," Callaghan recalled. On Saturday, motorcycle couriers would be dispatched with the newest edition of the documents to the country homes of the bankers and executives.

Callaghan was returning home in the early morning hours of March 7, 1987, after fifty-two straight hours of work, when he heard that the ferry *Herald of Free Enterprise* had capsized with heavy loss of life as it left the dock in Zeebrugge on its way to England. He concluded that the tragedy would be the Channel Tunnel's salvation. "I thought that had signed and sealed it for us," said Callaghan. "The ferries had been going on and on and on about how they were the only safe service to France. And that proved them wrong."

Morton quickly proved that he was more than a breath of fresh air; he was a whole gale. "When he came in he set about uprooting things, throwing out pieces of furniture," Noulton said. "There were a lot of puffing noises coming out of the building." Sound and fury were Morton's meat and drink. They nourished him even when they accomplished nothing very useful. "He wants action," Noulton said. "Even if you believe, and you can demonstrate to him, that an activity will bring no dividends, he wants you to jump up and down on the spot, and do something. . . . Someone had written about him, 'He is the sort of man who can't pass a pond without throwing a rock in it.' He doesn't like it to be placid. He is also not very good with organizations or with clear demarcation of responsibilities.

"He would give a task to the last person he had spoken to, even though it was the responsibility of someone else, and even though he might already have given it to someone else in a slightly different form. And he seems to enjoy this kind of creative tension within organizations where the fittest survives."

Morton did not suffer fools gladly—Deacon could remember the peremptory dismissal, in public, of someone Morton found wanting—but he was not much inclined to get rid of anyone once he had served any time at Eurotunnel.

"He is not very good at discarding people," Noulton said. "For someone who has got such an externally fierce and abrasive temperament, when it comes to doing the hard thing, and getting rid of people, he is not very good at that." Eurotunnel carried people on its payroll, he said, "that should have been seen off years ago."

Morton knew he had to take a drastic step: He had to postpone Equity 3. The boardroom overhaul and the failure of Equity 2 had left the company in disarray—disarray that was evident to anyone who might be thinking of buying or brokering the stock.

"In the end he was right, but there had been a longstanding commitment that Equity 3 would be raised in June of 1987," Noulton said. "And he said there wasn't any way that he was going to the markets in June. Now we were very nervous about any postponement of that. It was an admission of weakness, and we'd waited a long time for something that was an exhibition of strength."

The public announcement of this risky act was buried under a pile of artfully manufactured good news. On March 17, Eurotunnel issued a "briefing

Alastair Morton and André Bénard in July 1987.

paper" that said the project had thus far created 2,250 jobs and that Kent would have an added 5,000 jobs by 1990.

On the following day, Morton announced that Rory Macnamara of Morgan Grenfell, who was then thirty-two years old, would come over to handle Equity 3, which the press release still called the "summer share sale."

Two days after that, on March 20, Eurotunnel showed mock-ups of the shuttle cars to the press and government officials. The affair, held at the site of the planned international passenger terminal at Ashford, was uncommonly well done: There were cranes to hoist photographers up for better angles, two separate shoots arranged to take best advantage of natural light, executives on hand to answer questions and motorcycle couriers to carry film back to London for the evening news shows.

A new announcement rolled out every few days: A poll conducted during a "recent three-week tour of regional centres by a Eurotunnel exhibition train" had found "overwhelming" support for the Channel Tunnel; a meeting with Kent leaders provided an excuse for another press junket, with helicopter rides for journalists and lunch for everyone.

Morton chose a Saturday to notify the press that Eurotunnel had decided how to handle the rest of its financing: There would be a private placement in July and a larger public offering in the autumn. SG Warburg had joined the three French banks, Morgan Grenfell and Robert Fleming as financial advisers. The French press release said that the fifty billion francs in the whole financing package would cover construction costs that were estimated at twenty-seven billion francs; the balance would cover interest costs, Eurotunnel's expenses and inflation during the construction phase. There was no talk about cancellation or delay; the decision was presented as a calm and deliberate move by a company that knew what it was doing.

Though nothing in Eurotunnel's pronouncements mentioned it, delaying Equity 3 meant that Eurotunnel would have to borrow money from the banks to stay in business until the autumn. When the press release spoke of a "private placement" during the summer, it really meant some further borrowing. Indosuez had quietly put together a plan for £72.5 million in loans, to be repaid out of the proceeds of Equity 3. The other banks were invited to subscribe.

At this point, NatWest balked and refused to participate in the interim loan. In this, it was acting like the bank that it was rather than the co-venturer that it had been. If a loan were to be made, NatWest in effect said, it would be made on a normal commercial basis. What Eurotunnel was seeking was an advance against a sale of equity, not against anticipated revenue. NatWest thought that Eurotunnel should apply to an investment rather than a commercial bank.

"They were trying to break the founding shareholder relationship," Deacon said. "Equally, with Morton in the saddle, Midland was keen to be seen a good boy." Midland agreed to do the British part of the financing, enabling "Midland to gain some considerable Brownie points—not only with Eurotunnel, but also with the French."

The political process in Britain, true to its historic patterns, now ran contrary to everything else that had to do with the tunnel—that is to say, it worked with hardly a creak or groan to move the project forward.

The House of Lords' own Select Committee on the Channel Tunnel Bill formed on February 19, invited citizens to be heard, and promptly received 1,457 petitions. The Lords' hearings would mostly echo the earlier House of Commons sessions. Pleas about dirt, noise, pollution of streams and air, damage to areas of natural beauty and loss of jobs in the ports formed the bulk of the eight boxes of petitions that came to the committee. Rabies leaped slavering from many a page. The third petition received was utterly typical; it came from fifteen Dover-area residents with a litany of predictable grievances. At the other end of the line, the members of the Monday Pensioners Club, who lived near the proposed passenger terminal in London's Waterloo Station, said they would be afraid to leave their flats "because the group think it will be very bad here."

Four pages of childish signatures were attached to a petition from Park Farm County Primary School in Folkestone, which said that tunnel work shouldn't be permitted around the clock because "the noise levels will affect our sleep patterns and must therefore be detrimental to our powers of concentration during school hours." If the peers detected a teacher's hand in the composition, they let it pass. There were also some eccentric nuggets in this dross, such as the witness who claimed that the French were in the habit of visiting England with rats in their pockets.

The petitions themselves were redolent of tradition: Petitioners who were neither solicitors nor represented by solicitors had to file a Certificate of Respectability, signed by some local luminary—a retired military officer suited very nicely—who was willing to attest that the witness was a serious person. The parish council of Hougham Without, for instance, sent a representative who bore a certificate signed by Geoffrey Percy Sansom Thomas, Retired Air Vice Marshal, CB, O.B.E. The petitions' preambles, at least, were couched in antique legal form, and in some, the entire text might have been drawn from a much earlier century. Many were handwritten, and character often shone through the dull glaze of legalism.

To be sure, some of the character thus displayed was odd, as in the petition of Elizabeth Pollard Lloyd of Tonbridge, who objected broadly but specifically to a dozen clauses of the Channel Tunnel Bill. Her petition was impeccably drawn, though she showed rather too great a fondness for the uppercase:

"In the honourable the House of Lords of the United Kingdom of Great Britain and Northern Ireland in the House of Lords Assembled,

"The HUMBLE PETITION of Elizabeth Pollard Lloyd of 45 Woodside Road, Tonbridge

"Your petitioner is the owner of a residence known as 9 WHITFIELD COTTAGES, ASHFORD, KENT to which a VAST WEALTHY TRUST BELONGED—THESE DEEDS, THAT CONTAINED HISTORICAL MANUSCRIPTS THAT WENT BACK TO EDWARD THE CONFESSOR—AND THE DOOMSDAY BOOK, HENRY VII OF THE HEALING OF THE WAR OF THE ROSES AND WHO WAS THE FATHER OF HENRY VIII."

There followed talk of "SEA-MAPS OF SUNKEN SHIPS of great age, lying in American waters," and of "A VICTORIAN DOCUMENT OF A MEETING IN LONDON ABOUT THE LAST THIRTY YEARS OF THE 19TH CENTURY, 1870–1890 AT WHICH THE BUILDING OF A TUNNEL ACROSS THE ENGLISH CHANNEL HAD BEEN DISCUSSED AND THE DOCUMENT WAS SIGNED BY THE EARL OF THANET AND SIR EDWARD CARSON.... A SUEZ CANAL DOCUMENT SIGNED BY de LESSEPS.... VAST WEALTHY VICTORIAN TRUST DEEDS OF LAND AND PROPERTY—ETC WORTH MILLIONS."

Lloyd said she had given these valuable documents, which included deeds to Herstmonceaux and twenty-eight other British castles and very much else besides, to an Ashford solicitor to register. The faithless solicitor, she asserted, had "MANEUVERED THEM THROUGH OTHER CHANNELS," and she had not been able to recover them. Hence her opposition to the Channel Tunnel Bill.

Their lords were tolerant and even sympathetic listeners, but their patience sometimes wore thin. When a trucker noted that the Shuttles would not accommodate giraffes—as the ferries could—he was sent away quickly.

The hearings were somewhat of an empty exercise as far as the Channel Tunnel legislation was concerned, and the report seemed to be a supportive document to put in the Channel Tunnel dossier. But Eurotunnel, in its eagerness to please, had agreed to safety measures that were far more sweeping than anything ever before considered for the project.

One Eurotunnel blunder concerned rabies, a disease that is the subject of a curious British passion. No human has contracted rabies in Britain since at least 1902, the year it was eradicated from the canine population by slaughtering all dogs suspected of having the disease. It did not appear in wildlife. In the same year it slaughtered the dogs, Britain established a six-month quarantine period for any animal that could contract rabies. In the subsequent eighty-four years, twenty-eight animals—twenty-six dogs, one cat and one leopard—had died of rabies in quarantine. The only serious failure of the system occurred after the Great War, when returning servicemen smuggled home their mascots, but rabies had again been eradicated by 1922.

Nonetheless, rabies haunts the British; immigration posters at ports of entry give greater emphasis to the threat of rabies than to the threat of IRA bombs. Almost three quarters of the cases in the rest of Europe are in red foxes, and many in Britain feared that one might wander the fifty kilometers through the tunnel to spread the scourge.

Eurotunnel agreed to mount and maintain a security system that would have done Buckingham Palace proud. The first line of defense would be a line of fine-mesh boundary fences around the terminals, to prevent even small animals, including rodents, from entering (in France) or leaving (in England). These fences would extend down into the ground to exclude burrowing animals. Where the fence line was broken by gates, "an alternative barrier such as a cattle grid with a sunken pit will be used."

Inside this perimeter, all vehicles would be subject to checks and full searches by various enforcement agencies, for which adequate facilities would be provided on both the French and British sides. Security personnel would be trained to watch for attempts to smuggle animals into the United Kingdom. Their efforts would be augmented by roving dog patrols. Members of the public were to be encouraged to report anyone seen with an animal in the terminals or on the trains. Train marshals would be briefed to watch for animals in their shuttle cars.

During construction of the tunnels, "strict measures" would be taken to prevent the accumulation of rubbish that might attract animals. Dog patrols would be used in the tunnels, too, and procedures would be devised to capture or tranquilize any animal that managed to get through the fence line. Tunnel entrances, including the service adits, were to be kept under closed-circuit television surveillance; these openings would also be fortified with grid pits and electrified fence to kill any intruding critters. All pipes, drain channels, ducts and ventilation shafts would be either sealed or covered with fine mesh.

All these measures were to be in place before breakthrough. Afterward, the tunnels were to be kept "scrupulously clean and free from potential nutriments [sic]" to guard against "progressive colonization" by French rodents. In conclusion, the Committee report noted that Eurotunnel had agreed that "trains will be sealed in the tunnel and chemical accumulation toilets are to be used on all trains. Food will be banned in the service/maintenance tunnel. Special searches will be made until all animals are accounted for in the very unlikely event of their being released as a result of an accident."

Eurotunnel erred far more seriously in its undertaking on fire safety in the tunnel. The earlier House of Commons had distilled two decades and more of thinking about fires in a three-tube Channel Tunnel. Fire doors would close at each end of a shuttle car should fire break out; these doors would be able to hold back the blaze for thirty minutes. Passengers in the involved car would move to adjacent cars while the train continued through the tunnel.

"As far as possible, trains should attempt to continue out of the tunnel," the House of Commons report said. If that weren't practical, the train would uncouple and leave the burning car once it had been evacuated. If passengers were forced out of the train, they would move to the service tunnel for evacuation to the surface within ninety minutes.

In the House of Lords' Select Committee report, there was a significant addition. Where the House of Commons report had spoken of "fire partitions with a resistance of 30 minutes" between the shuttle cars, Eurotunnel's memo on safety in the House of Lords document said "the wagons will have a fire resistance of more than 30 minutes so as to enable, in appropriate circumstances, the trains to continue on their journey to clear the tunnel in the event of an outbreak of fire. Shuttle wagons will be equipped with fire doors or curtains also having a minimum fire resistance of 30 minutes."

Since the passage through the tunnel itself was to be about twenty minutes, the need for thirty-minute fire resistance in the cars was debatable. What was certain beyond all debate was that such a margin of safety would come only at considerable cost. To build a railroad car with fire-resistant doors at each end is financially and technically challenging; to build an entire railroad car—and the shuttle cars were to be the largest railway cars ever built—that could roll along for a half hour with a fire raging in its interior was quite another task.

The consequences of Eurotunnel's promise cascaded ruinously down through the entire project. Philippe Essig, the SNCF chairman, noted that the frame of any normal railroad car would be so deformed by a thirty-minute fire that it would be immovable. Preventing this deformation required the use of alloys that had never been used. "Only in the space shuttle in the States," Essig said. "Never in rail transit. Not one of the wagons of the TGV, of the German ICE, not the rapid transit in Paris, in San Francisco, in Washington, has been designed for that. If you have a fire in the wagon, the wagon will be bent after half an hour of fire."

Making the wagons fire-resistant, Essig said, meant making them 50 percent heavier. Because the concession required trains to be capable of running at 160 kilometers per hour, heavier shuttles required bigger locomotives. A train made up of the original shuttle wagons would have weighed about 1600 tons and could have achieved that speed behind any of several standard, off-the-shelf European locomotives; Britain, France and Germany all had production models that would have worked very well. But a train of fully fire-resistant wagons would weigh about 2400 tons, and there was no stock locomotive in the world that could pull that load at speed.

Eurotunnel, said Essig, was "obliged to design a special locomotive with six motor axles, instead of four." That increased the power requirements, which meant the tunnel's power system would have to be changed. "And so on and so on," Essig said. "This agreement given by Eurotunnel to the Select Committee was something awful. But it was not appreciated in all its consequences when the decision was made and given."

In France, the Senate had passed the enabling legislation unanimously on June 5, thereby completing, without exceptional drama, a legislative process fully as complex as that in Britain. The government had solicited comment, listened to it and rendered a decision. No one expected surprises, and there were none. "The fast track in Britain is more difficult than the DUP (declaration of public utility) in France," said Philippe Montagner of Bouygues. Most of the debate in France concerned the earthwork dams for the Fond Pignon, which were atop the hills backing the magnificent headland of Cap Blanc Nez. (The spoil pumped into Fond Pignon would bury one reminder of a shared unpleasant past: an emplacement from which German artillery fired into Folkestone during the last war.)

Debate about Fond Pignon consumed almost four months; most of the concern naturally came from local residents. "We had to see a lot of people from the region," Montagner said, adding that the process was simplified by the fact that the tunnel would emerge near Calais. "If it had been on the Côte d'Azur, it would have been more difficult," he said. "Kent is the best part of Britain . . . but Calais is not so very nice; it's a mostly industrial area."

The election that had made Noulton so nervous came on June 11 and maintained Thatcher's government in power; Parliament had earlier agreed to carry over the Channel Tunnel Act to the next session. On July 23, the queen signed the Royal Assent, using the wonderfully antique phrase that had come, many hundreds of years before, from across the channel: *la Reyne le veult*. On July 29, Thatcher and Mitterand met at the Élysée Palace, where they would not be annoyed by the xenophobic chants of British tunnel opponents, to exchange documents and formally ratify the treaty. Now all that remained was for Transmanche-Link to dig the tunnel and for Eurotunnel to raise enough money to pay for it.

Three weeks before the ratification, the first horizontal tunneling had actually begun on both sides of the Channel. On July 4, a Westfalia Lünen road-header broke through a temporary concrete face in the Sangatte shaft to start work on the land service tunnel's marshaling chamber. The next day, a British crew set about removing the head of the tunnel-boring machine, which had been left in place when the tunnel-boring machine from 1974 had been cut apart.

The gods could not resist a little cruel meddling in what should have been a historic moment, one that Eurotunnel might have used to bolster faith in the project. In the British tunnel, the cutting torches set fire to some grease. The engineer of a passing train saw black smoke coming from the mouth of the tunnel adit and called the Kent Fire Brigade. The brigade's services weren't needed; the tunnel's own workers easily extinguished the very minor blaze.

But it was a fire. Flexilink had been conjuring images of a subterranean inferno; the Kent firemen had been clamoring for funds and equipment to fight

A roadheader at work.

such a blaze. Eurotunnel had spent much money and time quelling these fears and demands. And now, on the first day of real tunneling work, there had been a fire.

Eurotunnel's immediate worry was convincing the public and the banks that the Channel Tunnel was a good investment. The plan was to nail down the bank financing by midautumn and to proceed then to Equity 3 later that same season.

There would be fifty underwriting banks, which would in turn parcel out portions of their participation to smaller banks. NatWest and the other four original Arranging Banks were on the hook for £170 million apiece. In the next circle were eighteen big banks—including Deutsche Bank and the other hard-liners that had pushed for improvement of the construction contract—each of whom was to provide £128 million. Farther out were seven banks, including five from Japan, that had pledged £98 million each; then nine banks that had pledged £64 million each and eight that had pledged £60 million each. In the outermost circle were Banque internationale à luxembourg (£39 million), Banque internationale pour l'afrique occidentale (£35 million) and the AL UBAF Banking Group of Bahrain (£30 million).

Banks could also provide—instead of cash—letters of credit that would secure debt financing from other sources, notably the European Investment Bank, the European Community's nonprofit lending institution. The EIB had agreed to put £1 billion into the Channel Tunnel project in May, an event that John Noulton characterized as crucial.

"If you looked at it really closely it didn't mean a great deal, because they weren't putting money up at their risk," Noulton said. "But the European Investment Bank does lend the project a certain cachet. . . . It sounded the right kind of encouraging note."

On August 25 the fifty Underwriting banks signed the necessary documents by which they agreed to underwrite the £5 billion loan that Eurotunnel needed to build the tunnel. The task then was to sell shares in this huge loan to other banks around the world. The standard sales tool for this sort of thing is the road show, a carefully choreographed and thoroughly rehearsed parade of a project's merits to calm the qualms of edgy executives. Eurotunnel accordingly set about taking its show on the road.

It wasn't one show, and there were many roads. Eurotunnel's partisans were divided into two separate task forces to cover more ground in less time. Even so, the road shows would consume more than three weeks.

"I was responsible for putting all the road shows' programs together," Callaghan recalled. "They all had to be in the local language. The scripts had to be approved by lawyers, which meant that what you presented in America had to be approved by American lawyers, French presentations by French lawyers, and so on. The presentations were done with slides in Arabic or French or German, depending on where we were."

Callaghan was also in charge of preparing the supporting documents that were sent ahead to the banks, to bring them up to speed before the Eurotunnel show arrived in their towns. "All banks interested in the project received two cardboard boxes full of reports and all the papers," said Chris Deacon. "They were absolutely deluged. It was a huge weight of paper."

The road shows came in two sizes: full-day for big cities such as London, Paris, New York and Tokyo, and half-day for such places as Oslo, Bahrain, Milan, Madrid, Frankfurt and Zurich. A full-day presentation featured thirty-two separate speeches (each accompanied by slides) that ran a numbing five hours and forty-five minutes. The half-day shows offered a mere three and a quarter hours of show-and-tell, plus a half hour of questions.

Eurotunnel did what it could to make people comfortable. Most of the road shows took place in good-to-better hotels: the George V in Paris, Le Meridien in London, the Parker Meridien in New York, the New Otani in Tokyo. Tokyo was typical of the big, important shows. It actually sprawled over six days; the cast came in on a Saturday and had the rest of the weekend to decompress, sleep off their jet lags and prepare. There was a press conference on Monday and meetings with the Japanese institutions that had become shareholders in Equity 2. The road show itself was on Tuesday, and a nice dinner was tacked on to end the day with a menu chock full of Japanese favorites: *Fondant de Légumes et Caviar, Sauce Coulis de Tomate; Consommé Royale Japonais; Rouget et Crevettes au Sauce Safran; Aloyau de Boeuf Rôti, Assortiment de Légumes; Salade Verte, Glace à la Pêche Dôme d'Or*, melon, coffee and *petits fours*.

For Callaghan, the responsibility was a pleasure. "In just career terms it was wonderful. It was sheer enjoyment," he said. "I mean, when NatWest found out the things I was doing, which I wasn't remotely qualified to do, they were horrified. The bank documentation which went out to a hundred and something banks around the world—I mean, I'd never written a bank prospectus in my life. When sober career bankers learned of it they were astounded. It was something they would have been allowed to do after thirty years in the bank business—*maybe*. If they were lucky."

Callaghan had a lot of professional help. Eurotunnel could not afford to stint on the road shows; if they flopped, the project could fail with them. They were therefore professionally mounted and thoroughly rehearsed, as much like a West End or Broadway show as time and acting talent permitted. The element of theater was real and strong—because, as Deacon pointed out, Eurotunnel "had to show itself as something it wasn't at the time: Professional, and of some size, and up to the job. . . . They had to create an extremely slick and professional show."

Morton ignored much legal advice and pleading. He did not need theatrical coaching; he had a great natural gift for the stage and for speechmaking. He brushed away the lawyers as if they were gnats.

"The joke was he would go to jail for saying that the tunnel was the greatest thing since sliced bread and would make a pile of money, which we weren't allowed to say," Callaghan recalled. "He went ahead and said it anyway."

Morton and NatWest were the stars of one group of road shows; Bénard and Crédit Lyonnais led the other. Deacon was with the latter, which he says got all the second-class cities. "They got all the goodies," he said. "They went to America and Japan. . . . I went to Milan and Brussels. We went to Bahrain to pick up the Arab banks; I remember the hotel had the only swimming pool I've ever swum in that was chilled rather than warmed. We went to Madrid and to most of the European capitals or commercial centers."

New York was a disaster; the lack of American interest was painfully evident. "We made a presentation in New York, and it was almost insulting," said Behr. "I had never seen so sparse and junior a group of people anywhere."

"The Japanese were the ones who came in really big, with a great deal of enthusiasm," said Colin Stannard. Japan was intent on becoming a presence and a force in European economic affairs, and Japanese bankers were looking for projects. There were inevitable cultural clashes as this took place. Stannard recalled that the Japanese banks expected Channel Tunnel contracts for their own favored customers in return for loans. "If we supply money, we also supply equipment" was Stannard's summary of the Japanese attitude. "We had to explain to them that they couldn't do it the way that they were used to," he said.

Howard Heydon was a spear-carrier in the cast of Morton's road show. He had a decidedly small part; he was allotted five minutes late in the morning sessions of the full-day presentations. However, no script was more rigorously edited than Heydon's. By August, he and Louis Berger International had become symbols of the sort of negative thinking that Eurotunnel's supporters wanted to extirpate. Callaghan, in imploring road-show speakers to stay with their texts and keep to the schedule, wrote: "Let's not reinforce LBI's [Louis Berger International] views on this by our performance. This is definitely not the time to show the financial community that we—Eurotunnel, consultants, Arranging Banks, EIB [the European Investment Bank] and Equity banks—cannot even work together effectively enough to bring a speaking session in on schedule!"

Five minutes was worse than insufficient, Heydon felt. It was an insult. It was not so intended; it was simply to minimize the effect of Heydon's deep and strong doubts about the project by limiting him to a few words whose impact would be diluted in the stream of positive views. By August 1987, Howard Heydon had become the Channel Tunnel project's Jeremiah.

He had, by then, been examining the project for seventeen months. He had moved to London and had continued to produce reports. His views about the contract's deficiencies hadn't softened very much. He was not cheered by the way the project was progressing in the field. The depth of his concern was reflected in a confidential letter he sent on August 25 to Deacon and Coindreau, summing up his view of the project's problems and pleading again that five minutes was too little time to "adequately set forth and explain our current opinions."

The problems "substantially endanger the success of the Project and they are symptoms of a project with the potential for major cost and time overruns. . . . This is probably the last chance for the Banks to use the weight of finance to get the Project onto a sound footing." He suggested that Eurotunnel consider finding the contractor in default.

Such views naturally enough earned Heydon the enmity of the contractors. But he was hardly more popular with the Arranging Banks that he endeavored to serve with such zeal. They saw him as a loose cannon, a threat to the project, someone to be shown the door as soon as possible.

Yet Heydon had endeared himself to the hard-line banks that harbored deep suspicions about the tunnel. Eurotunnel was looking to the central group of hard-liners—Deutsche Bank, Union Bank of Switzerland, Amsterdam-Rotterdam Bank and the Industrial Bank of Japan—for more than a half billion pounds sterling, and they thought Heydon might be right.

So Heydon could not simply be cast aside like the inconvenient prophet he had become. He could be maneuvered toward the sidelines, however, and other less strident consultants could be brought in to neutralize his acid observations. The Arranging Banks had a candidate in mind: Parsons-DeLeuw Cather, a firm with long associations with the tunnel project, a solid reputation for good work and a much more moderate voice than Harold Heydon's.

In November 1986, Heydon made a tactical error. Deacon and Pierre Coindreau casually asked him what he thought his role should be in the years ahead, as the project moved toward completion. Heydon answered for himself, saying he didn't think he wanted to spend the next seven years with the Channel Tunnel. The bankers took this for Louis Berger International's corporate answer. "They pounced on it immediately," Heydon recalled. "And within a few days, DeLeuw Cather was on the job, signed up, doing some other work."

When Heydon went to the first rehearsal, he was asked for a copy of the draft speech he was going to deliver. He told them he didn't have a text, that he was going to speak from notes.

"I got up on stage, gave the presentation, and you could have heard a pin drop," Heydon said. "I said, this place is screwed up beyond all recognition, and it's hopeless. I deliberately put in all sorts of really—well, things I wouldn't have said to the public. So there was a hush. I said, you don't need me any more, and started out the door, and one of the guys rushes up, one that Bechtel had hired, and wanted a copy of my notes. I said, I don't have a copy; much of that was off the cuff. But I'll tell you one thing: If you don't want that delivered publicly, I had better be able to talk to Morton before I leave."

Morton, Heydon said, "had never met me. He wouldn't meet me. So I wanted to get his attention. And I did."

The meeting with Morton, which Durand-Rival and Bénard also attended, was dramatic but without real effect; Heydon was required to submit a script, which others gutted. His first draft was almost three thousand words long; their final script had fewer than nine hundred words.

What words remained gave a sunnier view of the project than the earlier versions. Heydon was permitted to speak about his misgivings, but the shading of his remarks was subtly lightened to lift the gloom. The road-show speech was effectively Heydon's swan song. Berger stayed with the project, but very much on the sidelines, an observer rather than a participant.

"I think they were quite good," Pierre Coindreau said in summing up Berger's role in the project. "But the ball had started rolling and there was no way it could be stopped. And if you were the guy saying, no, don't do this, you must stop, think about it—you were simply pushed aside. . . . They made some mistakes, and they didn't help their own case. But the real problem was that they were saying and writing things which could not be written."*

Also, Coindreau said, the banks were running on an adrenaline surge in trying to get the deal done in a very short time. Anything that threatened the schedule was simply an obstacle to be shoved out of the way.

---

* A far kinder assessment of Heydon's role came more than three years later, in a letter from Dick Asjes, first vice president of Union Bank of Switzerland, to Derish Wolf at Berger. Asjes wrote that DeLeuw Cather replaced Berger "notwithstanding the strong protest of UBS, who . . . strongly supported Heydon/Louis Berger for their expertise. Looking back, most banks will appreciate the professionalism of Howard Heydon more and realize that without the technical requirements, milestones etc. that he was able to put in place that things would have been far worse." Asjes concluded by saying, "In our opinion Howard Heydon is one of the top engineers we ever came across."

"When you're negotiating a big credit agreement," he said, "you tend to lose touch with the realities of the deal itself."

Heydon's labor was not entirely unfruitful, but some of the fruit it produced was very bitter. Optimization, which Heydon ardently supported, became Eurotunnel's policy, then its weapon. It produced an interminable back-and-forth between the two sides: Eurotunnel would demand a bottom-line price for the tunnel; TML would reply by demanding that Eurotunnel agree on a finished and definitive design for which Transmanche could reckon costs. Philippe Montagner recalled speaking to a Eurotunnel executive who asked why he couldn't give him a fixed price. "I'll give you a price when you give me a fixed design," Montagner said.

"David Brown wanted a cutoff date: 'When we finish this, it's optimized.' Other guys were saying it was a continuing process that never ends," Pete Behr said. "Optimization just kind of got to be a runaway wagon."

The wagon had already rolled over Brown, who had had a fairly miserable year. Optimization demanded exquisite calculation and balance, because each change provoked a chain reaction that disrupted calculations and forced other changes, which in turn cascaded down through the project, down to the bedrock assumptions upon which the Channel Tunnel idea stood.

Investors were invited to think of the tunnel as a hole in the ground, but Brown's engineers were denied the comfort of such easy assumptions. Brown's engineers spent their strength daily on questions that seemed, at first glance, to be absurdly simple, such as how wide the running tunnels should be. A wider tunnel would be more expensive to build, but it might be cheaper to operate, since the aerodynamics inside were better: The piston effect would be diminished, so trains might more easily glide through the passage. Locomotives could be smaller and power consumption would be lessened. The engineers concluded, based on this and many other similar calculations, that the inner diameter of the running tunnels should be 7.6 meters.

A fair portion of that diameter was dictated by tolerances: How large a deviation from design could the project accept? The tunnel passage was going to be carved by very large machines operated by human beings. Mistakes were certain. "We knew we were going to get variations on the center line," Brown said. "There's a construction tolerance, so you don't have a line running down center, you have a circle. . . . If a TBM turns sharply—if there's bad ground or a driver falls asleep in early hours, which has happened—you may have an instantaneous error of close to sixty millimeters."

Eurotunnel and its consultants, particularly Atkins-SETEC, the maître-d'oeuvre, saw things differently. They wanted a smaller tunnel (the 1974 plans, which SETEC had helped draw, had called for a 6.85-meter diameter), built to smaller tolerances (60 millimeters rather than Brown's 120), with freight shuttles that could carry the large 4.2-meter-high trucks that were used on the Continent.

The catenary system naturally entered this discussion, since it would occupy some of the precious space above the railroad cars. Brown was told to examine a rigid bar, like an overhead third rail, as an alternate to the usual wire catenary.

Brown thought this would be wasted effort. Nonrigid wire catenary had a long history of good service. SNCF had done much research on it and used it for its high-speed TGV trains. SNCF and British Rail expected to run their trains through the tunnel, and these were designed to take power from wire catenary. Rigid catenary, on the other hand, was new, relatively untested and rare in the field. "The only place we could find it was in a five-hundred-meter tunnel in Switzerland, Zurich, for trains that went eighty kilometers per hour," Brown said. He was nonetheless unable to convince the MdO that rigid catenary need not be studied.

Brown saw sinister motives in these attacks on Transmanche's capabilities. He believed that Atkins-SETEC wanted the design contract for itself or, failing that, wanted to run up its consulting fees by making more work. "If you're sitting across the table, being paid man-hours by banks, you earn most by creating the most bother," Brown said. "They wanted studies done, because the more studies, the more fees." If Eurotunnel could be convinced that the contractors couldn't design the tunnel, he added, the MdO could have kept two or three hundred of its people working for years on the project.

This tunnel debate had an Alice-in-Wonderland air about it, since Transmanche had already ordered the big tunnel-boring machines. Orders for the marine running-tunnel machines were placed in August, after more than eighteen months of planning and design discussions with the manufacturers. (The service tunnel-boring machines had been ordered in November 1986, and work was far enough along for Thatcher to pay a ceremonial visit in September to the Glasgow factory where they were under construction.) The running-tunnel machines, which were also under construction, were designed to cut passages for 7.6-meter-diameter tunnels. But the debate over the proper tunnel diameter had achieved a life of its own and continued even as the machines worked their way out under the Channel. Eurotunnel did not formally accept the 7.6-meter diameter until long after the tunnels were complete.

In late 1987, Dherse called Heydon at home in Florida. He seemed troubled and asked if Heydon would meet him to talk about the project. Both had to be in New York soon after and agreed to meet there.

Dherse, like Heydon, had come to believe that the project should be stopped—for a year—and rethought. He took this idea to Bénard and Durand-Rival, and received the same answer that the two had given to Heydon: They turned it down flat.

"It was out of the question politically and financially," Bénard said. "You could not stop that project and get it going again." Dherse told Bénard it had to be stopped: The details that had been brushed aside in the early planning had returned and were a genuine threat to the success of the Channel Tunnel.

"Rationally true," Bénard admitted. But Bénard and Durand-Rival—and most others involved with the project—believed that while the project might survive the problems that beset it, delay would certainly be fatal. Soon after he met with Heydon, Dherse left the project. So in persuading Dherse, Heydon had lost him as an ally.

When Dherse left, Durand-Rival moved up to take his place and invited Bechtel to participate more fully in Eurotunnel's operation. Even before Durand-Rival's rise to the top post, Bechtel's role in the project had grown. In August, the inner circle of Eurotunnel executives had invited Bechtel and Atkins-SETEC, the MdO, to submit plans to improve project management. Both presented their plans at a Eurotunnel board meeting in Crédit lyonnais's boardroom on October 12—the same meeting, coincidentally, when Durand-Rival was officially anointed as managing director. Behr thought the presentation went badly, but Durand-Rival called him that evening to say that Bechtel's plan had been accepted.

The result was the Project Implementation Division (PID), which was established within Eurotunnel to oversee the project. It was to be—depending on which side of the contract one stood—a curse or a blessing to the Channel Tunnel. It was created with personnel from both Bechtel and Atkins-SETEC, but quickly became a Bechtel fief in Eurotunnel's kingdom. Atkins-SETEC's role in the project was split, with an inside unit, or "integrated MdO," which did engineering work within the PID, and an outside unit that retained the MdO oversight function. The effect, though, was to dramatically strengthen Bechtel's role in the project, while diminishing that of the MdO.

Bechtel benefited from the fact that all sides mistrusted Atkins-SETEC: Eurotunnel thought they had been influenced by their long relationship with the contractors, the banks thought they were too much a creature of Eurotunnel and everyone suspected they might say anything to keep the work.

As these evolutions were taking place, the Credit Agreement was moving steadily toward a successful conclusion, as were plans for Equity 3, the stock issue through which ordinary citizens would become shareholders in this grand venture. The Bank of England allotted time slots for such stock sales to preserve order in the marketplace; Eurotunnel's had been placed behind the coming privatization, in early November, of British Petroleum. This was certainly not an ideal place to be; BP's £6.9-billion issue would absorb a great deal of the capital pool. Would there be £770 million left on the floor for Eurotunnel? The answer was that there had to be, or the banks would not make the loans and the project would die yet again.

Certainly Eurotunnel did what it could to make its shares attractive. Investors expected perquisites along with their shares, and creating these fell, again, to Ian Callaghan and his colleagues. The idea was to offer free passages through the tunnel to buyers of the stock: The more shares one bought, the more passages one would get. It seemed simple; it was not.

"Oh, God, that took up many, many hours of legal and executive time," Callaghan recalled. "Tying up all the loose ends was a nightmare." Questions arose: What if a taxi driver bought enough shares to earn unlimited passages through the tunnel—could he then carry passengers across the Channel free of charge?

Eurotunnel hired public relations consultants to help hawk the shares. Marketing was easier in France than in Britain. First, the French were far more friendly to the project. Second, British rules about what might be said to lure investors were far more restrictive than the French strictures.

David Wilson, a Eurotunnel executive, complained that British television ads—after much negotiation with the broadcasting authorities—could only say, in effect: "We're building a tunnel, it'll make travel quicker, we're selling shares in it, write in for further info." In France, he said, the television ads said, " 'Become a shareholder in the biggest tollbooth in the world.' The image was coins spinning through space and pouring out of a tunnel."

There were more road shows, too, in thirty cities around the globe, for institutional investors. Eurotunnel set up a share information office in London and mailed a short form of the Equity 3 prospectus to everyone who called. "There were something like a half-million calls for the prospectus," Callaghan said. "My guess is that half were schoolchildren doing assignments." The office, at Winchester House in the City, also contained an echo of an earlier time: a scale model of the Folkestone terminal, complete with running model trains.

Callaghan thought that a private issue, like Equity 2, would have met the banks' requirements just as well and might well have been easier and cheaper to mount.

"We probably spent as much as BP did for PR, offices, toll-free phone numbers for people to call in and get prospectuses [to raise] a comparatively tiny amount of money," he said. "To my mind there was always a question as to whether the public issue was worth doing at all, because [with that] type of prospectus, the legal requirements are much much tougher, because you weren't dealing with major institutions. We spent a hell of a lot of money on advertising for the public issue—if you run thirty- and forty-second commercials in prime time TV, you're talking about a lot of money, plus you have to pay to make the films. . . . The videos had to be cleared, image by image, by lawyers."

Eurotunnel commissioned market research to try and identify likely private investors. These studies found that the young, affluent private investors who were playing a substantial role in the privatizations were unmoved by the Channel Tunnel. So, too, were the bigger, more sophisticated investors. Callaghan said that the research did locate a pocket of interest among older, fairly well-heeled investors who kept portfolios worth between £2,000 and £5,000. The trade called these people—for reasons that Callaghan never fathomed—"Belgian dentists." Britain was, if not exactly full of them, at least reasonably well stocked.

In all, Callaghan estimated that Eurotunnel spent between £60 million and £70 million in legal fees, public relations and advertising to sell investors and banks on the wisdom of putting money into the Channel Tunnel project. Equity 3 advertising alone cost more than £10 million.

The travel perks started at one hundred "units"—because of the binational structure of Eurotunnel, buyers got a share in Eurotunnel S.A., the French part of the company, and a twin share in Eurotunnel PLC, the English portion—for which the buyer was entitled to one round-trip passage on the shuttle within a year of the tunnel's opening. Buyers of five hundred units got one round-trip a year for ten years; buyers of one thousand units got two such trips a year until the concession period ended in July 2042. Anyone who bought fifteen hundred units would be entitled to unlimited passages until the concession expired.

The Equity 3 prospectus was a clearly written document that offered the usual cautions about the risks that awaited all investors, but it also painted a rosy picture of the tunnel's financial prospects. Traffic across the Channel was expected to double between 1985 and 2003. Eurotunnel expected to pay its first dividends in 1994. The initial payout was expected to be 39 pence on each £3.50 unit; this should rise to 85 pence by 1998 and £1.46 per share by 2003. The projected gross dividend yield over the life of the project was estimated at 18 percent per year.

Alastair Morton stumped for the issue with his usual brash confidence. In late September, he addressed a meeting of institutional investors in New York; his speech was entitled "The Greatest Project in Europe in This Century and a New Utility for Investors."

He was accompanied on this outing by Colin Kirkland, Eurotunnel's technical director. Kirkland had been with the project for a long time, and had helped with the legislation in Parliament and with the negotiations over the construction contract. He had proved to be an excellent spokesman, too: Morton, he told an interviewer, came to call him "Old Silvertongue."

Less than a month after the meeting with institutional investors, Kirkland was back in New York on an October Monday for another presentation. He recalled sitting in the dark as the slide presentation clicked across the screen.

When the lights went up, it seemed as if everyone in the audience had a cellular phone clapped to his ear. They were, Kirkland soon discovered, absorbing information about a catastrophe: Sixteen days before the Credit Agreement was to be signed in London, and precisely four weeks before Equity 3 was supposed to go to the public, the stock market had crashed.

CHAPTER

11

On the morning after the Black Monday market crash, Ian Callaghan was supposed to take a planeload of stock analysts and fund managers from London to Switzerland.

"One of the things we used to do very regularly was to take parties of investors to the rail tunnels in the Swiss Alps," he said. "There was this wonderful money-no-object attitude. We used to hire a plane and take twenty or thirty of them, fly them over there, take them through a tunnel, put them up and fly them back the next day. It was money well spent, actually, because it proved to people that even on this very, very low-tech Swiss arrangement, it wasn't an unpleasant experience. And they were able to talk to the guys who ran the tunnel, who could tell them in the thirty years they'd been operating they'd never had an accident."

Callaghan and Tony Gueterbock had each led several of these junkets, which often included members of the press and Parliament as guests. On Black-Monday-plus-one, Callaghan duly trudged out to Gatwick to lead yet another tour, fully expecting to find no takers. He was stunned to find a crowd of them.

"We actually had extra people," he recalled. "They all said, 'The last place I want to be today is in the office—take me to Switzerland.'"

Still, some thought that the crash was the death knell for the Channel Tunnel project. This pessimism, prevalent among Eurotunnel's investment bankers, was heightened when the British government decided to go ahead with its planned sale of British Petroleum just before Eurotunnel's shares came to market. This would flood investment houses with BP shares that they had agreed to purchase at a precrash price.

Eurotunnel had no option but to go ahead with its offer: Its funds were running out, and the bank loan depended on Equity 3. For once, though, the long-haul aspects of the project made Eurotunnel's task easier; the stock market crash was dismissed as a small bump in a long, smooth highway.

On Wednesday, November 4, Eurotunnel and the banks signed the Credit Agreement—a red-bound document, more than twenty centimeters thick and weighing more than four kilograms—in simultaneous televised ceremonies in Paris and London. "These five billions form five-sixths of our total, and put a 185-year-old dream on the way to realization," Morton told the world.

Despite its impressive volume, the Credit Agreement was nothing more than a piece of paper: Eurotunnel could not get any of those "five billions" until after Equity 3 went through—indeed, Eurotunnel could not draw down the loan until most of the money from Equity 1, 2 and 3 had been spent.

Nonetheless, £6 billion seemed a comfortable, even ample sum—indeed, £1 billion of the total was considered "standby" money, to be used to cover unexpected overruns. There were a few estimates of the tunnel's costs (at July 1987 prices) floating around at the time; these ranged from £4.874 billion to £5.227 billion. The latter estimate included £3.044 billion in construction costs; £608 million in corporate and other costs, a £530 million provision for inflation and £1.045 billion in financing costs. Once Equity 3 went through, the amount raised from the three sales of shares would total £1.023 billion.

That pathfinder, or preliminary, prospectus for Equity 3 came out the day after the Credit Agreement was signed. It spelled out, for nonbankers, the fees that the banks were charging Eurotunnel for the privilege of borrowing a great deal of money for a long period of time. They were not unusual for a loan of such size and risk, but they were considerable. There was an arrangement fee of a quarter of a percent and an initial fee of seven eighths of a percent, on the £5 billion total—that is to say, £56,250,000. There was also a fee of one eighth of a percent per year on any money that Eurotunnel had not yet drawn down, and further fees on the money that the company *did* draw down each six months. Further still was another commitment fee of one eighth of a percent per year that had commenced almost twenty months earlier, when Eurotunnel was formally awarded the concession.

Interest on the borrowed money itself was pegged to LIBOR, the London Interbank Offer Rate, which is similar to (but usually a bit lower than) the prime rate in the United States. The margin ranged from 1 percent above the London rate to 1.75 percent. Rates were to be higher during the construction period, dropping a quarter to one half of a percent after the tunnel was complete and operating. There were thus clear and powerful incentives for Eurotunnel to push to get the project finished on time. The obverse was equally true: If the tunnel opening was delayed, the interest charges could become ruinous.

As with any loan, the borrower would benefit from a long stretch of low interest rates and high inflation. If this happened, Eurotunnel would save on interest charges and would be able to pay back the loans with cheaper money. Of course, if interest rates rose and inflation remained low, Eurotunnel faced a much worse prospect. And there were already grim hints that the rate was beginning to drift upward. During 1986, it had lingered below 7 percent. By the time Equity 3 came to market, it was above 7.5 percent.

There was much that could not be reduced to clauses in a credit agreement. No words could at a stroke give Eurotunnel the administrative strength that it so conspicuously lacked. No words could reach beyond the bankers and Eurotunnel's management to move the contractors with sweet reason, nor could they persuade the Intergovernmental Commission or the Safety Authority to be sparing in the strictures they might impose.

And no words could stimulate the bankers to trust Eurotunnel in their hearts. "You have to trust management," one banker observed. "You've got to think that they know the business. Because if they *don't* know the business, you're screwed."

On November 18, as the evening rush hour was drawing to a close, someone dropped a lighted match on one of the aged, wooden escalators in the Kings Cross station on the London Underground. The match fell between the loose treads and ignited some accumulated grease. Within minutes, flames engulfed the escalator; fire and dense clouds of noxious smoke filled the ticket lobby at its head. Thirty-one died.

The fire's effect on the Channel Tunnel project was profound. Predictably, it raised the fervent British devotion to safety to fever pitch. Its other effect was indirect, through changes it wrought in the career of Tony Ridley, the director general of London Underground.

Ridley had broad and deep experience in mass transit. He had been the first director-general of the Tyne and Wear mass transit system in Northern England, starting in 1969, when the system was little more than a line on a map. Ridley managed construction there for three years, at which time a corporate headhunter recruited him to become managing director of the then-abuilding Hong Kong Transit Railway. He was active in the Union internationale de transport publique, a professional organization that put him in contact with mass transit experts throughout the world. A particular friend in this circle was Philippe Essig, who had been engineering and operations director of the RATP, the Paris mass transit authority.

Months before the Kings Cross fire, Ridley received a call from Alastair Morton, of whom he had heard but whom he had never met. It was a lunch invitation, and the pitch was direct: "Morton said, in effect, 'I'd like you to consider having an interest in this project and joining us,'" Ridley recalled. "It wasn't clear what I was to do. . . . He talked about some of the problems, which were—my words, not his—'The people in TML don't seem to know too much about transport systems; go and talk to Pierre Durand-Rival.'"

When they met, Durand-Rival and Ridley agreed that the term "Channel Tunnel" was a misnomer. The tunnel, Ridley observed, "isn't the greatest Civil Engineering project in the world. It's the greatest *transportation* system, which happens to run through three big and expensive holes under the Channel." Building the tunnel called for a lot of skill and cleverness, he would tell people, "but that wasn't the fundamental challenge."

However, Ridley did not agree to join Eurotunnel. "Pierre and I seemed to have a common understanding about what some of the issues might be," Ridley said. "But he was a very difficult person, with characteristics that in my view were not suited to leading a great project. Nothing to do with the man's basic competence. It was the personality and characteristics: 'Never trust the contractors, don't let the bastards get away with anything, look what a bloody mess they're making of things.' Whether it was true or not, it was not the atmosphere within which one carries out a great project.

"I went back to see Alastair Morton and said I didn't want to join. I said to him, 'I don't see a role for myself, and I've got a full plate at London Transport.'" Morton asked him to join the Eurotunnel board, which he did.

Then came Kings Cross, which changed a great many things, including perhaps the enthusiasm of investors for Equity 3. Market research had suggested that more than a half million Britons were ready to buy Eurotunnel shares, but only about 112,000 actually did in the days day before and after the Kings Cross fire. The underwriters were stuck with 20 percent of the shares in Britain and 15 percent of the shares in France. But all that mattered was that the tunnel financing survived.

The crew that had done the bank-loan syndication was pleased with what they had accomplished. "We sold fifty per cent of the debt, which was quite an achievement, really," said Chris Deacon. "We had underwritten five billion pounds, sterling equivalent, and we effectively got people to take two point five billion."

"We negotiated a seven-hundred-million-pound equity sheet, five or six billions in bank financing, a railway contract and a construction contract," said Ian Callaghan. "And all the stuff that had to go through Parliament, the bill and all the rights to the land, the planning permission, everything. That's a lot of work in eighteen months. Each of those contracts was bigger than any other contract that had been negotiated before, and the negotiations were with parties in twenty-three different countries with different traditions, different legal systems. Nothing had ever been done like any of this. . . . Just the method of voting in a company with linked [French and British] shares was a legal nightmare. Nothing fitted; nothing quite lined up. So we had to devise a whole new way of presenting accounts, because British and French accounting laws differ—and yet we had to produce a single set of accounts which people could actually understand."

The satisfaction was sweetest for those who had survived the process without cracking. For years thereafter, people who had worked on financing the tunnel often spoke as if they had survived a great battle and, like war veterans, some of those who had campaigned to finance the Channel Tunnel found it difficult to return to the humdrum daily life of business. As soon as things calmed down, Callaghan left Eurotunnel. He had heard of a small hotel for sale on the wild Atlantic side of the Isle of Harris in the Outer Hebrides. He bought the place and moved there; it was as near to Iceland as to London or, for that matter, the Channel Tunnel. The seven-room hotel kept him busy for seven months of the year; when it closed he wrote plays. His wife painted.

Chris Deacon tried to get away from the tunnel, but it would not let him go. Morton liked him and pressured Midland to keep him on the job. So Deacon stayed. The project had affected him in ways he had never foreseen.

"My father fought in Burma during the war," he said. "Dead now. He was in the jungle. Never talked about the war. When he died he was delirious, and the only thing he could talk about was his Sergeant. He kept saying, 'Are you there, Sergeant?' Obviously deep down in him there was this . . . *something* that he wouldn't talk to us, his boys, about. But deep down, the Japs in the jungle were there on his deathbed.

"People say to me, 'Oh, you do Eurotunnel, how very nice to be associated with that.' But only those who were involved in it really know what it was like. I genuinely feel like that about it. The previous generation had a wartime experience: It was something you went through, something that only people who have done it can understand. That's what this was for us."

The Credit Agreement specified that none of the loan could be drawn until £700 million of the money raised from equity sales had been spent. Well before the ceremonial signing of the agreement, it was evident that it would not be difficult to spend money quickly in building the tunnel.

The first tunnel-boring machine—the one that was to dig the British section of the undersea service tunnel—took its initial bite of chalk on December 1, 1987. The project was by that time about three months behind schedule, this being the sum of delays in the political and financing

Assembling a running-tunnel TBM under Shakespeare Cliff.

processes. Yet work was already well under way; the TBM's first bite was a symbolic event in a process that had begun months before with much less ceremony. By the end of the year, the Sangatte shaft was more than half finished and the marshaling chamber for the service tunnel TBM was complete.

On the British side, TML broke out of the old 1975 access adit at the shoreline under Shakespeare Cliff to begin creating the marshaling chambers for the other TBMs. At the same time, work crews began hand-mining a tunnel beneath the marshaling site; this was for the machinery of the conveyor that would carry excavated spoil to the surface via the 1975, or A1, adit.

Work also started on the 110-meter-deep vertical shaft from Upper Shakespeare Cliff that would carry workers down to the tunnels. By early 1988, work was under way on an additional sloping shaft, Adit A2, from the shoreside down to the marshaling chambers; this would carry material down to the tunnel on five parallel rail lines.

These were not small jobs. They involved the creation of almost three kilometers of tunnel and the excavation of 160,000 cubic meters of material. Adit A2 was more than twelve meters wide and more than seven meters high. Most of these passages and chambers combined some very old and very new tunneling techniques. Most were dug by hand, although the hands were assisted by some very powerful machinery. The lining was done by the New Austrian Tunneling Method, a state-of-the-art approach to tunneling that was a scant two decades old. NATM, as the trade called it, involved shotcreting—spraying special concrete onto the excavated surfaces rather than lining the passages with precast concrete or cast-iron rings. NATM freed the tunnel from rigid, regular forms, but it required quite a lot of planning to use NATM—it was important to understand the strengths and characteristics of the ground and brace it with rockbolts and reinforcing steel when needed—but it was fast, flexible and reliable.

Four other undertakings, far larger in scope and difficulty, were also under way: In Britain and France, work had begun on facilities to contain the huge volume of excavated material from the tunnels, and on fabrication plants for the reinforced concrete tunnel liner. If one looked at these works—and they were difficult to miss, since each sprawled over huge tracts of land or water—one saw clear evidence of the national differences that divided this Channel Tunnel into a great project and a quite distinct *grand projet*.

Some of the differences, of course, were dictated by logistics. The British had drawn a decidedly bad hand when it came to geography. The Shakespeare Cliff work site was atop one of the most sacred of the White Cliffs of

Lower Shakespeare Cliff in the 1880s.

The Lower Shakespeare Cliff platform in 1987, stacked with segments abandoned after the 1974 attempt failed.

Dover. The Lower Shakespeare site, on the Channel shore at the cliff's foot, was a mere toehold of land, cluttered with stacked tunnel segments from the abandoned 1974 project. The only access for motor vehicles was a small, steeply angled tunnel, carved in 1975, from the Upper Shakespeare site. This access tunnel was too narrow for vehicles to pass side by side. Worse, bureaucratic tangles associated with the Channel Tunnel Bill's passage through Parliament kept engineers from even entering the Shakespeare Cliff site until August 1987.

There were no easy solutions for the British. Kent did not want the spoil dumped anywhere in the county. Kent was similarly unenthusiastic about a major fabricating facility for the concrete liner. Transmanche-Link concluded that it would have to deposit the soil in the Channel at the foot of Shakespeare Cliff and would have to build the tunnel segments at a site quite distant from the tunnel works.

Dumping the spoil at Lower Shakespeare offered some considerable advantages. It was perfectly accessible, lying just at the mouth of the adits. The spoil could be spread out to form a generous tract of land, upon which TML could build a marshaling yard to support the construction work in the tunnels: There would be room to unload and stockpile prefabricated concrete sections, to assemble and repair work trains and locomotives, to build a ventilation system, an electrical substation, a batching plant for grout and concrete. And, finally, there was rail access to the site, via British Rail's shoreside line between Dover and Folkestone; this meant that the liner segments could come by train, rather than truck, from wherever they were manufactured.

The problem was, the nation did not want some four million cubic meters of sodden chalk marl simply dumped in the Channel. If TML wished to use the area, it would first have to enclose it with a seawall. The lagoon behind the wall was to be so solidly sealed that none of the spoil would leach through or under the barrier to stain the Channel's waters. This was a very big job. The seawall frame would be the largest driven-sheet-steel structure ever undertaken. The spoil platform would enlarge England by thirty-four hectares.

The engineers began by driving a 1,700-meter-long double wall of steel sheets into the Channel bed. The space between the walls—8 meters to 11.36 meters, depending on how deep the solid chalk lay—would be filled with concrete. Temporary steel-sheet double walls, infilled with spoil, would run out from the shore to meet the seawall to create small lagoons that could be used immediately while the permanent wall inched southwestward, about 200 meters offshore, toward completion.

Building the seawall was not a simple matter of pile-driving steel and slopping in concrete. The first step was to dredge the surface deposits off the seabed. Next, a platform rig would drive the steel; the walls were linked every few meters with driven sheet pilings that formed contained cofferdams. After divers had cleaned out the debris, these would be filled to a meter above sea level with special concrete placed underwater. A second mass of concrete would be added later to raise the height to four meters above the sea. A third layer of concrete, 6.6 meters wide and sloping slightly to seaward, would bring the top of the wall to 7 meters above sea level. Topping that would be a 1.22-meter-high concrete "personnel barrier" to keep humans from slipping into the water.

Steel from the inner face of the wall, and from the temporary partitions, was pulled out and reused after the concrete set. In all, the seawall would consume 180,000 cubic meters of concrete and 32,500 tons of pilings.

The spoil, which would come to the surface as crushed rock, could be piled above the level of the wall; the highest permanent portion of the site would eventually be sixteen meters above sea level. At times, spoil was temporarily stockpiled in mounds that rose to thirty-two meters above the sea. Eventually, the band closest to the seawall would be stabilized with a concrete apron. Inland of that, TML proposed to build a microcosmic nature park, with hills and valleys, footpaths and boardwalks, car parks and picnic areas. There would be wetland areas tucked into folds of the man-made land, a timber bridge over a ravine and a broad seafront promenade atop the wall.

By August 1987, events had moved so rapidly that there was an instant need for a place to put spoil from the adits and the marshaling chambers. The engineers quickly cobbled together a temporary lagoon at the edge of the existing platform. Work started in late August was finished by mid-November—despite the interruption of the great October storm that ravaged the south of England.

The concrete tunnel liner benefited, at the outset, from the foresight of an earlier age. Before work had halted in 1975, engineers had installed strain gauges in the walls. These were maintained for ten years and gave a continuous reading of how the segments reacted to the load that burdened them.

When David Brown's people came to the job, they upgraded the instruments and sat down to examine what the gauges revealed. The calculations showed that the segments could be made significantly thinner, with considerable consequent savings. An undersea segment that would have been 350 millimeters thick in 1974, Brown saw, could be shaved down to 290 millimeters. Some of the savings came from the better understanding of forces that the old instruments conferred; another portion came from advances in the design of concrete and concrete-reinforced structures.

Under land, the savings were even more dramatic, since the overburden was far more crushing than it was out under the water. Tunnel segments had to be designed to withstand the weight of anything that might be built above, such as a road and the weight of its passing traffic. "Under land, we were looking at the potential of one-meter-thick segments," Brown said. Such gargantuan rings would have required a larger tunnel-boring machine to cut a sufficiently large passage. Good data and careful design work enabled Brown's engineers to thin the underland segments by almost half, to just 540 millimeters.

A particular worry with the tunnel segments was concrete cancer, a deterioration caused by the invasion of chlorides. The contract had strictly limited the amount of water that could leak into the tunnel: "Not more than one drip per minute" could fall from the top half of the tunnel onto equipment below, and no continuous leak could exceed four liters per hour unless it was diverted directly into the drainage system. Nonetheless, there was bound to be some seawater in the tunnels, and the speeding trains would very efficiently turn this into a fine mist that would land on all surfaces. If the chloride ions managed to penetrate the concrete, the interior steel reinforcing would corrode and expand, cracking the lining. After much calculation and many tests, the chemists came up with a precise mix of cement, pulverized fuel ash, crushed granite and superplasticizer. Mixed with water and cured in a two-stage process—one hour at 20°C, followed by five hours at 50°C—and molded around a welded cage of twenty-millimeter-thick steel wire, it made a ring segment that could do the considerable job asked of it for more than a century.

The ideal place for making the segments, of course, would have been at the mouth of the A2 adit. There was no room there, so Brown looked elsewhere. No one in Kent wanted the plant as a neighbor. In 1974, RTZ had found a site near Ashford where local opposition was insufficient to quash the plan, but this was no longer available.

"We looked at a number of sites for the precast plant," said Brown, "and it just so happened that, by accident, one of my friends was the managing director of BP, UK Oil, in London, who were wanting to get rid of their Isle of

Grain refinery." The refinery had already been removed, leaving a long, flat stretch of barren marshland.

Within TML, the Isle of Grain was no one's idea of a perfect place for the precast plant. Among the people of Kent, it was rather the best choice: far away from most everywhere and already spoiled. It wallowed in the mud in the Thames Estuary, no longer an island but rather a sore thumb protruding from the Hoo Peninsula. Even before it became home to a sprawl of refineries, it was at best a place of middling beauty and charm. The Isle of Grain was about thirty-three air miles from Folkestone, but by rail, Brown calculated, it was close to about ninety miles. A one-way trip took three hours.

Still, it had much to recommend it. The twenty-nine-hectare site was large enough. It had a deepwater dock and was accessible by road and rail, so raw materials could come in from almost anywhere. The rail link to Folkestone was roundabout, but at least it existed, so the segments could reach the work site with a minimum of handling. The logistics of shipping and receiving would be of extraordinary magnitude: The plant had to ship 422,755 segments over three and a half years of operation. Two hundred thousand tons of cement were needed. Fortunately, there was a supplier about twenty miles away, at Northfleet, and this could be shipped by rail. The ninety thousand tons of pulverized fuel ash and forty-five thousand tons of reinforcing could come in by truck.

The biggest single ingredient in the concrete was granite: A million tons of it would go into the British portion of the Channel Tunnel. It was special granite, too, and the source was a mountain on the west coast of Scotland, north of Glasgow. Tarmac, a big user and supplier of construction aggregates, had put Transmanche onto the trail of this mother lode, which was owned by Foster Yeomans, another aggregates supplier.

"Yeomans said to us, 'Well, we have got an option on a mound of granite in Scotland, but we have not got the resources or the finances to develop it,'" Brown said. The mound was, in fact, a rather imposing mountain, and it represented an opportunity rather than a barrier for TML, which was glad enough to help finance the venture. There were environmental problems in removing a handsome eminence from Scotland's landscape, but Yeomans was able to get permission to remove the interior of the mountain, leaving its exterior intact. The granite was transported by ship to the Isle of Grain.

Work began on the Isle of Grain site in November 1986; it took eleven months to ready it for production. Eight parallel assembly lines ran the length of the place. Four concrete-mixing plants at the water's edge fed two lines in each of four parallel production buildings just inland. Farther on were four long storage areas, each served by several overhead cranes. Rail spurs ran down the aisles between these lines.

A lot of hand work went into the segments. There were thirty-five different models; they varied in thickness and shape, and in the holes that were molded into them. Three large holes ran down the center of the inner face of a typical segment. The top and bottom went all the way through; these permitted grout to be pumped into the space behind the rings. The center hole was a cast-iron-lined handling socket by which the piece could be lifted: A rubber-clad device could be fitted into the hole and expanded, like a bottle stopper, to grip the segment. Tunnelers called the rubber gripper a "bull's prick." They applied a mixed but equally accurate animal metaphor to the handling socket: This they called the "elephant's foot."

In segments meant for the sides of the tunnel, two additional rows of holes would be molded into one side of the grout holes and handling socket; these were for affixing brackets for pipes and wires.

The steel reinforcing cages were hand-built and hand-welded. When production started in October 1987, there was a problem with the concrete mix: It left gaps under the reinforcing wires when it settled in the mold. The solution was to make the concrete a little finer by cutting down the amount of coarse granite in the mix, replacing it with fine. A problem with the surface finish was solved by coating the molds with a special oil.

Each production line had nine workstations, where the molds were cleaned, prepared, fitted with reinforcing cages and filled with concrete. Each station was supposed to finish its work in ten minutes. Segments then moved to curing tunnels, where they were bathed in steam at 50°C for six hours. They were then lifted from the molds, wrapped in special jackets to guard against thermal shock and too-rapid drying, and stockpiled outside. If all went well, a production line could turn out 144 segments a day. At peak, the eight lines could fill three 24-car trains a day with segments.

The difference between the French and British precast facilities was stark. The French side's task was smaller in bulk—252,000 segments—but because of the anticipated difficult tunneling conditions the French had to make 72 different types of segments, compared to 35 in Britain. The French precast plant was smaller in area, twenty hectares, but they had the luxury of being able to put the plant next to the Sangatte shaft, so that completed segments had only to trundle a few meters to where a special crane lowered them to tunnel level.

Early on, the French had considered building their reinforcing cages in the same fashion as the British, using standard hand-building methods. When they asked for proposals for constructing the steel-fabricating unit, though, one manufacturer suggested a highly automated operation, and this the

Hand-assembling steel reinforcing for a British tunnel-liner segment.

French adopted. Human beings assembled the elements of the reinforcing from eight- and twelve-millimeter wire. The wire panels were fed to the machine, which shaped them to the required radius and hung them on a monorail carousel, which delivered them to a welding machine, which took the shaped panels, assembled them in the proper order and welded them together.

At this point, the cages were handed back to a gang of eight workers who finished the cages, cutting out wire where it was in the way and adding it where it was needed. The system could produce twenty-five cages an hour, which set the pace for the whole production line. The cages were trucked to the casting plant—a journey of a hundred meters—and loaded on a conveyor, which took them off to be encased in concrete.

The British admired the French plant. "Absolutely fantastic," Andrew Mc-Dowall said of the cage-making system. "All done by machine—coiled the re-

Machines built the reinforcing cages for French tunnel segments.

inforcements, spun out, laid out. . . . The welding was done automatically and all the rest. . . . We had umpteen steel fixers in there, doing it all the British way." The delivery systems, McDowall noted, were similarly dissimilar: "They had overhead traveling gantries. Computerized. No men in 'em. They'd pick up a palette of units as they came out—they made a ring at a time, I believe; it went onto the palette a complete ring. The crane would pick up and put down, no manpower, in exactly the right spot. When there was a call from the shaft for ring such-and-such, the crane would run along, pick up the right one, put it on a little railway and it would run down to the shaft."

This was too admiring a view, although the French did not discourage their British colleagues from holding it. In fact, the French system was rather too fine for such massive items as tunnel segments, and there were problems. The automatic cranes had so many safety devices that their operation was hampered, and the French ended up unloading them and using forklifts to store the segments. Tinkering with the production line cut fabrication time significantly, but the cranes could not be made to run faster to handle the increased daily capacity. Worse, the cranes at the Sangatte shaft could only handle palettes that had been stacked with extreme precision; the tolerance was a minuscule one centimeter. This was beyond the capability of the automatic cranes in the storage area; 60 percent of the palettes failed to meet it. Those palettes then had to be repacked by humans.

To build a ring in the British portion of the running tunnel, eight segments were held in position by the TBM ring erector and a keystone-shaped segment was rammed in to form and keep the circle. In the service tunnel, a ring was six segments and a key. In the French works, all rings were of five segments plus a key, and the segments were bolted together to form the ring. Further, each ring was bolted to the next. Wherever one edge touched another, there was a gasket to make the joint watertight. This was necessary because of the water that lay outside the French rings under enormous pressure—ten atmospheres, equivalent to one hundred tons per square meter—in the fractured ground near the coast. Grout was pumped behind the rings. After it had set, the bolts were taken out and reused.

In theory, the French did not need a drainage system in their part of the tunnel to remove water. "The British accepted infiltration and put in a drainage system," said François Jolivet. "We didn't accept infiltration." He paused to smile. "But we put a drainage system in, anyway. Sometimes the British are more pragmatic than the French."

Fond Pignon, the earthen vessel that the French built to hold their 3,000,000 cubic meters of tunnel spoil, was a huge job that would eventually cover fifty hectares. The dam that formed the bowl for the thick soup of slurried chalk from the TBMs covered eighteen of those fifty hectares. When it was complete, the dam—almost forty meters high and over a kilometer in length—would itself contain 1,864,000 cubic meters of crushed white chalk dug from five borrow pits in the bowl.

The Shakespeare Cliff seawall was finished by early 1990, but not before it had become the subject of a furious battle between Eurotunnel and Transmanche-Link. "That wall," said André Bénard, "the cost of which had been estimated at £28 million by the contractors, was a fairly simple piece of civil engineering. . . . We were warned in September '87 that we may have to pay £40 million. A week later, it was £50 million. A week later, it was £70 million. So, of course, we had to call the contractors and say to them, 'Stop this nonsense straight away.'" The contractors, of course, had a different opinion about the expenditures. The British contractors said very bluntly, "You'll pay what it costs," he recalled. "The French contractors were a bit more worried."

Fond Pignon, where the French dumped their tunnel spoil.

"TML didn't do a good job of justifying the extra cost," said Pete Behr. "I think they came up with the true cost [later], but it wasn't clear that the engineering was good, or if the solution was the cheapest one available. . . . It became a symbol to TML of Eurotunnel's intransigence, and a symbol to Eurotunnel of TML's incompetence and duplicity."

The seawall controversy established a destructive pattern; the same harsh dialogue was to be repeated often (and often with more heat) in the years that followed. The contractors wanted Eurotunnel to trust them to build the tunnel according to the contract. Eurotunnel always felt that it was being jobbed, that the contractors were treating it like a cow to be milked. There was evidence to support both views, though neither side could see the other's across the vast and widening gulf that already separated Eurotunnel from Transmanche-Link.

Building the seawall at Shakespeare Cliff.

Both sides tended to think proprietarily about the money. "One thing Durand-Rival did that came from Fos: He'd get approval from the board on a budget [item], then he'd take something out," Behr said. "He'd then try to get the work done for the smaller sum—in essence trying to pay ninety dollars when he had a hundred in his pocket. It was done in an open fashion: 'Here's the budget, a hundred dollars. See if you can do it for ninety. If you can prove you need the hundred, I'll give you the other ten dollars.' "

On the other hand, Behr recalled a meeting with McDowall. McDowall began asking acquisitive questions about the one billion in standby funds; Behr had to discourage him. "They acted like it was all their money," Behr said of TML.

Fueling the money dispute was an inexhaustible series of arguments about the nature and scope of the project and the respective responsibilities of Euro-tunnel and TML.

"Starting from the beginning there was a big day-to-day dispute with Eurotunnel on the engineering and the transportation system," Jolivet said. "The main reason related to our role as contractor: The contract said we were responsible for both engineering and construction, and we have to achieve the performance described in the contract. It was an obligation of performance, not the means of achieving it.

"But Eurotunnel decided that *it* must decide if the way we were doing it was acceptable to them. They asked to review all of the technical documents. . . . They reduced our role to [that of a] classical contractor, not responsible for engineering decisions—but they wanted us to keep the overall responsibility. We disagreed; that's why there was a permanent conflict.

"The contract says we have to give information to Eurotunnel so that Eurotunnel, as operator, can possibly introduce change. They used this code of the contract to say, 'What you decide from a technical point of view is not acceptable to me.'" Eurotunnel began issuing instructions, which Transmanche held to be changes for which Eurotunnel would have to pay, Jolivet said. "I tried to understand why they were acting that way," he added. "In my opinion, the men within [Eurotunnel] were not confident of TML. They decided they needed to manage the project themselves."

Philippe Montagner of Bouygues traced all of the tunnel's problems with costs to a "change in the spirit of the bid. When we bid, the concept was, we would design and build and test. That's our job. Eurotunnel's [would] be to operate, do the commercial part, marketing, find the finance." But Eurotunnel, instead of recruiting operating and marketing people, instead hired engineers like Durand-Rival—"a man who made a lot of big projects, but who wouldn't accept the word of the contractors." Montagner noted that contractors were accustomed to working in the developing world, for governments that were inclined to accept the word and representations of contractors. He recalled Durand-Rival saying, "I am not an African nation. I won't wait seven years to find out what I'm getting. I want to check everything." This attitude, said Montagner, basically created another source of design for the project.

The vagueness in the bid and in the construction contract now came back to haunt the project. Montagner's and Jolivet's views were merely one sort of interpretation that could be put on the documents. The same could be said of the views of Bénard and Durand-Rival and Morton. The documents were like the Bible, subject to differing interpretations. The trouble was, both Eurotunnel and TML thought they possessed the revealed truth.

Other documents began to intrude and to complicate the relationship between the parties. "Eurotunnel went ahead and agreed the usage contract with British Rail," said Andrew McDowall. "It was very much different from what we'd anticipated. They went ahead and signed the agreement. There are bits in there that cut across the contract; that were different from the proposal."

Morton had renegotiated the Rail Usage Contract with British Rail and SNCF soon after he arrived and used the new pact as propaganda to bolster faith in the tunnel. "In fact, he didn't do anything with the rail contract," said Chris Deacon. "He just dressed it up as if he had. The truth of the matter is the railways had Eurotunnel over a barrel. I know, from talking to the advisers on the railways side, that the view which the railway boards took was, 'Well, we know we've taken them to the cleaners, but we've got to dress it up in the press. . . . We'll get the money points, Eurotunnel gets the glory, because if ET doesn't get the glory we don't have a project.' "

The renegotiation did change the schedule of payments that the railways were to make, front-loading them so that Eurotunnel would get the money sooner rather than later. But the changes that disturbed TML had to do with such questions as: How fast could the British Rail and SNCF through-passenger trains go in the tunnel? SNCF wanted to be able to run its TGV trains through the tunnel at 200 kilometers per hour, at least; 250 kilometers per hour would have been better. The shuttles were to run at 160 kilometers per hour. A TGV would therefore run into the rear end of an in-transit shuttle unless the latter had started its journey well before the pursuing passenger train entered the tunnel.

This created a grave problem. The tunnel was designed around the shuttles. The Submission to Governments had said that high-speed trains and shuttles would pass through the tunnel at the same maximum speed: 160 kilometers per hour. This passage time defined what was called a "standard path." With a train entering every three minutes, there would be twenty standards paths in each hour. Trains that ran faster or slower wrought havoc with this neat arrangement. A 200-kilometer-per-hour train would complete the passage in fifteen minutes. If it was to emerge from the tunnel three minutes after the preceding shuttle, the high-speed train would have to enter the tunnel nine minutes after the shuttle. The two standard paths that would have begun during those nine minutes would be lost. Things worsened if low-speed freight trains were thrown into the mix, as the Rail Usage Contract permitted: If you put two high-speed trains and two slow freights through in an hour, they would consume twelve of the hour's twenty standard paths.

Beyond timetable concerns lay others: Changing the speed of trains meant changing the signaling system, the rails and railbed, the power of the locomotives, the design of the piston relief ducts and much else. So there was much reason for go-slow caution when it came to questions of speed.

On February 17, 1987, Colin Stannard—then Eurotunnel's commercial managing director—wrote a confidential memorandum to representatives of

SNCF and British Rail, setting forth the company's position on a number of major usage contract points still not agreed. On the question of speed, Stannard wrote, "The Concessionaires will carry out studies to establish the necessary design changes and their cost implications in order to permit trains to run through the Fixed Link at speeds of up to 200 kph. . . . However, the Concessionaires shall be under no obligation pursuant to this clause unless they are satisfied that the Railways have used their best endeavors to maximise the speed of their trains throughout all other parts of the London/Paris and London/Brussels routes."

This promise to study the possibility of high-speed trains was consistent with Eurotunnel's contract with TML, which said that Eurotunnel accepted the principle "of passing the Railways' trains through the Fixed Link at a speed of up to 160 kph." Of higher speeds, it said only that "the parties shall debate in a positive manner the implications of operating trains through the Fixed Link at speeds greater than 160 kph (for example 200 kph) with a view to establishing the additional terms which would be necessary to permit such speeds."

Stannard's memo added a comment: "Eurotunnel are already examining the implications of running through the tunnel at 200 kph. The current view is that the additional fixed equipment cost is not likely to be large (in the context of the total tunnel cost) although the additional maintenance costs have yet to be assessed. However, it is considered to be extremely difficult to overcome the operating problems of mixing trains running throughout at 200 kph with shuttles and freight trains; the initial conclusion is that the acceptance of any speed above 160 kph could seriously reduce the effective capacity of the tunnel."

Three weeks later, despite those doubts, Eurotunnel directed TML to design for 200-kilometer-per-hour trains. In a March 6 letter to Jolivet and Reeve, Eurotunnel's project manager wrote that the catenary system should be able to provide power to TGV trains running at that speed. The letter also required that the tunnel be able to handle the increased traffic expected in the future. Twenty-four standard paths would be needed ten years after the tunnel went into service. At saturation, this would increase to thirty.

The flaws in the contract that led to this sort of debate and confusion were evident to some at Eurotunnel. To Joe Anderson, one of the Bechtel engineers, they were glaring. His solution was simple: Change the contract.

Anderson was a Scot, born in Glasgow. A life in engineering had worn away much of his accent but had left his devotion to home intact: He knew Scots history and he always remarked, in speaking of his colleagues, which of them were Scots.

He differed from many of his peers by having an enduring and happy marriage, a success perhaps due in part to the fact that his wife, Sandra, the daughter of an American engineer, had been inured to the hardships of the engineering life. They met on a job in Turkey. When work took her family to the Philippines, Anderson followed. When Sandra's father went to a project in Arizona, Anderson found work in Utah, a scant few hundred miles away, whence he continued and completed the courtship.

He had worked for several companies, some British, before winding up with Bechtel. In 1973, he was working on the huge James Bay hydroelectric project in Canada. The lead contractor there was Rio Tinto Zinc, and Alistair Frame approached him one day and asked if he'd like to get involved in an attempt to build a tunnel under the English Channel. Anderson declined.

In the years after, Anderson had been involved with a string of major projects. His mandate was to monitor big civil projects for Bechtel from San Francisco. In 1987 he was thinking of retiring. He had just finished work on a huge project, the Jubail Industrial City in Saudi Arabia. He had a nice house in Atherton, California, not far from Stanford, and a head full of ideas about a waste-disposal system. A life in engineering had left him in vigor, health and strength. He was calm and thoughtful, with something of a card-player's air of calculation about him, confident rather than confiding, friendly but without any false warmth.

While he was visiting Turkey in mid-1987, Riley Bechtel, who was stationed in London, called. "He asked me to come back by way of London to hear about this *opportunity*, as we would have called it." He did, and there met and talked to Behr and Durand-Rival.

"They were having problems," Anderson said. "I agreed to come out for ninety days to do a technical audit, to look at the way the project was organized: How is it being designed, how is it being built, what different companies are involved, what consulting engineering companies. The contractor's operation: How is *he* organized, how is he going to get the design completed and how is he going to get the construction done? How has the owner's organization been structured?" The result of this audit had been the Product Implementation Division (PID), which Anderson organized. He also agreed to stay on to run it as one of Eurotunnel's deputy managing directors.

Anderson saw that the contract contained some bad elements that were likely to cause problems. "I saw there were two or three areas of the contract that were going to be a can of worms," he said. He was particularly worried by the lump-sum prices, which seemed too low. It seemed clear to Anderson that there were going to be a lot of claims down the road. The lump sum, Anderson noted, governed some of the project's most crucial elements: the catenary and train control systems, the rails and ties, and—perhaps most significantly—the signaling system. The signaling system, he said, was "definitely in an evolutionary stage." All of these also were elements upon which the tunnel's safety depended: There could be no skimping on them; only the best would do.

"There's really no such thing as a lump-sum," he said. Lump sums always ended up being negotiated between the parties. Lump sums varied according to risk. On a project with little risk, the lump sum would be inflated by perhaps 8 percent; this would rise to about 25 percent on a high-risk project. Risk, in turn, varied in relation to the state of the design when the contract was signed: More information meant less risk and less protective padding in the contract price. The best case for a lump-sum contract is, finish all design work before setting the price.

"But design is so costly that contractors don't want to invest too much money unless they're certain they're going to get the job," Anderson said. On this project, the design work for the Submission to Governments alone, he said, cost nearly £50 million. The contractors were still running big risks; the geological work was still far from conclusive: "Not much was known about the faults," Anderson said, adding that "aerodynamics [within the tunnel] weren't well understood, because you needed an expensive model."

Anderson knew that it would be difficult to convince the parties to compromise. After Eurotunnel won the concession, he said, the sides "went from being great friends to friendly enemies to being quite violent enemies." But it was still possible—the project had not gone too far to preclude it—and Anderson was one of the few people who might have been able to broker such a deal. He liked Durand-Rival and got along with him. "I enjoyed working with him," he said. "He told you what he thought. He let me concentrate on the civil part—the tunneling, the excavation and the terminals—and he got more involved in putting together the operating end of the company through André Bénard."

Although Anderson had never met McDowall before, the two men had much in common. In the 1950s, before he joined Bechtel, Anderson had worked for Wimpey, and he and McDowall had a lot of friends in common at the company. Even McDowall's natural allies admitted that he could be difficult to get along with, but McDowall nonetheless found it easy to work with Anderson. Anderson also knew and understood the contractors, particularly the British companies. "I knew the British construction industry; I'd grown up in it," he said. "We were all more sympathetic to contractors than, say, PDR (Durand-Rival) was." Knowledge of the construction industry didn't dull Anderson's critical acuity, however. Although some individuals acted from higher, often patriotic motives, he said, "Most of the contractors were just hard-money bidders."

Anderson took his thoughts about the contract to Durand-Rival, who took them to Bénard and Morton. "I said the best thing to do is renegotiate," he said. "I was pointing out that here was a problem we were going to be fighting over. . . . This was February, March of 1988. I didn't get much encouragement from Eurotunnel; they preferred to stick with the contract." He remained convinced that Eurotunnel's refusal wasted an opportunity. "I always felt that the job could have been saved a year and a lot of money if they'd decided early on to do what they eventually did: Apportion the risk," Anderson said.

Jolivet, too, hoped to change the contract, and he too was rebuffed when he submitted some proposals to the chairmen of the French companies in TML. To illustrate the project's structural problems, Jolivet drew a circle and added the organizations like stones on a necklace: the banks, Eurotunnel, Transmanche-Link, the national railways, the Intergovernmental Commission and the Safety Authority.

"The key factor was that no one had full power," Jolivet said. "The banks were two hundred in number; they decided to be represented by twenty-seven of them. So when you say 'the banks,' you have no one guy for the banks. Eurotunnel was two chairmen, TML was two directors-general, two boards. British Rail was on one side, SNCF the other. So you have organizations and not individuals. Difficult to establish confidence. There was no common communication system among the parties. They were not together around one table to discuss the project."

He returned to his necklace diagram. "The key issue for success is the capacity of all these people to take into account the overall interests of the project, despite their individual interests. People who study project management [say] that the key factor of success is communication and mutual trust." He shook his head ruefully. "And we had not, on this project, mutual trust. Everybody was—not negative, but thinking in terms of failure. The banks' attitude was: 'I have to protect my money if the tunnel fails.' Eurotunnel, 'I have to prevent TML from failing.' The IGC, 'I have to deal with details, since we don't know if Eurotunnel can do it.' Success must be based on trust. Instead, there was a failure-based mentality."

Jolivet saw parallels in the contract itself. "In a family, the marriage contract is to organize divorce, not love. The contract is to deal with separation. Today, the overall policy is to manage by lawyers rather than managers." While Jolivet agreed that lawyers provided necessary services and advice, he said it was fatal "to do one hundred percent of what they say. It's unworkable if you accept one hundred percent. They have to give opinions; it's their job. But they are not to decide what has to be done. . . . If you have a contract which defines the roles—how to work together—it's quite positive. But if it is oriented toward dispute and how to fight together, it's negative. In such a project, you *must* be partners. You are in the same boat."

Instead, the system set the project on a ruinous course. "The project has created a great deal of tension between the individuals, because it's not geared to solving the problems," Jolivet said. "It's geared to placing the blame."

CHAPTER

12

B y early 1988, Eurotunnel had solved its management crisis, after a fashion—it had the Project Implementation Division in place, it had strong
and aggressive leadership in Morton, Bénard and Durand-Rival, it had legions of Bechtel people in house and on call. By March of that year, the last of
the secondees either joined Eurotunnel or returned to their various companies.

Eurotunnel knew more about what it wanted by this time, and it had the
strength and leverage to demand it. The contracting companies were now cast
in the role of servants to their own creation. This altered status rankled. As
Eurotunnel's management grew better able to handle the project's demands,
those same demands began to overwhelm TML's management. Transmanche,
like Eurotunnel, was very much an infant organization. Jolivet and Reeve and
McDowall had formed and shaped it from the muddle of ten striving and proprietary companies. It hadn't been easy.

"TML was *bicephale*—two headed," Jolivet said. "There were two directors-
general, two supervisory boards, two [main] boards. There was liaison between
the boards, but mainly people were thinking along national lines first. The
overall concept was that we'd build two joint ventures: Transmanche Construction was the company responsible in France; Translink JV in Britain. Together they formed TML, a joint venture in which all risk was shared equally.

"It created a community of interest at the top level, but we started with national organizations. The main reason was, if we put only one director-
general, if he was French he would not understand the British practice and
context, and vice versa."

Jolivet and Reeve first organized the engineering unit and produced a
bilingual manual that would explain the project to the legions of workers who
would shortly be enlisting. Staff instruction was particularly important in
France, where almost all of the workforce was to be recruited locally to help

bring down the Nord-Pas de Calais region's unemployment rate. French hirees received three days of indoctrination as part of a training program that cost 120 million francs.

On the British side, the core of the workforce came from the tunneling fraternity—men who had spent their working lives underground, who would laugh at any suggestion that three days of instruction could help them build a tunnel to France. They brought a great body of knowledge to the project, along with a reputation for wildness and a contempt for the preachings of safety officers.

By early 1988, Jolivet said, "There were six hundred people working together on the engineering, in twelve to fourteen different design offices in the Paris vicinity and London vicinity." Bringing English and French engineering together was a difficult but necessary undertaking. "It *had* to be Franco-British," said Jolivet. "The transport system couldn't be split; you can't have two types of equipment. It was not so easy. Take the question of voltage: The standard is 380 in France, 420 in Britain. We decided to have 400 volt. When you have people coming from two nations, each believes that only their own regulations are right."

Reeve's view of the French, Jolivet said, was that they were too dogmatic: They drew up a detailed plan and stayed with it, even when the results did not match expectations. Jolivet agreed, but added the French view: The British hated to plan anything, lest it hinder their ability to adapt to changing conditions. The Channel Tunnel project provided endless evidence to support these views, which in time became useful, if conventional, wisdom.

Both sides recognized the frequent need to compromise. Some of the deals thus struck dealt with matters of some importance. A remarkable instance was the decision that set the service-tunnel diameter. The construction contract specified that the service tunnel would be 4.5 meters in diameter. "On the British side," Reeve recalled, "we designed a four-and-a-half-meter tunnel because that was quite sufficient, in our view, to take all the services. On the French side they said, 'No-no-no-no-no, you've got to have five meters, because we need to get the earth-moving equipment in, and turn it round to build the cross-passages, all this sort of thing. We *have* to have five meters.'

"And we said, 'For Christ's sake, we can't build a bloody four-and-a-half-meter tunnel one side and a five-meter tunnel the other side.' We didn't want to increase the costs, and *they* said, 'Well, we can't afford to reduce the diameter.'" Reeve found that the French had done all their cost estimates on a five-meter tunnel.

"In the end *we* said, 'OK, why don't we reduce yours to four-point-eight meters, which you can live with, and we'll increase ours to four-point-eight

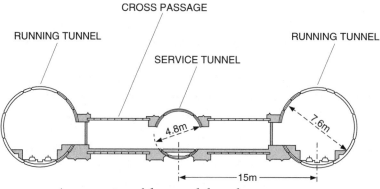

CROSS PASSAGE

RUNNING TUNNEL

SERVICE TUNNEL

RUNNING TUNNEL

4.8m

7.6m

15m

A cross section of the tunnel through a cross-passage.

meters, which we can live with, and the cost is the same as it would be with two different diameters," Reeve said. "And that is how the four-point-eight-meter tunnel came to be."

Where such compromise was impractical, national differences were simply ignored or papered over: The French portion of the tunnel was built to French codes; the U.K. portion was built to British standards. This was made simpler by the fact that there was nothing like a standard for tunneling practices in either nation. "I mean, had there been a French tunneling standard and a British tunneling standard," said Gordon Crighton, "I doubt if we would ever have started."

The Channel Tunnel, Jolivet thought, was in much too much of a hurry. It would have been far better and safer to allot twelve or even fourteen years to plan and build it, rather than seven. He knew this was impossible in a pri-

A cross section through a piston relief duct.

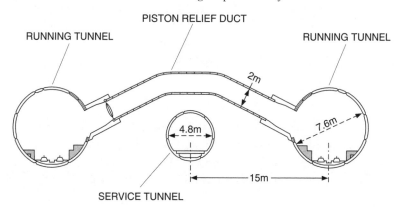

PISTON RELIEF DUCT

RUNNING TUNNEL

RUNNING TUNNEL

2m

4.8m

7.6m

15m

SERVICE TUNNEL

vately funded project, but that didn't affect the logic of his argument. He and
Reeve faced much the same problem as Eurotunnel itself: They had to create a complex administrative structure to oversee design and construction of
a project that was already well under way, gathering momentum as it rumbled
toward a critical deadline. David Brown was designing on the fly, making decisions that would be cast in concrete long before they were ever ratified by
Eurotunnel. If any of them had stopped, the project would have crushed
them and rushed on to disaster.

The whole cobbled-together structure now functioned like a hydraulic ram
to pressure TML. The banks and their consultants pressured Eurotunnel,
which passed the pressure along to Reeve and Jolivet. But Eurotunnel now
had Bechtel and the Project Implementation Division to critique everything
that TML did or suggested; they in turn had the full, even eager, support of
Morton and Bénard and a blunt tool in Durand-Rival.

"Starting from the beginning there was a big day-to-day dispute with Eurotunnel on the engineering and the transportation system," Jolivet said. "The
main reason related to our role as contractor: The contract said we're responsible for both engineering and construction, and we have to achieve the
performance described in the contract. It was an obligation of performance,
not the means of achieving it. But Eurotunnel decided that *it* must decide if
the way we were doing it was acceptable to them. They asked to review all of
the technical documents."

Eurotunnel saw things differently, of course. "One time, Jolivet asked me
if we could help," said Pete Behr. The request was for people that Bechtel
might know who could assist with cost control and project management.
Behr did not doubt that TML needed help. "I'd ask for manpower forecasts.
Jolivet would come up with something; Reeve would come up with zero.
They couldn't do these things."

By early 1988, Jolivet was convinced that the hostility between Eurotunnel
and Transmanche could wreck the whole project. "I said to some of the French
chairmen of the mother companies, 'We can't work with the two organizations
fighting each other. We have to merge Eurotunnel and TML,'" Jolivet said. "I
proposed that, but I wasn't authorized to go further, as the answer given to me
was: 'The people involved in this project are too numerous. . . . We have no
way, no possibility to change the contract.'"

Jolivet's perception about Eurotunnel's lack of trust was correct, Behr confirmed: Durand-Rival had concluded soon after he arrived that Jolivet and
Reeve were not up to building an advanced transportation system by themselves. Durand-Rival also wanted to deal with one person at TML rather than

the two directors-general. Eurotunnel pressured TML to install a single chief executive who would be responsible for all the contractors. The job fell to Andrew McDowall.

McDowall was not as harsh as many in his judgment of Durand-Rival. This was a generous act, because McDowall often bore the brunt of Durand-Rival's hammering. "Very few people at Eurotunnel trusted John Reeve," said McDowall. "John was perhaps a bit too quick on his feet and too intelligent for his own good. And then François Jolivet could wrap up Rival in the technical design side, so Rival didn't like him too much either."

For his part, McDowall had more to worry about than a truculent and demanding Durand-Rival. The French and English in TML might paper over their national differences, but there was no such simple solution to deal with the wide and deep differences among the ten companies. No amount of argument could persuade the companies to relinquish control to a single leader. "There was always the worry that if you got a lead contractor, the others would be out," McDowall said. McDowall tried in vain to point out to the British chairmen that naming a lead contractor would not in any way affect their profits or the project itself, since most of the work was to be done by subcontractors. (The exception was the railway electrical system, which was done as a joint venture by Spie Batignolles and Balfour Beatty, because of their wide experience with that sort of work.) His arguments fell on deaf ears.

This sniping and backbiting extended down through all levels of TML; one company or another was always complaining about a rival. "Same thing went on on the other side, except the French never talked to you," McDowall said.

Transmanche-Link's problems weren't restricted to the executive offices. David Brown was being asked to perform prodigies of design to satisfy the often contradictory goals of optimization and economy. Aerodynamic tests on one-to-twenty-scale models of the tunnel and its trains, long delayed by lack of money, had at last been carried out. They showed, to no one's great surprise, that the cooling system—removed from the tunnel plans months earlier to make the project's price tag more attractive to lenders—was going to be needed immediately. Without cooling, temperatures in the tunnel would soon approach an equatorial 55°C.

Design consultants came up with an extravagant solution. "Initially they came up with a number that looked like about £300 million," Behr recalled. "They were going to put hundreds, if not thousands, of air conditioning units in the tunnel." Maintenance, too, would be fabulously costly. Then someone calculated that chilled water running through ordinary pipes could do the job. The estimated cost was a mere £150 million, and Behr approved it. It was a rare victory of economy over cost.

The signaling system, as first imagined by the would-be builders of the tunnel, was to be a simple affair, quite like the trackside system that RTZ had designed for the 1974 project. While such systems were cheap and proven, they were hardly suited to the tunnel's dense mix of fast and slow trains. The 1986 Concession Agreement required an in-cab signaling system with some sort of control to stop a train automatically in case of danger. The agreement also specified that the system be able to control trains running at up to 160 kilometers per hour on three-minute headways—that is, running three minutes apart through the tunnels.

The Concession Agreement allowed for some delay in meeting these standards, as long as the signals as built could be upgraded in the future. There was a powerful incentive for TML to keep the cost low on this item: It was part of the lump sum, which meant that any cost overrun would come out of the contractors' pockets. "We only had, from memory, £22 million in the bucket for it," said Andrew McDowall.

There were, however, extremely powerful forces pushing for an enhanced signaling system. None of these was constrained by concern about the costs. The first was Eurotunnel, which naturally wanted the best possible system. With the cost fixed, Eurotunnel could demand the best that any amount of money could buy. Not surprisingly, it did.

Also interested was SNCF. In France, signaling technology had been carried along on the wave of innovation that had developed the high-speed TGV trains. Each new TGV line had carried the signaling technology further. The TGV Atlantique between Paris and Bordeaux used a system called the TVM300, the initials signifying *Transmission Voie Machine,* or track-to-train transmission. At its heart, this was simply an elegant elaboration of long-standard technology: A train entering a section of rail closed an electrical circuit flowing through the rails. In older systems, this set the trackside lights in adjoining sections of track, or blocks, to alert other trains. The new TGV systems fed more information—about speed, for instance—to signal rooms along the route, whence it was relayed, by radio transmission via the rail, to other trains. The information was picked up by the train and displayed in the engineer's cab.

When SNCF set out to build the TGV Nord line to link Paris with the Channel Tunnel, it ordered development of a still more advanced system, the TVM400. This was to be a technological leap to carry train signaling into the computer era. The rails would carry far more information and would carry it in digital form so that computers could use it directly to optimize performance.

Yet there were serious questions about the TVM400's suitability for the tunnel. It was, after all, designed to send occasional trains rocketing along dedicated rail lines that were uncluttered by freight or low-speed passenger trains. The Channel Tunnel environment would be filled with trains with very different capabilities of speed, acceleration and braking. These trains would be running three minutes or less apart, through a tunnel rail system that was part commuter subway, part freight spur, part high-speed through-train main line. In the French countryside, the TGV signal blocks were measured in kilometers, and the signal rooms that relayed information to the trains were fourteen kilometers apart. In the tunnel, the blocks would be five hundred meters long and there would be eighteen signal rooms—ten in the tunnels and four in each terminal.

One who foresaw problems with the signaling and train-control system was Joe Anderson. "A lot of that stuff was leading edge technology," Anderson said. "There were a few companies that were very expert in it; some in Sweden, some in Switzerland and France. But there wasn't a lot of it."

Anderson also foresaw a problem in convincing the Safety Authority that the system was suitable. "You can't institute a system until it's been proven," Anderson said. "It's not only got to be up and running, it's got to be proven. . . . That means it has got to be run on a reliable basis for a period of time. And there was no system anywhere in the world that was exactly like what were trying to do."

Anderson brought his observations to his superiors at Eurotunnel, with the suggestion that something be done to forestall a looming problem. But, he said, "We didn't get much encouragement from Eurotunnel; they felt they would rather stick with the contract as written." This was not the only time Anderson had tried—or would try—to address a problem before it arose. The response from Morton and Bénard here was typical.

"Their policy was not to tamper with the contract," Anderson said. "They were going to leave it, because that was their rock. They felt that was the strongest thing they had. Which is a typical banker's approach: 'Don't confuse me with the logic of what's got to be done; you signed this contract and by gosh we're going to make you honor it.'" Anderson said he wasn't against the contract: "All I was trying to point out was, here's a potential problem down the road that we're going to be fighting on on a financial basis. And even if they *had* agreed to do something, it would still have taken a lot of effort and time to resolve it."

TML asked four companies—one Swedish, one Italian, one German and one Anglo-French—for bids on the signaling system. This was TML's right and duty under the contract; the plan was to evaluate the four systems, invite bids from those judged acceptable, then choose a winner. The principle, David Brown said, was, "May the cheapest win, as long as it's technically acceptable."

Within Eurotunnel, there was only one system among the four that would be acceptable: the system that the Anglo-French company GEC-Alsthom was developing, not coincidentally, for SNCF: The TVM430. "Beginning in 1988, Durand-Rival was saying, 'You must go down this route for the signaling system. There is only one signaling that is right for this job,'" said David Brown.

Several people, within TML and without, saw the powerful hand of SNCF in Durand-Rival's preference. They also saw a larger plan to bring GEC-Alsthom in as a partner or prime contractor for TML. GEC-Alsthom was a powerhouse of a company, a fifty-fifty joint venture of Britain's General Electric Company and France's Alcatel Alsthom compagnie générale d'électricité. GEC is entirely separate from the General Electric Company in the U.S., but it played a similar role in bringing electricity to its homeland. The GEC-Alsthom venture, which had done key work in developing France's TGV trains, supplied a fifth of GEC's revenues.

"SNCF with its suppliers were quite clearly concerned about Swedish, German, Italian involvement in French territory," Brown said. "They saw an opportunity of breaking into the UK market, once they'd actually got the tunnel system installed around their technology: If the UK were to go for a high-speed line between London and the tunnel—or extend one onwards past London—logically, you would say, 'Well, we've invested all this money in these high-speed trains from London to Paris, all this in-cab signalling system. What do we want to have another signalling system for? We've got it all, just extend it through here.' A nice political-commercial maneuver: You've then got yourself a nice inroad into the UK."

"A lot of decisions on the transportation system were politically driven by SNCF," said John Noulton. "Decisions about signalling, trackform, et cetera, had more to do with the country they were built in than whether or not they suited the Channel Tunnel. The problem with the transportation system is it's a lump-sum contract, so Eurotunnel found it very difficult to get in among the details. They [SNCF] *did* get in, to influence the choice of those items."

Whatever SNCF thought, TML still held to its opinion that the signaling system would be chosen through competitive bidding, and TML was leaning toward a system proposed by a Swedish company that had entered the contest in joint venture with Spie Batignolles and Balfour Beatty. If their bid came in with the anticipated numbers, the Channel Tunnel would have TGV signals to the French portal, a Swedish signal system beneath the waters and British Rail's best railside signaling beyond. "The third party," said Brown, referring to SNCF, "was not happy."

Evaluation of the proposed systems nonetheless went forward, looking toward an invitation for bids from the various companies. Brown could not foresee that events were rushing toward quite a different destination: The signaling system would shortly become a famous controversy in this famously contentious project, the subject of a long, complex, very heated Clause 67 claim.

Clause 67 of the construction contract contained the agreed means by which intractable disputes between Eurotunnel and TML would be settled. These, it said, should be referred to a panel of experts. The panel would have a disinterested leader acceptable to both sides and a balance of partisan members—that is to say, members nominated by TML and Eurotunnel, from each side of the Channel.

The panel was to render decisions within ninety days (though this deadline was rarely met); these could be appealed to an arbitration panel whose decisions, guided by the rules of the International Chamber of Commerce, were final and binding.

In a better world, no contract would need a Clause 67. Even on this imperfect sphere, such clauses are little used on projects where sweet reason and compromise govern. To Pete Behr, the panel system set forth in the tunnel contract was stricter than many. "It's common to have some sort of pre-arbitration agreement, but I thought this one was a little more formal and complex than most. . . . This was something I hadn't run into before, and I didn't much like it," Behr said.

Behr, among others, had tried to keep the panel as far from the project as possible. He had served as chairman of the claims panel of the huge James Bay hydroelectric project in Quebec and knew that it was far better to resolve claims in the field than in a paneled office.

"I tried to map a disputes process that would minimize the need to use the panel," he said. "It had a lot of go–no go diagrams, so that things kept getting recycled." If the parties couldn't settle things among themselves, Behr hoped to be able to broker settlements—anything to avoid the panel. "The idea of the panel was to avoid arbitration," he said. "We tried to devise ways of avoiding the panel."

On the other hand, Clause 67 held considerable appeal for both Eurotunnel and TML. Eurotunnel saw it as a way of enforcing its demands for optimization and of slowing payments. The contractors saw it as an antidote to other hated provisions of the contract, particularly Clause 1.(2), which gave Eurotunnel broad powers to assign costs to TML, and Clause 7.(2), which Eurotunnel said gave it the right to demand optimization.

Clause 1.(2) said that no "addition admission or adjustment" would be made to the costs for anything that arose from a "wrongful act or admission ('WAO') on the part of the contractor his servants agents subcontractors suppliers of others for whom the Contractor is responsible."

The definition of WAOs, as they were thereafter called, was indeed very broad. A WAO was "any act, omission, mistake, error, fault or lack of care; or any circumstance amounting to a breach of the Contract; or any unreasonable conduct which would be actionable at law which a competent and experienced designer or contractor should not have allowed to occur or to be repeated." Roger Freeman, TML's chief lawyer, had never seen anything like it in British contracts and thought it smacked of French practice. Whatever its source, it offered Eurotunnel a formidable line of defense against any claims by TML.

For Freeman, the Clause 67 panel was the counterbalance to Clause 1.(2). "The panel is our remedy to it," he said, adding that its members functioned as "marriage guidance counselors rather than divorce lawyers."

The panel was not all that TML wished it were. Clause 67 required TML to keep working while the panel considered any conflict. Coupled with Eurotunnel's power under Clause 1.(2) to deny additional payments, this meant that TML had to keep working even if Eurotunnel withheld payment. In fact, everything conspired to press TML to keep working—even in matters such as the signaling system, which TML fervently believed to be a change for which Eurotunnel would have to pay. Working under protest might save the project, but it put TML in a progressively deeper hole: It had to continue paying its subcontractors to continue work. The more Eurotunnel withheld payment, the more the ten companies had, and were, at risk.

This ignited paranoid fantasies that had been smoldering within TML for months. Anderson said the companies felt that they might have to wait years to get, say, £8 million on a £10 million claim. While they waited, the £10 million sat on the books as a liability. If claims of this sort accumulated, he said, "It might be enough to tip the scale on a hostile takeover."

The contractors also had another dilemma: They were still shareholders in Eurotunnel, and the more they took out of it, the less their investment was worth. "It became a business question," Anderson said. "Was it better to try and safeguard the value of the project and maintain the equity in the stock, or was it better to try and get cash on the barrel for the work they'd done?"

Eurotunnel was far from immune to such fearful fancies; there was a genuine concern that the banks and contractors would conspire to drive Eurotunnel under and form a new company without the old shareholders. The banks wouldn't suffer, because they had a first lien on everything and could make a deal with the contractors to finish the project. All the banks would have to do would be to deny Eurotunnel the right to draw down its loans. Eurotunnel wouldn't be able to pay TML and would have to declare bankruptcy.

Given this fevered scenario, Eurotunnel's refusal to pay TML can be viewed as a defensive measure: Eurotunnel could (and did) withhold payments, arguing that the work or material was deficient. Such arguments could be dragged out over quite a long period of time—during which time Eurotunnel would be proof against financial assault by the banks and contractors.

So both sides found uses for conflict, and Clause 67 eventually came to govern the project to a degree that Behr and others found discouraging. "The whole project management came to be run along legalistic lines," Behr said. "Not good. Quantity surveyors were into everything. The contract was constantly quoted, constantly referred to. I've had jobs where I've never looked at the contract after it was signed." Here, he said, "Everybody kept reading the contract rather than looking for ways to make it work."

In late March 1988, the British Marine Service Tunnel TBM had struck bad ground. Water—a lot of water—was jetting into the tunnel, soaking everything, submerging the construction railway tracks that fed men and equipment to the TBM and removed tired men and excavated rock to the surface.

From the start of tunneling in December 1987, everything had gone as expected. "We started off driving, started off from the 1974 drive, which was done in perfect dry ground," said Gordon Crighton. "We had assumed that would have the same stuff."

For the first six hundred meters, the assumption held: The chalk marl held back the waters, and the TBM bored steadily ahead. It left its chamber beneath Shakespeare Cliff, heading northeast, edging offshore, then turning on a long arc to the right to head for the rendezvous with Brigitte. The machine was not far into this sweeping turn when water began pouring in.

Water itself was not a problem. Tunnels, even those under land, were wet; it was the dry tunnel that was rare. And going out under a large body of water required caution, so the worst-case scenario—a collapse at the face, a complete and sudden inundation—had governed Crighton's planning.

"We had pumping capacity," he said. "We carried with us two pipes, four hundred millimeters in diameter, all the way across. You don't do these things lightly. In other words, if there was inrush of water at the face, we could have pumped—and pumped like hell—until the guys were out. We carried these massive pipes with us, and massive pumping capacity, which we never had to use, thank Christ. If you're tunneling under water, by Christ, you're conscious of it every day in your life. You're aware of it all the time." Further, all of the electrical equipment in the tunnel was built to withstand immersion; everything was insulated.

But if it did not present a danger, water nonetheless did present Crighton with some very serious problems. One was overbreak, the tendency of the water-soaked layers of rock to break apart and fall into the tunnel behind the shell of the TBM. "If you get water coming through, it lubricates the rock and it makes it fall," Crighton said. "That's the problem—not the water itself." The overbreak wasn't minor. "Hunks of rock were coming down," Crighton said. "A lot of rock. Quite huge. I mean, there's photographs of a guy, six feet tall, standing in a four-meter-wide hole above the crown." Such rockfalls were a lethal hazard to the men who erected the lining rings, who worked outside the shelter of the TBM's shell.

Overbreak had been foreseen as a possible problem, and Crighton was ready to deal with it: Cast-iron rings could be bolted together in the shelter of the TBM's shell to take the place of concrete rings. But these were terribly costly in terms of both time and money. As Brown and Crighton had noted early in their planning, cast-iron lining was three times as expensive as concrete and took three times as long to install. Still, it would serve for any short stretch of bad ground.

Geologists had cautioned that water might have seeped down from the Channel here and there on the British side, collecting in pockets in the all-but-impermeable chalk marl. This was quite a different problem from the one faced by the French, who knew they would have to tunnel through badly fractured rock whose fissures were direct conduits to the Channel above, and who had designed their TBMs to deal with this. A pocket of water was a local phenomenon, a nuisance. Crighton fully expected to encounter pockets that might possibly extend for thirty meters along the tunnel's course.

So when the water first gushed, Crighton did not panic. As it happened, there was a simple test by which he could tell, with perfect accuracy, that what he had encountered was an isolated, finite pocket of water. All he had to do was scoop up a sample and taste it. Water that had seeped slowly down through the chalk to collect in a pocket would have lost most of its salt content by the time it reached the tunnel's depth. It would be about a tenth as saline as the water of the Channel.

Crighton tasted the water. It was pure seawater, as salty as the Channel above.

"We had never expected saline water *anywhere,* and we found this was 100 per cent saline," Crighton said. "We got a wee bit worried, quite frankly, because I knew it was being fed from the Channel. I also knew that we couldna' drain the Channel. We'd have had to drain the Atlantic, and the Pacific as well."

Still, all of the geologic evidence suggested that this was just a local phenomenon, a fluke produced by a small fault. "We built cast-iron and kept going. And . . ." At this point, Crighton paused, remembering the time with evident horror. "And . . . the wet patch *continued.* And it got worse. And worse. And there was a wee bit of despair set in, in the way of: *Are we ever going to get out of this? Is this what we're going to be going through for the rest of the tunnel?* Because if it was, there is no way we could have gone across to France with the machines we had. That was when we'd gone about two hundred meters in the broken ground and had put up cast iron, and there was despair."

It took geologists some years to come up with a good, satisfying theory of what the service tunnel had encountered. The upheaval that formed the Alps had wrinkled the earth's crust into a series of ripples that locally ran northwest-southeast, on or parallel to the tunnel's path. Dover and Sangatte are both on the edge of the same structure, the Axis of Artois, whose rocks date to the Jurassic period.

The geologists found, though, that the mountain-building did not produce only northwest-southeast structures; there was also wrenching that produced some north-south features. Geologists suspected that these features existed, but had never found evidence to support the theory until the TBM blundered upon it.

One of the north-south structures was a graben, a geologic formation produced when the crust stretches and cracks and a block of rock drops. In section, a textbook graben looks like a keystone that has half-fallen through the arch it supports. Here, the graben produced a trench in the shallow sea, which filled with chalk-marl sediments. After the passage of some millions of years, the crust moved again and pushed the graben closed. As the compression continued, the graben bulged upward and what had been a trench became a ridge. This stretched and cracked the sediments that had been laid down in the trench. Normally, the clay in the marl fills and seals cracks. But this upheaval was too great; the cracks remained cracks, as Crighton discovered to his dismay.

The water was under great pressure, and if it caused no danger it nonetheless did cause much discomfort. Among those who spent long shifts in drenched clothes was Helen Nattrass, the senior geotechnical engineer for tunnel construction, who headed a group of thirty geologists.

Nattrass was one of very few women who worked in the tunneling end of the tunnel project. She was short and sturdily built, with an owlish look and intensity to her gaze. She kept strangers at a distance with blunt speech and a keen, ironic wit until she was sure they would give her the respect she had earned rather than the hard time she too often received. Once they understood who she was, and accepted it, she relaxed. She came to be very warmly regarded. John Hamlen, a tough, high-ranking TML engineer, spoke admiringly of her as "a real peculiar lady—drinks beer, an expert on real ale, follows the horses, speaks about seven languages, plays just about every musical instrument there ever was." He recalled warning Nattrass, when she was being interviewed about the job, that the TBM's toilets were rudimentary and designed for the convenience of the male anatomy. She told him not to worry.

Geology was not Nattrass's first choice for a career. She would rather have been a musician—or, more accurately, she would rather have been a professional musician than the performing amateur that she was. She sang, composed and played viola in a string quartet. Her social life centered about music; it was through music groups that she found friends in Canterbury when she moved there from her native York.

But she saw that a life in music would require sacrifice and, perhaps more important, compromise. "If you want to be a performer, you have to realize that you're going to spend six to eight hours practicing a day," she said. "That's not taken into account, though; you only get paid for performing in public. And what are you going to perform? It's only what lesser mortals demand." She foresaw a lifetime of Handel's *Messiah* and years of Vivaldi's *Four Seasons,* and took up geology.

She went to work for TML in February 1987, after the boreholes had been drilled but six months before the Shakespeare Cliff work site opened.

"The first real job was proving wrong all the bright schemes dreamed up by all the boffins," she said. These schemes, dreamed up in laboratories by scientists who (she said) had had too long to think about them, included using radar and seismic testing in a fan of boreholes. "Brilliant if you've got the right conditions," she said. "Trouble is, the [seismic] difference between good chalk and useless chalk is almost nil."

Other boffins arrived in the tunnels with machines from their labs that required 240-volt current. Nattrass had to explain that in underground construction, 240-volt was used only for the permanent installations; for safety, all the working current was 110-volt, carried by yellow wires. (Permanent 240-volt work was blue; higher voltages, such as were used by the locomotives, were red.)

Gradually, with Nattrass's nudging, the emphasis swung to drilling the ground itself, with the drill rig that one day would be used to locate the oncoming French TMB for breakthrough. The purpose, of course, was to keep the tunnel in the twenty-meter-thick bed of the lower chalk marl.

Drilling had side benefits, too. The material from the holes spoke volumes about what lay ahead. When the sediments that made up the rock had been deposited, layer by layer in the ancient shallow sea, they included the bodies and shells of foraminifera, the tiny marine animals whose shells formed the chalk. The layers took on the character of the life that lived and died in the waters: Species flourished and faded, life teemed and ebbed. In time, the tunnel geologists could tell with very great precision where they were by remarking which of the ancient creatures they met. The ground was ideal for this; the layers were many and each had a distinct composition.

"We did an extremely detailed correlation of the micropalea through there," said one of the geologists. "We developed this as a method of controlling probe holes—forward probes on the TBM—because we found that just drilling blind, you'd no idea whether the probe had turned." The geologists examined the face and peered at the walls of the cross-passages and piston relief ducts to see what was there, micropaleontologically speaking. An intimate knowledge of the foraminifera allowed them to map the layers. Initially, this was a fairly crude sequence, drawn from relatively few samples. But as the tunnel progressed, accuracy improved. This satisfied the geologists, who were delighted to see their science put to the service of an undertaking where practicality governed. By checking the samples in the probe, the geologists could follow the path of the drillrod, deducing where it might have sagged. Eventually, they were able to say within a meter where a 330-meter-long probe had ended.

When the TBMs hit bad ground, the accumulated knowledge of foraminifera had more than doubled the length of the usual probes. Each 200 meters, when the TBM was shut down for a maintenance shift, they would drill 220 meters ahead—a distance that the machine could cover in about a week, under normal conditions. The work was "fast, rough and ready," Nattrass said. Here, "the only object was to find out if there was a catastrophic amount of water." The hydraulic drill rig was mounted on the TBM; the bit went through a gap in the cutting head and into the rock face, angling five degrees up to allow for sag during the drilling. Every so often they would drill down through the floor of the tunnel to find out how far above the Greensand they were.

"I remember the worst drilling shift," Nattrass said of those days when the tunnel was in bad ground. She had started work in the morning. A relatively inexperienced geologist was due to replace her for the night shift. She decided to stay.

" 'The water had been a little bit savage in the previous shift, and I thought to myself, 'He won't know what to do.' So I didn't go home. At about 4 am I was getting tired, so I thought to myself I'd get some rest. I went to the famous tea urn, then I went in the driver's cab and went to sleep.

"You know when you have a dream, and when you're waking up, what's outside comes into your dream? I kept thinking, dreaming about waterfalls. I woke up to see a jet of water zapping past."

The water was jetting through the hollow drill pipe. The custom was to measure the flow by letting the water run into a bucket that had a white line painted inside to mark thirteen liters, and timing how long it took to fill. This time, the jet was so powerful that the water splashed out of the pail. Nattrass and some tunnelers found an unoccupied set of oilskins and used the trousers as a sort of funnel, letting the water shoot down one leg and into the bucket.

"It was about three hundred liters a minute," she said. "But that was more an order of magnitude than an accurate measurement." The drillers stanched

The operator's cabin of a tunnel-boring machine.

the flow by putting a check-valve in a section of the drill pipe, and drilling continued—indeed, had to continue, because if it halted, the ground around the pipe would "relax" and trap the drill, making it impossible to remove so that the TBM could resume boring.

The TBM found better ground for a bit, then again ran into badly shattered rock that streamed water and broke overhead. Geologists could explain the overbreak—the rock had been laid down, millions of years ago, in layers that differed substantially in their composition, and these horizontal layers split off easily—but could offer no technical advice on how to solve the problem. The bad ground ran for a kilometer, then another, with no signs of improvement. The machine dove deeper into the seabed to try to escape the strata most given to overbreak; this helped but did not come close to eliminating the problems. TML was looking at the ruinous prospect of driving a cast-iron-lined tunnel to France.

"We kept soldiering on through this," said Crighton. "I mean, if this had been a traditional contract, quite frankly, we would have stopped. We would have said to the client, 'Right, pal, what next?' But *we* were doing the lot, so we said to ourselves, 'What next?' And of course we looked at maybe re-designing the lining, maybe redesigning the machine. . . . We looked at all sorts of things. Hell, we knew we couldna' go on with cast iron. We knew that it wasna' viable."

Something had to be done to permit the British tunnelers to use the con-crete lining rings in the bad patches of wet and breaking ground.

"Eventually the solution to the thing came from a guy that was working on the machine, a guy who was on the TBM," Crighton said. "He didn't come up with the ultimate [solution], but he came up with the original idea, which we developed."

The idea was to build stainless-steel "fingers" that would trail behind the TBM, in the ten-o'clock-to-two-o'clock arc. These would shelter the crew that erected the rings from overbreak. The fingers would be flexible, as they would have to be if the TBM were to be able to move ahead. As it happened, the fingers were not quite the thing. "We had pieces of rock falling between the fingers," Crighton said. "It wasn't too clever a thing to think, well, maybe we'd better put a sheet across the top." The result was a stainless-steel hood, thin enough to flex but strong enough to hold against overbreak, which served very nicely. It was not nearly as good as driving merrily through good ground—Crighton figured that it added at least 10 percent to the time it took to erect a ring—but it worked.

The success of the hood restored spirits marvelously. The ground got bet-ter for a time, then worse again. This time, though, there was no despair. In all, the bad ground ran for almost three kilometers, beyond which conditions were as good as had been hoped.

The French contractors did not gloat over these British troubles—their necks were in the same financial noose—but they could not resist taking some satisfaction from it. The French machines were designed to handle just the sort of conditions that halted the British service-tunnel TBM. The British machine *required* good ground. All of the British TBMs were simple machines, at least when they were compared to their French counterparts, which were basically tunnel-boring submarines, sealed against the intrusion of water. Philippe Montagner used the term "rustique" to describe the British machines. Given his feeling that the British were geared toward solv-ing problems only when they arose—rather than at the planning of the proj-ect—in the British TBM's problems, Montagner saw a vindication of French methods.

There were other differences, too, between the French and the British works. The French changed into their work clothes in a bright and spacious room called the *salle des pendus,* the hall of the hanged men. The name came from the storage system: Each worker had a chain that ran through a pulley in the high ceiling. Clothes and belongings were hung on the chain and pulled up to the ceiling; the chain could be locked at the floor. It was very space-efficient; it held a great many sets of clothes, each suspended like a felon from the roof beam, with none of the clutter of a locker room. From there the French workforce "jumped into a train that was carried down [the Sangatte shaft] on a huge elevator to a waiting loco-motive," Behr said.

In Britain, the men changed in locker rooms and lumbered down a labyrinth of adits and shafts, Behr said, each lugging a gas mask in case there was methane. "You would say that the British works were designed by Charles Dickens," Behr said. "The French [works] were designed by Jules Verne."

The Salle des pendus, *the hall of the hanged, where French crews stored their clothes.*

Andrew McDowall didn't argue with this view. "We go about it in a totally different way," he said of the two nations. "As Alastair Morton used to say to me, 'When I go to France, it looks as though it's organized. When I go down the British end, it looks a sheer bloody muddle. But I've no doubt the Brits will muddle through.' And that's precisely really what happens. I have to say that. The difference in the quality of approach, and of the temporary works, was unbelievable."

This should have surprised no one; the difference between the peoples had been noted long ago and ever since. The British propensity for wading rivers, and the French for seeking out bridges, had long been scrutinized. "For the Englishman, to understand is, in a way, to mingle more or less with the object which is to be understood," wrote Salvador de Madriaga, an astute Spanish observer of the various European characters, in 1928. "For the Frenchman . . . to think is to look with the eyes of the mind. And for intellectual vision, as for physical vision, there is a given distance which is the best possible one between the eye and the object."

British tunnel segments went underground by train.

French segments went underground by crane.

Indeed, the British did manage to turn their experience in the bad ground to the profit of the venture, and the French would soon enough find trouble of their own, despite all the planning.

At this point in the project the brilliance of having the service tunnel as a pilot hole for the main running tunnels—an idea that dated back to Charles Dunn's 1959 plan—was now fully revealed. The hard times that the service-tunnel TBM spent in the bad ground were a warning of what the running-tunnel TBMs could expect when they reached the same area. "This was always to be the tunnel where we found out what the ground was like," Crighton said. "We knew the running tunnels were going to come into the same ground, so we actually drilled across, ahead of the running tunnels, and injected grout." The cement-like grout sealed and healed the broken ground.

"It cost megabucks to do that kind of thing," Crighton said. "It was an operation we hadn't prepared for. But then, of course, when the running tunnel machines came through, they went through that ground beautifully, and it was a success."

Injecting the grout was a delicate and demanding matter. It required a special product, an epoxy that would penetrate the cracks and set hard under water. It had to be brought in dry, in "bullets"—the cylindrical railcars that carried dry grout and concrete down from the surface—and mixed at the TBM. It had to set fast, but not before it had penetrated the fractures in the rock through which the big running-tunnel TBMs would carve their 8.36-meter-wide passage. The pressure under which the grout was injected, like the setting time of the grout itself, could not err much on either side of an ideal: The pressure had to be sufficient to force the grout into the fissures, but not so powerful as to cause further damage to the rock.

Eurotunnel did not look on any of this with either pleasure or sympathy. Indeed, it seemed to Crighton that the client turned a blind eye to the problems. In a sense, Eurotunnel could not afford to acknowledge that there were problems with the tunneling, because the banks were worried and restive. Eurotunnel's ready money from the sales of its stock was running low, and it would soon need to draw down part of its loan. This wasn't unexpected; the Credit Agreement with the banks stipulated that drawdowns could start after July 1, 1988. The trouble was, an important number of important banks were saying that they wouldn't put up their money.

"There is a mechanism—and this is the bane of this project—a mechanism in this agreement which is a control measurement: the cover ratio," said Chris Deacon. "A cover ratio is a present-value relationship between a flow of income and a flow of costs. If the flow of income is greater than the flow of cost, you have a positive cover ratio."

Eurotunnel, of course, would have no flow of income until the tunnel opened for business. So the cover ratio (actually three cover ratios, related to bank debt, total debt and debt service) was calculated using revenue projections.

"The revenue forecasts were reported on and updated every six or so months, and [so were] the costs," Deacon said. "So every six months, effectively you got a new series of project economics. You fed them into the computer and you came out with a different number and you kept your fingers crossed." If the bank debt cover ratio slipped below 1.2, Eurotunnel couldn't borrow. If it slipped below parity—if projected revenue fell below costs—the loan would be in default, a far more serious matter that would permit the banks to take over the project and substitute another owner for Eurotunnel.

Unfortunately, crossed fingers hadn't been effective in stopping a steep increase in inflation and real interest rates. This was the worst-case scenario that Eurotunnel dreaded: Inflation would drive up construction costs; rising interest rates would increase the cost of borrowed money. It meant, Deacon said, that "there was a risk that the cover ratio was going to be breached for first drawdown, and the banks were flexing their muscles."

The cover ratio wasn't the only ground upon which the banks could refuse to fund the loans; the credit agreement also included a list of "conditions precedent" that had to be met before any drawdown. Tunneling problems meant that certain milestones would be missed. Further, the banks' advisers had to be satisfied that design work on the tunnel had reached a reassuring level and that TML had a program to build the tunnel at the cost and within the time specified in the construction contract.

At this time, as spring gave way to summer, the tenuous client-contractor relationship between Eurotunnel and TML went to pieces. Distrust became hatred, anger became fury. "You could feel pressure building through '88," said Jolivet. "Individuals in Eurotunnel and TML got along pretty well. But the institutions did not."

Roger Freeman, the TML lawyer, felt that the vitriol was restricted to the highest executive levels of each organization. At most levels, he said, the Eurotunnel-TML relationships were professional and good. But the top level, he said, was something else entirely. "I don't think I've ever seen the level of antagonism I've seen here," he said.

Morton had access to one weapon that was denied TML: the press. The construction contract, in a section that covered copyrights and confidentiality, said that TML could not "impart to any publication, journal or newspaper or any radio or television programme any information relating to the Works" without prior written approval from Eurotunnel. In Morton's hands, this became a gag; TML's voice was not heard for years in the public debate about the Channel Tunnel. Morton's voice, on the other hand, *was* heard—he raised it often, often in anger, and brought it down upon TML with punishing force.

McDowall, stung by a particularly harsh article about TML's management problems—an article he believed was either written or planted by Morton—notified Morton that he was going to give a public reply.

"Morton said, 'Under Clause nine, bracket three, you know quite well you're not allowed to make any public statements without my clearance,' and that was true," McDowall said. "An untenable position as far as I'm concerned. I said, 'Well, I'm going to.' He said, 'I'll have you removed if you do,' or words to this effect. He then confirmed that with a fax, straightaway, about quarter to four in the evening. The fax read, 'Reference our conversation earlier this afternoon, I confirm that you only can make a public statement if you confirm you're going to finish these tunnels on time.'

"So I sent that straight off to the newspapers and the television, I was so browned off and fed up with the way he was behaving. So it came up on all the screens. 'Dear Andrew . . . Alastair Morton,' with those few words. Morton went up through the bloody ceiling. The banks got very upset with me . . . nevertheless, I shut him up. I'll tell you, he didn't do that for a little while afterwards."

The banks, particularly the European banks that had been hard-liners in the negotiations over the construction contract, were horrified by this relentless bickering. Something was needed to persuade the banks that Eurotunnel and TML could cooperate—or be forced to cooperate—to complete the project.

The mechanism was to be a truce between the warring parties, set down first in a formal Memorandum of Understanding, to be followed, before the end of January 1989, by a yet more formal Joint Accord. Although these appeared to be an armistice and a treaty between the warring parties, they were in fact elements of a peace brokered and dictated by the banks.

Chris Deacon and Pierre Coindreau, with a few colleagues from the other key banks, created the accord. "If Eurotunnel was going to draw down, Eurotunnel had to have an agreement with TML on project progress and organization—which at that stage didn't exist. Things were going wrong at that stage," Deacon said. "Rather than having the banks instruct, we always tried to give Eurotunnel the strength."

The first step, Deacon said, was to get the banks to agree in principle to put up the money. As before, the toughest banks were German and Swiss; Deacon decided to go around them and deal with the Japanese banks.

"I thought—bearing in mind our experience with the Germans—that the way to deal with drawdown was: Why pick up with the hard boys first? What we really should be doing is to pick up the softies—which term I used; there was a perception that the Japanese were very keen to lend money at that stage," Deacon said. "So it seemed to me that the simplest way to approach drawdown was to do a deal with the Japanese, and then to dare the difficult Germans and Europeans to go against what the Japanese were set to do.

"So I went out to Japan, uninvited. Normally with the Japanese you have to be invited, and they make a fuss; this time I just went to them. And I did a deal with a chap at Sanwa, a chap named Moriwaki, who has since had, proverbially, to fall on his sword over this job. . . . I liked the guy, and we did a deal. We sorted it out. It's very unlike the Japanese, actually, but anyway we did this deal. And he said, 'Leave it to me; I'll sell it to the other banks.' "

It took three more visits to Japan to cement the deal, but it held up, and the other banks bought it. It said that the banks would allow the draw to take place, but the proceeds would be held by the banks in a special account. "The banks were transferring money from one pocket into the other, and drawings were only permitted from that fund when certain conditions were met," Deacon said.

The documents that supported the Memorandum of Understanding bear evidence of the fevered haste with which the agreement had to be cobbled together. When details were presented to the central group of banks, at a September 1 meeting in Midland Bank's theater, nine letters from the banks' technical adviser were offered; each said that a certain condition precedent had been met, or that reasonable progress had been made toward that end. All of the letters were signed by the same person and dated August 30—two days before the banks' meeting.

On the surface, and perhaps to some little depth, the deal was attractive to both Eurotunnel and TML. Eurotunnel would get its money; TML got a one-month extension, to June 15, 1993, to complete the work. If that deadline was met, TML would receive a £40 million bonus and all liquidated damages would be reimbursed. In addition, all of the milestone dates were pushed back a few months, and seven new supplementary milestones were added. TML would receive a £2 million bonus each time it met one milestone. These, said Pete Behr, were incentives to TML and were designed to be met.

More satisfying still: Both sides agreed on management changes. What this meant in practice was that each side was able to get rid of a hated member of the other. TML chose Durand-Rival; Eurotunnel chose McDowall. Neither would leave immediately, but neither would have much to say after the Joint Accord was signed in January 1989. TML believed that the project was being ruined by too much oversight and that the removal of Durand-Rival would ease this problem. Eurotunnel felt that TML suffered from inept management that had shared its power among too many people; McDowall could be replaced by a chairman in whom more power could be united. Both sides felt that some of the venom would be drained out of the relationship.

Nothing could have been more reassuring to the banks than the men who were chosen to replace McDowall and Durand-Rival. Tony Ridley, who resigned from London Underground as a public gesture after the Kings Cross fire, would become Eurotunnel's managing director. Philippe Essig, Ridley's longtime friend in the world of mass transit, would become chairman of TML.

In this case, the incestuousness that lay like a guilty secret at the heart of the project promised to engender genuine amity. Both men were esteemed by both sides. Both had sat on Eurotunnel's board—Ridley since October 1987, Essig since April 1988—and Morton had actually put Ridley forward as a candidate to lead TML.

"In the summer of '88, I met Alastair and Sarah Morton at Festival Hall," Ridley recalled. Morton began telling Ridley that he had to join, and Ridley had begun to demur, when Morton cleared things up.

"I want you to join TML," he told Ridley. "I've spoken to Frank Gibb [the chairman of Taylor Woodrow and a Eurotunnel board member] and he knows he has to make changes."

Ridley had a series of meetings with Gibb and Sir Clifford Chetwood, Wimpey's chairman, who acknowledged that TML management needed an overhaul. Then Essig's name came up, and there was some discussion about having Ridley and him serve as joint chairmen of TML. "Philippe said *non*," Ridley recalled. "There would be only one chairman and it would be he."

Three days before Christmas, Morton and Bénard invited Ridley to breakfast at the Goring Hotel. They offered him the managing director's job at Eurotunnel, he accepted and all shook hands. Morton and Bénard then left for vacation: the former to Africa, the latter to the South of France.

Gibb called Ridley the next day. He apologized for the fact that things had taken so long, then invited Ridley to join TML.

"Bloody hell, Frank, I can't," Ridley told him. "I've just agreed with Alastair and André to be MD [managing director] at Eurotunnel." Gibb called Bénard, who confirmed that Gibb was a day late with the offer. So Ridley stayed with Eurotunnel, where he would be joined shortly by Alain Bertrand, an SNCF engineer who became managing director for technical matters. Essig agreed to lead TML, and a search began for a technical man to oversee construction.

Essig had a formidable résumé. He was a *polytechnicien,* and also a graduate of the elite École nationale des ponts et chaussées. He had spent ten years running and building railroads in Africa. In 1966, he returned to France to work for, and eventually head, the RATP, the rapid-transit system for Paris. He had spent the four years before he came to TML as chairman of the board at SNCF and, in the last year, as France's secretary of state for housing. When he joined TML, he was fifty-five years old. He was accessible and friendly by nature and cultured in manner. He believed that a spirit of cooperation could save the Channel Tunnel from the worst of its difficulties.

There was an element in the Memorandum of Understanding of peculiar significance that Eurotunnel grasped and TML did not. The Memorandum contained a series of conditions, dealing with progress in completing the work, that would have to be met. If they were not, the banks could declare the contract in default. In that event, the banks would own the project: Construction would cease for lack of funds, the concession from the governments would be withdrawn, and the banks could substitute an entity of their own choosing to be concessionaire.

Or so it seemed. In fact, the conditions imposed by the Memorandum of Understanding were not quite as absolute as they were meant to seem.

"I can remember getting summoned to the Eurotunnel board on one occasion and grilled on the meaning of this," Deacon said. The Memorandum, he told the board, "looked like a legal constraint, and it was designed to look like a legal constraint. But if you read the small print it wasn't."

With a full understanding of the Memorandum, Eurotunnel could hold it over TML's head and summon the specter of default. "The conditions were used as a weapon by Eurotunnel in order to get what they wanted from contractors," Deacon said. "That's effectively the way the project has been managed ever since."

13

Philippe Essig arrived at TML with a broad, even Olympian understanding of the Channel Tunnel project, and almost no idea of the nature or depth of its problems.

He knew that the Railways Usage Contract was unfair, because he had been chairman of SNCF when the original version was signed. He knew the main players—indeed, the good quality of his relationship with Morton and Bénard recommended him for the job. He understood Eurotunnel's management problems and the unusual role of the banks. He understood the client-contractor relationship as it existed in France, and how it differed in Britain.

All this he knew when TML approached him in November 1988 about his becoming chairman. He was to discover, with Ridley, that however much they strove to change the future, they could not change the past; that change and warm feelings were easy to command but impossible to compel. The ink was hardly dry on the Memorandum of Understanding when the past again asserted its power: Morton lashed out at TML in a public statement, saying, "We don't have a tunneling problem, we have an equipment and management problem." The contractors, in turn, released damaging information about overruns in the target costs.

This skirmish made Essig's diplomatic mission far more difficult when he assumed his official duties on January 11, 1989. Five days later, TML and Eurotunnel signed the Joint Accord with a public display of affection that certainly helped repair the damage caused by TML's rash release of bad numbers. The investing public, reassured by the sight of contractor and client agreeing to cooperate, pushed Eurotunnel's share price steadily higher.

Insiders saw evidence of a very different sort. Essig quickly found that the accord might not guide all future relations between Eurotunnel and TML. At his earliest meetings with Morton and Bénard—usually over a simple lunch of sandwiches in Bénard's office in Eurotunnel's headquarters, which adjoined Victoria Station—it was agreed that McDowall would of course leave the scene. Essig argued that this should be done after a decent interval of a few months, after public attention wandered and Essig learned about the organization he was to lead.

Essig received no direct feedback and concluded that McDowall's sacking would receive the low priority he thought it merited. Instead, it was brought up—unexpectedly, Essig felt, and treacherously—at a February meeting attended by the agent banks. Morton warned that he wouldn't make Eurotunnel's monthly progress payments to TML if McDowall remained. The Agent Banks supported this stance. McDowall was duly shunted to a post that had no say in how the project was run. He remained there another nine months, helping Essig when and where he could.

Essig soon found that there was a much more serious problem than bad blood between the parties. McDowall had warned that optimization of the fixed equipment was driving costs up at a dangerous pace. David Brown recalled McDowall saying, at a meeting in mid-1988, "Unless you do something about it, the cost could potentially go up by £500 million." This was a fantastic number: The original lump sum was hardly more than £1 billion, and the market capitalization of all ten contracting companies combined was about £6.6 billion.

All through February and March, Essig—who had never heard McDowall's dire prophecy—accumulated evidence that cost overruns on the transportation system were indeed far more serious than he had imagined. To his horror, Essig found that costs had soared to levels that threatened TML, Eurotunnel and the project itself with utter ruin. It took until late March for him to grasp the actual sum of his problems: The lump-sum costs, he found, had risen just as McDowall had predicted, by about £500 million. If these costs were to go unpaid—and there was nothing in the contract that would force Eurotunnel to accept them—each of TML's member companies was looking at a catastrophic loss.

Why and how had this happened? In the first place, the Joint Accord had solved the wrong problem. "There was no special concern about the drift in costs," Essig recalled, "only concern about the slow progress of the TBMs and the possible delay in finishing the project. The Joint Accord was oriented to the problem of delay."

There was reason enough to fear delay: A lost month could cost Eurotunnel £100 million in lost revenue and additional interest; that same lost month could cost TML a substantial amount of money in liquidated damages under the contract. So the Joint Accord concerned itself with time: The contractors asked for a six-month extension; they got one month, with bonuses to offset penalties that the inevitable six-month delay would bring. Essig thought it a fair and workable accord—for the problem of construction time. "But in fact the biggest problem, the biggest issue, wasn't addressed," he said. "It was a terrible mistake."

It is nonetheless difficult to imagine an accord that could have solved the Channel Tunnel's cost problems at the stroke of a pen. As Essig was soon to appreciate, they sprang from several sources and ranged from the obvious to the most subtle. Great changes had wrought much havoc, but so, too, had very minor ones. Changing the signaling system, for instance, added tens of millions of pounds to the lump sum, but even tiny changes in specifications had had profound effect. A heavier bracket in the tunnel wall might require larger screws to hold it in place. The per-unit cost of such tinkering could be measured in pennies, but the aggregate cost of thousands of brackets and fifty million screws could be enormous.

Further, the project had acquired a dangerous, irresistible momentum. Eurotunnel seemed powerless to resist the Intergovernmental Commission; TML could not argue Eurotunnel's demands. Each of these grave problems derived from single bad decisions, Essig thought: Eurotunnel had not resisted the incursions of the IGC—as it came to be familiarly if not affectionately known—and TML had continued to work even when Eurotunnel withheld payment. "When you work for the London Transport or the Paris transport authority, or SNCF, at the end of the day they pay—they pay the additional costs. They pay because there is no limit to public funding," Essig continued. "In their [the contractor's] minds it was impossible to believe that the owner would not pay for the additional costs. They had no resistance to changes in the design. You have to see that there was no counterforce to limit the costs. None. Every force was pushing in the same direction: '*Oh, you want it bigger? Why not?*'"

Everywhere he looked, Essig saw examples of rampant growth in the project. "Eurotunnel, through the process of optimization, obliged TML to design the power system to be able to run the trains in any situation which could appear in the future," Essig said. "And so the power capacity of each station, in Coquelles and Folkestone, was increased from one hundred to two hundred megawatts. To give you a comparison, two hundred megawatts is the totality of the power required by the RATP, the Paris transit authority. This is the *entire* RATP, including the RER, the rapid transit." Essig laughed ruefully at the numbers: The RATP ran about six hundred trains simultaneously during peak hours; the RER ran an additional one hundred or so.

Still, Essig had reason to hope that the friendly spirit of the Joint Accord might help. He had already established a good working relationship with Tony Ridley, who shared his view that cooperation was vital to a project's success.

Philippe Essig.

Ridley was fond of pointing to his experience in building the Hong Kong mass transit railway. "If you talk to anyone who ever worked on it, whether they were government, employer, consultant, contractor or banker, they will all tell you it was the greatest project in the history of the world," he said. "There was a great spirit of cooperation; there was a tremendous spirit of achievement. That's where I developed for myself the concept that owners and contractors either win together or lose together. There has never ever been a successful project where one side won and the other side lost."

The first meetings buoyed the hopes of both men.

"The first thing I recall doing was going away to some hotel on Wimbledon Common—my senior guys and his senior guys—to sit down and say, 'Look, the root of the issues here are arguments, rows, indecisions, unhappiness, uncertainties about the transport system design. Let's sit down and thrash through the issues,'" Ridley recalled.

This thrashing-out ignored the tunneling problems, which frightened the bankers far more than anyone else. "Almost every tunneling that's ever been has problems at startup and goes like the clappers toward the end," Ridley said. "The problem is that history doesn't give confidence, and bankers who've got a hell of a lot of money at stake are not easily convinced that that's the way it's going to work out."

The real problem, Essig and Ridley agreed, was the transportation system. "The transportation system was always at the heart of the project, and therefore at the heart of the problems with the project," Ridley said. He and Essig formed an executive committee, agreed to regular meetings, agreed to share or alternate the chairman's role. The guiding principle was simple, Ridley said: "We're all in this together."

So when Essig brought the bad news of the £500 million cost overrun, he had reason to hope that he and Ridley could arrive at some agreement that would preserve all parties and the project itself from disaster.

Ridley, at least, did not disappoint him. He was shocked by the size of the problem, but did not waver in his resolve to make things work.

"Philippe wanted to put some realities on the table," Ridley said. "I was of a mood to hear realities. The difference between Philippe and I and the others was not that we were better or worse than them, but that we were new boys, and neither of us was personally committed to what had been said before. And I have always believed that you can never run a successful project by kidding yourself. I understand the legal ramifications, the contractual ramifications, the negotiating ramifications. But if you kid yourself, you're in the shit."

The trouble, said Ridley, was that Eurotunnel believed that the lump sum preserved it from any increase in costs. He referred again to his experience on the Hong Kong project, where every civil engineering contract had a 10 percent contingency, every electrical and mechanical contract included a 7.5 percent contingency. Beyond these cushions was a further 5 percent contingency. "That's the way I'd done it, and the way I thought it should be done," he said. But there had been no such thinking about the Channel Tunnel. When Ridley asked about contingencies, he was told that there were none.

Ridley asked how this could be. The response he got was, "If we admit there is any contingency, those bastard contractors will have it from us."

This posture was most rigid when it came to the tunnel's fixed equipment. The logic was that a lump sum by definition excluded any extra payments. Why should there be contingency funds when a contingency could not exist?

"Well, you don't need to go very far, or talk to many people who have run big projects, to find some people who would disagree with that view," Ridley said. "Even in the best-run circumstances, owners *do* have to make decisions, after they've started, that have cost ramifications. But the whole spirit in the existing [Eurotunnel] organization—and these are not wicked people I'm talking about—was: 'These bloody contractors will do us if we blink. So don't admit anything . . . they're not going to get a penny more than *they* calculated—not we, *they* calculated—when they won the concession. They're not *our* estimates, they're bloody TML's estimates.' "

Essig sat down with Ridley, Morton and Bénard in an informal meeting and set forth the bad news. Eurotunnel's response was as swift as it was predictable.

"Ridley, under the instructions of his board, asked me to guarantee the lump sum," Essig said. "That was the start of the second part of the war." Essig continued to discuss the contract with Morton and Bénard through April and May, but Eurotunnel continued to assert "that the contractors would have to take the consequences," Essig said. "Eurotunnel refused to negotiate to solve the problem. It was a very big disappointment."

None of this affected the excellent performance of Eurotunnel stock, which continued to rise in price. The shares had come to the marketplace at 350 pence and, after slipping in price to below 300 pence for a time, rose to more than 500 pence per share by the fall of 1988. The publicity surrounding the Joint Accord—Ridley and Essig were photographed toasting each other in wine and beer—offered further encouragement; the shares more than doubled in price, to nearly 1,100 pence, by the time Essig had made his disturbing report and received his discouraging answer.

Nonetheless, the shares held steady, for the simple reason that the stock markets did not know of the new turmoil that now threatened the project: The investing public was fed only a steady diet of good news and cheery projections about the Channel Tunnel's profitable future. In October 1988, Eurotunnel had released new traffic and revenue predictions that were substantially more encouraging than those from July 1987 and from the 1985 Submission to Governments. Eurotunnel now expected £580 million in revenues in 1994, rather than the £538 million it had foreseen in July 1987. The 37 million passengers that the Submission to Governments had predicted for the year 2003 had jumped to 41.3 million.

To be sure, these encouraging numbers were rather more sober than others that some of the project's adherents had brandished through the decade. A September 1987 report from Warburg Securities, the lead broker advising Eurotunnel on Equity 3, had predicted that the shuttle alone would bring in £836 million in the year 2003; Eurotunnel's 1988 study put it at a mere £454 million. The 1984 Five-Bank Report had been even more hopeful; its base-case forecast had put Eurotunnel's total revenues for 1993 at more than £1.6 billion (in 1984 funds); Eurotunnel now thought it might be around £873 million in 1988 funds.

As Essig strove to breach Eurotunnel's stony defense of the lump sum, Joe Anderson received a call from Jack Lemley, an American construction engineer whose considerable skills included an ability to win claims on major projects. Lemley had left the corporate world of the big engineering firms a short time before and set up his own consulting business in his native Idaho.

"I was doing a job for the Nationalist Chinese government in Nepal when an executive search firm called my office in Boise and said they were trying to find a candidate for CEO of the Channel Tunnel," Lemley said. "When I called in from Katmandu, in from the bush, I didn't believe the message. So I finished what I was doing and got back about two weeks later. There was a stack of messages. So I returned the call."

He received assurances from the headhunter that TML was indeed looking for a chief executive, and that he was a candidate. Lemley then called Anderson.

"Is this job for real?" he asked.

"Read me the description," Anderson said, and Lemley complied.

"Yes, that job exists all right," Anderson said. "It's the one Andrew Mc-Dowall has right now."

Anderson, despite a twinge at what he felt might be a conflict of interest, encouraged Lemley to take the job because he knew tunneling, as Jolivet and Reeve did not.

Lemley fit the image of a big-job engineer: He was tall and rugged, direct in speech, accustomed to command and entirely comfortable with it. He shook hands with a powerful but controlled grip and regulated his language in much the same way: When a situation called for politeness and tact, his speech was mild. When circumstances demanded something more persuasive, he had the necessary reserves. If he did not always find it easy to like the people with whom he worked, he nonetheless loved the work itself.

A formative event in his career came when he was working for Guy F. Atkinson and Company on the New York City Water Tunnel Number Three in the early 1970s. An engineer friend lost his touch or nerve and was treated badly by Atkinson, Lemley said. He was given a string of bad jobs and finally committed suicide. Lemley thereupon saw the true danger in his work and decided he would never let the job get to him.

The interviews that brought him to the Channel Tunnel were representative of the project as a whole—that is to say, divided along national lines and not terribly well organized.

"I came over and was interviewed over a five-day period by each of the five British chairmen," Lemley said. "At the end of the week nobody said anything to me; Pam and I—my wife—we had theater tickets. We went to the theater on Friday night; Saturday we got on the plane and went back to Boise. When we arrived there on Sunday, there was a message that the French chairmen wanted to talk to me. So I got on a plane on Monday and arrived in Paris on Tuesday, was interviewed by the five French chairmen individually. That took about three days. Then they decided they would offer me a job, but they wanted me to go through some psychological testing. So I came back to London and I went through a couple of days of psychological testing. Then I negotiated a contract with them and went back to Boise, hired a couple of people to take over my clients and was back here seven days later."

The psychological testing seemed designed to find out, Lemley said, "if I had enough steel in my spine to stand up to the problems." He did a little testing of his own, questioning his interviewers about the project. "I wanted to know about control systems, project management, project control, sched-uling, cost control, accounting—all the business and management systems that it takes to run a project like this," Lemley said. "I extracted different an-swers from each of them, so I knew damn well they didn't know what was going on here in detail. They had an overview of it but they didn't know what kind of control systems were in place across the project; they didn't have a good picture of where the project was. So I had a pretty good idea of what to expect when I got into the job."

When Lemley joined TML in May, the project was about a year behind schedule. He detected no sense of urgency. "In engineering, people were not trying to firm up designs and build things," he said. He did two things imme-diately: He reorganized his management structure, and he ordered a zero-based budget on the entire project, which took the original cost estimates, added all subsequent changes, projected future costs and came up with a new overall estimate. The management changes were painful for many; the budget study—the first since the project began—was shocking to almost everyone.

Jolivet and Reeve were removed as directors-general. Lemley felt that both were very capable; what was lacking was a commonality, a rapport, anything synergistic. This was a terrible blow to Reeve and Jolivet, and though Lemley offered them jobs near the pinnacle he now occupied, both chose to leave.

Daniele DeMori Calderon, a Frenchwoman who was Jolivet's assistant, said that when he was forced out, "it was terrible. He [Jolivet] didn't even come to say goodbye." Calderon, a shrewd judge of character and a keen ob-server of the internal politics of TML, recalled a bitter comment Jolivet made in the troubled days before his departure. "The French want to complete the project," he said. "The English want to make money." For years afterward, Lemley sent word through Pierre Matheron, inviting Jolivet to attend cele-bratory events. Jolivet never came.

Reeve had impressed even his enemies with his devotion to the project. To Andrew McDowall, it was all inevitable. "I knew when I took this on that if I made it halfway through, that would be it," said McDowall. "I said it to every-one. John Reeve never accepted it; John Reeve thought he was there for the whole thing and probably would get a knighthood or something out of it." Reeve stayed on as a part-time consultant to TML.

Lemley's arrival, and the departure of some of the original leaders, changed the personality of the project. Lemley made a powerful impression on the staff who remained. Calderon, who stayed to assist Jolivet's successors, found him "very particular, hard to work for. And, my God, he can be so deadly! When he says something he means it, and when he has someone in to talk to them, his choice of words is so, so . . . *what he says has the impact of a machine gun.* He is lonely, the way Jolivet was lonely: He can't trust anyone but himself. For the French, it is hard for them. He isn't particularly warm."

Lemley did not order a bloodbath; his chief concerns were about systems rather than people. "The management systems on the French side were not what I would like to have seen, but they were able to manage the project with them, and they were coherent, one system to another," Lemley said. "But they didn't interface with the systems being used in Britain, and there was no overall plan."

Shortly after he arrived at TML, Lemley pulled the computer lists that showed who had been in the tunnels and found that he had been down in the tunnel more often in his few weeks on the job than either John Winton, the U.K. construction director, or John King, director of U.K. tunneling. Lemley fired Winton. "I wanted to fire King also," he said, "but I couldn't wipe them all out without losing the whole organization."

The problems were concentrated in the British management organization. "There was no doubt we had the technical capabilities in the engineering department, and the construction capability in the construction phase," Lemley said. "But we simply didn't have the engineering management that could properly pull the engineering together. . . . I discharged five or six people who were senior managers for the UK operations and replaced them, and in the engineering group I guess I made three changes."

All of the management changes were on the British side. Lemley was impressed by the French operation, particularly with the two people at its head, Pierre Matheron and Jacques Fermin, the assistant construction director in France. Fermin, he said, "was absolutely first-class. His work was flawless."

Lemley was much taken with Matheron's approach to the work. During one of his first visits to the French site, Lemley wanted to go down in the tunnel to look at something. Matheron offered to accompany him; Lemley said he needn't bother.

Matheron's response was, "No, I haven't been in the tunnel for about a week. You know, you really have to look the crew in the eye to know how they feel, how they're reacting. And it's time: I really should go back down in the tunnel."

Down at the heading, Lemley said, "He worked his way through the whole machine: Stopped and talked to people. And he and Jacques Fermin impressed me as having a very intimate relationship with their crews. They knew what the crews were doing, and what they were thinking and how they were working. That was not the case on the British side." The management systems on the U.K. side, he said, were entirely inadequate.

On the French side, Lemley's was a personal reaction to men with whom he felt comfortable and with whose aims and methods he was in sympathy. But the skills and organization he so appreciated were hardly infallible. Like their British confreres, the French sometimes created problems for themselves. Self-generated troubles are usually the most difficult to correct, and French touchiness effectively barred any British assistance.

McDowall had had concerns about French grouting procedures from the start—when the French TBM pulled ahead, it left a gap between the tunnel bore and the lining that had to be filled—but found it very difficult even to investigate. Good grouting was crucial because it made a strong single structure of rock, grout and tunnel lining. Without grout, the tunnel segments would rattle around in the TBM cut like loose teeth.

"The important [segments] were the ones under the bottom, which were going to take a hundred million tons of bloody traffic a year," McDowall said. "I made them drill holes through the unit, and so did Joe Anderson, and we found just bloody nothing underneath 'em. So that was a big problem. I said, drill holes through every other one; I want to make absolutely certain. There was almost a riot in France."

This was not the only and not nearly the worst problem in the French works. There was a serious lack of progress in the early days: The French Marine Service Tunnel TBM went only fifty meters in its first three months of work; at the end of a year it had gone only a kilometer. Questions from the British side of TML and from Eurotunnel were turned aside. The service-tunnel TBM had difficulty with its slurry-pumping system, according to Jolivet. "It was necessary to extract chalk with water," he said. "In terms of cooking it was a good texture, but not in terms of working with it in the tunnel."

Then the big running-tunnel machines seemed to be having problems. In both cases, the French refused to let the TBM manufacturers send their representatives down to the machines. Eventually Anderson forced an entry and found that the French had fitted the cutting head with picks that were too short; they were grooving the chalk rather than breaking out chunks of it. It was easily solved by replacing the picks with longer ones; the delay had been unnecessary.

The French reacted in similar fashion, shortly after Lemley arrived, to a nearly catastrophic problem with their big marine running-tunnel machines. The machines were designed to operate under the ten atmospheres of pressure that were expected in the broken ground near the French shore. They were equipped with thruster rams capable of pushing against the face at that pressure, but on the way down to that extreme the French drove them against the face at full force. The cutting heads weren't able to withstand this pressure and the ends of the arms that carried the picks bent back about four inches.

The French again were reluctant to let anyone but their people look at the machines. "We had to go in and strengthen the heads, and we had to lighten the loads on them," Anderson said. "We started grouting ahead of them from the service tunnel." The result was a three-month delay, but Anderson noted that it might have been far worse. "They were lucky they didn't have a failure that would have forced them to remove the whole machine, because that really would have been catastrophic," he said.

Anderson was so concerned with the French refusal to cooperate that he considered trying to get Matheron fired from the project. Behr talked him out of trying. "I told him, 'Forget that, Joe, because he's too strong. And you'd be wrong.'" So Matheron stayed as Reeve and Jolivet departed. With them and their colleagues, Calderon said, went some measure of the spirit that had buoyed the project through its difficult but exhilarating first stages.

But for Lemley, projects did not run on fellowship; decision was all. "This industry, it's not really a democracy. It's run by people who make decisions. You have to build a consensus, but you still have to make decisions," he said. "You make the decisions, at times, based on what information you have, and hope like hell that you're not too wrong."

The cost forecast that Lemley ordered on his arrival more than confirmed Essig's gloomy findings. It put the construction cost of the entire project—lump-sum, cost-reimbursable and target costs—at £4.7 billion, more than 80 percent higher than the £2.6 billion in the construction contract. The forecast document that TML presented to Eurotunnel bore Lemley's stamp; it was far more complete, far more rigorous than the forecasts that had preceded it. The document for the U.K. side alone had seven sections, each of which concluded with a graph showing the number of man-hours of work for each month for five years into the future. It broke down how many TBM crewmen would be needed at the peak of construction (664), how many workers on the construction railroad in the tunnel (788); everything down to the number of workers—eight—whose duties involved "tunnel hygiene." The total British tunnel workforce at peak (which was expected in December 1989) was calculated to be 3,587—or 3,411, if locomotive performance could be improved. This was far more than the 2,100 or so that had been predicted just a few months earlier by Lemley's predecessors; most of the difference was made up of electricians and fitters that revised logistics required. In sum, the forecast was heavy with supporting documentation of the sort that might help still or settle an argument.

If Lemley didn't change his views, he did add to them. He, like Essig, came to feel that Eurotunnel was wasting and misdirecting its energy. Instead of working to create an organization that could deal effectively with the railways and governments and, eventually, operate the tunnel's complex transportation system, Lemley said, Eurotunnel devoted all of its attention to TML. This was an echo of an old cry that dated to the earliest days of the project: McDowall had said that Eurotunnel should "let the lads get on with it"; David Brown had asked that Eurotunnel supply the performance specifications for the trains and then stop dabbling. Crighton, too, believed that the contractors should have been left alone to practice their craft.

Jolivet, too, had tried to persuade Pete Behr that Eurotunnel and Bechtel should retire to the sidelines and let the contractors build the tunnel. But the idea remained an article of faith within TML; to Eurotunnel it was heresy, and Lemley had no greater success than his predecessors in converting the client to this view.

Lemley believed—and said to anyone who would listen—that if Eurotunnel continued to act as a shadow contractor and failed to build itself into a strong operating organization, there would be two consequences: First, the IGC and the railways would continue to dictate changes that would force the project's costs ever higher. Second, Eurotunnel would someday find itself owning a very sophisticated transportation system that it was not competent to operate.

Few items had been examined in greater detail than the signaling system, and it had now come time to make a decision. Shockingly, Eurotunnel ordered TML not to open the bids that it had solicited for the system. Instead, TML was directed to give the contract to GEC-Alsthom for the TVM430, a system based on SNCF's TVM400. SNCF had pushed hard enough to work its will on Eurotunnel, which simply turned and handed the order to TML.

There were grave implications in the act. First, it infuriated the companies that had tendered bids—bids that had taken much time and money to prepare. These companies immediately brought suit against TML. Second, it required TML to adopt a complex and expensive system—as events were to prove, the choice of GEC-Alsthom at a stroke quadrupled the signaling system's cost—that might well be ill-suited to the task. "The system of the TGV Nord was not as developed as they believed," Essig said. SNCF engineers told him that "the change in the signal system between the TGV Atlantique and the TGV Nord was a leap. And they told me that the change between the TGV Nord and the Eurotunnel system was *another* leap." Further, the TVM430 didn't satisfy the British, who insisted on a fail-safe system in which the engineer was merely an observer of an entirely automatic train.

All but lost in the furor surrounding the signaling system was a TML discussion with the Safety Authority about the width of the pass doors in the passenger shuttle wagons. These were fire-retarding features at each end of each car. They were complex and crucial elements of the rail system, and they were to create costs and difficulties of incredible proportions.

Passenger shuttle trains were made up of three types of cars: loading wagons and single- and double-deck vehicle carriers. These were arranged first into "triplets" of vehicle carriers, whose mechanical systems would be linked, with power converters in the end wagons. Once they were assembled, triplets would stay coupled except during in-shop maintenance sessions.

The next level of train organization was the "rake." In passenger shuttles, a rake was four triplets with a loading-unloading wagon at each end. A full shuttle train would have two rakes, one double-deck and the other single, with a locomotive at each end. In all cases, even in the quite different shuttles that were to carry heavy trucks, vehicles were to drive onto the train via a loading car, then continue through the train, from car to car, until each had its full complement of vehicular cargo. Five passenger cars could fit into a single-deck shuttle, ten into a double-decker. Single-deck shuttles could also carry buses.

Once the shuttle was full, the ends of each wagon had to be shut in case fire broke out in one of the vehicles. The concession required this, but it did so rather ambiguously:

> Shuttle rakes must be provided with intermediate fire doors or curtains with a fire resistance time of at least 30 minutes to prevent the spread of smoke along the train in the event of fire occurring on board. As far as is practicable, the design of shuttle rakes should be such as to enable, in appropriate circumstances, a train to continue on its journey to clear the tunnel in the event of an outbreak of fire.

Such loose talk left a great deal to the imagination of designers. Were there to be doors, or would curtains do? If the doors or curtains were designed to hinder the spread of smoke, what was the meaning or significance of the half-hour "fire resistance time"? The earliest documents spoke of having a fire curtain at one end of each car; a second was quickly added.

Seeking to allay the mild fears of the House of Lords' Select Committee in 1987, Eurotunnel had made its costly and ill-considered promise: The shuttle wagons would have thirty minutes' fire resistance. What evolved thereafter was a steel shutter door flanked by two sets of double pass doors at the end of each wagon. During loading or unloading, the central steel door would roll up into the overhead like a storefront grate, and each pass-door structure, frame and all, would fold back against the wall of the car. If there were a fire in a shuttle wagon, the pass doors—which were double, hinged at the side to

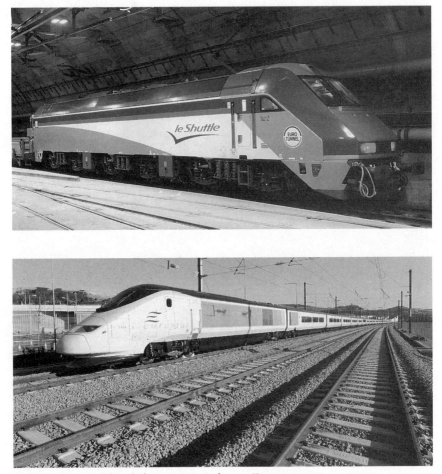

Top, *a shuttle locomotive.* Below, *a Eurostar passenger train.*

swing like saloon doors—would allow passengers to move to another wagon while the train sped on toward the surface.

In normal railcars, such doors are sixty centimeters (six hundred millimeters) wide; in buildings, such an opening is usually seventy centimeters (seven hundred millimeters). Although the concession agreement was silent about passage between wagons, the Safety Authority indicated in September that it wanted seventy-centimeter pass doors. Eurotunnel preferred sixty centimeters. It was important to decide rather quickly what the dimension would be—the width of the pass doors also determined the width of the central steel door—but it seemed a rather minor matter in the grand scheme of this grand project. After all, the difference between sixty and seventy centimeters was trivial: less than four inches, about the width of a man's hand at

Pass-doors at the end of a passenger shuttle.

the knuckles. This sensible judgment was wrong, however: Those ten centimeters would prove to be an almost unbridgeable gulf.

There was a bizarre element to this and to all discussions about the rolling stock: The contractual process to build it was already far advanced; there were signed letters of intent with various joint ventures, gathered under an umbrella organization called the Euroshuttle Consortium Shuttle Group, to manufacture the wagons and locomotives. Bombardier of Canada, joined by French and Belgian partners, had the contract to build 252 passenger shuttles. Breda Construzione Ferroviaria and Fiat Ferroviaria, both of Italy, would build 270 heavy goods vehicles, or HGV wagons, that would carry trucks. A Swiss-British venture would build 40 electric locomotives.

Five days before it announced the letters of intent on July 26, 1989, Eurotunnel alerted the public that the price would be high. "It is clear that the value of these orders will be substantially higher than was foreseen in the November

1987 prospectus," the company press release warned. "Other project costs are likely to show increases, and Eurotunnel is discussing these with TML." Some months later, Eurotunnel released the numbers: The rolling stock contracts totaled £600 million, compared to £252 million in the Equity 3 prospectus.

The pass-door problem fell, with many others, upon Bryan Driver, a career railwayman who had joined TML at the invitation of Andrew McDowall and John Reeve. The three met at a formal affair in London in the summer of 1987, shortly before Driver, who was president of British Rail's containerized freight subsidiary, was to take early retirement. McDowall recruited him on the spot, though Driver couldn't begin until the following February. Driver, who was setting up a consulting business and wanted to get other clients as well, agreed to give TML six months of three-day weeks.

"It was, of course, four and often five days a week," Driver recalled with a rueful chuckle. "By May, I was asked to go as a full-time executive director of the company. I knew it wasn't something you could do part-time."

Driver was a man of deep experience and pleasant manners, with something of the bishop and the colonel about him. He dressed well and conservatively, but he gave himself no airs: He was genuine and direct, with the latter softened by politeness. He was from Yorkshire, but his career had removed most traces of it from his speech: Fellow Northerners could hear it; southerners could not.

He liked France, liked the French on their terms. When the TML job led him to rent a house near the Coquelles terminal site, he fit in well: His neighbors always gave him a friendly wave, and he appreciated the worth of those gestures. His house stood at the edge of the Field of the Cloth of Gold, the scene of another memorable meeting of the French and English, when Henry VIII met François Ier in 1520. Driver liked to point out a spot behind his house where, he said, Henry had pitched his tent.

When he came to TML, he was in charge of the tunnel's railway—the signaling system, the rolling stock, everything. This was more than enough to make him groan, and he offloaded some of the responsibility to others. He kept the rolling stock, which seemed quite enough to occupy anyone. Each car, each type of train, was fraught with complications. The passenger shuttles were the largest railroad wagons ever built. Each was 26 meters long, 5.6 meters high, more than 3.3 meters wide. Both double- and single-deck wagons could carry twenty-four tons of vehicles. They were so large that they could operate only under controlled conditions outside the tunnel. Aboveground, fences were needed because of the famously strong winds off the Channel, which could quite easily derail a shuttle.

Driver also had to deal with daunting problems with the HGV wagons, which were to carry trucks. The problem here was that the HGV wagons could not be built. The design requirements for speed, payload, axle load and an enclosed structure did not add up: If you enclosed the wagons, they would be so heavy that the axle load would be exceeded. You could tinker with the axle load by redesigning the wheels, but only if you gave up some speed. You could reduce the payload, but only by excluding the forty-four-ton trucks then coming into use on the Continent. The best solution seemed to be to build open or partly open wagons, but that—like everything else about the rolling stock—was a matter that required the Intergovernmental Commission's approval.

John Noulton became chairman of the IGC in the spring of 1988, which meant that he ran the body administratively. When he took the post, the IGC did not have much to do and occupied itself with questions of sovereignty and frontier controls. Some of these had a comic air: The customs of each nation would be in the terminal of the other, so that passengers could show up, clear customs, take the tunnel, disembark and keep going. This meant that French customs officers, who were armed, would be stationed in Kent, where the police eschewed firearms. Noulton brought up the question after tunnel opponents raised the specter of a British citizen shot dead on his native soil by a French customs agent. The French agents said they could be brought up on charges of being out of uniform on duty if they were forced to check their weapons at the border. The matter was settled—not without some difficulty—by having the chief constable of Kent issue a blanket authority for the agents to carry arms, with the understanding that they would do so only on occasions for which the chief constable gave specific permission.

Customs gave rise to other battles as well.

"We had a discussion about on-train controls," Noulton said, referring to the through-train passenger services that the national railways would operate through the tunnel. "This went on for years. The British immigration and customs people are not used to carrying out controls on trains. They prefer to stand still and have passengers come to them, like the airport control. And they said, 'All these passengers going through Waterloo [Station in London], the easiest thing to do is for us to have our people there and let people walk through.' And the French said 'No, no, do it on the train. Much easier to do it on the train.' The counterargument to that was, 'You will need detention rooms on the train, and all sorts of things, and you'll have to interrupt people when they're having their lunch to turn out bags and things.' And the French said, 'Well, you don't actually *do* that, anyway. It's a cursory check, and after all, all these people are just traveling within the community, so what the hell, it's like going from Glasgow to London.' The other argument they said was,

'Unless you do controls on the train, you won't be able to run services from, say, Manchester or Glasgow, because you're not going to have customs security and immigration people standing there all day for one train.' And the British passport people said, 'No, of course we're not. They'll just have to get out in London and change trains.'

"Everybody said that will be just ruinously damaging to the service. This argument went on and on and on. And in the end they agreed to do on-train controls for those trains that went past London."

It was not just the IGC and debates about customs that were taking up valuable time. In Britain, the Safety Authority swiftly achieved a powerful position from which to oversee the project. In France, it was called the Comité de sécurité, or Safety Committee, and functioned from the same office as, and as an appendage of, the IGC. In Britain, the Safety Authority was given its own headquarters in Church House, near Westminster Abbey, to emphasize its independent status.

"When we set up this Safety Authority—I remember this well—we had a lot of debate about what its composition should be," Noulton said. "We concluded that it should have a fairly light touch on the project. The theory was that ET was a competent client with good, solid engineering expertise. It would employ competent contractors, specialists in their fields. . . . There would be an independent technical auditor, whom we called the maître d'oeuvre, who would also have a view of it. All of these people were professional, competent engineers. And by this time it was apparent that the banks themselves would have a technical adviser who would also be looking at these matters.

"So you didn't need to have another army of people second-guessing all these professionals. You needed a fairly small group of competent people who could look at it in the round and make sure that proper regard was being paid to national standards. But of course it's not worked like that; I mean they've got deeply involved in this, almost to the point where they're mainly designing the thing themselves."

Fire influenced all thinking about the tunnel. Fire drove the design of the rolling stock. Fire was the great fear, the issue that the ferries ignited and fanned in the hope of defeating or damaging the tunnel. When it came to questions of fire safety, the worst-case scenario always governed: The passenger shuttles were to be able to contain fires from blazing automobiles and exploding fuel tanks for a full half hour without the least distortion of the wagon frame; the locomotives should still be able to drag what amounted to a furnace on wheels out of the tunnel while passengers retreated to safety in other wagons, behind impregnable fire barriers. There were some early attempts to design fire curtains for the wagons, as the concession permitted. These would have been much cheaper and much lighter in weight, but the efforts came to naught; the Safety Authority wanted something much more substantial.

After setting things right with the Safety Authority and the IGC, Driver had much occasion to test and measure the threat of fire. TML did a long series of tests at a laboratory in Cerchar, north of Paris. "We burned a few cars," Driver said. "We built mockups with features of the single-deck tourist wagon. I used to amuse my family by saying, 'Well, I'm going off to Paris to burn another coach.'" The technicians started engine fires, toilet fires; they set fires in luggage, they set fires everywhere in the passenger compartment. It was not as easy as one might think. The fires did not thrive, and not for want of encouragement: The technicians disconnected fuel lines to feed their engine-compartment blazes; they put firebombs in luggage. Nothing produced a blaze that could not have been quenched by a modest but efficient fire-fighting system.

The rolling stock was full of such systems. The HGV wagons had a foam system for the central ditch that ran under the trucks to catch any leaked substances. The passenger shuttles had a water-spray system supplemented by another that used halon gas to smother a fire.

Driver recalled one test, in which a fire was set in a bus seat on the mockup shuttle. The fire burned less than merrily. After a half hour, it had managed to spread across the seat, but had not been able to leap to the adjacent seat. Finally, after thirty-two minutes, the technicians turned on the halon system, which put the fire out, completely, in eighteen seconds. Tests had shown that even aged and moderately infirm passengers could evacuate a bus in less than three minutes.

Halon, a gas used to smother fires, itself caused some hand-wringing. Driver had to bring in world-class experts to assure the Safety Authority that halon, in the low concentrations used in the tests and intended for the tunnel, was not a threat to even ill and feeble passengers.

When the Safety Authority voiced its preference for seventy-centimeter-wide pass doors, it did so in the context of a series of IGC meetings with TML and Eurotunnel that stretched from the summer of 1989 well into the fall. It was one issue among several: The fire tests at Cerchar, and their relationship to the question of nonsegregation, were discussed at length (the Safety Authority was still far from convinced) as were such things as video surveillance cameras on the shuttles.

During the summer, Driver and Alain Bertrand, Eurotunnel's engineering chief, met informally with Bryan Martin, who had replaced Rose as chairman of the Safety Authority. Martin suggested that it would simplify their work if the Authority drew up a list of nonnegotiable requirements. Bertrand agreed; Martin said he would try to deliver the list around September.

The video cameras ended up on the list, and so, too, did the seventy-centimeter pass doors. These and the other items on the list came to be called "binding requirements." By the time the list was forwarded to TML and Eurotunnel, design work on the pass doors was fairly well advanced, helped by the fact that Eurotunnel had given a £1 million study contract on the subject to De Dietrich, a French company that was in particularly good standing with SNCF. This gave De Dietrich a great head start over any other bidders, which it was able to exploit later. De Dietrich produced a design and prototype with the central roll-up door flanked by double pass doors. However, the pass doors as designed were sixty centimeters wide.

Progress on all of the hard rolling-stock issues was elusive, and relations among the parties became strained. Emotion joined technical considerations in the discussions. Someone decided that a retreat might help: Get everyone together on neutral ground for a weekend to sort out and talk over the issues. It would be best done away from the withering gaze of the press.

The Isle of Guernsey was chosen as the site of the meeting, on December 6 and 7, because "it was felt there was a risk the media might learn of this very emotional seminar," Driver said. "We would go to Guernsey to maintain the lowest possible profile." This was a foolish hope; Guernsey is empty and echoing in December, and the arrival of a few score of serious businesspeople—the Safety Authority alone was sending a delegation of fifteen—was bound to attract more attention there than in the center of London. "Every taxi driver on the island knew about it," Driver said. He nonetheless joined the crowd of others in the Old Government House in St. Peter Port, a genteel, quiet hotel of a certain age, for what came to be known as the Guernsey Seminar.

Before he caught his flight from Gatwick, Driver received word from the rolling-stock people at TML that it would be difficult to switch to seventy-centimeter pass doors "without significant redesign by De Dietrich," Driver said. "And it would be very costly. I went to Guernsey knowing that 65 centimeters might be achieved without major redesign and cost consequences."

When the issue of fire barriers came up at the seminar, Driver could see that Bryan Martin, the Safety Authority chairman who had produced the agreed list of binding requirements, was growing agitated at Eurotunnel's stance that sixty-centimeter pass doors were impossible.

"I walked up to the front and said, 'Let me put forward a proposal,'" Driver recalled. "'Six hundred millimeters complies with normal railway design. Seven hundred is a binding requirement by the Safety Authority, supported by the IGC.' I said that to achieve seven hundred millimeters would be difficult, causing delay. I said it would be costly."

Driver said that he couldn't make a specific proposal, but that something between six hundred and seven hundred would be achievable. "I invited the Safety Authority to reconsider, to tell Eurotunnel to redesign the pass doors at six-fifty.

"Well, the chairman went absolutely mad. It was the first time I had had that problem. I think he felt that he had to keep a grip on the binding requirements, and he saw his grip slipping. He said there was no scope for compromise. He rejected it out of hand."

What Driver did not know—and did not learn for another ten months—was that just after the seminar, Bryan Martin and Alain Bertrand signed a paper that confirmed that the binding requirements were, in fact, binding. There was a quid pro quo: If Eurotunnel implemented all of the binding requirements, the IGC would approve nonsegregation in the shuttles, meaning that drivers and passengers would be permitted to stay with their vehicles. This was critical for Eurotunnel, since it saved the time and confusion of getting people out of their cars and into a regular railroad coach before the trip started, and back into their vehicles when the trip was complete. Without segregation, Eurotunnel could not keep to a tight, profitable schedule.

The IGC fulfilled its part of the bargain by duly approving nonsegregated passenger shuttles. But Eurotunnel was not quick to fulfill its end of the deal.

"We'd already designed the doors, we'd tested them and all at six hundred millimeters," said Lemley. "Eurotunnel said, 'Don't change that, don't go to seven hundred as we agreed with the IGC yesterday. Stay at six hundred and we'll someday get this changed with the IGC.'"

TML continued to ask Eurotunnel for a formal order to build the shuttles with sixty-centimeter doors; it took four months to secure one. On March 1, 1990, Eurotunnel sent Driver an instruction on the IGC's sixty-centimeter doors that read, "We will dispense with this requirement due to its severe structural and schedule impacts. We may require TML's assistance in preparing our report to the IGC."

The accompanying cover letter expressed amazement that TML would need such an order. "We are surprised that TML needs an instruction to perform what is good commercial practice on our behalf. . . . We herewith formally instruct you to perform in accordance with our letter."

The cover letter also ordered TML to "advise when you have prepared your in-house assessment of cost and schedule" that would be involved in changing the pass doors. Driver's assistant attached a handwritten note, saying that Eurotunnel "is looking for a detailed time/cost assessment. . . . We must produce evidence that we have made a serious assessment, otherwise we shall be at risk if ET claim 'wrongful act or omission,' as I have a feeling they may do."

According to Lemley, just such a study was done. Had the change been made at that time, before the shuttle wagons had gone into production, changing over to seven-hundred-millimeter doors would have cost about £5 million—a genuine bargain, as events were soon to show.

14

I f the safety issue was still clouded by acrimonious debate, at least all of those involved in the Channel Tunnel could find solace in the physical progress of those digging beneath the sea. Two months before the December 1989 meeting on Guernsey, Eurotunnel was able to announce that about 37 kilometers of tunnel—nearly a quarter of the 150-kilometer total—had been completed; that the French land service-tunnel TBM had completed its journey from the Sangatte shaft and had broken through at the Coquelles terminal site, and that its British counterpart would soon do the same; that the French marine tunnel-boring machines had achieved good rates of progress "after the cutting heads were reinforced." In releasing so brave a statement, Eurotunnel was betting that the past was past and that the encouraging present would continue without interruption until trains were running beneath the Channel. The tunneling was indeed going better, but the improvement was very recent, measured in weeks rather than months. A new stretch of bad ground could resurrect all of the problems that Eurotunnel now sought to bury under boldly optimistic words.

A month later, Eurotunnel found cause for public celebration when the U.K. land service tunnel-boring machine broke through at Holywell Coombe, one hill short of the tunnel mouth itself, after an eleven-month, 8,135-meter-long underground journey from Shakespeare Cliff. (The rest of the work to the tunnel portal was to be done by hand: a cut-and-cover section through the valley at Holywell, then a hand-dug section through Castle Hill to the terminal site.)

This November breakthrough, two weeks ahead of schedule, was televised live by the BBC's regional service. Eurotunnel served up a fairly lavish reception for several hundred guests in the cut-and-cover section. The guests were treated to a laser show in the tunnel; the tunnel's neighbors were afterward treated to a fireworks display that was visible for miles.

A month after the fireworks the British marine service tunnel-boring machine had traveled 13,666 meters from Shakespeare Cliff; its French counterpart had come 6,638 meters from its starting point in the Sangatte shaft. This meant that 17,696 meters separated them. If they kept their rate of progress, they would meet in mid-November 1990—two and a half months late, but far sooner than it had seemed possible until quite recently.

Credit for this belonged to the Creator (the ground on the British side was providentially better), to TML's new chief executive and to the unimpeded operation of The Crack.

This last was a mysterious spirit or mood that governed the British tunnelers. The Crack was very difficult to define or explain; it was the body of knowledge and attitude that made a man a tunneler. Tunnelers were citizens of a separate and largely secret society, set off from the rest of the world the way sailors were. The Crack was the glue that held their culture together.

"I've looked it up, and all I've managed to find out is that it stems from the Irish construction industry at about 1840, but nobody knew where it came from," said Tim Green, who ran the construction railway in the British tunnels. "But it is a most incredible thing, The Crack. It is benign. . . . If you can join in The Crack, it is a very powerful management information tool, both up the way and down the way. But if you did try to overuse it as a management tool, it's become bad Crack. The Crack becomes bad as soon as you push too hard. It has to be casual, it has to be *en passant*." If you had good Crack on the job, all would go well. If you had no Crack, or bad Crack, nothing would go right.

"If they know what the Crack is, it means they've been around," said David Denman, the agent in the British marine service tunnel. "They fit in. They know when to have a respect for somebody. They understand the position of the agent who's running the job. They know the engineer, what he does. They know the pecking order. They'll know other people within the industry."

Denman had acquired The Crack in twenty years spent as a tunneler before he came to the Channel Tunnel in the early summer of 1988. He, like many others, was a reluctant recruit. He had come back from a three-year mass-transit job in Singapore not long before and taken a tunneling job in London. Then, in a move that he could hardly explain to himself, he quit and went to work for his brother, who had a landscaping business. "I decided I'd had enough and I decided I didn't want it," he said. "I could see no future. I just needed a rest, I think."

At about that time, a manager at the Channel Tunnel called to see if Denman wanted work there. "I wasn't really very interested," he said. "Don't know why." Five months later, there was another call, and Denman went down to see how things stood. "I got the impression, actually, that the whole

Tunnel Cross Section Diagram

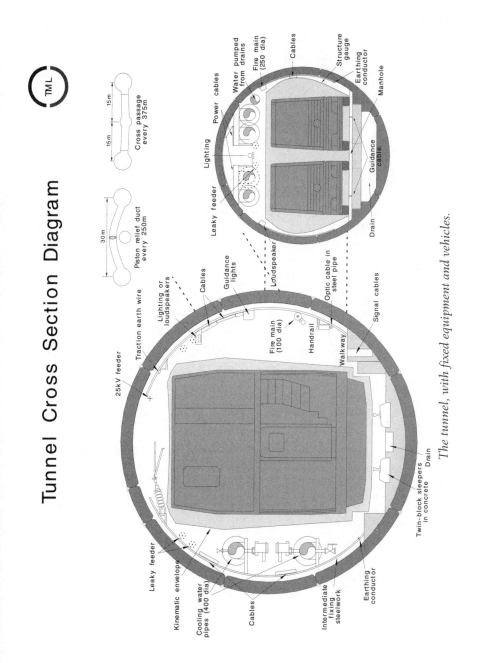

The tunnel, with fixed equipment and vehicles.

thing was in an absolute state of chaos," he recalled. "The guy who was going to interview me hadn't actually turned up. Somebody else interviewed me, and they thought I was going to work for him." Denman's original contact called back later, telling him to ignore everything the interviewer had said.

"They didn't know what salary it was going to be, they didn't know what the job was going to be. But basically would I like to come down: There was this job, take it on trust." Denman paused for a wondering laugh. "This is the biggest job in the world; this is the number one tunneling job. So when you've got that sort of thing going on at interview time, you've got no option: You've *got* to take the job, out of curiosity."

Denman was hired as agent for the Land Service Tunnel, whose machine was just then being assembled in the erection chamber at Shakespeare Cliff. "The chamber hadn't even been finished and they were building the machine in it," he said. "It was absolute chaos." The Marine Service Tunnel, which Denman would later take over, was then in the midst of its hellish passage through bad ground.

Denman had to assemble a workforce of about 120, with a good representation of experienced tunnelers, in six weeks. As he set about this task, Denman found further disarray. There was a personnel office, but it only supplied raw data—a request for miners would bring a list of perhaps two hundred names and a stack of *curricula vitae*. The office was clearly swamped; thousands of applications were pouring in, drawn by press accounts of the fabulous wages that tunneling paid. The one thing most applicants had in common was an almost total ignorance of The Crack.

"I got my little book out and put a few names down that I knew," Denman said. "Spread the word round. Spoke to my boss; he had a few names. A couple of lads I had working for me, they had a few names. . . . I phoned 'em up, got CVs sent in, and I made arrangements to see them myself. Once I'd done that, I then went back to personnel, and said, 'These are the guys I want.' A few got blacklisted, and they wouldn't take them for one reason or another; they'd been naughty boys or something. Effectively that was how people got people in." That dodge provided a core of tunnelers; the rest of the force, laborers, were called "cannon fodder" and could safely be requisitioned from personnel.

Tunneling was hard work that attracted tough men from regions that offered few opportunities for employment. Most were Irish, most of the rest were from Scotland or the depressed north of England. There were enough Liverpudlians to drive the local publicans to near distraction by endlessly playing Gerry and the Pacemakers' "You'll Never Walk Alone" on the jukeboxes. All were inured to the hard life of a tunneler; all rejoiced in it. It was the badge that set them apart from the gray and feeble mass of humanity who lacked their skills and their appetite for discomfort.

Before the Second World War, most British tunnelers came from the roughest part of London's working class. "After the war, Londoners became sort of fat and lazy and didn't want to do the tunneling," Denman said. "That's when the Irish came in. They're good strong lads—salt of the earth—but they don't like paying tax."

When they took over the tunneling trade, the system was such that no Irishman worth his salt needed to worry much about taxes. Tunneling, like the construction industry, functioned on a system called The Lump. A tunneler could in essence declare himself self-employed by filling out a form and getting a book of tickets that were called 714 Certificates.

"If the guy gave you one of these, then you could pay that guy without making any deductions for tax," Denman said. "And you also could pay his whole gang on it. . . . Almost anybody could get one of these, quite bona fide. He could move around, change his address, put as many people on it as he wanted, get paid cash up front. Then all he had to do was disappear back to Ireland every so often and come back with a different name. So you could never catch up with these people. They were working, earning big money, getting it tax-free."

Even then, tunnelers made top money: In the later 1970s, Denman said, £200 a week was about normal for a tunneler, exceptional for any other worker, and the tunnelers kept everything they made.

Shortly thereafter, the rules governing The Lump were tightened up considerably, and the tunnelers found themselves confronted with the unpleasant prospect of paying taxes. "At the same time the unions, who were looking for people, found a whole industry full of disgruntled Irishmen," Denman said. "So of course the unions and the Irishmen joined up, and they actually pushed prices up and up and up, and for a few years—and there wasn't a lot of work around—it got pretty nasty. . . . That was when a lot of the firms really started to mechanize, because the labor had become so expensive."

Tunnelers made people on the surface more than a little nervous; Kent gave them the sort of welcome it would have offered an invading army of barbarians. TML had built a sort of camp for them, forty-two barrackslike buildings, each with twenty-eight single rooms, set on a hillside overlooking the main road between Dover and Folkestone. It was called Farthingloe Village by TML and more humorous names by its inhabitants—Colditz and Stalag Luft 17 were two offered to a visiting journalist. Farthingloe had a canteen, a general store, a laundry, a barber, tables for pool and tennis, a gymnasium, two bars (pints of bitter and lager were attractively priced at 80 and 85 pence, respectively) and five television rooms to diminish the need for arguments. There was a chapel installed in a restored eighteenth-century barn. Everything was clean and decent and more than a bit Spartan, but it served well enough for men who came home—for home it was to many of them—exhausted from their labors, after a long trip back from the face in a badly lit, bone-rattling work train.

Good citizens often noted with disapproval that the tunnelers were uncommonly well paid. "I must admit I get upset when people say they get paid too much," said Gordon Crighton. "I say to them, 'Well, you go do it. *You* go underground six days a week,' cause they did six shifts—ten hour shifts, rotating around the clock. You've got no weekend, you can't plan. You're on a ship, you're a prisoner of the job, you're living in Farthingloe, in bloody Alcatraz down there. You're worth the wage you get. The lowest-paid laborer on the tunnel was getting 600 quid a week. A top foreman was 2,000 quid a week. The top foremen were hundred-thousand-a-year men, and worth every bloody penny, worth every penny." Crighton noted that tunnelers often had to endure long lean spells when there was no work.

The British press shared and stimulated the region's fascinated ambivalence about the tunnelers. The tunnelers sometimes amused themselves by playing to stereotype with journalists, who didn't hesitate to report bar bragging as sober truth. They styled themselves "Tunnel Tigers," a term no journalist could resist. The results were often unfortunate, as when one national tabloid painted a lurid picture of Folkestone besieged by an army of thuggish tunnelers. TML thereupon forbade its workers to talk to reporters, but the press's infatuation with the subject did not die, nor did the articles about Farthingloe cease. Efforts by even the respectable press sometimes added fuel to the flames of local indignation. Denied access to Farthingloe and turned away by the family-minded workers who lived in trailer camps nearby, reporters trolled through the pubs, with predictable results. The *Independent* accosted some tunnelers in the Hare and Hounds on the Dover Road and grilled them about their work and philosophy; the subheadline on the piece read: "They travel the world in search of highly-paid work, women and great binges. The tunnelers are the blue-collar aristocrats."

The accompanying article was replete with similar condescension: One tunneler came from "Donegal in western Ireland, where drinking and digging are held in similar awe." Other judgments studded the piece: "It is only 8 o'clock but already the tunnelers' table bears an extensive assortment of empty glasses and bottles. Finding space for the next round poses a serious problem. . . . Next to the ability to drink copious amounts and remain upright, chasing women—and more importantly boasting about chasing women—is central to being a tunneler. . . . Predictably, memories of life abroad are dominated by epic tales of drinking."

The *Independent*'s piece was not negative on balance, and it did note some of the interesting small changes wrought by the tunnelers' presence, such as the Irish cigarettes and copies of *Construction News* in the news agents' shops. The travel histories of the British miners were explored: Men met old friends here, with whom they had worked on jobs in Hong Kong, Cairo, Sri Lanka, the United States, Oman. It concluded with a quote that caught perfectly the swagger and simple truth of the trade: "You've got tunnels being built in London," a tunneler said in the crowded bar at the Capel Court Country Club, where one could drink during the many hours when pubs were closed. "Why don't you go and talk to workers there? The Channel Tunnel is no different from building a tunnel under a river. In this case, it's a bloody great tunnel under a bloody great river."

This was a sentiment with which John Hester could agree. Lemley lured him over from the States because "British tunneling simply was not functioning the way it should. I needed someone who understood machine tunneling. . . . He was still located in Texas running six or seven underground projects. Nobody I knew of had ever run six TBMs at one time with the size and logistics we had here. I did a really wide search in my own mind, and I felt he was one of the few men who could do it. . . . What was needed was experienced leadership *in the tunnel*."

In Hester, Lemley saw many of the virtues that he respected in Pierre Matheron. "He spends his time in the tunnel," Lemley said. "He knows what the crews are thinking, what their problems are and what has to be done to keep them moving forward. And I agree with that completely. I just don't think that executives in our business can sit away from the work and understand what the problems are on a real-time basis. You have to be willing to get dirty and have a relationship with people that might not have a college education or have nice smooth hands."

Hester went in November 1989 to look over the project to see if he wanted the job. "We were just starting the marine tunnels, the two big marine drives," he said. "All four of the big machines were basically just starting. They had been trying to get North Marine going for a long time, but they weren't going anywhere." Hester took his time, walking to and through each of the machines and talking to people on the job. Then he went back to London to have dinner at Lemley's apartment. He recalled the conversation:

"Well, are you going to come over here?" Lemley asked.

"Nope," said Hester.

"Why?"

"It's tough to get a good reputation in the US. I don't see any reason to ruin it here."

Hester went back to the United States, where his boss encouraged him to take the Channel Tunnel job and promised to keep his job open in case he didn't like it. On those terms, Hester joined the effort, as reluctantly as the people, like Crighton and Brown, for whom the long job seemed as much a sentence as an opportunity.

Hester was adamant in his belief that the Channel Tunnel project was being driven by a taste for novelty rather than a respect for experience. "Put it this way," he said. "People who can spell tunnel, people who know how to write letters—not people who drive tunnels—sit around and talk about all the great advances in tunnel boring machines. *There are no advances in TBMs.* The TBM that drove the Channel Tunnel is no different than the one Beaumont built back in 18-hundred-whatever. It's just that the components are better. The basic idea is the same."

He was particularly scornful of the computers that had been built into the Channel Tunnel TBMs. "We can program this computer and put it on a TBM and we push a button and it goes through its logic and turns on all the things in the proper sequence and it does, oh, such a fabulous job," he said, his voice strangled with sarcasm. "And it allows you to do a lot more things at the same time, because it's not dependent on a man thinking any more. But unfortunately, those things don't work worth a shit under salt water. And the other thing: *There's nobody on the job knows how to fix the goddam thing when it goes down.* So it's stupid, stupid as hell, but they did that. They stuck these goddam things all over here, and we took them all off. As many as we could."

Hester liked his TBMs to be solid, simple and very dependable. "Instead of pushing a button if you want something to turn, you go up and you pull a lever. And the hydraulic oil goes through the valve, goes to the motor and *turns* it. And we know how that works. The average mechanic on a TBM can sit down with a hydraulic schematic and say, 'By God, you put it in here and it goes out there'—and they can fix it. But these electronic boys, stickin' all this garbage on these machines, have set tunneling back probably twenty years. I mean, tunnels are not driven in computer-friendly conditions, and the type of people that are involved in tunneling don't know how to fix 'em."

Hester's overhaul of the machines was not restricted to unplugging the computers; he also cut the machines to pieces to free up space. "We used up enough oxygen and acetylene to run a normal tunnel job, cuttin' the garbage off the back of these fuckers, just to get places for people to work, to create the little place where the man can stand, to create the ladder where he can get up to his place without breaking his goddamned neck.

"If you don't talk the language," Hester continued, "they're not going to lis-ten to you. If you can't sit down and discuss a tunnel with them, and know what you're talking about, they don't want to talk to you. They're not going to pay any goddam attention to anything you've got to say."

This had been a problem in the Channel Tunnel, because some of the people who were giving orders were good construction men but not tunnelers. Even good, solid construction men were excluded from the fraternity, Hester said: "He could walk in and sit down in a room and try to talk to these construction managers, who were the tunnel bosses, and he might order them to do something. But as far as they were concerned, it was, 'What's he doing here?'

"The man you have to listen to on a tunnel job is the man that's working at the face. The hell with all the rest of these goddam people. If you want to know what's going on and how to drive the goddam tunnel, and what's wrong in that heading, you go talk to that lead miner and his crew."

(This independent spirit sometimes pushed matters too far; Crighton recalled that in the first weeks of the job, some "cowboys"—experienced but headstrong tunnelers—were leaving out bolts because they felt they weren't necessary. Crighton fired them on the spot.)

Although Hester's principles were not observed to his satisfaction in the British works, they were at least honored underground, where the tunnelers had The Crack and knew that many of their bosses neither had it nor understood it. In France, on the other hand, Hester would have been beyond comprehension: There was no Crack in the French tunnels; there could never be any; things were not arranged that way. As Jolivet had noted, one of the purposes of the project was to provide local employment to the depressed Nord-Pas de Calais region. According to Philippe Montagner, the goal was to hire 80 percent of the tunnel workforce from the region. In fact, the local recruiting was even more successful than that; toward the end of the project, almost 95 percent of the workers were local recruits, and many of them shifted over to work for Eurotunnel when the project neared completion.

These recruits went through Jolivet's 120-million-franc training program, which instilled the necessary skills and work habits. A British tunneler was the sum of his experiences; the French tunneler was a graduate of a special course of instruction. The works were designed to use the skills that the recruits had learned, and not to demand more.

"They had to be taught from the word go. They worked *under factory conditions*," Hester said of the French workforce. "I went over and watched them drive tunnel. I thought it was *boring*. They didn't even see the grout; it went in over the top. There was none of this running around, hooking up grout hoses. As soon as their little grout pump went down, the guy cleaned it and he painted it. And it was beautiful. I mean, the whole machine was sparkling white; all them had their little paint cans and when they weren't working they were painting. It was like being on a ship."

The French tunnel works (shown in the lower photo) were neat and, to some tunnelers, boring. The British works looked more like tunnels, less like factories.

Throughout the tunnel, any hand-mining that had to be done was done by British tunnel miners. This even included work that was done near the French portal. The reason, Hester said, is that the French didn't have any miners. The French used small roadheaders to cut their cross-passages and piston relief ducts; the British used air spades wielded by burly miners.

An air spade is not an elegant instrument. It is a pneumatic jackhammer with a broad chisel blade at the business end. It takes strength and endurance to use one; it has to be hefted and held firm as the blade hammers away at the rock face. The relationship between action and reaction means that an air spade is as hard on the man as on the rock. An air spade is noisy and brutish, but an experienced man can do lovely work with one, cutting stone with the finesse of a chef carving a roast. According to one estimate, British tunnel miners cut almost ten miles of passages by hand.

There was a benefit to doing things in the French mode: Statistics suggested very strongly that it was safer. "That side was a factory," Hester noted. "You take a little guy off the street, you train him, you put him in there. He doesn't come with all the bad habits. He's taught what to do, and he does it. Here, you've got the big macho Irish miner. He comes with all the baggage."

The French rings were designed for the conditions that were expected on the French side: They had gaskets to make them waterproof, they were bolted together to ensure alignment and they were built inside the French machine, which itself was sealed against water intrusion. A gasket between the exterior of the ring and the inside of the TBM's cylindrical body held out water until the ring slipped clear as the machine pulled forward. Grout was pumped behind the ring, and after it had set to maximum strength in twenty-eight days, the bolts were taken out and reused farther down the tunnel.

The British rings, on the other hand, were designed for ideal ground—intact chalk marl that would stay obediently in place and hold back the waters that lay above. Like most ideals, this type of ground proved to be in short supply. Even out past the disastrously bad ground that had driven Crighton to despair, the British machines still operated with hoods to shelter the ring builders from overbreak. They built expanded rather than bolted rings: The segments were held in place while a smaller keystone-shaped piece was shoved in by a hydraulic ram to form and hold the pieces in a circle. Such rings are at their best in clay, where they can be expanded to push against the ground behind them, Denman said, and maintain their shape and strength without benefit of grout. But the Channel Tunnel rings were hybrids; they had pads on the back to hold them clear of the cut to leave space for the grout. "I've never fully understood the logic behind them," Denman said.

The rings certainly cried out for initiative in the assembling. "The lining-up is by the skill of the miner," Hester said. "They used little pieces of wood,

British tunnel segments were fitted into place by hand.

little shims, all stuck behind it to make sure they match. In France, bolts hold them; if the bolt fits, it's lined up. You don't have to have any skill with it. These [in Britain] were built in the open. You had to understand a little bit about the ground: What was going to fall, what to scale off, what to leave. This was more of a skilled miner operation."

The keystone also called for skilled handling by the British tunnelers; it was shorter than the 1.5-meter-long segments in the service tunnel and left a gap when it was driven in to expand the ring; this had to be covered with a shutter behind which grout was pumped.

Hester found that the heavy and smothering hand of regulation was already upon the project in Britain. This came from two sources: One was the long-held but now-withering tradition of "demarcation," the rigid definition of job duties. Labor unions had taken demarcation to extremes after the war; on the Channel Tunnel, demarcation was management-driven and existed with equal vigor in the TML offices on the surface and down in the tunnels. The other source of regulation was the same that was driving the design of the tunnel rolling stock to absurd extremes: the official British belief that extremism in the pursuit of safety was no vice.

He ran into demarcation barriers on his first visits to the tunnel, when he found a TBM shut down—broken down, as the three electricians and three mechanics who were sitting there told him. Hester asked why they weren't trying to fix it; they explained that they didn't fix the machine. That was handled by the Plant Department, which was sending someone in to do an inspection, a necessary preliminary to repairs.

"I said, 'Aw, come on,'" Hester recalled. "He said, 'No, we do the maintenance, grease it and all, but if it breaks down, we have to call the plant department to come in.'"

By the time Hester arrived, this was a very deeply rooted problem. "The job wasn't organized right," he said. "When you're on a tunnel job, you're not there to see how well you can make locomotives run, how fancy a machine you can build, all this horseshit. You're there to drive the tunnel. Whatever it takes to drive the tunnel is what you're supposed to be doing. This project has lost track of that a little bit. . . . We had a plant department that was independent of the production people, a railway that was running independent of the tunnel drive. There were little kingdoms all over the place."

John King, as tunneling director, might have been able to stifle those customs, Hester said. "But John King had been away from tunneling for a *looong* time, and he didn't see it. He was in the forest trying to find a tree."

There was certainly a dense forest of regulations in the tunnel. Hester recalled talking to a mechanic in one of the tunnels, who told him that a crane was not working. Hester suggested that they turn the machine on and try to diagnose the problem. The mechanic said that was impossible: Before you could do that, procedures dictated that the machine had to be isolated electrically. "There were four or five things you had to do," Hester said. "You had to lock the whole thing out [of the electrical system]. You couldn't take a piece, move it over, hit the button and see if it worked. It was a procedure. These goddam people believed that you could write procedures, and somehow everybody was going to work safely."

Hester tried to sell the idea that a well-informed workforce, alert to the fact that safety was a shared responsibility, would create its own safe environment. "They didn't believe it," he said. "They had procedures."

Denman was intimately acquainted with procedures; he was awash in them. He had crates full of them, and so did everyone else on the job. Denman tended to doubt the value of all this paper, since it was not backed by practical instruction. The procedures were unread because they were unreadable, written as they were to satisfy the whims of bureaucrats rather than the needs of a workforce. Denman knew of cases where all of this became surreal: Some of the men in his tunnel could not read.

"It came to a point, I think, where everyone became punch-drunk with it, certainly in regards to things like writing procedures," he said. "There were procedures for everything. There were people being employed just to write procedures. The *quality* of the procedure—whether it was necessary, whether the guys understood it—didn't matter as long as they'd signed for it."

The source of this manic pursuit of safety by dubious means was the British government's "health and safety executive." There was no doubt that this tunnel, like any other, could be a dangerous place to work. The danger was one of the reasons tunnelers got good money. In the time of The Lump, well within Denman's memory, an injured man might well get a hasty bandaging from his mates and head for the ferry to Ireland, before the authorities could inquire too closely about who the injured man was, and who he might have been on other jobs.

Those days were gone, but the tunnel was still full of risk and the possibility of tragedy. A fitter in Denman's tunnel, David Simes, became the second fatality on the Channel Tunnel job. On the service-tunnel TBM, the top ring segments were carried to the erection chamber by an overhead conveyor. The lower ring segments were carried forward through the TBM by a mobile crane that rode, underslung, on an overhead rail that ran the length of the TBM's back end. The crane was controlled by a worker who walked along with it, guiding it with controls that were on a wire pendant. It was quiet—"So quiet they had to add warning noise to it," Denman said.

It was this crane that caught and killed Simes, who had apparently gone back to the TBM to retrieve something. He was in a blind spot; the crane operator didn't see him.

"He was the first guy I'd lost in a tunnel in twenty-odd years, and it was a very traumatic event," said Denman, who had hired Simes. "I didn't know what to do about it. I blamed myself. I had to: I was the agent, I was in charge. It was a tragedy. What was I going to do?" After much soul-searching, Denman rephrased and shortened the procedures, and held mandatory classes in which they were read and discussed.

Hester believed that some of the devotion to procedures originated within TML, in part from fear. "I think there was a fear on the part of the so-called leaders of the job, that you might void a warranty if there wasn't a proper inspection on a machine," he said. "Or that Eurotunnel might hit you with a wrongful act or omission if you didn't follow a procedure."

In a sense, getting the tunneling up to speed was less a problem than getting the project clear of the procedural swamp into which it had strayed. "It was easy to get this job going," Hester said. "They had the wrong people in the wrong places, but the people were here." Management was a problem only insofar as it had failed to create an organization that could drive tunnel.

Events would show that Hester was merely the final ingredient in a stew of talent; the tunneling was already making good progress by the time he arrived. Lemley received the credit for this in many quarters, and in many ways he deserved it. Once people like Denman—and there were many like him— were given the authority they needed, the daily progress by the TBMs improved steadily. The British genius for solving problems—a skill that even the French recognized and admired—had cracked some very difficult ones: Hester was of the opinion that the worst ground on the French side was better by far than the worst ground on the British side. Even before the ground improved, the British tunnelers were gathering speed.

Still, to outsiders—even such interested ones as the bankers in Eurotunnel's syndicate—it seemed that Lemley had worked a miracle, and his standing grew daily. This led to a strange meeting between Lemley and Alastair Morton late in 1989, at the Hyde Park Hotel in London.

Morton, said Lemley, spoke of "trying to find a new approach to the job." The nature of this new approach gradually emerged: Morton was offering Lemley a job with Eurotunnel. Once again, it was a job that did exist and was at that moment held by another person: Tony Ridley.

Lemley guessed that Morton "wanted to withdraw Ridley's authority. I think he was feeling I was outgunning Ridley and he was going to replace him with either another structure or another person."

Morton's offer was generous: "I would run the project for Eurotunnel, and he was going to pay me what I was getting from TML," Lemley said. "Plus, he was going to give me a lot of stock options in Eurotunnel."

Lemley felt that Morton was trying to buy him. "I interpreted his motive to be that he couldn't beat up on me so he was going to try to buy me," he said. "I concluded that if he bought me, he'd probably sell me quick, too." Beyond that suspicion, Lemley was offended: He was being asked to sell out his employer.

"I wouldn't take that offer, Alastair, if you gave me the whole fucking company," Lemley told Morton.

15

If Lemley knew with fair certainty what tasks lay ahead when he accepted the job from which Andrew McDowall was soon to be removed, he certainly did not know how close that job was to extinction.

Roger Byatt of NatWest told Lemley later that the Channel Tunnel was in such trouble when Lemley joined that the banks thought seriously about not funding it further. In the summer of 1989, the banks were approaching a point of no return. By the end of July, Eurotunnel had drawn down £850 million of its loan. This sum was far less significant than the state of affairs within the project: The tunneling was going badly, the rolling-stock prices were high and likely to go higher, TML wanted the contract changed to reflect enhancements ordered by Eurotunnel and the IGC; Eurotunnel was refusing this request and withholding payments from TML.

Eurotunnel and TML cherished and deepened their resentments toward each other: TML railed against Eurotunnel's Project Implementation Division, which now had a staff of more than 350, and against Alastair Morton, who seconded every second-guess that the PID made concerning TML's actions. Eurotunnel questioned TML's competence and honesty.

The loan remained where it had always been, in real if unacknowledged default; Eurotunnel was able to draw money only under waivers from the banks. The wishes of the banks governed: The syndicate could dump Eurotunnel and find a new owner if it wished. There was much to recommend this drastic course. The banks would be foreclosing on something worth substantially more than they had invested. All that Equity 3 had bought would belong to the banks; the shareholders would be removed at a stroke from the playing field. The best case—a new operator, a new reign of reason, a completed tunnel awash in revenue—was more than agreeable; the worst case— a loss of £850 million spread among a good many banks, each of which would survive the experience—was not beyond contemplation.

As before, though, the banks stayed with the project. A series of crises rippled through the fall of 1989: On September 21 and 22, Eurotunnel met with the twenty-two instructing banks in Paris to discuss its default. The Credit Agreement stipulated that Eurotunnel must at all times be able to show that it had available financing sufficient to meet the estimated cost-to-completion of the project—that is to say that there would at least be a positive cover ratio of equity to debt. By now, however, the cover had slumped to below parity, which meant that Eurotunnel did not have enough financing to finish the project.

Essig's warning, and Lemley's new estimate of £4.7 billion, made it certain that the £5 billion available to Eurotunnel was sadly short of what was needed to pay the construction bill, operate Eurotunnel and pay the banks' interest and fees. In Lemley's phrase, the estimate broke the banking case; the default could not be concealed behind vague phrases. There were various estimates of what that full sum might be; the median of these was about £7.5 billion. One possible solution was for the contractors to provide additional equity by taking Eurotunnel stock in lieu of cash payments for their work. The contractors, fully aware of Eurotunnel's tenuous hold on existence, refused.

The four Agent Banks—who had become the dominant voice in the negotiations—set forth the minimum conditions under which they would continue to ask the syndicate to continue funding the project. It was, in a sense, a replay of what had happened a year before, when the banks forced Eurotunnel and TML to put their hands to the Joint Accord. This time, the central terms had to do with cost rather than the delay that had bulked so large in the Joint Accord. Now the banks wanted economies: They wanted the price increases to cease, they wanted the project trimmed to save money, they wanted agreement on how cost overruns would be shared by TML and Eurotunnel.

Cost reductions were most important. Both sides agreed in principle and disagreed on the specifics: According to Philippe Essig, TML offered a list of modifications to the tunnel and its attendant systems, while Eurotunnel wanted the savings to come from what it saw as high TML overhead in managing the work sites.

The banks set forth their minimum conditions three days after the Paris meeting with Eurotunnel; three days after that, TML submitted a list of "potential cost reductions/scope changes totaling approximately £250 million," according to a later document that incorporated, for the signature of both sides, the results of months of haggling. Most of this saving was to come from lowering the maximum speeds in the tunnel from 160 kilometers per hour—as required by the contract—to 120 kilometers per hour.

Lowering the speed, Essig noted, would permit the use of stock rather than custom-made locomotives, would halve the amount of power needed to run the system and would eliminate, at least for the time being, the need for a cooling system. He had further ideas: A simple signaling system, capable of being upgraded later, would save quite a lot of money, since it would simplify everything from the locomotive cab back through the control rooms. Essig also thought that the safety systems in the shuttles, which the IGC was busily enhancing in its quest for perfect safety, should be reviewed with an eye toward reducing costs. Taken together, these measures could cut costs by as much as £470 million, Essig thought.

Eurotunnel made no public acknowledgment of the TML suggestions. On September 30, the four Agent Banks informed the more than two hundred other banks in the syndicate that Eurotunnel wasn't in full compliance with the Credit Agreement. The Agent Banks did not, however, give notice of what the agreement called a "Potential Event of Default." This would have had far more serious consequences, since Eurotunnel would have had just ninety days to restore its finances to full compliance with the loan terms—an impossible task, as Eurotunnel made clear after a joint board meeting in Paris the next day, when it notified the London and Paris stock exchanges that "no agreement has yet been reached between Eurotunnel and TML on how to handle the situation which arose in July from the large cost increases advised by TML." The announcement put the overall cost of the tunnel at £7 billion and said further financing would be needed to complete it.

A week later, in announcing its half-year results, Eurotunnel said that it was getting along well with TML's new management and added, quite casually, that a contract for the signaling system had been awarded to the Tunnel Signal Group, a consortium of U.K. and French companies. Tunnel Signal Group was the GEC-Alsthom venture, and the contract infuriated TML at this moment when it seemed that the project could be saved only by the grace of amity and goodwill.

The chief obstacle to a settlement, to a renegotiated contract that would guarantee economic survival to contractor and client alike, lay within Eurotunnel. André Bénard clung sternly and absolutely to the contract as it stood, resisting all suggestions that it be changed. Essig had been trying for months to open some sort of negotiations. It was all in vain; the response was "that the contractors would have to take the consequences," Essig said. "Eurotunnel refused to negotiate to solve the problem. It was a very big disappointment."

Essig's proposed economy measures were similarly received. "I thought it would be possible to agree through a common review by all the parties," he said. "I was much too idealistic."

Bénard was the hard core of Eurotunnel's resistance. This was unusual, in Essig's eye. Bénard, he noted, need have had no personal attachment to the contract, since it was signed before he came to his office. Also, as a Frenchman, he might be expected to favor the French rather than the British view of contracts. The British, said Essig, were governed by "the religion of the contract: The contract is the contract, you must abide by the contract or you must go to arbitration or to court. In France, the success of the project is most important. We consider modifying the contract much more easily than the British."

It seemed that Bénard's long and easy familiarity with and respect for things British had not been without effect; Essig saw that Bénard "was probably much more British in his approach to the contract than French." Indeed, Bénard once chided Essig on failing to appreciate the British view. "Bénard once said to me: 'You have too French an approach to the contract,' " Essig said.

Bénard went on to criticize SNCF, saying that the railways "are not aggressive enough, that we too easily consider success," Essig added. "I thought—and still think—that success is as important to Eurotunnel as to TML. A delay of one month costs them, what, £80 million? We had a common interest in success. Bénard emphasized the contract, the network of contractual obligations, impossible to modify. So if you had a claim, refer it to a panel. No use to talk about it. Of course, this is a caricature of what went on. But it gives you an idea."

The banks were not interested in the theology of contracts; they had a potential savior in Lemley, and they wanted the project—and their money—saved. By mid-November, there was open speculation that Bénard would be forced out if he did not accede to a contract revision. Bénard did not lack support for his views; others on Eurotunnel's board were tacit backers. But the banks knew what they wanted, and if Bénard did not agree, the flow of money would cease.

Lemley had demands of his own, the principal one being that Eurotunnel be compelled to stop acting as shadow contractor. He wanted the Project Implementation Division scaled back and assigned to tasks other than—as he saw it—second-guessing TML's conduct.

"There's not anything very pragmatic about André," Lemley said of Bénard. "My view of him: A man who has had an outstanding and basically brilliant career in business; in his time with Shell there was very little that one could criticize." Lemley noted that during the 1970s oil crisis, Bénard was one of the central players who negotiated between the West and the Mideast. "He came from there to a startup company," Lemley said. "He came to the company without a Shell-type organization and a Shell-type culture behind him. He came as a developer, and I don't know whether he assumed that because he *said* something that it simply was going to happen. Well, it doesn't happen around here that way. He doesn't have that kind of a culture or organization behind him, and he doesn't have the same deep pockets that Shell had. This is a one-project development thing: ET has one project, one single aim in life and that's to turn this into a transport system. And their pocketbook isn't big enough to fund what they're trying to build here."

All of this came to a head at a November 16 meeting at which the instructing banks were to discuss whether they would continue funding the project. On the Monday before, Eurotunnel announced that it would cut back its Project Implementation Division by assigning 90 of its 360 staff members to other duties in the following weeks. Eurotunnel indicated that this was simply a planned shift of emphasis, a turning toward training staff to operate the tunnel. However, it was almost universally viewed as a concession. The magazine *New Civil Engineer* quoted a TML official as saying, "The agreement [the Joint Accord] was that we would put our house in order by pulling in new heavyweights and Eurotunnel would cut back on its PID checking and second guessing everything we did."

Both Bénard and the Channel Tunnel survived the banks' meeting, and negotiations between Eurotunnel and TML continued. Ridley was the one who carried these forward, as best he could, with Lemley.

"Philippe [Essig] quickly fell out with Alastair and André, and particularly André," Ridley said. "In my view—I don't know this for a fact, and I wouldn't like it to be quoted as a statement of fact, but just a perception—that André, who didn't appear to like the left in French politics, thought [Essig] was a crazy French socialist, and a *Christian* Socialist. I remember André saying to me something like—and I don't know whether he used the word agnostic or atheist—'I was brought up as an atheist, and we learned to tell the truth. Essig is a Christian Socialist and he tells bloody lies.' I don't know whether the quote is right, but that was the message."

Ridley had been making an honest effort for months to find some common ground upon which his own board, and that of TML, could meet and shake hands, and from which both might set forth to complete the Channel Tunnel.

"At some stage, which I can't recall, I decided that the contract that we had between us and TML was for the birds," Ridley said. "The nature of the contract was such that it was contributing to the problems and was not an aid to the successful completion of the project." He felt that the contract encouraged confrontation, that it contained elements—such as optimization—that could be used as weapons. The contract provided each side with these weapons, and each had fallen into the habit of using them.

"I thought it might be possible to put together a reformulation of the contract which would aid in the collaborative approach to the project," Ridley said. These were words that might—indeed had—come from Lemley himself, and their negotiations approached something very like collaboration.

One possibility Ridley put forward to the Eurotunnel board was for a "lump-sum, all-up contract" that would have recognized and admitted the increased costs but basically capped the price. "I think it would have been fair to Eurotunnel if I could have guaranteed—and people suspected that I couldn't guarantee—that that would've actually been the limit, within reason, of the cost escalation," Ridley said.

"To some of my colleagues, such a suggestion was like spitting on the Bible," Ridley said. "I think André felt like this. I think some of the lawyers felt like this. And therefore I was given authority to go back and renegotiate certain things within some fairly constrained limits—I think it's true to say—with a number of people on my team keeping a close beady eye on me."

Behr, for one, doubted the value of Ridley's effort, convinced that Ridley was too sympathetic to TML's views. Ridley nonetheless continued the negotiations, which had begun during the summer of 1989, on into the winter. "I had countless sessions, where we invented a thousand and one formulae," he said. "And I couldn't do a deal with Jack, because I couldn't go far enough on behalf of Eurotunnel, and he was not prepared to go far enough to meet us. . . . I went back to André and Alastair." To them he quoted a famous line about the end of the brief Peace of Amiens between France and England during the Napoleonic era: "Normal relations between England and France were resumed; they were at war." "Well, that's what happened after I failed to deliver," he later recalled. "The war party took over again."

The fear of a coup by the contractors resurfaced, Ridley said. "There were other suggestions inside Eurotunnel that TML were going to create such mayhem that they were going to drive down the price of Eurotunnel shares, and the contractors were going to buy up Eurotunnel on the cheap." The guess was that if the shares could be driven down to 150 pence (they then stood at about 550 pence), the contractors would have the company for themselves. Ridley knew of no evidence that such a campaign was contemplated, "but there was a lot of talk about it inside Eurotunnel. I think the cochairmen may have held this view."

Lemley and Ridley did continue to search for costs that both sides agreed could be cut. By December they had identified almost £117 million. TML was also studying the HGV wagons, with a view toward making them simpler, lighter and much cheaper. The suggestion that this be done came, to Lemley's surprise, from the *maître d'oeuvre* at an October executive meeting of Eurotunnel and TML. Signing of the formal rolling-stock contracts was then imminent, based on the letters of intent signed in July with the Euroshuttle consortium. These specified closed HGV wagons. Any change would have to be approved by the Intergovernmental Commission. As events had shown, the IGC was inclined—indeed avid—to err on the side of greater safety, whatever the cost. Although decades of experience in the Alpine tunnels suggested that open HGV wagons were safe, closed HGV wagons might be safer, and this would almost certainly guide the commission. Looking at open HGV wagons thus seemed an empty exercise; relying on them for savings seemed foolhardy. But the study proceeded; by January 1990, with the lower costs of simpler HGV wagons figured in, the agreed-on savings reached almost £143 million.

Although Bénard's hard-line defense of the contract stood in the way of a negotiated peace, TML's anger focused on Alastair Morton. One of the inflexible demands that Lemley brought to the table was that Morton step back and let others run the project. As things stood, Morton had the last word about everything, and the word was most often *no*. As Ridley lost favor within Eurotunnel, Morton and Bénard stepped in to do the negotiating. By mid-January, Ridley was out of the picture, and Morton's aggressive personality asserted itself.

"Someone was quoted as saying, 'Alastair sees this project as being like a five-year takeover battle,'" Ridley said. "It's my judgment that Alastair is one of the brightest people, one of the quickest and most nimble people I've ever met. If I were ever in a takeover battle and wanted one ally, the guy I would go to is Alastair Morton, because his ability to deal with the banks, public relations and lawyers, and to put it all together, is absolutely brilliant. But takeover battles last three weeks or three months, and big projects, in my view, are not like that."

By January, the banks had been able to convince both sides to agree to a renegotiated contract that satisfied no one fully, but that each party—banks, contractor and client—could tolerate. The principal change was to raise the target cost, which covered the tunnels themselves, from £1.14 billion to £1.58 billion (at September 1985 prices), "above which all [target] costs will be shared 30/70 between TML/Eurotunnel without limit." Before, TML's responsibility was limited to 6 percent of the target cost.

In return, TML got a promise of management changes within Eurotunnel. "TML wanted an authority in Eurotunnel that could make decisions other than Alastair Morton," Lemley said. "So we struck a bargain whereby Eurotunnel agreed to reorganize their Project Implementation Division, and in turn TML agreed to have an unlimited cost sharing on the target works part of the contract, which was the tunneling."

These changes, which would open the way for the banks to continue funding the project, were incorporated in Heads of Agreement to be signed in January. These were to be followed by a formal contract amendment, to be signed on February 19. On January 8, 1990, the day before the Heads of Agreement were to be signed, the four Agent Banks wrote to Essig, confirming that they would support the new contract elements. Part of the understanding was that Eurotunnel would raise additional money by selling more stock. The banks wanted this done quickly, by June if possible; Eurotunnel preferred to wait until the fall.

The Heads of Agreement were duly signed the next day, clearing the way for Eurotunnel to secure urgently needed funds. The agreement also called upon Eurotunnel to pay £13,292,379 and 291,934,612 French francs to TML; bills for these sums had been accepted by Eurotunnel on December 22 but had not been paid.

Now the chief concern was to secure another £2 billion in bank loans to pay for the added costs that had been acknowledged by all sides. Selling this idea to the syndicate banks would not be easy under any circumstances. If the Heads of Agreement seemed not to be working, it would be all but impossible.

To some, the Heads of Agreement were far too weak and limited to solve the Channel Tunnel's deepest problems. Philippe Montagner was one of these, and in the weeks after the agreement was signed he drafted a remarkable document, which he entitled "Personal Reflections on the Evolution of the Project." On February 13, he sent it to André Bénard. In its very length—twenty-two pages—the document spoke volumes about the depth of Montagner's feelings—this was a Bouygues man after all, a man who had risen high in a company that considered brevity to be a dependable measure of executive ability. This summing-up of the project's history and difficulties, by someone who had been present at its inception, was infused with both anger and anguish. Stripped though they were of any ornament or verbosity, twenty-two pages were hardly enough to contain what Montagner had to say.

He began by noting that all parties—Eurotunnel, the *maître d'oeuvre*, TML and the banks—agreed that the project's costs had soared, but each had a different estimate of where the overall cost then stood. "Such an increase and such a divergence among the estimates show that the cost of the Project has not been mastered," Montagner wrote. Worse, Montagner was convinced that the Heads of Agreement, just signed after long and difficult negotiations, would prove insufficient to the task of solving "the very grave crisis that lies in the way of the project." The remainder of his letter was a litany of the many now-familiar and frustrating problems that had beset the tunnel project. Summing up, he wrote that the "misuse of the contract and changes in the understanding [between the parties] have brought on a hellish cycle of inflation in the costs of engineering, of management and of the technical solutions chosen." Montagner concluded with gloomy warnings and some advice. "The parties are now at an impasse, in a dispute of exceptional dimensions, which will worsen things and can only aggravate the current situation. Such a dispute is no way to control the industrial problems now before us, which from now on will decide the success of the project."

Montagner said Eurotunnel should be headed by an *homme d'exploitation,* a commercial man who could balance the business of running the tunnel against the cost of building it. The independent *maître-d'oeuvre* should be reconstituted to run the construction phase, while Eurotunnel prepared for the great task of operating the Channel Tunnel.

This was the heart of TML's position: Morton—and Bénard as well—would have to step away from running the project and set their hands to making Eurotunnel an operating company.

"Through the month of January, Alastair would have me come to his office a couple of different times, and we went over ideas about reorganization," Lemley said. In his view, Morton's offer was always "basically just a rehash of the people that were there; no real change, no chief executive in charge of the PID. So come the end of January, the banks wouldn't extend their banking waiver, because they were in violation of the Credit Agreement, and they owed us somewhere around £80 million pounds."

This £80 million had been certified by Eurotunnel, but there was no money to pay it without a further drawdown from the banks. Lemley now had it in his power to stall that drawdown, and he did, refusing to agree to the management changes that Eurotunnel suggested.

"Eventually, Eurotunnel agreed that they would appoint a new chief executive, which the contractors had been asking for," Tony Ridley said. "But then to their more than slight chagrin, the new chief executive turned out to be a man called Alastair Morton, and they went absolutely berserk."

Lemley recalled the incident: "Alastair called me down and he said, 'Our board has approved a new organization and now we want the amendment to the contract signed.' And I said, 'Well, let's see the organization.' And we went through it, and he had himself as chief executive, and it was not at all what we had agreed to do." Lemley told Morton that the decision was up to the executives of TML's partner companies, but that he didn't think they would agree. This prediction was borne out a few days later, Lemley said, when the partners met, agreed that Eurotunnel had to make more significant changes and refused to sign.

"At about that time, I went to Nanterre, the French court, for a judgment against Eurotunnel on this [£80 million] pay estimate that they had certified but they hadn't paid," Lemley recalled. "So we were in court trying to get a declaratory judgment in France, and I think the British agent banks were starting to get very nervous about the situation, and they had the governor of the Bank of England, Robin Leigh-Pemberton, call a meeting in the governor's chambers. Leigh-Pemberton and two of his aides set up the meeting; it was on a Friday afternoon.

"I arrived there with the chairman of each of the British companies. Eurotunnel was represented by Morton, Bénard and their British non-executive directors." Representatives of the British Agent Banks—very senior executives, Lemley said—filled out the cast.

This was on February 16, and only the weekend separated the project from the critical February 19 deadline, by which time the Heads of Agreement had to be ratified. Leigh-Pemberton opened the meeting and had everybody give his version of the events that had led them hither.

"Eurotunnel's non-executive directors were appalled that their contractor would try to dictate an oganization to them." Lemley said. "We said we weren't trying to dictate the organization, but if they wanted us to change the contract we wanted a proper person that'd run the PID. So after maybe forty-five minutes there was a caucus called by the governor, and we went out into another room."

Once outside the meeting room, Lemley called his office and found out that the French court had given TML the judgment against Eurotunnel.

"By that time the stock exchange had closed, and we couldn't do anything about collecting over the weekend," Lemley said. "So as the meeting reconvened, the governor asked if any of the parties had changed their position, and we said no. Everybody said no; nobody had moved in their position.

"I said, 'Well, there *is* one thing that is germane here, I think, and that's the fact that we do have a judgment against you in Nanterre, and we intend to collect on Monday.' There was a lot of muttering around the table: The non-executive directors of Eurotunnel were muttering about having to withdraw the stock from trading; the banks were muttering about having to appoint a conservator, and the governor suggested maybe another caucus. So we stayed in the meeting room and ET went out, and came back in about a half an hour and suggested John Neerhout as the new chief executive for the project development."

Neerhout was executive vice president and member of the management committee of the Bechtel Group, an exalted position. According to longtime Bechtel executives, Neerhout had broken out of the pack in the 1970s by turning around a South African project that had gone sour. His ability recommended him to all his superiors, and his toughness made him acceptable to Bechtel's hard drivers. He was short on affability. "Typical Bechtel, I must say," said Eurotunnel's Tony Gueterbock. "Not a glimmer of emotion anywhere, see what I mean? He has a sense of humor, but it takes a long time to come out."

Neerhout had a long behind-the-scenes association with the project—it was he who had put Behr into it—and a long association with Lemley. The two had played the same roles earlier in their careers, on the other side of the world, on the Oktedi project, a gold and copper venture that Morrison Knudsen did, under Bechtel supervision, in West Irian on the island of New Guinea. Neerhout ran the job for Bechtel, Lemley did the same for Morrison Knudsen. There was an uneasy relationship, at best, between the two.

"John was quoted as having been telling people that, well, he had fired this guy Lemley before and he'd do it again if he had to," Joe Anderson recalled. "That was the rumor. I heard it while I was in England; I'd never heard about it before. Someone else had told me; I knew nothing about it. And I'm sure if they told me it got back to Lemley, and Lemley hated it. . . . So they didn't get along that well."

Lemley—who said that he hadn't been driven off the West Irian job, that he had seen it through to completion—admitted that Neerhout was intelligent, but only after first noting, "He's a bastard."

Neerhout was therefore not a diplomatic choice for chief executive, not the one who might easily bridge the gulf that separated Eurotunnel from TML. The contractors' feelings appeared with stark clarity when a press release was readied to announce Neerhout's selection: The original draft in French included, as a grace note, the phrase, "TML a fait part de sa satisfaction pour cette nomination." Jean-Paul Parayre, who headed the French group in TML, sent a note to Bénard, asking him to strike the phrase from both the French and English versions of the press release; Bénard complied.

When Neerhout was named at the meeting, Lemley couldn't object to him on the basis that he was unqualified. "But we did ask who would he answer to, because we wanted a person independent of Morton," Lemley said. "And Morton said, as I remember, 'He'll answer to me.' And we said that wasn't sufficient; we wanted him to report to the non-executive directors of the board. And that was finally agreed, and there was a handwritten agreement signed by the five chairmen, Morton and Bénard . . . that outlined the deal."

Leigh-Pemberton held the document, which contained a clause that invited the parties to come back if there was ever a situation serious enough to require the Bank of England's intervention.

"On that basis, the governor said that he felt the stock could be traded until midday on Monday, and the banks agreed not to foreclose until the agreement was signed between ET [sic] and TML, with the understanding that it would be before noon on Monday," Lemley said. "After we got all that done, I went home. It was about seven o'clock. Now, in the meeting they had stated they were going to fire Ridley. . . . When I walked in the house, Ridley was on the telephone and wanted to know what had happened. So I told him."

This did not come as much of a surprise to Ridley; Morton and Bénard had both hinted at it. "At some stage [in the weeks leading to the Bank of England meeting] I remember Alastair saying to me—can't recall his words precisely—'One of us has got to go and it ain't gonna be me.' " Ridley said. "I effectively said, 'Well, you were here before me, Alastair, and I understand and I agree,' or words to that effect. Because although I've always believed his style was wrong—and I don't step away from that—clearly he had a longer history with the project."

Ridley added that there were hints—from Bénard—that Morton believed Ridley coveted his job. "I said, 'You've got to be joking,' " Ridley said. "Bénard's response was, 'Oh, it's obvious.' "

Lemley emerged from the Bank of England meeting nervous because he had not consulted TML's French partners before signing the agreement. He called Essig in Paris; he said he would gather the French leaders for a Monday morning telephone meeting.

"We were in Balfour Beatty's corporate offices, the five British chairmen and I," Lemley said. "The five French chairmen were gathered someplace, and we had a meeting. The French were not very happy about the settlement; they felt that we hadn't gotten what had been agreed to in early January, so there was a bit of a dust-up over that."

From the other side, it seemed that TML was stalling, intending to throw the project into receivership. In a Eurotunnel-sponsored account of the events, Graham Corbett, Eurotunnel's managing director for finance, said that TML "simply went off the air" as the Monday deadline came and went. "Throughout that previous week we had been approving invoices for payment one by one, but we were down to our last £1 million. For a company our size that means as near as you can get to bust. It was the only time I doubted whether we would see the project through."

Monday passed, Tuesday morning passed. In the afternoon, by Eurotunnel's account, Bénard scheduled an emergency board meeting for 8:30 Wednesday morning at Le Bourget, outside Paris. The dissolution of Eurotunnel was to be on the agenda. At five in the afternoon, after a further series of telephone negotiations, the two sides found it possible to agree. The necessary signatures were in place by nine o'clock that evening.

Montagner soon had a sense of what lay ahead: On February 27, Bénard replied to his "Reflections." Had it been an English business letter, it would have been remarkable for its impersonal, all-business tone. In France, where even a dunning letter from the tax collector is couched in polite phrases approved by the generations that have used and polished them, Bénard's letter—written in French—was little better than an insult, a brush-off, a blow.

"Having barely signed an accord, you tell me that you aren't in agreement," Bénard said in his first of five points. "That's not acceptable. The two sides are linked by the accord. For my part, I defend my point of view up to a point, I accept yours up to a point, I sign without reservations and I execute the accord. I expect no less of you. . . ."

"I deplore, in a word, your commentaries on the increase in capital," Bénard continued. "We will succeed in this project together or not at all. We are working to succeed; your comments won't help us.

"Eurotunnel's executives understand the problems well. They are all men of experience who, without claiming to know everything, work day after day to resolve the difficult problems that we faced.

"I share your opinion that a different spirit is needed to guide the project, and I hope that the new teams at TML and Eurotunnel will be able to establish the rapport that will make it possible. But you cannot be ignorant of the responsibility that Eurotunnel's board has to obligations given in the shareholders' prospectus or in the banks' Information Memorandum. Those documents were based on estimates made by the [contracting] companies in 1986. The first result of the considerable price increases of which you have notified us must be a renewal of the hard work of 1987. To this undertaking, we must first of all have the necessary trust, and then share it. If TML doesn't understand this, all of our efforts are in vain."

It was a shockingly brusque and dismissive letter. It was perhaps understandable, since Bénard had only days before been forced, by TML's hard bargaining, to schedule a meeting to discuss Eurotunnel's dissolution. Still, it was odd: The head of another of the French companies, Serge Michel of SGE, had written a similar letter to Bénard at almost the same time. Bénard made similar points in his reply, but couched them in polite language: "Thank you for your letter of February 21. As you asked, I have sent it on to the executives of Eurotunnel. In the meantime, I am drawn to offer certain observations that aren't new, but upon which I cannot remain silent, given the gravity of your remarks." These observations were offered in phrases that could not have given offense. Bénard closed by looking forward to a meeting with Michel, adding, "I would like, at all events, to assure you that in all that concerns Eurotunnel, we will stay steadfastly loyal to the accord that we have signed. I have no doubt that TML will do the same."

So the question for TML now became: Which of these faces would Bénard—and Eurotunnel—show in the months ahead?

16

TML could thank Bénard for one thing, at least: He eliminated prefer-
ential buying by Eurotunnel, the practice that had brought in the GEC-
Alsthom signaling system, to the contractors' great dismay.

"There was a period of time when it looked like there was a lot of preference being given to French companies," said Joe Anderson. "They decided
they would sole-source certain things and save all this talk. . . . That was definitely going on." Bénard, he said, "stepped in and stopped that." However,
some single-source deals, already in the works when Bénard acted, went forward to completion.

One was the contract for the pass doors in the shuttle, which went to De
Dietrich, the French company that Eurotunnel commissioned to study the
problem. Bryan Driver, who was running the rolling-stock program at TML,
thought the De Dietrich system was good but complex and expensive. Another proposal, submitted by Tebel-Darchem, an Anglo-Dutch joint venture,
matched the merits of De Dietrich's at lower cost and with greater simplicity.

A more important question lingered over this debate, of course: What precisely would De Dietrich build? Eurotunnel had instructed TML to keep the
sixty-centimeter-wide fire doors that the Safety Authority had expressly rejected at the Guernsey seminar. The authority hadn't budged since: It had
kept its part of the bargain by permitting nonsegregation in the passenger
shuttles; it expected Eurotunnel to do the same. Eurotunnel expected to
change the authority's mind.

In mid-March, Eurotunnel's Alain Bertrand wrote to the IGC, expressing
great concern about seventy-centimeter doors, noting that Eurotunnel "is
taking all the necessary practicable steps to meet the requirements," but that
replacing the sixty-centimeter doors would increase the cost by £6 million,
cause a three-month delay and add as much as three hundred kilograms to

the weight of each shuttle wagon. "Having thus carefully studied the implications of your request, we believe there is no reasonable practicable solution" but to build sixty-centimeter doors.

This brought an encouragingly mild reply from the IGC: It couldn't say yes, but it could and did say that the Safety Authority understood the problem. Eurotunnel chose to bet that it could convince the safety people to accept the narrower doors. In doing so, it was taking a hand in yet another high-stakes game: In January, during the hurly-burly that surrounded the Heads of Agreement, Eurotunnel and TML had presented a semiopen design, with lattice sides and a full roof, for the HGV wagons. This was halfway between the closed wagons that the Safety Authority wanted and the wide-open models that Eurotunnel wished to use. The semiopen wagons bore the usual defects of compromise: They could not contain the hypothetical fire that burned so bright in the authority's mind, yet they were too heavy to achieve the minimum speeds demanded by the concession. Though there was no guarantee that the Safety Authority would accept this hybrid, the Euroshuttle Consortium was ordered to start work on it.

In late May, TML agreed to help Eurotunnel prepare its case on the pass doors. Driver asked the Euroshuttle companies to assemble a dossier examining the whole pass-door question. The idea was to give the IGC a way of changing its mind without losing face—as Driver noted in a memo at the time, it seemed that the Safety Authority, having given way on the nonsegregation issue, was standing firm on the wider doors "more a matter of principle than of technical safety origin." The dossier was to emphasize the safety of the narrow doors and the expense of the wider ones.

"This approach is a gamble and much will depend on Alain Bertrand's willingness to try this proposed line of reasoning," Driver noted in his memo. "If he doesn't accept it, or if the SA will not be persuaded, then Eurotunnel is in serious trouble and we cannot help them any further."

Euroshuttle, in collaboration with TML, obliged with a forthright assessment of the issues. Daniel Des Landes, Euroshuttle's project director, wrote a letter noting that the issue of pass-door width had "resurfaced." The letter said that accommodating wider doors could require lengthening the wagons; this was "out of the question," since it would essentially set the project back to zero. Everything—even the workshops in which the cars were already in production—would have to be redesigned and retooled. Parts that had been manufactured already would have to be scrapped. In sum, Des Landes wrote, changing the the fire doors "would generate a delay of several months as well as an impressive cost impact on the project."

Three days after this was delivered to Eurotunnel, Bertrand wrote back to TML. The dossier, he wrote, had "essential elements for a good demonstration, but this demonstration is not enclosed. You know that we have undertaken to write the safety part of the dossier, and that you promised to present the technical part so that we would not have to alter it." He asked TML to redraft it.

This was not at all what TML had agreed to do, Driver said, and his office wrote back immediately to note "it was not the intention for TML to write the paper for submission to the IGC and we do not propose to do so."

Eurotunnel, to be sure, was awash in concerns at that moment. It had scheduled a special board meeting in Paris to authorize an increase in its share capital. This was a requisite if bank financing were to continue; Eurotunnel told the public that it had been negotiating with the Agent Banks and that everything was contingent on "raising a sum in the order of £500 million of additional equity or quasi equity" before the end of year.

In fact, the deadline was even tighter; the banks had first asked that the equity financing be done by June, then relented and moved it back to October 15. The reference to "quasi equity" was a signal that there were some unusual problems with the stock issue. The syndicate banks were demanding a *guarantee* that the new equity funds would be available, or else they would not permit any further draws on the loan after June 1. Since Eurotunnel had exhausted all of its Equity 3 money and was drawing as much as £100 million a month, this was a death threat.

Morgan Grenfell proposed the solution: Underwriters would commit themselves to paying at least £2.40 per share when the issue came to market. If the tunneling did not encounter any unusually grave problems, the agreed price would be £4 per share—about 20 percent less than the then-current price of the existing shares. In late May, Eurotunnel's standing received a further boost when the European Investment Bank pledged £300 million; this was to be a twenty-five-year loan, available once the tunneling was finished.

But neither this show of support nor the standby commitment could work miracles or convince fearful banks in the far-flung syndicate to commit further resources to the troubled venture. By the end of July—by which time 90 percent of the new £2 billion in loans was to have been subscribed—the Agent Banks had been able to scare up a mere £800 million.

On August 13, Eurotunnel notified the stock exchanges that the syndication was "making slower than expected progress" and was unlikely to meet the August 31 deadline. Ninety-one banks, whose participation represented 31 percent of the total loan, "have so far declined their support," Eurotunnel said. Another twenty-six banks, representing 13 percent of the loan, hadn't replied. The remaining ninety-three banks had announced their support. The Japanese banks that had been avid participants at the start had now become the core of the opposition.

Faced with that opposition, the Agent Banks asked the syndicate banks to extend the waiver to permit Eurotunnel to continue drawing funds through September. "Unless syndication can be completed shortly thereafter the rights issue planned for October will be delayed," Eurotunnel warned.

Ten days later, the *Financial Times* noted a feeling of gloom and crisis around the project. The bank syndicate had pledged a mere £1.1 billion, the piece said, adding that the bankers now seemed to be terrified by the enormous scale of the project. September 1—the day on which the historic breakthrough was to have occurred, according to the schedule in the original construction contract—passed without anything to cheer. The best that could be said was that the syndicate banks agreed that the project should not be scrapped—there was no trouble getting agreement on continuing the waivers; the reluctant banks simply wanted someone else to put up the additional money.

The project's momentum had now overtaken the Agent Banks, too: If the syndicate banks wouldn't participate in the new financing, Eurotunnel wouldn't be able to sell its shares. In that case, the Agent Banks would have to continue to advance money to keep the project from collapsing on their heads.

Nonetheless, the pressure on Eurotunnel—particularly from the press— was enormous. The suggestion that the project was about to fold was ever in ink; Morton was driven to file formal complaints with Britain's watchdog Press Council. Morton admitted that "our forecast of total funds required to 1995 is £7.66 billion plus an acceptable funding margin. Ergo, extra money is needed and if not raised the project will be at risk." But, he added, £3 billion remained of the funds pledged in 1987, so the crisis was still some distance away. He had hardly uttered that assurance when another crisis rose up before him: The ICG rejected the shuttle design with the six-hundred-millimeter-wide doors.

Eurotunnel decided to make a last-ditch fight. On October 8, Morton wrote Essig on the subject, with a copy to Driver. The letter, in French, was full of fellow feeling: Morton noted that the dossier "has been the object of a collaboration *très poussé* between our teams since 1987." He praised Driver by name, saying that he "was constantly at Alain Bertrand's side in the difficult '89 negotiation, notably during the Guernsey seminar. He heartily supported the cause of the 600mm doors on that occasion." Morton noted that the shuttle-design proposal "was prepared jointly by TML and Eurotunnel." Morton rejoiced that TML was ready to support Eurotunnel in a last stand against the wider doors.

The tone of the letter made Driver uneasy. He showed it to his assistant, Bernard Pavot. "I think he's trying to implicate you," Pavot said, confirming Driver's suspicion. He immediately wrote to Essig, explaining his misgivings, saying that Morton's letter "could be an attempt, perhaps a first-step of an attempt, to link TML and me in particular with the quarrel which exists between ET and the IGC. . . . If my suspicions are well founded, then we must be prepared to reject totally any move by ET to shift the blame." To ensure against this, Essig wrote a polite response to Morton, which generously gave Eurotunnel full credit for everything that had happened.

Part of the last-ditch campaign was to be a demonstration, a test evacuation through a six-hundred-millimeter opening, to show that narrow doors would provide an adequate escape route. The Casualty Union was called in to provide verisimilitude for this bit of theater. The Casualty Union is a volunteer group that provides the "victims" for any disaster one might care to stage. If the Red Cross wished to train its people for, say, one of the major railway accidents to which the British had grown accustomed, they called on the Casualty Union for a platoon of players.

"They will come," Driver said. "They will simulate everything. They'll moan and groan and writhe and scream. . . . They can be sick, lame, lazy, everything you like. Forty of them were going to come, with a fair share of sticks and crutches."

This simulated disaster very nearly came to genuine grief. When Driver arrived at his office on the appointed day, an assistant told him there was a problem: The Casualty Union staff member who was arranging the mock disaster had herself fallen victim to a real illness and had been unable to issue the call for volunteers. The bearer of these tidings told Driver they would have to postpone the test for perhaps two months.

"I said, 'Like hell we will; I'll get a team, and we've got to get it before ten o'clock,' " Driver said. "So I found a number of people in the London or Sutton area, whom I knew, of different ages and abilities. And I told them what I was looking for. I said, 'Why don't you come? It will be a free lunch, and you'll have a lot of fun.'

"One was an elderly couple—he could only get out in a wheelchair—and I said, 'Come on; you'll have a great day.' They were approaching seventy years of age. I said, 'Have you got any friends? Please bring them.' " Driver quickly collected two dozen volunteers, whose ranks he supplemented with a draft from within his own office. By ten o'clock, he had just the motley assortment that the occasion demanded.

They performed admirably, and Driver delivered the great day he had promised. "They wanted to be part of the tunnel project," he said. "They understood what we were trying to do was make this safer for everybody, and they thought it was great fun." Even the wheelchairs rolled through the six-hundred-millimeter gap with ease. When it was all over, Driver had the local florist take violets to the ladies that had contributed their pretended sufferings to the event. The men got thanks without flowers. The exercise convinced the *maître-d'oeuvre* at least, and so the pass-door war would go on a little longer.

By this time, the pass-door issue had become just one more wave in the sea of regulation upon which Eurotunnel rolled and pitched. The IGC and the Safety Authority were feeling their strength, and found much to say about everything. The shuttle cars were forced to evolve to meet an ever-lengthening list of concerns.

Noulton, who had left government to take a job with TML, found that the IGC's passion for absolute safety had wrought mighty changes in the shuttle wagons. "There's an atavistic fear in this country of anything new," Noulton said. "The fire brigade people got on the bandwagon, because they wanted to get lots of money out of us and lots of training and lots of new equipment and lots of new personnel. So they started winging on about the longest crematorium in the world. So everybody had a field day."

Fire burned on as the great fear, fanned to white heat by the press. Even the Kent Fire Brigade, never given to minimizing the hazard of fire in the tunnel, grew sick of the press attention. The brigade's chief, writing in a professional magazine, noted, "A very small fire . . . which was put out with a hand extinguisher" resulted in the brigade "being virtually under siege for nearly 24 hours because of the sensationalist local press statements." He was also dismayed by other fire officials who spoke of "the longest crematorium in the world" and "Armageddon" in the tunnel.

"There is no rolling stock operating anywhere on the Continent—or, indeed, probably in the world—which would be able to meet the safety requirements that have been put on ours," Noulton said. "All these dangerous French trains, German trains? Deathtraps that wouldn't be allowed in the tunnel."

"Rail travel is known to be the safest form of travel, bar none. There isn't any safer form of travel; the figures tell this time and time again. And if you look at accidents that do happen to trains, they are caused by driver error, invariably—and we've eliminated driver error. The driver cannot override the system. If he tries to, the train will stop, and all the trains behind him will stop, so we've eliminated driver error. I mean, he's there to reassure the passengers, basically. . . . He isn't there to drive the bloody train. I mean, we don't want *people* driving *trains*.

"The second [major cause of rail accidents] is derailment. Well, you've seen the structure of that tunnel. On one side we've got this great walkway.

On the other side we've got a lower walkway. . . . If the train comes off that track, it will be held in an upright position. It'll bump along the blocks and come to a controlled halt. But it won't tip over and it won't run into anything."

Like anyone (outside the IGC and the Safety Authority) who had anything to do with safety in the shuttles, Noulton could quickly work himself into a lather when discussing the subject. He did so here, continuing his litany of empty worries and idle threats to the public's well-being. Head-on collisions? Difficult to imagine in one-way tunnels. Smoke? The ventilation system guaranteed a safe haven in the service tunnel.

"These aren't trains we're operating," Noulton said in summary. "They're Boeing 747s without wings."

The shuttles came to be packed with the whims of officials for whom the bottom line was safety, not cost. There were, for example, three separate and entire systems to detect fire in the passenger shuttles: an infrared system that could "see" the fire, a smoke detector, and an opacity meter—a device that measured the amount of light that could be transmitted through the air between two points, a device more often used on industrial smokestacks to measure the particulate content of smoke. There were two fire-fighting systems. There was a video surveillance system, with two cameras in each car.

Each shuttle wagon was loaded with other systems as well: electric, electronic, hydraulic, pneumatic, air-conditioning. There were fifty kilometers of cabling in each wagon. Computers collected enormous amounts of information—there were ten thousand control points in each train—and fed much of it to the onboard desk of the *chef de train,* or train captain. The captain's desk had a state-of-the-art touch-screen monitor that enabled him to check on the status of all systems in any car.

"He gets a menu," said one American engineer who worked on the cars. "He punches in car 17. Another menu flies up with all the systems on it: Fire suppression, fire detection, door status, fire door status, lighting status, power consumption, toilet status . . . all computerized, all digital. Each of the systems has its own control system full of chips. It's unbelievable. And that all has to work, OK? It has to endure vibration, shock, all kind of things." The train captain also faced a vast array of monitors that fed images from the surveillance cameras in each wagon. Essig and many others argued vainly that this was useless, that no one could pay attention to a whole bank of monitors.

By early October, the financial crisis had eased. Eurotunnel's board learned, at its October 5 meeting in Paris, that the bank syndicate would supply an additional £1.8 billion. This, coupled with the £300,000 pledged earlier by the European Investment Bank, raised the company's total credit from £5 billion to £7.1 billion—sufficient for Eurotunnel to plan its share sale for November.

(This financial coup was very nearly overshadowed by an embarrassing accident in Folkestone. One of the big running-tunnel TBMs, which had completed its uphill drive to Holywell Coombe in late September, had been sold for a substantial sum to another tunneling project. But in trying to remove the huge machine from the pit into which it had been driven, something went wrong. The TBM slipped from its slings and tumbled back into the hole. It was cut up for scrap. No word of the misadventure ever reached the outside world; photographs of the event were suppressed.)

Persuading the Japanese banks had required the extraordinary—and extraordinarily discreet—intervention of Margaret Thatcher. "I was told that Mrs. Thatcher, who had refused to give any government money to the project, wrote a letter to the Japanese prime minister," Essig said. The text of the note has never been made public, but its plain sense is part of Channel Tunnel lore: Thatcher wrote that she was astonished to learn that Japanese banks were reluctant to lend more money to a project that had—that very clearly had—the wholehearted support of the British government. The words had the desired effect, and Eurotunnel was soon setting up telephone lines to receive inquiries from would-be investors and assembling a new batch of travel perquisites to accompany the shares.

In the weeks that followed, the tunnel's fortunes looked good in some lights, bad in others. On October 25, Eurotunnel announced that "signature of the extensive documentation for its Extended Syndicated Credit Agreement has made satisfactory progress. It began simultaneously in London and Paris this morning." The agreement itself would be ready for signing shortly; Crédit national had eased its terms on another four billion francs in further financing; the TBM in the British service tunnel had halted about three hundred meters from the French machine and would shortly send its drill probe forward to connect Britain to Europe.

All banks had signed by noon the next day, and six days later, newspapers were trumpeting that the borehole had been "less than the width of a handkerchief off target"—an exaggeration that fell within the license granted to publicists. The precise difference, measured some days later, was 358 millimeters in the horizontal (almost precisely fourteen inches) and 58 millimeters in the vertical (a hairsbreadth more than two and a quarter inches).

Other signs were less encouraging. The prospectus that Eurotunnel issued early in November said that TML had submitted 201 claims for extra payment, of which 87 were settled or withdrawn. Most of the outstanding claims had to do with "alleged changes to the design or construction of the System," and were part of the lump sum.

In the two weeks that followed, Eurotunnel had good news to report: The big running-tunnel TBMs were breaking records; the French and British machines were approaching each other at 578 meters per week in the north tunnel and 535 meters per week in the south. At that rate, they would meet the following summer—as originally planned, having made up all lost time. On November 20, the Land Running Tunnel South TBM broke through at Holywell, a month ahead of schedule.

One week later, Eurotunnel hand-delivered a letter to TML: A formal notice to instruct Euroshuttle to build the seven-hundred-millimeter firedoors in the passenger shuttles. All efforts to convince the Safety Authority to ease this requirement had failed. TML duly instructed the consortium to change the design in the least expensive way and to prepare estimates of how much the change would cost in both money and time.

Three days later, De Dietrich halted production of the six-hundred-millimeter pass doors. On the following day, a British hand reached through a hole in the chalk marl beneath the Channel and grasped a French hand. The link had been forged.

17

When the orchestral thunder of construction was at its fullest, anyone—engineer or not—could comprehend the magnitude of the venture. Every shift began and ended with a reminder of how far things had gone, how far away was the safe and smiling world of the earth's surface. The descent took two and a half hours, the ascent took the same. "It was a serious thing to go underground," said Helen Nattrass. Land tunnels had a shaft every kilometer or so, she said, and daylight was seldom more than twenty minutes away. The Channel Tunnel was very different. "Down there, you went down for the whole shift," she said. "Eight hours down there seemed like sixteen." The isolation, the sense that the only way out was the long route by which you had come in, was almost tangible.

On both the French and British sides, the circulatory system of this great body of work was the construction railway. In Britain, the heart of this vast and complicated network pulsed under Shakespeare Cliff, at the bottom of the access adits; in France, it was at the bottom of the Sangatte shaft. Fresh workers departed from these chambers on work trains loaded with segments and grout and concrete. The same trains returned hours later, stripped of the tunnel segments, with muck skips full of excavated waste and manriders full of exhausted tunnelers. The construction railways also had to transport everything mechanical and electrical that was to be installed in the tunnels, and the personnel who were to install them. On the British side alone, work trains would log 150,000 kilometers a month; seventy trains—thirty-five in-by, to use the parlance, and an equal number out-by—would run the 22 kilometers of the service tunnel in a single shift. This movement went on twenty-four hours a day without benefit of a signaling system, along tracks that were often blocked by work cars and other equipment.

Tim Green, a sardonic Scot who had come to the project in 1989, ran the British construction railway. He was admiral of a large undersea fleet of vehicles: There were 183 locomotives of thirteen different types, including self-propelled manriders. He had 1,209 cars in his rolling-stock fleet: 343 Mulhauser side-tipping muck skips, 554 flatbeds for carrying concrete segments, 34 unpowered manriders, 51 concrete-mixing cars, plus a mixed brood of flatbeds, cement cars, cable-drum cars and mess-and-toilet wagons.

Locomotives were in short supply, so Green and his crews cobbled together fifteen other "prime movers"—self-propelled work cars that could inch along, from one work station to the next, using winches or hydraulic rams. These were useful, he said, "where somebody had to do something twice every segment, where every 750 millimeters you had to stop."

Green had recruited most of his locomotive drivers from the construction industry and had trained them on simulators. "Train drivers who came from BR very often brought all manner of habits that I didn't want," he said, adding that he preferred to look far afield for his recruits: "I literally tried to dodge the odd local. I liked traveling men because they're lean and hungry and used to the construction industry. We were working almost exclusively six days on, two days off, which means you never get a weekend."

Although Green had come to the tunnel from a thirty-year career with British Rail, even longtime tunnelers like Denman acknowledged that he had The Crack. He was a thin, gingery man, with a fine cutting edge of wit. "If you look at his background he's got all the wrong sort of qualifications," said Denman. "You'd never ever think he would fit into the scene. But Tim is one hell of a guy, smashing guy. He was given an almost impossible task to do down there, to run that railway without upsetting everybody, and he did it."

In the four years he had the job, Green oversaw several logistical services in the British tunnels. During tunneling, everything moved on the narrow-gauge construction railway. Later, after the tunneling was done, he operated a standard-gauge service on the new track in the running tunnels, and a rubber-tired fleet on the new concrete roadbed in the service tunnel.

These transport systems offered nice measures of the Channel Tunnel's size and complexity. The narrow-gauge construction railway was twenty thousand tons of rail, in six- and nine-meter lengths, 37.5 kilograms to the meter, laid nine hundred millimeters apart. All of the rail was leased from British Steel, which had found this way at last to participate in building the fixed link. There were more than two hundred kilometers of track in the tunnels and another fourteen on the surface at Lower Shakespeare Cliff.

Green liked to tell people that he operated the third largest railway in the United Kingdom, after British Rail and the London Underground, and the latter was only half again as large as the Channel Tunnel's system. At peak, the construction railways logged enough train-miles each month to circle the earth four times. Over its five years of operation, there were train-miles enough for five round-trip journeys to the moon.

Remarkably enough, almost all of the hauling at this peak time was done by diesel locomotives. The early presumption had been that the seventy-eight electric locomotives in Green's fleet would do most of the underground work; diesels would devour oxygen and replace it with foul exhaust. But the electric locos, like the delicate computers on the TBMs, were not at their best in the harsh tunnel atmosphere. With water raining down on them, and moisture precipitating out of the water-saturated atmosphere onto their every surface, the electric locos began shorting and burning out. Half of the Mark I Hunsletts were converted to diesel after it became apparent that the tunnel ventilating systems—long ducts that followed each of the TBMs and carried fresh air pumped from Lower Shakespeare Cliff—were more than adequate to their assigned tasks. In the service tunnels, 250 cubic meters of air were pumped in each minute, and 200 cubic meters extracted; the numbers for the undersea running tunnels were 300 cubic meters in, 250 cubic meters out. Most of the time the men and diesels used about half of the air that the system delivered. "We occasionally used .6 of the air, and when the vent wasn't working particularly well, it did get pretty blue down there," Green said.

The U.K. construction railway began on the surface, amid the mounds of concrete segments that poured in from the Isle of Grain. It ran down the broad oval of Adit A2, through a bewildering maze of tracks in the marshaling area and thence off into the tunnels, right into the long framework trails of the tunnel-boring machines.

No single train made the entire passage; trains were uncoupled and reassembled at the bottom of the adit. The first stage in making up a train began on the surface, when the segments went aboard the flatcars. "You had to get right segments for each ring," Green said. "There was an ordering system from underground—'The next ring I want is, three of those segments and four of those'—which meant we had to put the trains down in order. If you got one out of order, and you suddenly came across a bit of SCI [cast iron] in the middle of some concrete, that would be a monumental cock-up. Only twice or three times in, well, half a million segments did we manage to get things in the wrong order. That was usually because some field superintendent had nicked a train to go and get *his* tunnel working at the expense of his mates." Cooperation governed inside each of the six tunnels; ruthless competition ruled relations between each tunnel and all the others, and any superintendent would cheerfully beggar his neighbor to reach the bonuses that were paid for rapid progress.

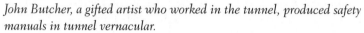

OK Charlie, it's done now and there's nothing to be gained by bluff and you are going to get a 'going over' by your supervisor. Well deserved too. So, first thing to do is get it moved where it won't present a hazard. Next move is to find out how to 'estimate' how much material is needed for a particular job, and don't be afraid to ask! Most people like to help, and you've all the qualified people you need here, right! Don't make the same mistake again. Mistakes can teach you valuable lessons if you don't have too many. So learn from them.

John Butcher, a gifted artist who worked in the tunnel, produced safety manuals in tunnel vernacular.

Green had ample room on the surface for his operations, thanks to the decision to dump all the tunnel spoil at Lower Shakespeare. The earliest plans had been to send the land tunnel-boring machines downhill from Folkestone; the spoil was to be used to level the terminal site. This was scrapped for the logistical convenience of operating all of the tunnel drives from one central facility at Shakespeare Cliff. But the open simplicity that Green enjoyed on the surface disappeared at the bottom of the adit, where a big and busy rail yard had been stuffed into three cramped tubes. Rack locomotives came and left here, endlessly crawling up the sloping adit with empty segment flatcars and returning with loaded ones. The segment flatcars joined empty muck skips and manriders—the men came down through the vertical shaft from Upper Shakespeare Cliff—and a locomotive hauled the train out to one of the TBMs. At peak, two thousand tons of spoil came up the conveyor per hour, in which time five hundred tons of segments and other gear were sent down and then out into the tunnels.

The trains also had to carry other necessaries, such as rails to extend the construction railway as the TBM progressed, ducting to extend the ventilation system, grout, concrete and materials for the cross-passages and piston relief ducts.

And water. There was fresh running water out in the tunnels, but it was there for the convenience of the machines: It was used to control dust and wash down the machinery to guard against saline corrosion. The only thing this water did for the workers was to make them more uncomfortable; it kept the humidity high as a complement to the high temperature that the big machines generated. The ventilation system removed some fraction of the waste heat, but most of it stayed down, soaking into bodies. The humidity was always near 100 percent, and the temperature was often 38°C—100°F. "You would stand down there and just feel the perspiration pour off you," Green said. (After construction was complete and the waste heat dissipated, the ambient temperature in the tunnels dropped to 17.5°C, or about 64°F.)

The drinking water—the water that kept the tunnelers alive in the hellish heat and humidity near the face—all came from a tap at the base of the adits. A tunneler drank an average of six liters of water on an eight-hour shift. At peak, Green was shuttling in a thousand tunnelers per shift, which meant that the trains had to ferry in eighteen thousand liters of drinking water—almost five thousand gallons, carried in five- and ten-gallon plastic jugs—each twenty-four hours.

Once clear of the marshaling yard, the trains had to weave their ways through very crowded tunnels. There were crossover switches every 375 meters, so that trains could switch tracks to avoid congestion. This allowed workers along the route to park a needed car near their work site: Hand-miners cutting a cross-passage, for instance, could keep a muck skip at hand; a crew installing the butterfly valves that controlled the passage of air through piston relief ducts could inch along on a flatbed work car.

These constrictions meant that "we had to work single-line along big lumps of the tunnel," Green said. Single-line working meant that in-by and out-by trains would both be using the same tracks; the trick was to make sure that they did not try to use the same track at the same time. Automatic signaling systems had been doing just that for years, but the construction railway did not have automatic signals—indeed, it had no signaling system at all. Green had advised against having one, on the belief that none could be made to work in the tunnel. There was very little room for signals, particularly in the service tunnel, and extending the systems to follow the TBMs would be complicated. Green's belief had its proof in the French tunnels. "The French, you see, went for a signaling system on their construction railway," Green said. "It cost 18 million quid, and it was in use about two percent of the time. It was a trackside system, and didn't work cause it was too wet and shitty."

British trains were guided by operations board controllers, or OBCs, rather than trackside lights. OBCs were humans, and accumulated evidence suggested that they were born rather than made. The OBC sat in a metal box, a two-meter-by-four shipping container that had been converted for his use if not comfort. The furnishings were a long bench with a radio base station on it and a white magnetic board on one long wall. "No windows," Green said. "A coffee-making machine, rather a dirty floor." The white board held a diagram of the track system in the tunnel and a supply of small magnets. Each magnet had the number of a locomotive. The OBC controlled the trains by radio, speaking to the locomotive drivers.

"The first OBCs sat or stood with a hand-held radio," Green said. "They could see the arse end of a TBM and there was one train. Then all of a sudden there were two trains, and he could still see the arse end of the TBM. Then the TBM got out of sight and there were three trains. And the OBCs just grew with it." The only possible training for the work was apprenticeship under an experienced OBC, and it quickly became apparent that it required a certain type of thinking.

Young men seemed to do better at learning the job, but youth alone was no guarantee of success: Some trainees lasted only a few hours. "They'd look bright people," Green said. "We'd put them on, and by lunchtime they'd say, 'This isn't for the likes of me.' And they'd be right. . . . It isn't intelligence; God knows what it is. It's just the ability to control something. The computers we had down there were between their ears." Green was fairly certain that he himself did not have whatever it took to be an OBC.

The best of the OBCs was a young Kentishman named Mark Nadin, but who was known as Pykie to everyone in the tunnels. "Pykie" was a Kentish dialect word for Gypsy or Romany. Green did not know if Nadin had Romany blood in his veins, but it was certain that as Pykie he showed an uncanny ability to keep trains from disaster.

"Pykie could come on shift and in three minutes he'd know where every one of thirty or forty trains were," Green said. "He would move those trains through these single-line working bits. He never had two opposing each other. If in the middle of that there was an emergency, like a derailment, he'd handle it totally calmly and efficiently. He really was very good." Most of the time, Pykie did not bother moving magnets around on his white board; he kept track of all movements in his head.

The most perishable product that Green's railway carried was concrete, which was mixed wet at the surface and sent down in bullets, cars whose pointed bodies rotated. The mix had to be adjusted as the tunnels lengthened and the trip time increased. Occasionally, one of the bullet trains would derail or get delayed. When that happened, no effort was spared to get the bullet back to the surface before the concrete set hard—it was useless as concrete after such an aborted journey, but at least one could get it out of the bullet.

If the concrete set hard, the only way to get it out of the bullet was by hand. The bullets held either six or nine cubic meters, and there was room

A concrete bullet car.

inside for only two men, their tools and ear protectors. "Jesus, that was hard work," Green said. "And yet we had some guys who wouldn't do anything else; they loved it. If they got a piece out the size of a football, they'd cheer, because most of it came out as dust." Green was particularly proud of the fact that he managed to halve the frequency of "incidents"—breakdowns and derailments—that allowed such disasters to happen.

Green liked to think of the tunnel as a complex of long factories that, taken together, stretched about 150 kilometers. He was allotted about two meters of the width of this exceedingly narrow world, through which he was to transport all of its needs and all of its waste product. The months before the breakthrough were the most difficult; the service tunnel was often as crammed and cramped as those wasted bullets of rock-hard concrete.

"The one word I learned down there was *logistics*," said David Denman, whose skills deepened as the tunneling became more complex: He began work with "two or three men, a couple of engineers, and myself," he said. By the time his marine service tunnel had gone sixteen kilometers—about two thirds of the way to breakthrough—Denman was in charge of a factory that operated around the clock, with a workforce that often exceeded five hundred on each of the three shifts.

It was a very crowded world. The TBM operator sat a few meters back from the cutting head, usually with an engineer for company. A few feet farther back was the build chamber, where the rings were assembled; this was where the shift boss and tea urn sat. "The engineer's got the brain power, the shift boss has got the experience in the tunneling," Denman said. "Put the two of them together, and between them they'll run your tunnel for you."

There also would be a leading miner and his crew at the back end of the TBM, setting the rings with an erector operator who ran the machine that handled and placed the segments. There would probably be an inspector of some sort, perhaps an electrician or a fitter, perhaps others drawn by the tea urn. "It was always quite busy at the front end," Denman said. "The tea urn always tended to keep it busy. Move back another twenty feet and there would be a couple of guys grouting. If there's a train just come in to the TBM, a crane operator and a couple of general operatives will be unloading the train."

The next 150 meters behind the TBM would have an engineer or two, a foreman, a couple of fitters, an electrician, a couple of grouters working up high and the locomotive driver.

Two hundred meters back from the face, Denman said, "You would have guys doing what we call finishing works and backgrouting. There'd be a half-dozen there, plus a couple of general operatives doing all sorts of bits and pieces—cleaning up, packing stuff up, perhaps working on the ventilation cassette, maybe extending all the pipework or tidying up the track."

There were always people congregating at the back of the TBM, waiting for a train back to the surface. "It's like a bus stop or a railway station: the end of the line," Denman said. "You'd get some Eurotunnel people, some from our own different departments—your quality assurance, your safety people, tunnel engineers, geotechnical people, the surveyors.

"You'd find people working on the ventilation right throughout the tunnel. There'd be groups of them all over the place. . . . A little way back from the TBM, perhaps a kilometer or two, you'd start to get the hand-tunnel gangs working on the cross-passages."

A hand-tunnel gang, Denman said, had six to eight miners, and there would be gangs spread out over a few kilometers, hacking away with air spades to create the cross-passages. Many of these were dead-end holes until the running-tunnel TBMs reached and passed them, at which time they'd be cut through and fitted out. There were some early attempts in the U.K. tunnels to cut the cross-passages with excavating machines, as they did in France, but they were abandoned quickly. "Just a mistake," Denman said. The hand-miners used small conveyors to take the excavated material out of the passages and into the muck skips that they kept standing by.

"They were like a bunch of nomads, moving down the tunnel behind us," Denman said. "They'd be spread out over four or five kilometers behind the TBM, so when the trains went in they had to dodge round them. You'd also probably find, in there somewhere, a few guys doing track maintenance."

Farther back, large crews worked out of sight in enormous pump stations and sumps under the main tunnels. There were five of these between Sangatte and Shakespeare Cliff. The end ones, at the shafts, were designed to catch water coming down from the landward tunnels. The undersea sumps collect water at the low spots in the tunnel, whence it is pumped to the surface. The path through the chalk marl was like the letter W with an extra peak, so there were three low spots. Two were on the U.K. side of the works—Pump Station G was about 6 kilometers from Shakespeare Cliff; Pump Station K was near the tunnels' midpoint, 16 kilometers from Shakespeare Cliff. The French pump station was 8.8 kilometers from the Sangatte shaft.

The British sumps, which were larger than the French, were not good workplaces for claustrophobes. The main structure was a long tube, 170 meters long and 5 meters in diameter, that lay at right angles to the service and running tunnels. This was lined with cast-iron rings and represented a considerable tunneling achievement in itself. If you stood on the floor of this tube, the floor of the service tunnel was 10 meters above you, and the only way to get there was via two shafts that led up to two long equipment rooms. These rooms were 1,106 meters long and were wedged lengthwise between the service tunnel and the two running tunnels. Everything that went into or out of the sumps had to pass through the access shafts. Roadheader excavating machines had to be taken apart for the passage in and out.

"They were *massive* underground developments," Denman said. "There were vast amounts of rock to get out, it all had to come out through the service tunnel, and it all had to be done at the same time as we were driving the tunnel, at the same time they were developing the cross-passages." As a measure of their size, a 3.3-meter-diameter cross-passage involved the excavation of about 220 cubic meters of rock; a 2-meter-diameter piston relief duct, about 100 cubic meters. Each pump station required more than 11,000 cubic meters of excavation.

Yet all of these works were dwarfed by the huge, cathedral-like undersea crossover caverns that would allow trains to switch from one running tunnel to another and thus permit the tunnel to continue operating when maintenance or mishap took a section out of service. These were the largest undersea structures ever attempted. Few structures differed so fundamentally between the French and British works as the crossovers, largely because (as Pierre Matheron observed) when it came to geology, the British had been

A cross-passage on the French side.

more successful than the French in negotiating with God. The British had in-herited a nice construction adit and an intact section of tunnel from the 1974 effort; the French had the useless Descenderie. This allowed the British marine service-tunnel TBM to start early and to get well ahead of the big running-tunnel machines. Calculation suggested that it would reach the crossover site, eight kilometers from the Shakespeare Cliff shaft, nine months before the running-tunnel TBMs. The British therefore decided to build the cavern by hand, working from the service tunnel, and have it ready by the time the running-tunnel TBMs arrived.

The French, on the other hand, had started their three marine drives at about the same time from the Sangatte shaft. Although the service tunnel was ahead of the others, the lead represented no more than two months—far too little time to prepare a crossover chamber. So the French decided to let the running-tunnel TBMs grind ahead, building rings normally but drawing

The British crossover cavern was carved out before the tunnel-boring machines arrived.

closer together as they approached the crossover site, 12.5 kilometers from Sangatte, so that their paths could be enclosed in the chamber when it was built. Once the running-tunnel TBMs were beyond that point, the French crews would dig their way over from the service tunnel and encase the two tunnel tubes in a long concrete shell. They would then remove the chalk marl from the shell, exposing and removing the concrete rings. The whole interior would then be finished to create a single chamber in which the tracks would cross.

The very top of the British crossover was about thirty-six meters below the bed of the English Channel, which was about thirty meters deep at that point. The entire structure was as well-sited in the strata as engineers could have hoped: It sat on a bed of what the geologists called 6A material, a firm clay-rich chalk marl. The weak Gault Clay, which tended to well up like toothpaste from

The French excavated their crossover after the boring machines had passed.

a tube when it was uncovered, was a full five meters below the cavern's invert. Overhead were two meters of exceptionally impervious chalk marl, and above that were ten meters of good-quality unweathered upper chalk marl. So when a clairvoyant predicted that the tunnel would soon collapse and flood, it was of interest chiefly to the lurid tabloid that learned of the prediction and printed it.

Nevertheless, during construction, cracks in the shotcreted roof began to appear. About six meters back from the face, the foot-thick shotcrete layer had cracked on both sides of the crown heading. The cracks ran for about sixteen meters, and the steel reinforcing bars had buckled. In three hours, the roof settled more than sixty millimeters, almost double the maximum predicted movement. The crack was in four-day-old concrete, which should have set to a strength that would support any predictable forces from the rock.

"The roof started to come down on us," Lemley said. "After we shotcreted, it started to deform and come down; the movement was exceeding what we'd predicted. It's not unusual in tunnels; it's something that you watch for. In a lot of mines you find around the world, they still use timber supports, because the timber pops and cracks as it takes load, and you can see the material compressing. The old miners say it talks to you. And you listen to it, and if it's talking too loud, why, you know you have to do something. But if it's speaking in a normal voice, then you can be comfortable working there."

The shotcrete and the rockbolts and trusses that were used in the chamber were doing what they were supposed to do, Lemley said; they were yielding. However, he said, the yielding "had gone outside the limits of what we considered predictable behavior." It did not take long to diagnose the problem: The excavation had passed a transverse crack in the rock, which interrupted the even distribution of pressure on the shotcrete shell. Further, drilling found a layer of impermeable clay about four meters above the crown. A mass of water was resting on top of the layer, bearing down on the vault.

"A hydraulic head built up over the chamber, and the water couldn't migrate through the rock," Lemley said. "It started to add load to the crown of the chamber. . . . We drilled several holes into it and drained it off, and the loads kind of stabilized. So it wasn't a long-term problem, but for three or four days we paid very careful attention."

Drilling and draining didn't do all that was needed, Crighton said. The men had read the lurid account of the clairvoyant's prediction, and they had seen the cracks and the buckled girders. "Now how do you combat that?" said Crighton. "Well, you go down there. You say, 'I'm with ye.' And you stand there. That's what we did, what Johnny Hester and I did, I'll tell you that. . . . You've got to go down there and stand under the thing and say, 'It's all right, fellas—Look, I'm here.' Because you've got to convince the fellas that's diggin' the hole that you know what you're talking about."

Construction resumed, with six-meter-long drainage holes driven up along the length of the crown. Excavation exposed the shells of the side-wall drifts, which were broken up and removed. The roadheaders then removed the central "bench," the ground between the side-wall drifts. (The shotcrete for the temporary side walls was stabilized with special rock dowels that wouldn't interfere with the roadheaders.)

In August 1990, Running Tunnel North's TBM broke into the cavern. This was a rare event in machine-bored tunneling, a chance to stand back and look at a machine that usually lay embedded in the rock through which it burrowed. After it reentered the ground at the French end of the cavern, no one would ever see its skin again: Within months, the machine would be driven down into the bed of the Channel, gutted and pumped full of concrete, there to rest forever. There was a similar chance to look upon a TBM

Jack Lemley, left, on a visit to the tunnel.

a few weeks later, when Running Tunnel South's machine repeated the
process. Once it departed, tunnelers set to work to finish the chamber.

The cavern lining was a coat of several layers. The first was shotcrete over
mesh; next was a double layer of fabric, the inner one of impermeable yellow
polyvinyl chloride to exclude seepage water. (Each of these layers required
more than an acre of material.) Last was an inner layer of shotcrete, which
varied in thickness from six hundred millimeters in the crown to a meter at
the abutments on each side at floor level. This lining work was done in thirty
arches over the chamber, each 5.5 meters long, each using 169 cubic meters
of shotcrete.

Great masses of concrete formed the floor and the end walls of the cavern.
The floor was eighteen meters wide, and at its center the concrete was more
than four meters thick. The end walls, which were subject to enormous
loads, were three meters thick.

A running-tunnel boring machine, in passage though the British crossover.

The problems in the cavern were "bad but controllable," Gordon Crighton said. "In any engineering job there are problems. If there were no problems, then ye wouldn't need engineers; they could put a bunch of bank clerks in there. . . . Making provisions for problems: that's what tunneling's all about."

When the British Running Tunnel North TBM broke into the crossover cavern in August 1990, the worst problem in the British tunneling effort was miles away, beyond Shakespeare Cliff, up in the running tunnels that were being driven uphill toward Folkestone.

The land tunnels were often ignored by the public and in Eurotunnel's press releases. This was a real injustice, because some of the most innovative engineering went into them, along with heroic effort. (The terminals on both sides—noble works of monumental dimensions—were given similarly scant attention, in part because construction went smoothly.) The landward tunnels used several techniques: TBMs worked uphill from Shakespeare Cliff to emerge at Holywell Coombe. The Holywell valley section was done by cut-and-cover: The path was excavated, lined with a long concrete box and covered over. This section gave engineers the opportunity to move the service tunnel out from between the running tunnels and add another crossover between the running tracks. The final section, under Castle Hill, was built with NATM, the New Austrian Tunneling Method, which used shotcrete—sprayed concrete—to form a bearing structure.

Each of these stretches presented problems. Castle Hill is a landslip area. The Gault Clay causes these slips—the surface of the Gault gets wet and slippery, and the chalk slides off. The tunnel portal is in just such a zone—there are two slip blocks behind the portal—and engineers had to "toe weight" the area by dumping fifty thousand cubic meters of fill at the foot of the slope. The portal was then essentially built from the top down in the hillside: The side walls and roof went in first, then the hillside was cut away. The result did not only have to please structural engineers; as Britain's gateway to Europe, it also had to satisfy the Royal Fine Arts Society. It did.

The Gault created problems in every section of the landward tunnels. Under Castle Hill, when the ground relaxed after excavation, fissures developed that allowed water to seep through, increasing the possibility of slippage. In Holywell Coombe, the Gault was an unsteady foundation for the massive concrete "boxes" that were poured to form the tunnels in the open cut. In the bored tunnels, the clay welled up into the TBMs and all but choked them. But while those working on the land tunnels struggled, for people like Denman events were building to a climax: The undersea breakthrough would soon link the two nations. The only question now was, how should the moment be celebrated?

CHAPTER
18

The breakthrough that would unite the nations had no such power over the companies whose fortunes it would so deeply affect. For Eurotunnel and TML, the breakthrough was just another source of hard feelings. The argument this time was over a simple question: Whose celebration was this to be?

For Lemley, the event belonged to the people who had created the tunnels. For Morton, the breakthrough was a public-relations godsend in a difficult hour, when the lending banks were governed still by their doubts and fears, and when investment banks were trying, with middling success at best, to kindle interest in Eurotunnel's new stock issue among investors.

Lemley wanted a stand-alone TML celebration that would commence with the breakthrough at precisely ten o'clock in the morning of December 1 and would peak at a lavish evening party in Dover Castle. The ten contracting companies had put up more than £300,000 for this gala, and the centerpiece was to be a video. Most of this video had already been produced, and it was excellent, a stately procession of images that captured the great esthetic truth of the Channel Tunnel project: It was as beautiful as it was awesome, a great simple harmony created from confusion. Tens of thousands of hands had been plunged into muck, thouands of minds had toiled in a mire of facts and details, to create this clean-lined, powerful tunnel as their monument. The video lacked only an ending, and the breakthrough—the moment when a French hand grasped an English one through the rock—was to provide that. Graham Fagg and Philippe Cozette, the workers who had been chosen by lot, would play that final scene.

It was artful scripting, bringing the great undertaking down to perfect human scale. After the British TBM's drill probe had found the French machine on the night of October 30, the British had driven ahead, lining the

French tunnelers celebrate the breakthrough by signing the last ring in the service tunnel.

tunnel as before with concrete segments. (During this stretch, the original borehole was collapsed and lost.) When the British machine was about fifty meters from the French TBM, it was driven off-line to the right, into the narrow space between the paths of the service tunnel and the south running tunnel. In departing from the direct line, the TBM built a few cast-iron rings on the true alignment; thereafter, the tunnel was lined with shotcrete. The TBM stopped when it was head to tail with its French counterpart, and British hand-miners angled a short drift over to the face of the French machine, which the French, unhindered by nervous government safety experts, would soon cut apart with acetylene torches. The miners actually cut a small though unofficial hole through the last curtain of chalk marl, through which cigarettes could be (and were) pushed from one country to another. French recipients could enjoy these smuggled goods immediately; the British had to defer the pleasure, since smoking was forbidden in their tunnels. It was this hole that Cozette and Fagg were to enlarge until they, and others selected by influence and standing rather than lot, could step through.

Timing was crucial to the TML celebration. Tape from the morning breakthrough had to be returned to the surface and added to celebratory video in time for the whole to be delivered to Dover Castle. Weeks before the event, Lemley asked Noulton to work out details with Eurotunnel. There were two points on which Lemley did not wish to compromise or even negotiate: First, there would be no live television coverage; the breakthrough would be celebrated within the TML family. Second, nothing could interfere with the timing, because delay could spoil the party.

According to Lemley, Morton agreed that "we could take the day of the breakthrough and have a celebration, but he put an embargo on us inviting politicians." Then, a week before the celebration, "all of sudden it dawned on him that this was a pretty significant event." Morton agreed that the breakthrough timing was very important, but his thinking was distinctly at odds with Lemley's. "It needed to be between 1:00 and 1:30 [P.M.] French time for television," Morton said. "If you hit that slot, it was going to be live on breakfast television on the East Coast of the United States; it was going to be live on late evening newscasts in Japan. It fitted into both, and it fitted into London as well."

Morton first managed to get Noulton and Lemley to agree to live television coverage; Eurotunnel arranged and paid for a fiber-optic cable in the tunnel. Then, after Lemley went to Italy to check on construction of the HGV wagons at a Fiat plant, Morton began pushing Noulton, and later Matheron, to move the time of the breakthrough as well.

Denman was pleased that the honor had fallen to Fagg. "Couldn't have been a better choice," he said. "Thank God they pulled out a good one: A local man, been there all the way through, had been there on the '74 tunnel as well. Been around a lot. A nice guy, a TBM operator right the way through from Day One." Denman arranged to pick up Fagg from his house in Dover on the breakthrough day. He arrived at five in the morning on December 1.

"Shit, you're early," Fagg said in some surprise, Denman recalled.

"I know, we've got to be down the hole, in there at six o'clock," Denman said. It would take two hours to reach the face, and Denman had to make certain that everyone knew his part and everything was ready to hand.

"What?" said Fagg. "I haven't got me sandwiches yet."

"Sandwiches? What do you want to take sandwiches for?

"Well, I get hungry down there."

"You'll be in *France*," Denman said. "There'll be champagne and all. You won't need *anything*."

"No," said Fagg. "I've got to take me sandwiches with me." Denman, bowing to a superior need, waited while the sandwiches were prepared and packed.

Fagg was not the only one with whom Denman had to wrestle. He had had a hard time convincing his wife to come down from their home in Surrey, southwest of London, for the celebration.

"She got pretty fed up with hearing about the bloody Channel Tunnel all the time," Denman said. "She began to hate the place, she really did."

He could understand: He lived down near the tunnel during the week—at Farthingloe, for a while—and came home, tired, for the weekends. "All I wanted to talk about was the Channel Tunnel; all she wanted to talk about was anything *but* the bloody Channel Tunnel." Feelings ran particularly high when his beeper would go off on the weekend. She wouldn't go to tunnel parties; she had even missed the breakthrough celebration for Denman's first tunnel, the land service tunnel.

"She had a good reason," Denman admitted. "She was in the hospital having a baby." Denman was interviewing someone for a job when his beeper went off, notifying him that he had a daughter. He received congratulations from the applicant, whom he thereupon hired.

But Denman was not having any excuses this time. "When it came to the breakthrough I said to her, a couple of weeks before, 'You've got no excuse. It's a big do, it's important, and you're coming down.'" He had taken the precaution of arranging for his sister-in-law to babysit; he had hired a car to pick up his wife and take her to Dover.

"After the do, we'll be driven home," he said. "We'll pick up the children, and we'll go home. Don't argue. It's all arranged." She agreed.

Arranging matters at the face was more difficult. "It was more of a problem figuring out who was going to go through to France than actually building the tunnel," Denman said. "There was a lot of people falling out with one another. It got really bitchy. I got fed up with it—They were arguing who was going to go through second, who was going to go through third."

The bickering was intense, because only fifteen souls were to be permitted to pass through the hole and proceed on to France. Another forty would be allowed to stand in the tunnel and observe the event. This mirrored the arrangements and numbers in France. Neither side found it easy to decide *which* fifteen of its multitude of deserving workers would be honored.

Denman had brought a hip flask of whiskey with him; he and Hester passed it around, careful to save some for the rite of passage that was soon to occur. Denman found himself standing next to Morton, who was waiting to go on camera with a television crew and who tried to edge Denman out of the shot.

Fagg and Cozette stepped up to the carefully preserved rock faces and set to work with air spades. The chalk was dry, pale gray and rather hard to carve for two men who had hitherto done their digging with the aid of very large and powerful tunnel-boring machines. A fist-sized hole appeared, opened, dilated. At twelve minutes after the hour, Cozette, urged by Fagg, pushed his right arm through and followed it with his head and left arm. He rose up and smiled, his face bathed in the glare from the television lights and splashed by white flashes from the still cameras. The act was repeated in reverse: Fagg, filmed from the French side, pushed half-through the hole, resettled his hard hat on his head and waved. Cameras whirred and flashed.

Graham Fagg, left, *and Philippe Cozette pose by the* *breakthrough hole they cut.*

The great undertaking had succeeded: There was now a passage under the English Channel.

The aperture grew, as did the amount of flesh that could and did pass through it. Fagg was the first to step through bodily into the French tunnel—he and his colleagues had been working in France, of course, for several weeks; Point M was quite near the northern end of the Fosse Dangeard, well inside French territory. Morton was second through the gap; Lemley was third. The list of the others gave a fair measure of the competition for the honors. The chairmen of the British companies were in the next group; John King, Denman recalled, was about tenth in the parade, followed by Alan Myers, who managed all of the hand-tunneling and was the master hand at NATM.

Denman was thirteenth, and he managed to bring along one of his engineers. "There really were only about four of us of the crew that was down there, that represented the sharp end, who went through," he said.

Through to France, that was: The number of people who made a quick round-trip through the hole that day grew steadily, once the formalities were over; Denman thought that several hundred on each side, at least, stepped through and back. "Loads of people went through, but only fifteen went on to France, on a French manrider," Denman said. "The French did likewise."

André Bénard was not present on either side of the breakthrough; he was in Paris, recovering from heart bypass surgery. Matheron telephoned him from the tunnel to give him joy of his achievement.

As soon as they were through, many of the British miners lit up cigarettes. Denman pulled out his flask and shared a drink with Jean-Yves Demeillat, his French counterpart. Demeillat, a huge bearded bear of a man, was called "Le Capitaine," in part because of a resemblance to Captain Haddock in the beloved Tintin classics, in part because he had, indeed, been to sea, as a chief engineer on supertankers; the Channel Tunnel was the first submarine work he ever attempted. He shrugged off the career change. "There's very little difference between a fully automated supertanker and a tunnel boring machine," he said. At sea, if something went wrong, you had to repair it with whatever was available. There was the same pressure under the Channel: If something went wrong with Brigitte, his TBM, it had to be fixed on the spot.

When the British drill probe had found Brigitte, it was Demeillat who had removed the bit, the first object to have made the historic passage. This went to Matheron; the British were left with some hard feelings but few options.

Demeillat shared the drink with Denman, handed back the flask and headed for Britain.

"I got the impression there was a very lukewarm reception when the French arrived here, from what I could gather," Denman said. "We actually got mobbed with the French. Graham Fagg lost most of his bloody clothing

Jean-Yves Demeillat, left, greets his British counterpart, David Denman, center, after the breakthrough.

in bits. I got dragged off by some guy from the BBC World Service who wanted a bit of an interview." After the interview, Denman asked where the broadcast would go. Europe, the BBC man said. North America, the Far East, Australia. Around the world. Denman thought he was joking; he was not. Denman's wife had already seen him on the live television broadcast from the tunnel.

"So we had all our passports stamped," Denman said. "We were dragged off to a beer tent; they were going mad over there. Cameras everywhere. It was good fun."

The British tunnelers ended up on an airplane late in the day, heading back to Dover. "That was absolutely unbelievable," Denman said. "We'd all had a few drinks by then, and we were floating. It was smashing: We just couldn't believe we'd actually done it." It was strangely moving to fly over the Channel, to look down and see France and England and to know that the tunnel—their tunnel—lay beneath the waters.

The British tunnelers got back tired, still in their work clothes. The Dover Castle festivities gave them a second wind. "The do they put on was absolutely out of this world," Denman said. "We always knew the Americans did everything grand, but Jack Lemley went over the top that night. They say it cost half a million pounds, and I can well imagine it did." The castle was set up as a medieval fair, with strolling minstrels, jongleurs, fair ladies singing madrigals.

There were some glaring anachronisms—can-can girls and Victorian-style market stalls serving meat pies—but no one seemed to mind.

Denman spent much of the evening shaking hands with distinguished strangers. Then there was a tap on his shoulder; he was told to go around to the back of the stage.

"The stage sort of came forward, and Jack Lemley went out and there was a speech," Denman said. "Then we were all mentioned by name—We got pulled out to the front of the stage, and they started playing *God Save the Queen* and *Rule Britannia,* and then they had the *Marseillaise.* There was stuff coming down from the ceiling; everybody went mad. I stood out there thinking, *What the hell?* I looked down; I could see my wife's face beaming— you know, as if to say, '*I like this tunneling.*' I was totally taken aback.

"After that, when we got back home, she said to me, 'I take it all back. I can see now how much that tunnel meant to you.'"

For most everyone, the breakthrough merely enhanced long-established behavior patterns: Morton and Lemley, and their surrogates and their institutions, remained locked in contention. Pierre Matheron, on the other hand, found a crafty way to use it to the project's advantage.

The French absorbed a fair amount of painful ribbing after Denman's TBM crossed the border. British jokesters had sent a fax to a TML executive committee meeting just after the crossing, notifying Matheron that the British were digging French soil, that they had found a fossilized squashed frog and that they would take good care of French territory. (Tim Green was accused of being the fax's author; he pleaded "jointly guilty.") More innocently, Hester had arranged for some of the TML office secretaries to pay a festive subaqueous visit to France.

On the night before the breakthrough, Matheron and his wife had come through the Eurotunnel exhibition center in Cheriton, near the British terminal.

"Matheron came walking in," Hester said. "Never said hello. Walked over to me and he said, 'The score today is one, England; Nothing, France. At the end of the job it will be two-one, France.' And walked off.

"So that started it. He couldn't have done anything better for the project. I mean, it created this huge competition of who was going to get into France. He told the press of this: That he was going to put two machines in [Britain.] So what happened was the damnedest logistic battle you've ever seen in your life, from there on out."

At one point, Matheron called Hester and said he was conceding the race in Running Tunnel South. "Then he threw everything in the world into running tunnel south," Hester recalled. "But we knew about it right away. We had people over there, that went back and forth. He'd get a report at seven o'clock; we'd have it at seven-thirty. He didn't win, but he didn't lose by much."

There were real stakes in this symbolic contest. "We were manufacturing segments," Hester said. "They didn't want to make too many, we didn't want to make too many, and you couldn't end up short. So the decision had to be made on when we'd shut down the Isle of Grain, and when he'd shut down his plant. So we had this critical few months to jockey for position."

The game called for some quite delicate skills, as Tim Green had discovered when the north running-tunnel TBM broke into the almost-complete crossover. The machine wouldn't need Green's services as it was hauled through the cavern, so he promptly threw four extra trains into the south running tunnel.

"I choked it," Green said. "When we were at the crossover, eight trains was never quite enough, twelve trains choked it up, but ten trains were very nice."

Eurotunnel had its own contests to worry about; it had to sell enough shares to stay alive. It did, but not with any particular ease. Two weeks after breakthrough, Eurotunnel "welcomed the overall success of its rights issue," adding that it had been "92% subscribed overall." Eurotunnel stretched gamely to describe this middling success as "a triumph of binational cooperation."

This faint success was followed by some very bad news. On January 16, Bryan Driver sent a fax to Lemley at the Century Plaza Hotel in Los Angeles, where he was attending a professional conference. Driver's message was simplicity itself: "AS PER ATTACHED," it said. "REGARDS."

The attachment was a nine-page communication from the Euroshuttle Consortium that detailed the costs of reworking the shuttle wagons to provide seven-hundred-millimeter-wide pass doors. The numbers were horrific: The change would add 576,821,479.69 French francs to the contract price and thirteen months to the delivery schedule—ten months if various fire and pressure tests didn't have to be repeated.

This setback—the sum was equivalent to about £58 million—was particularly alarming because Eurotunnel still was pursuing a similar strategy with the design of the HGV wagons, betting that the Safety Authority would not insist that they be closed and fire-resistant. Euroshuttle was still working on semienclosed wagons with lattice sides, though even these were still too heavy to perform as the concession required. By mid-March 1991, the designers had been able to get the weight down only to 35.5 tons—almost two tons overweight.

Worse, there were ominous signs that the Safety Authority would be as un-compromising on the HGV wagons as it had been on the pass doors in the passenger shuttles. After an April meeting of representatives from Eurotunnel, TML and the *maître d'oeuvre,* a summary document concluded that "Modifi-cation/alteration of the carrier waggon design, sufficient to allow compliance with all concession requirements, would now be very difficult to achieve and could therefore have severe ramifications as regards cost and programme." It noted elsewhere, "It seems the SA does not accept the semi-open concept and wishes to revert to the lightweight design with light containment."

The idea of light containment was to contain a fire for a short time—five minutes, perhaps. This would be a dubious benefit—the truck drivers were to be segregated from their vehicles, and five minutes was not time enough to clear a burning train from the tunnel unless it were very near a portal—but

The lattice-sided frame of a shuttle car for trucks.

such a requirement would require still heavier HGV wagons. Eurotunnel's rolling-stock experts grew ever more alarmed, but the dilemma left them little option: Work on the lattice-sided HGV wagons continued.

Not all was gloom, however. The tunneling was going very well; the service tunnel was finished by mid-February and Tim Green's railway was linked to the French construction railway.

Politics had dealt Green a disappointment. For months, he had been ferrying TML's office workers down into the tunnel for visits on Saturday mornings. He had cleaned up a manrider for these trips and given it a glass roof; the tunnel crews called it the Disneymobile.

In the months before the breakthrough, it dawned on Green that he could with reason expect guests of more elevated standing to make the descent. Because the breakthrough would occur quite near the fifth anniversary of the Treaty of Canterbury, Mrs. Thatcher was almost certain to pay a visit. The Disneymobile was clean and useful, but the occasion would demand more. Green sent one of the manriders back to the manufacturer for a £50,000 retrofit.

"It had got carpet on the walls and carpet on the floor and bloody sprung seats," Green said of the result. "It was really superb—had room for about twelve, like a club car on a train. It became known as the Maggiemobile. Then, of course, the rotten gal got bloody sacked five weeks before breakthrough. . . . So she never rode in the Maggiemobile." Green was consoled by the fact that the party in power didn't change, and so the carpets of Conservative Blue could remain.

"It was the Disneymobile and Maggiemobile that went through point M and right out into the fresh air in France, the first time we connected the two construction railways together," Green said. "So that was the first train that went through, the first international train: One of my little construction trains." There were three cars—the Maggie- and Disneymobiles flanking a nonpowered car. There was a test run, then a ceremonial passage on April 3. The next day, Green's crews took out the connection and began removing the construction railway. (When all tunneling was complete, five hundred of the original twenty thousand tons of rail were found to have disappeared during the installation, repair, modification and removal of the construction railway. Green considered this about right, considering the size of the job.)

As it turned out, tearing up the construction railway was a little premature; it would have been quite welcome when crews later began installing fixed equipment in the service tunnel. But the service tunnel was destined to carry a rubber-tired fleet of service vehicles, and the plan now called for installation of the concrete roadbed. That created a need for a new fleet of rubber-shod service vehicles; Green drew up some specifications and went out for bid. The winner was a Finnish-made tractor, a standard model modified with a second driver's cab at the back end—there was no room to turn anything around in the tunnel—and a passenger pod in the middle. The tractor could pull two trailers, each with a passenger capacity of thirty-four. Green had nine of these rigs, but the construction crew needed other vehicles. They ended up with two sorts of Japanese-made tractors, large and small.

"We had to start by removing the grass-cutting attachment from the little tractors," Green said; the little tractors had been designed to mow lawns.

Superimposed on all of this was a fleet of 125 mountain bikes that Green added, against his initial better judgment.

"The French had done it before me, and in the end I got instructed to put them in," he said. The French had bought butcher's bicycles: heavy, sluggish vehicles with big bins on the front. They were not geared for pedaling a dozen kilometers up a gentle but relentless grade from mid-Channel to Folkestone.

But Green soon revised his opinion of the wisdom of a two-wheeled fleet. "They made a lot of sense, because we had a number of people who would want to go in and perhaps spend five or six minutes at every one of twenty cross-passages in a row." Workers on these missions lost huge amounts of time waiting for the next regular shuttle, so Green began shopping for bicycles.

He found a small, new British manufacturer, Saracen, that could supply nice twenty-one-speed machines for £195 each. Green had each adorned with a large reflective number and required anyone who used one to sign a log, but some genius managed to make off with one in the first week; Green not only didn't find the culprit, he never figured out how the thief had managed to remove it from a very secure work site. No other bikes disappeared entirely thereafter, but some of nicer fittings—seats particularly—disappeared, replaced with less elegant and much-used pieces.

The bikes quickly established speed records in the tunnel, despite hastily drawn safety regulations that limited them to twenty-five kilometers per hour. "If you happen to be going from here to Pump Station G, down a one percent grade with a geared bicycle, and if you're young and fit, fifty kilometers per hour is no problem," Green said. Indeed, tunnelers who had long since left youth behind had no trouble leaving motor-driven vehicles behind, too, even going uphill. Green had to reprimand a tunneler of more than sixty years for passing a motor vehicle that was traveling at the statutory twenty-five kilometers per hour. The elderly rider had come ten kilometers uphill from Pump Station G when he passed the motor vehicle; he did not slacken until he reached the U.K. portal, five kilometers farther uphill.

Green's switch to rubber tires in the service tunnel came at a good time for the project: The French were critically short of construction locomotives;

Lower Shakespeare Cliff at dusk, at the peak of construction.

Green was able to send over thirty-five—some through the tunnels, some by ferry. The arrangement did not please the bean counters in Translink, who had to account for the locos on their books. They wanted to sell the locomotives to Transmanche g.i.e. "I shamed them out of it," Green recalled.

In May 1991, TML was preparing for another breakthrough, in Marine Running Tunnel North. This would take place 17,932 meters from Shakespeare Cliff, a point that lay several hundred meters inside British territory. When the French machine crossed the border in early May, the belief among the British workforce was that the French had been allowed to win. The British machine had stopped work in April, and a Eurotunnel press release offered a mysterious and meaningless explanation: "In order to recover delays due to tunneling problems in 1989, it was agreed that the meeting point of the two TBMs be moved closer to the British coast."

Lemley denied that anything but engineering determined the outcome of this perceived race between the nations. "We let the tunnels stop where they naturally progressed to," he said. "We did stop the British machines and permit the French machines to finish, but we made that decision because French health and safety laws were much more permissive, and we were able to cut up the French machines. But there was no conscious decision to let the French come across just to salve national feelings."

Though the question of *where* might occupy various minds, there was no uncertainty at all about *how* the breakthrough should be handled—at least, not in John Hester's mind. This time, he would not allow ceremony to interfere with proper tunneling. The British TBM would dive down into the seabed, where it would be entombed in concrete. Then the French machine would tunnel ahead, over the top of the entombed British TBM. The French machine would be gutted, and liner rings would be built within its hollow shell.

"The only thing I had to check was the turning radius and where the Gault Clay and Greensand were," Hester said. "So I went down, took my little ruler, measured all the clearances underneath the decks, drew myself a little picture, and came up and got my boys together and said, 'Now look: This is the way this is gonna be done. If I see one picture that looks different than this, whoever has instructed it to be drawn, and whoever is drawing it, will not be on the project five minutes after I see it, OK? I'm not gonna have any of this bullshit anymore with these big openings, where it takes spending two or three million pounds to finish the goddamned tunnel.' "

Hester went over to France to explain the plan to Matheron and Jacques Fermin. "So I drew this on the board for them, showed them why we should do this," Hester said. "And Fermin looked at it and said, 'Right, that's the way you should do it.'

"So Matheron was looking at it, and you know, Matheron is not only a great construction person, he's also quite a showman, and he said, 'No-no. If you want to do this, you're going to have to do something for me.' "

Matheron's demand was not easy to meet. As things stood, the French TBM would break into the sloping, shotcrete-lined cut left by the British TBM as it dove into the seabed. This meant that the French machine would break through at the bottom of this cut and crawl ahead, enlarging the opening until it was full face.

This creeping entrance affronted Matheron's sense of theater. What he wanted was a full-face breakthrough. To give this effect, he wanted Hester to hand-mine out the top of the sloping cut. He further wanted Hester to build a brick wall across the face and to finish it so that it resembled rock. This was the surface through which Europa—for that was the name of the French TBM in this tunnel—would make her grand, full-face entrance.

"I mean, that's a lot of work, cutting the top out of one of these big tunnels and making a face out of it," said Hester. Nonetheless, he didn't hesitate: "I said, 'Pierre, you've got it. We'll do that, don't worry about it, we'll take care of it.' "

In mid-April, about a month before the breakthrough, Fermin and Matheron came to Britain for a meeting. By this time, the British machine was on its downward course. Matheron asked Hester whether he was going to start cutting away the top. Hester said he was not.

French tunnelers wave through the face of their TBM after its breakthrough in Marine Running Tunnel North.

A French tunnel-boring machine breaks through over the grave of its British counterpart.

"Well, what are you going to do?" Matheron said.

"Nothing," said Hester.

"We made an agreement," Matheron insisted.

"I lied," Hester said.

"Matheron got so goddamned mad he slammed his fist down on the desk, walked into Lemley's office and told him he quit and wasn't going to work on the goddamned project anymore," Hester recalled. "Oh, my God, the screaming match . . . Fermin was sitting there with this sly grin on his face, because I think he knew all along that it was a dumb idea, and that I wouldn't do it."

Hester was not dead to the idea of drama, however, and gladly collaborated on a small extravaganza in which the big French machine drove to a welcoming arch, to be greeted by suitable lights, cameras and music. It was a good show, and Matheron allowed himself to be mollified.

These more or less friendly combats mirrored far more serious struggles between TML and Eurotunnel over the costs of the fixed equipment in the tunnels, which was covered by the lump-sum part of the contract. The times were difficult; every day required decisions on much disputed items. Bitterness was vivid. According to Philippe Essig, legal maneuverings between TML and Eurotunnel began to accelerate in 1991.

The successful completion of the tunneling had created a sense of confidence within Eurotunnel that Essig felt was dangerous. What lay ahead were long negotiations over scores of details, and Essig cautioned that there might be delays. TML could not solve the problems unilaterally, yet Eurotunnel refused to become involved, insisting that the contract, lump sum and all, would decide all questions.

"They thought I was using delay as blackmail," Essig said. "It was not blackmail. Ah, well, there is always blackmail when you're building something, when you are negotiating. But this was really a warning to them. . . . When you're in a dispute where everything requires a legal agreement, the process delays things by itself." Lawyers had to agree on everything down to the smallest technical points, on subjects that often lay outside their professional competence. Eurotunnel and TML were sunk in the legal and business equivalent of trench warfare, and progress, Essig felt, was likely to be slow.

For Essig, 1991 "was a difficult year. I had less and less means of negotiation with Eurotunnel." Attitudes within TML were hardening, even among the French partners; there was less inclination to compromise, more will to fight. Essig proposed that TML accept Eurotunnel securities in payment for some costs; both sides rejected the idea.

"It was difficult to get a common approach, a common point of view within TML," Essig said. "The British were much more orientated toward taking everything piece by piece, system by system, subsystem by subsystem," to derive a bottom-line cost for everything. The French thought that the knock-on effect, whereby each change required other changes throughout the project, made it impossible to reach the bottom line via the British route. The French experts preferred a global claim on the fixed equipment, an overall number drawn from actual expenditures.

After months of debate, the French view prevailed and TML submitted a global claim in July 1991; it said the fixed equipment cost, stated in constant 1985 prices, had risen from £620 million to £1.27 billion. It asked Eurotunnel to pay the cost, plus a £160 million management fee to TML. Neerhout's PID responded with a demand for substantiation and for legal and contractual reasons why Eurotunnel should comply.

The July global claim was the public expression of a deeper resolve within TML, according to Essig. "The members assembly decided to fight strongly against ET, and it was agreed that I would leave the project," he said. He understood: His name was associated with compromise and cooperation. The same combative spirit that earlier had claimed his friend Ridley at Eurotunnel now removed Essig from the field.

According to Lemley, Essig's removal was part of a move by the French companies to take control of TML's affairs. Lemley himself was invited to renegotiate his employment contract in a way that would have stripped away much of the unusual power that he held—power that exceeded some of the strictures in the joint venture agreement, conceded in a dark hour to someone who might save a foundering project. Lemley refused.

The global claim, said Alastair Morton, was the first gun in what he called "the War of the Lump Sum." The contractors "told us that they considered the contract was at an end, and they should be paid cost-plus," he said. It would take almost two years to decide this issue.

One of the battlefields of this long war lay under the tracks of the running tunnels. The track design was basically French: The rails were not to rest on ties that ran across the entire track bed, but rather on rows of short concrete blocks. These were encased in rubber "shoes" that would absorb noise and shock. To lay track, 182-meter-long sections of rail—each with three hundred blocks attached—would be set on the surface of a first pour of concrete in the tunnel. This concrete bed was poured in place by a special work train that would return, once the rails were in place, for a second pour that would embed the blocks.

Several suppliers bid to supply the rail system. "As we went into the procurement process, we had five systems that were approved," Lemley said. "We went out for tenders, and Eurotunnel tried to interfere in the selection. They

Track-laying in the French tunnels.

had originally pre-qualified the tenders, and then they tried to withdraw approval of a couple of the systems. I went ahead and solicited bids from all the originally qualified tenders. Eurotunnel got nasty with me about it."

Lemley sensed the heavy hand of SNCF in the dispute. The French railways had a regular supplier and pushed hard to get this system into the tunnel. TML favored another model, the Sonneville block, which a former SNCF engineer had designed.

The engineer had tried without success to get SNCF to use his system. "As I understand it, he believed strongly enough that he had a better mousetrap that he left there and started trying to sell this system around the world," Lemley said of Sonneville. The system had been used elsewhere; it was also £4 million cheaper than the nearest alternative—and, Lemley added, "It looked to me like it was a proper system." Lemley decided to go ahead and use Sonneville blocks.

"The French railways put enormous pressure on TML for over a year in the IGC, and literally wouldn't approve it," Lemley said. "We had to go through an approval process that Eurotunnel fought for a long time, and that the IGC fought. They couldn't beat us; we were going ahead with it.

"So then they started picking on the components of the system, and trying to disqualify the components, to throw enough barriers in our way that we would get discouraged and revert to the SNCF system. And I decided I was going ahead regardless.

"In one meeting, Neerhout refused to accept some of the concrete sleeper blocks that were built. And I said, *That's just fine. I'll load the god-damned things on a barge and dump 'em in the Channel, then, and we'll start over. But we're going to build what we set out to build here.* And he accepted the whole lot as fit for purpose in that meeting, when he decided I was serious and I was going to go ahead and dump them in the Channel." This was in late 1991, Lemley said, and occurred after months of wrangling over the trackbed: "At the time, track installation was already behind schedule." It was a typical skirmish, Lemley said: "The blocks give a good idea of how it all went."

There were other forces, too, that were pushing the project into ever greater expense: Behind everything was the culture, the habits of thought, of the transportation industry. This was one of the first things that struck Keith Price, another American from Morrison Knudsen whom Lemley brought to the Channel Tunnel project.

Price filled the American stereotype to bursting. He looked as Western as he was, with a Wild Bill Hickock moustache and a gunslinger's swagger. He roamed the frontier of insult humor, of profanity, of iconoclasm, but he was polite to the ladies and could play the gentleman when the situation demanded. When John Hester reduced a secretary to tears, Price called him out and forced an apology. Under all, he had a young man's enthusiasm for building things.

"Mr. Price is like the common denominator [among the Americans]," said Daniele Calderon, who became his secretary and aide-de-camp. "He does things quickly, takes decisions quickly. There's no long conversations first, like with the English and French. But I like the way they treat other people: Mr. Price will talk to a cleaner as well as a [director-general]. . . . With Mr. Price, when you need information or a decision, you don't go through channels, you go to the person who has the information or who can make the decision. The French, some of them, were very hurt by that."

Calderon was both charmed and offended by Price's resistance to pomp. For instance, he refused to use the china cups in which coffee was served in TML's executive offices in Shearway House. "He *hates* china cups," she said.

"I made a deal with him: I said, 'When we have someone in from outside I'll bring you coffee in china cups.' But if I bring him a china cup any other time he hates it."

Price had an unofficial role, too, as a buffer between Lemley and everyone else. "When there's anything to complain about, they come to me," he explained cheerfully. "And when anything goes wrong, Jack rips my ass."

Price's all-American brashness was an undoubted breath of fresh air, but he could do little to dispel the poisoned atmosphere that hung over the project. Eurotunnel and TML were settled in their trenches, settled in patterns of thought and action that would carry them through to the end of the project.

The cooling system was another typical skirmish. "The cooling system was not originally part of the contract," said Roger Freeman, the TML attorney. "It was introduced later. There was a dispute over the value of that variation." There was a sort of compromise that let work continue while negotiation plodded along. Then Eurotunnel dictated a price, which TML felt was inadequate.

"So we said, 'If you don't pay us on the basis you were previously paying us, we shall stop work,'" Freeman said, adding that the threat to halt work was intended mostly as a negotiating tactic. "Eurotunnel, in that situation, could have gone to the panel, but that would have taken ninety days. Instead, they chose to apply to the High Court in England, to ask the High Court to grant them an injunction to stop us from stopping work."

The High Court agreed with Eurotunnel, but did not issue an injunction because TML had agreed to continue work while the dispute lumbered through the courts. The Court of Appeal agreed with TML, sort of: It didn't say that TML had the right to stop work, but that the contract's arbitration clause, and not the English courts, should govern in the dispute.

Eurotunnel thereupon appealed to the House of Lords, the highest judicial body in the country, and lost. Neither side gained any ground in this, but the press gave it heavy, hand-wringing coverage, which made the banks nervous and unhappy.

The chiller at Shakespeare Cliff, part of the tunnel cooling system.

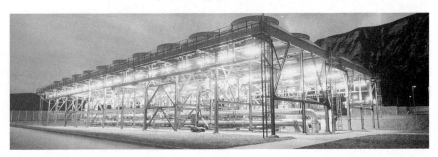

The banks had other bad news, too: Essig's warnings about delay were proving to be correct. In February 1991, Eurotunnel's board admitted publicly that the tunnel opening would be delayed, that it would miss the whole summer of 1993. In private, the board resigned itself to an even longer delay, until perhaps the late spring of 1994. This gloomier view found its way into the press, which did not hesitate to report that the tunnel would open a full year late.

Eurotunnel denied—continued to deny—that the tunnel would be that late. In October 1992, when Eurotunnel released its half-year results, it acknowledged a further delay, saying the tunnel would open around Christmas 1993, about a half year late. The meeting, and the press conference that accompanied it, offered a quick education in Eurotunnel's—and particularly Morton's—view of the project.

To anyone even slightly familiar with the history, it was apparent that attitudes were little changed, but that the outlook was getting steadily worse: Interest by now was costing Eurotunnel £1 million a day, and Morton admitted that revenue would increase more slowly than hoped after the tunnel opened, due in part to a winter start-up. Fewer people traveled in winter, Morton explained, and so there would be less word-of-mouth advertising during the tunnel's first months.

Morton opened the meeting with the press by saying "We are not—*not*—planning a rights issue before we open. Anybody want to leave now?" He said that Eurotunnel had drawn down about two thirds of its available credit, leaving £2.5 billion that would be ample for the remaining work. Eurotunnel had won the War of the Lump Sum in arbitration, he said, and admitted that the banks had been extremely nervous before the ruling.

He also acknowledged that TML and Eurotunnel had both worked hard to settle their lump-sum money differences, but with indifferent success: The sides had been near an agreement in August, when Eurotunnel offered about £980 million for the fixed equipment, along with "various combinations of shares and redeemable, subordinated, zero-coupon convertible loan stocks" in lieu of cash. This deal collapsed, and the dispute went on, with the sides about £130 million apart.

Here, Morton permitted himself a few harsh words. He expressed incredulity that TML hadn't yet finished fitting out the tunnel. "It's hard to believe TML could lose six months in fitting out, but they did," he said. Of TML's actions in refusing to sign the August peace treaty: "The French word is *chantage*. You could, if you were feeling malevolent, translate that as blackmail. Or you could say 'contract pressure' if you were feeling kinder."

There had certainly been problems for which TML bore responsibility, Lemley said. "I don't suggest that we've done everything perfectly. We have not; we've had plenty of failures of our own," he said. "We had some major failures in design of piping fixtures in the tunnel, approximately £20 million of rework and redesign that had to be done. . . . It's our responsibility, and we've had to face up to it and make the corrections." But beyond those problems lay a broader management failure by Eurotunnel, Lemley said. "They haven't tried to manage the process with the governments in a pro-active way, and we're still seeing changes in criteria imposed on the system that's being installed. That has a cost impact that ripples through everything."

He seldom had to look far for evidence to support his views. "Use yesterday as an example," he said, a few weeks after Eurotunnel's October 1992 meeting. "We sat in a meeting between myself, my senior staff and Eurotunnel's senior staff, the MdO and the banks' technical adviser." Toward the end of the meeting, the issue of controlling access to the tunnel property came up. The government had steadily increased its demands, and Eurotunnel passed them along: video cameras for surveillance at the Lower Shakespeare Cliff site, special fences, motion detectors on those special fences, infrared cameras for night surveillance, cameras that would take a picture of the underside of each vehicle that passed through the tollbooths.

"None of that was anticipated at the time that we tendered this, and they're asking for a system that is beyond what most military installations have in place," Lemley said. "We had agreed in August as to how this would be designed and developed." Now, in November, TML said that Eurotunnel was again moving the goalposts; Eurotunnel's managers denied it: The design, they said, was frozen.

"We walked out of the meeting and there have been three contacts within the hour . . . asking for specific different changes to that system," Lemley said. "This has gone on and on and on, ad infinitum. Here we're already at a point where the systems can't be completed, as they're now conceived and designed, until December of 1993. So they can't be finished until a week or so before the project is scheduled to open. And they're *continuing* to ask for changes."

By this time, more than a year before the scheduled opening, Lemley was warning anyone who would listen that Eurotunnel would not be ready to operate the tunnel when TML finished its work and handed over the keys.

Each day brought some fresh problem to Lemley's attention. The messenger was usually Keith Price, who spent his days (and many nights) struggling with the Cerberean problems of the Channel Tunnel.

There were, for instance, the rabies traps. "Britain considers itself rabies-strict, and I can tell you first-hand they mean it," Price said. "They worry about rabid foxes coming through the tunnel from France. There are certain zones, just outside the tunnel, where any animal seen in that zone will be destroyed. No questions asked. Today. Been going on since the tunnel was punched through. They just don't take chances. So we, as part of concession, had to devise ways of preventing animals on foot from entering the tunnel. Or if they did enter it, from leaving."

The solution was an electrified grid in the tunnel that would kill any fox, dog, cat or rabbit that stepped on it. There would be six grids, one near the entrance to each tunnel, each running from one side of the tunnel to the other, under the tracks. Each would be about three meters wide to keep animals from leaping over it. "If an animal attempts to walk the tunnel, he gets to this place and it zaps him—150,000 volts, but it's pulsed," Price said. If the intruding foot belonged to a human being, he added, "You'll never have to worry about getting rabies. It could be lethal."

There was some initial protest—"Some tree-hugger resistance, because we're going to kill animals and rabbits and stuff," Price said. "That kind of died out once they discovered we weren't putting this in to kill animals, but to keep rabies out of Great Britain. Depends on how you say things."

By itself, the system wasn't complex. "Primarily, it's the same basic stuff you use in an electric fence." Price said. "It's a little higher voltage, but it's made by the same people." However, it used electricity, and this raised some possible problems.

"Everything we design and build here is thoroughly analysed," Price said. "On this project, we spent close to 100 million pounds doing these kinds of studies. We spent a lot on the rabies thing. First there was the concern about its effect on pacemakers, because it sets up quite an electric field." Heart specialists concluded that the antirabies grids posed no threat to pacemaker-equipped passengers. But this did not answer Price's other worry, which concerned the train signaling system. This system was like something snatched from somewhere in the next century, something satisfying to draw on paper but terribly difficult to build and to put into operation. Computers in the control center, on the British terminal, would automatically determine an optimum speed profile for each train. If a fast shuttle were entering some kilometers behind a slower freight train, the computer would decide how fast each train should travel at each point of its passage to make best use of the tunnel's capacity. These signals would be transmitted through the rails as radio signals. "The track is the antenna, and there's a pickup that rides just above the track and picks up the speed, signals and other things for the train," Price said.

The electromagnetic fields generated by the rabies traps could interfere with the reception of those signals in the speeding trains. "So we had to install *another* system in the signaling system," Price said. The new system would shut off the rabies trap when an approaching train was about three hundred meters away and would turn it back on after the train passed.

The rabies trap, however, was only one possible source of interference with the signaling system. "We've got plenty of electricity in the tunnel," Price said. "Each of those two hundred rooms [in the cross-passages] is a miniature substation. We've got twenty-five-thousand-volt catenary all the way through." There were two other radio systems as well, for voice communications in the tunnel and between the control center and the trains.

"Main power comes in each end of the tunnel," Price said. "Very high voltage. It runs down; there's a separating point in the center. French side is supplied by France, UK by UK. The last I knew, San Francisco city limits was nine hundred megawatts, total connected load. This is about six hundred. The trains are ten apiece—actually about six a loco, but if you've got both locos full-on, you're drawing ten megawatts. That's a lot of power."

Handling that power required much care, as Price found out when he began to test the system. Power for the trains had to be fed through balancers that changed the three-phase incoming current into single-phase current for the catenary. These were the largest devices of their kind ever built. "We have exceeded the state of the art several times on this job, and these are very sophisticated, big, solid-state type devices," Price said. "Transformer-type things, and by their very nature they would give off large electromagnetic fields. *Large*. And you can't see those, it's like radiation."

Stout chain-link fences surrounded the balancers to keep passersby from wandering into these fields. For the first test, a subcontractor fired up the balancer to about one-third power. The electromagnetic field instantly melted large holes in the fence and welded the gate shut. "It was just inductive; the fence acted like the secondary of a transformer," Price said. "In the range of a thousand amps." The solution was a better grounding, or earthing, of the fence.

Certain problems with the signaling and train control system were of the worst sort, in Price's view. He was immediately impressed by the systems' profound complexity, particularly in the fan of tracks in the terminals.

On each side of the Channel, the mammoth shuttle trains had to be switched off the single tunnel track, directed onto one of three loop tracks and guided onto one of the ten platform tracks. (The terminal accommodates sixteen platform tracks; others will be added when and if traffic requires them.) The trains had to be slowed and stopped automatically. When they were loaded, they were to depart under automatic guidance, accelerating gently out of the fan and onto the main tunnel line.

The diagrams of this system were bewildering; the reality was almost be-yond imagining, even for an engineer like Price, who had a good background in control systems. "You start thinking: To make that happen here, it's fuck-ing unbelievable," Price said. As late as March 1993, design work on the sig-naling system was still only about 85 percent complete, Price recalled. "You think I haven't got some lay-awake nights?" he said. "We seem to be making it, but you have to stay on it every second."

To see how the system worked in practice, Price went to France and rode in the driver's cab of the TGV Atlantique. "And I thought, 'There's something fucking wrong here,'" Price said. "I noticed, as we left the Paris high-speed-rail-TGV terminal: *Lights.* Trackside lights. Green, yellow, red. And I noticed the train goes normal train speed till it gets out of the terminal area and maybe a few more kilometers, and then *boom,* he kicks it in the ass. And there's no more trackside."

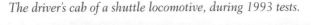

The driver's cab of a shuttle locomotive, during 1993 tests.

Price went next to the TGV Nord, where the TVM430's immediate ancestor was in use, and asked what happened when a train approached a terminal. The answer was trackside signaling: It was easier to use, simpler to build and served very nicely because the trains weren't running at high speed.

"So then I get back in here, and I said, 'Why are we using this son of a bitch in the terminal,' " Price recalled. " 'It's not going to work. It is too complex and *you don't need it.* Put TVM in the goddamned *tunnel. . . .*' I keep hearing, 'You don't know what you're talking about.' "

Price consulted Sofrerail, the SNCF subsidiary that was designing the signaling system. There was a computer that could help; one could program all of the system's logic into its software, along with the very precise distances between the data devices on the tracks. The computer would cost £5 million. Price asked a Sofrerail expert if the machine was necessary.

"He said, 'You don't need it *as long as you don't change anything.*' But he said if you change *one* track circuit it's going to take you a goddamned year with people working to figure out if that affected something else. Regression analysis: If I do this, what else in the system might be affected?" Price bought the computer. Within a week, he had news that infuriated him.

"I discovered, through my pardon-the-expression French Mafia connections, that one of Eurotunnel's finest is out on the goddamn street, shopping for a standard signaling system they would intend to install *after* we spend all our goddamned money trying to make TVM430 work," Price said. "So I'm not giving [the computer] to the client unless he pays dearly for it. And I will take that son of a bitch when I'm done with it and set fire to the fucker right out in front of his office and keep his ass away with a shotgun before I'll give the son of a bitch to him. That's where we are.

"Keep in mind our contract's fixed-price," he added. Why would Eurotunnel insist on a system it might not employ? "Because they're not credible people. They *like* to spend our money."

Price struggled on into the summer of 1993, working to get the system ready. In July, Morton succeeded in turning Lemley's flank and striking a deal directly with the contractors. Neville Simms of Tarmac, who had become chairman of TML's member's assembly, was the catalyst: He called Morton and suggested an informal chat to discuss terms. Morton needed a hard date when he could have the tunnel; TML needed a guarantee that the member companies would not end up bankrupt. The Bank of England stepped in again, hosting a string of early-morning meetings. On July 27, both sides signed a protocol: TML agreed to turn over the project on December 1.

"Relations were just dreadful, and they didn't improve until the protocol was signed," said Roger Byatt of NatWest. But both sides were under intense financial pressure to settle their differences. TML was facing the onset of liquidated damages in August. "Penalties for TML were so severe—£100 million plus—that they had to cooperate," Byatt said.

On the other side, the banks would not—could not—continue to advance money to Eurotunnel. In the summer of 1992, "the banks were very concerned about escalating costs, poor Eurotunnel-TML relations, the probability of delay," Byatt said. It was clear that if the banks ran a banking case at that moment, Eurotunnel's finances wouldn't pass. "So we didn't run it. It was like stopping the clock on negotiations. There were a series of meetings that went from bad to worse. By early October, we had to run the banking case." The result was as feared; the Credit Agreement had been breached.

"We couldn't indicate that the breach would be healed," Byatt said. "So we couldn't advance more money." The banks set a deadline in November, by which time Eurotunnel would have to resolve its differences with TML, get a firm date when the tunnel would be ready and assure the banks about the eventual total cost. "They couldn't do it," Byatt said. "So we issued a waiver of the breaches of the covenant."

There were many meetings in the first half of 1993, Byatt said, and all failed. "At the end of May, we said to Eurotunnel, 'We can't go on,'" Byatt said. A June 15 letter spelled out all that had to happen before the banks would agree to continue funding. It was this grim letter, Byatt said, that triggered the series of early-morning meetings at, and under the eye of, the Bank of England. Eurotunnel did not even have the cash, then, to keep its part of the bargains; Byatt had to arrange a £120 million cash advance.

The settlement was not universally popular within Eurotunnel. Pete Behr said that Frank Kane, who had replaced Neerhout and was the point man in negotiating with TML, went out afterward and had yellow-and-black rep-striped ties made, with a hornet embroidered in black on one of the yellow bands. These were worn by people who shared his dim view of the protocol, people who were "mad as hornets," Behr said.

Part of the deal was that Morton got Lemley's head: He would leave the project at turnover and would have little to say about affairs between TML and Eurotunnel. This did not bother him overmuch; he had long since decided to leave when the project was finished.

Before then, however, Lemley had to deal with Price's signaling problem. "We found out finally that one of our very senior engineering people had cut a deal with Sofrerail to make a major change in the signaling system," Lemley said. "He never surfaced the information, and we can only run one train in each direction, now, until after March [1994]. They've got to completely redo their software for that signaling system, and we're caught in the middle of this. There was an instruction out that there would be no changes to that system until after handover, and our French people, the technical people, went ahead and did it in secret."

Price and Lemley found that the decision had been made in August and that work had been done already on site. "Then we had our guy in the box," Lemley said. "He tried to change some minutes of meetings. We wouldn't allow him to change them, and it trapped him. So then, all of a sudden, when people started feeling the heat, why, we got reports coming out of everywhere."

Why had this been done? "They're protecting Sofrerail's reputation, partially, but this is the French system, where the *Polytechnique* fraternity is stronger than their ties to the company," Lemley said. "There was a *polytechnicien* inside TML, one inside Eurotunnel and God knows what in Sofrerail, but it surfaced that they cut this deal between them, and they just lifted up the rug and swept it under, put it back down and figured that we were so goddamned dumb we wouldn't figure out what had happened."

Lemley was at pains to exempt the French construction organization, under Matheron and Fermin, from this criticism. "He would never have let the signal thing go as it has," Lemley said of Matheron. "He was selective about what he brought to the office, but he didn't let things fester that were major issues."

This change in the signal-system software was not the only pressing problem as handover—now postponed to December 10—approached. When the protocol was signed in July, there was a "punch list" drawn up of work that remained to be done before the system would be considered complete. There were 22,000 items on the punch list.

From the academic post he now occupied—Rees Jeffreys Professor of Transport Engineering at Imperial College, London—Tony Ridley observed an odd provision of the protocol: Eurotunnel had agreed to take delivery of the tunnel before commissioning was complete.

"I think I could have forecast—and indeed did forecast—everything that's happened," he said, during the months between the handover and the first day of the tunnel's operation. "The one thing I didn't forecast, which I find absolutely mindboggling, is that in the settlement in December last, Eurotunnel took over the responsibility, albeit with TML's help, for commissioning the system. . . . That is virtually unprecedented in my experience."

Commissioning was usually a joint effort in large projects, Ridley said; a time when both the builder and the client shared the facility and worked together to get it up and running. Under the protocol, the tunnel became Eurotunnel's responsibility at the December handover. The length of the punch list indicated how complicated commissioning would be; the history of the project indicated how hard it would be to secure cooperation between Eurotunnel and TML.

But neither side had the time or strength, now, for another round of struggle. The protocol merely embodied the inevitable; everyone—banks, contractors and Eurotunnel—had fought themselves into exhaustion and out of options.

19

In the end, everything came down to a single day: Friday, December 10, 1993. At dawn, not even the weather looked promising; the ragged last gusts of a three-day gale rattled windows under a rolling mass of low, leaden clouds. The seas in the Channel were gray-green, broken, still strong, and a consolation for the backers of the tunnel: The gale had played predictable havoc with the ferries, and Dover was still full of delayed trucks.

For the rest, things looked grim. This was the day that had been set down for the handover, the day when all work would be done and all regulations met, the final deadline in a string that stretched back through years of a troubled past.

The ceremony that was to mark the moment was fixed and invitations had gone out to the celebrants. There was a tent standing in the French terminal at Coquelles, and all that was to occupy it in a few hours—a choir in white, tables of food, crates of champagne, platoons of uniformed attendants, lights and projectors and thirty gilded hard hats for the top TML executives—had been marshaled for deployment. There was a train waiting in Victoria Station to take two hundred celebrants through the tunnel to Calais, and another train in Paris waiting to carry an equal number of French guests on a quick round-trip to Folkestone. The handing-over ceremony was scheduled to begin at 7 P.M. in the tent at Coquelles.

There already had been problems; Lemley had planned the event to reward and honor the people who had actually built the tunnel. The ten contracting firms had rather different ideas; they saw it as a chance to coddle and impress prospective important clients and their own top executives. Lemley had been left—officially—with a pathetic thirty places on the triumphal train; he had pulled a number of strings to extend the train by a few cars and increase his places a fewfold. But in the last few hours before the train was supposed to pull out of Victoria Station, it seemed that his efforts might have been in a vain cause and that the celebration might turn into a spectacular debacle.

For one thing, the Health and Safety Executive wouldn't allow the sleek new Eurotrain to make the historic run: It hadn't been tested. Nor would HSE permit TML to use the opulent Orient Express coaches; their elegant wood paneling was considered too much of a fire hazard. The honored guests would have to make their way to the Channel Coast in a British Rail coach of the better sort, a first-class carriage normally used on longer runs between cities. This train could go only as far as Folkestone, however, because the locomotive took its power from an electrified third rail and the tunnel's power was in the overhead catenary. So the guests would have to switch at the tunnel portal to a string of disappointingly banal British Rail commuter cars. The top permitted speed would be a paltry 100 kilometers per hour—60 miles an hour, instead of the 160-kilometer/100-mile-per-hour design speed.

Worse, the tunnel was not finished, at least not to the degree specified by the July Protocol. TML's people had managed, by superhuman exertion, to whittle the punch list down from 22,000 separate items to a mere hundred or so. Twelve of the Protocol's thirteen milestones had been met, and only the last, the one that meant that the tunnel was in commission and ready for use, remained. A staggering amount had been accomplished, but the work wasn't finished. Twenty-four hours earlier, Tom Clay, an American engineer who was in charge of this final push, had calculated that it would take until December 15 to clear up the last items on the punch list. None of these items was of overwhelming or even unusual importance; taken together they did not even excite the British safety authorities, except to restrict the ceremonial traffic in the tunnel to one train at a time.

The trouble, again, was with the banks: If Eurotunnel accepted the tunnel from TML before all the punch list items had been corrected, it might damage the legal integrity of the entire Protocol. Accepting the tunnel as it stood might, in effect, void the guarantee, or so the banks feared. And thus it was that Roger Byatt of National Westminster Bank found himself enmeshed in a dizzying round of telephone calls and faxed documents on that Friday morning, striving to craft a document that bound TML and guaranteed that it would get paid, that protected Eurotunnel and the banks, that respected the various laws of different lands—and that pleased everyone, or at least did not mortally offend.

The Protocol required sign-off certificates from the banks to show that they were satisfied that the tunnel was certifiably complete and that Eurotunnel could therefore take the keys. But those certificates could be signed only after someone at each bank examined an inch-thick stack of supporting documents—and these had not been ready until late Thursday night, London time. There was no time to ship the documents to more than two hundred banks all over the world, much less to await a considered response from each bank.

Byatt and his colleagues in the core group of four banks had managed to convince the syndicate to accept the assurances of the twenty-two instructing banks. But now, as Friday morning slipped away, there was not even time to get the documents out to the instructing banks, not even by chartering aircraft. Byatt therefore had to convince the syndicate to accept the word of just the four Agent Banks. "We have to say to the other banks: 'We've looked at the documents, and we're happy with what we see,' " Byatt explained. "We have to give them assurances that there's nothing sinful here. Then we have to assure Neville Simms. We have to say to him, 'Even though you're only getting four, rather than twenty-two signatures, this isn't sinister, it's not a device to screw you, to come back in a few weeks and say that you're not going to get paid.' "

The glossy printed program for the day said the train would leave Victoria Station at 2:40 P.M.; guests had been told to check in at the Simplon-Orient Express Office by 2 P.M. At 11:20 A.M., some of the French contractors balked. Byatt spent a tense few minutes shuttling between telephone and fax machine as subordinates negotiated feverishly. The last fax with the last needed signature came to Byatt's desk at precisely 11:35 A.M.

By that time, the day had improved, too. It was brilliantly clear; the weakening wind had swept the gloomy clouds out into the North Sea, along with every mote of dust or wisp of haze. It left behind a sky of intense and unbroken blue and a still-green landscape washed with the deep gold of a sun not yet winter-pale. Byatt, like everyone else, dutifully reported to Victoria a bit before 2 P.M.; for this once, at least, something about the Channel Tunnel ran without friction or delay: quite the contrary. With everyone aboard, and with hardly a lurch, the train pulled out and began its run down through Kent at 2:20 P.M., a full twenty minutes early.

There was, of course, champagne; Pommery was dealt to the guests with a generous hand and the train covered long stretches at good speed. The only off-moment came at Ashford, where the train paused next to the site of what someday would be the international terminal for the through-passenger trains coming from and going to the Continent.

"Well, it's coming along," said one guest, looking at the site, which to an untrained eye showed not even the outline of a railway terminal. There was a muted chorus of grunts that might have been taken for assent. Then the train moved on.

Things fell apart at Folkestone, where the commuter train, already freighted with the TML workers for whom Lemley had engineered space, waited alongside one of the loading platforms meant for the Shuttle. The Shuttle, of course, was far wider than the standard passenger cars, so gangplanks linked each car to the platform. The London train rolled in on the other side of the platform and halted.

Word came that the French train was running forty-five minutes late. Since only one train was to be permitted in the tunnel at a time, the British couldn't budge until the French train emerged in Britain, looped through the Folkestone terminal and completed its return journey to Coquelles. Most passengers from London elected to remain, during the wait, in their more comfortable first-class carriages; many amused themselves, as the sun set and darkness gathered, by raising their brimming champagne flutes to toast their co-celebrants across the platform. Darkness fell, more and more legs began to be stretched on the platform and still the French train did not appear.

This should have created more consternation than it in fact did. The schedule called for a return to London by 10:30 P.M. to allow passengers to catch the last trains to their scattered homes. The schedule also called for almost ninety minutes of ceremony at Coquelles. If things ran an hour late—as seemed increasingly likely, as the French train fell further behind schedule—a lot of people were going to find themselves stranded in Victoria Station with an overnight wait for the next train home. A lot of other people had told spouses to fetch them at 10:15. Yet there was little fretting among the celebrants; no one complained. There was some impatience shown by the British TML executives, who sent word across the Channel that there could be no delaying departure of the return train: It would have to leave Coquelles at 8:40 Calais time, 7:40 London time. It began to seem as if the ceremonial key to the tunnel might have to be tossed from a moving train.

The British train, loaded at last with all its contingent of guests, edged into the tunnel mouth to switch onto the mainline tracks a few minutes after 4 P.M., then pulled back to await the signal to move. Safety announcements droned out of the public address system; details were offered as to how one would escape in the event of accident—at a walk, of course, not a run. These received about the same attention as the lifejacket demonstrations aboard airliners.

A ragged cheer greeted the French train as its lighted windows glided through the terminal a bit after five o'clock. More waiting followed. A growing sense of anticlimax stilled conversation. People sat staring out into the darkness, glancing with increasing frequency at their watches. Then, at 6:07 P.M., the train began to move. It was now ninety-seven minutes behind schedule.

It gathered speed quickly as it entered Running Tunnel North and moved down into the chalk, down toward the seabed. The tunnel walls became a gray blur with single white stripe—the cooling pipe—running at about eye level on the right side. The interior lights were shut off to allow a better view as the train approached the British crossover chamber, but in truth there was not very much to see: The white stripe disappeared at the crossover, and the flat mass of the great chamber doors replaced the curved tunnel wall for a few instants. All the wealth of detail that had absorbed the thoughts and labor of thousands of men and women—the cross-passages, the chiller pipes, the piston relief ducts—flickered by too rapidly for the eye to grasp. The experience was more felt than seen: The train, which lacked the mass and insulation of the shuttle wagons, swept along with a roar that made conversation difficult. The wall streamed by endlessly and a sense of the awesome dimensions of this tunnel took root and grew: Mile after mile of wall flew by the windows; the roar did not change pitch. Time seemed to slow. Five minutes went by. Ten. Fifteen. Twenty. Twenty-one, twenty two.

And then, in an instant, the roar dropped away, the tunnel wall disappeared and a clamor of approving sounds filled the cars. The clean, white forms of the French terminal structures rolled past, the carriages slowed and drew to a halt, the doors opened and a wave of music swept in. The song, played by a French Dixieland band, was "It's a Long Way to Tipperary," the tune to which a generation of Britain's youth had marched off to die in France, not very far from this red-carpeted platform, in the horror of the Great War's trenches.

All impatience fled from the lights of a hundred cameras; everyone was shot a dozen times on the gangplanks. Gaiety reasserted itself strongly. Sir Alastair Morton—in an incongruous outfit whose most striking elements were a belted rust-brown overcoat of generous proportions and a broad-brimmed, flat-crowned, blue waxed-cotton rain hat—pushed a bow-wave of journalists before him as he moved, waving, across a walkway to the huge tent. Byatt, unremarked by the crowd, walked a few paces behind, beaming happily at no one in particular. The debarkees made comic attempts at French, with particular emphasis on the word *merde*.

The tent was not some flimsy canvas streched over some poles—it was more like a steel-framed industrial shed or medium-size arena that happened to be sheathed in bright white canvas rather than wood or metal. It had a high stage at one end and three grand tables, lit by rows of intense overhead spotlights, running down its length like railway platforms. A large cloakroom took up half of one wall, and ten columns rose in two long rows; these latter were topped by the revolving corporate symbols of the ten contracting companies. A thousand guests trooped in and filled in the remaining space so thoroughly that it wasn't possible to browse along the tables to systematically sample what one imagined was an impressively varied array of food and

The Sangatte facility, with the great shaft at top right, in early 1994.

drink; all that stood up above the crowd were the columns and the stage. The band moved in and took the stage and began to work its way through a string of standard jazzband favorites: "I Can't Give You Anything But Love" and "Ida, Sweet as Apple Cider."

There was enough space, once away from the dense pack along the tables, to walk among the celebrants with reasonable ease, and this many did, searching out and greeting friends and associates. Lemley, Essig and Matheron came together at the foot of the stage and spent several minutes in earnest conversation. Photographers stalked through the crowd, hunting familiar faces. French and English blended together into a roaring, incomprehensible gabble.

The lights went down and, to a burst of tuneless but dramatic music, a film began to flicker upon the white canvas wall above and behind the stage. It was a handsome, professional piece of work, a succession of images: the

raw terminal sites, the immense machines, the maw of the great shaft at Sangatte. As these flashed out above the now-stilled throng, the wind off the
Channel began to ripple the canvas screen, and the images began to shim-
mer: Roadway viaducts waved sinuously like titanic serpents, manriders tumbled down tunnels, a TBM snaked its way through a crossover chamber that
pulsed like a human heart. Tendrils of electric cable spooled out, a drawing
of a sleek locomotive shivered as it took form; HGV wagons, with their
cutout sides, became huge stained-glass windows.

As the film ran, a mysterious band of white-clad figures entered the tent
from slits on either side of the stage. They stood by, craning to watch the film.

The handover was routine: Neville Simms uttered conventional sentiments in English, and Philippe Montagner, his co-president of TML, repeated them in French. The mysterious white-clad figures took the stage;
they proved to be members of a local French choir. They were one hundred
strong and gave strong, confident voice to a pleasant anthem that spoke of a
path beneath the sea. This was answered, from part of the crowd, by a drink-
fueled rendition of "Swing Low, Sweet Chariot," the anthem of the English
Rugby Union. As this died away, a path cleared through the crowd to let
thirty children carry the gilded hard hats to the stage. After appropriate ap-
plause, celebrants were invited to step outside for the presentation of the
keys; each was handed a plaid blanket as a shield against the chill.

Outside, under brilliant lights, with the towering metal wall of a shuttle
wagon for a backdrop, Simms and Montagner handed a symbolic key—a
two-foot-long object with the words "10th DECEMBER 93" and the TML
emblem—to Bénard and Morton. As Bénard brandished the key, the shuttle
slid silently toward the tunnel, revealing the vast sweep of the French terminal. Then, in a nicely choreographed performance, the tunnel's rolling stock
began to weave among the platforms: single and double-deck shuttles, HGV
wagons, flat loaders, shunting and tunnel locomotives.

On the flatcars were tableaux vivants, gangs of tunnelers frozen in midtask:
digging, hauling, stretching, bending, heaving, in every posture of work. The
white choir glided through, waving and singing the anthem. Figures on other
loaders held staffs whose ends poured forth fountains of gaudy firework
flames. Two fireworks panels blazed forth: One said "WELCOME," the other,
"BIENVENUE." More firework fountains gushed from the catenary supports
overhead. Rockets shot skyward, trailing gold sparks, to burst above the
crowds with cannon-shot booms that, had the wind been in the east, might
well have carried over the water—as the thunder of artillery had done from
the battlefield of Waterloo—to echo in Folkestone's amphitheater of hills.

The noises of this celebration were, however, less striking than the silent
running of the trains. They slipped through the spotlights without a sound,

gliding with an animal grace—a little sinister, like great predators moving toward prey—among the platforms. They were evolved: These were not roaring saurian behemoths wreathed in steam; they were big cats that moved with serene and soundless confidence.

In an important sense, nothing could have been more French and less English than this ceremony; nothing could have illustrated more clearly the gulf that even now separated the two nations. A choir of women and children *standing on a moving flatcar?* Unthinkable in Britain. *Tableaux vivants gliding beneath live catenary cables whilst fireworks thundered out overhead?* Gallic madness. *Rockets sent skyward through a network of cables?* Magnificent, but not good procedure. *Guests permitted to clamber up a temporary scaffold for a better view?* Horrors.

Nothing bad happened, though, and after a brief revisit of the tent, when smiling platoons of bilingual French hostesses told the delighted guests that they could keep their cheery plaid blankets as souvenirs, an announcement boomed out that the train for Folkestone was at the platform, ready for boarding. This took fifteen minutes, and at 8:30 London time the British Rail cars edged out of the French terminal. "I'm told that the engineer might make a mistake," Keith Price shouted over a few score conversations in one car. "He might take her up to a hundred miles an hour." Cheers greeted this.

The train took about five minutes to trundle down to the French portal. There it accelerated sharply for what seemed a very long time. The roar grew in volume, but as it did, the ride grew smoother and smoother. There was no clacking, no swaying in the car; it ran flat and fast. The sound reached a hundred-mile-an-hour pitch and hung there in a single, long, drawn-out

The handover ceremonies, December 10, 1993, at Coquelles.

note. "She's getting the benefit of the aerodynamics," Lemley said. "She's down on the rails and rolling." The elation in the car grew; a burly man in a signal-yellow jacket and white hard hat hijacked a drinks cart and steered it down the train aisle when the caterer's stewardess went off in search of more whiskey. Drinks were poured from daring heights, toasts and voices were raised above the sublime howl of the speeding train.

A crowd surrounding John Hester, at the front end of the car, bellowed for Lemley, who was working his way forward, shaking hands as he went. "I've got an emotional night going here," he said to no one in particular as he edged through the car. He disappeared into a noisy mass and emerged with a miner's oil lamp, a gift of powerful symbolic value from Hester, a value that Lemley clearly felt. He made his way back through the car, stopping at each seat to shake hands. "Thank you for your help," he said to each. "I may not see you before I leave, but I wanted to thank you."

He finally reached Price and tried to thank him, too, but Price rose to his feet on the handshake and threw his arms around Lemley.

"Thank *you*," he said. "Without you, you bastard, I might not have been here for this." A few minutes later, at 8:52 P.M., the train roared out of the tunnel, into a clear and chilly English night and an uncertain place in history.

At 9:42 on the evening of November 18, 1996, Train No. 7539, a heavy-goods shuttle carrying 29 trucks in two rakes, left the Coquelles terminal for Folkestone. It accelerated to 66 kilometers per hour before pausing for 32 seconds, just outside the tunnel portal, to await a signal to proceed.

As the train moved into Running Tunnel South, four witnesses—two security patrolmen, a dog handler and the service tunnel access controller—saw a fire under one of the vehicles near the middle of the trailing rake. It was a good-sized fire; the witnesses said the flames were about two meters high and two meters wide.

They notified the terminal controller, who in turn notified the Rail Control Centre in Folkestone. By that time, a smoke detector in the tunnel had detected the fire and relayed the information to Fire Equipment Management Centre outside the British portal.

At 9:51 P.M., with the train running at 140 kilometers an hour, the driver received a fire alarm from the unmanned rear locomotive. By that time, the Rail Control Centre had received four more alarms from the tunnel fire detection system and signaled the driver that he might have a fire aboard. He was told to proceed to an emergency siding in the Folkestone terminal. A few moments later, the driver of a following train in the south tunnel encountered heavy smoke and slowed down.

The rail controllers stopped other trains from entering the tunnel, slowed five trains already in passage to 100 kph and ordered the piston relief ducts closed to keep smoke from spreading.

The driver of the stricken train, following procedure, continued toward the British portal at 140 kilometers per hour. He managed to reach and pass through the French crossover before an electronic message at 9:57 P.M. indicated that one of the propping jacks, used to stabilize the shuttle cars during

Eurotunnel served a celebratory feast in the British crossover cavern for the official May 1994 tunnel opening . . .

loading, seemed to be in the down position. This could, if true, derail the train, so the *chef de train,* or conductor, tried to uncouple the damaged car to allow the shuttle to continue.

Before he could, the driver's STOP lamp came on, and he halted at a cross passage. As he did, the power went down and a wave of smoke ran forward over the train. It was so thick that the driver couldn't read the number of the cross-passage. Smoke began seeping into the amenity coach behind the locomotive, where thirty-one passengers (one a pregnant woman), the conductor and a steward were sheltering. The train was nineteen kilometers from the French portal, thirty-two kilometers from the British portal.

At 10:13 P.M., the control center turned on the supplementary ventilating

fans, which were designed to blow air through the service tunnel and out into the running tunnel to clear the air around a fire. But the fan's blades were left at zero pitch and thus pushed no air. This dangerous error wasn't corrected for a full seven minutes. By then, the *chef de train* had opened a door to try to see the cross-passage. He saw nothing; a cloud of smoke rushed in; the passengers were forced to lie on the floor, choking.

Up to this time, the fire apparently had grown slowly; the wind of passage flattened the flames and kept them from spreading. But when the fans stirred the air to a 2.5-meter-per-second flow, the fire seems to have intensified quickly. The fans did allow the crew and passengers to escape into the service tunnel after a bad twenty minutes on the coach floor, but the firefighters who shortly thereafter crept out to confront the blaze confronted a monster. A truck loaded with twenty tons of frozen fat had taken fire; explosions sent shock waves through the tunnel.

. . . as Marc Isambard Brunel had in his
Thames Tunnel more than 150 years
earlier.

At 10:42, the passengers boarded a passenger shuttle train stopped in Running Tunnel North and arrived in Coquelles at 11:24. From there they went to hospitals for treatment. The fire was declared extinguished at 5:00 the next morning. Temperatures had reached an estimated 1,300 degrees Centigrade, hot enough to destroy the tunnel liner. In a fifty-meter stretch, the forty-centimeter-thick lining was reduced to an average of seventeen centimeters of thickness; all of the steel reinforcing was exposed. Where the fire was most intense, only two centimeters of the lining were left.

Five hundred meters of track had to be rebuilt, as did eight hundred meters of catenary and 1.5 kilometers of the signaling system, the track circuits and electrical supply cables. Fifteen shuttle wagons and the rear locomotive were badly damaged. Ten shuttle cars were destroyed, though all were able to be towed out of the tunnel on their own wheels.

It was a culminant event: Within three years of the day TML had handed the keys to Eurotunnel, almost every fear about the English Channel Tunnel had been realized.

There had been a bad fire, and it had been handled in a way that did not engender confidence. There were immediate and persistent reports that the fire was the result of sabotage. Loading the train had been delayed because of a demonstration by workers in the French terminal, a result of Eurotunnel's critical financial problems: Five weeks earlier, it had announced that it would lay off 657 of its 3,500 workers over the following fourteen months to save cash. It was said that a disgruntled tunnel worker had been seen tossing a flare onto the moving shuttle in Coquelles.

After the fire, Eurotunnel noted accurately that the safety systems had worked and no life had been lost. But the fire had been badly handled and the truck drivers had had a far nearer brush with death than anyone cared to admit. Many of Eurotunnel's critics might have said, with much accuracy, that they had forecast such.

Three months after the handover—thirty months before the fire—Tim Green had criticized Eurotunnel's hiring practices, which (like his own) avoided experienced railway workers. "From what I can see, they're picking all the wankers," he said. "They've produced a hierarchy that isn't very experienced and they're frightened by experience. . . . The operators they've got are nowhere near running a railroad. We're all getting a little bit depressed because we've put a lot into this job and we want it to succeed."

In fact, Eurotunnel had been late in training its workforce. In October 1992, at a time when Eurotunnel was still hoping to open the tunnel by Christmas 1993, Morton had told shareholders that the company would spend 400,000 man-hours in the following 18 months to train about 1,800 employees of its transportation unit. At that time, Eurotunnel had 450 employees.

As Tony Ridley had feared, commissioning the tunnel had been a terrible ordeal for Eurotunnel. The months after the December 1993 handover had been a litany of delays and excuses.

Keith Price recalled trying, in the first months after the handover, to help with the commissioning. "The attitude was, 'We don't want to hire any old-time British or French railroad people; they're too hard to retrain and we don't want them to do things the way they learned to do them,' " Price recalled.

One vivid incident concerned a high-speed brake test on a five-kilometer stretch of track in the tunnel. Price arranged to leave the French terminal at 4 P.M., only to find that someone had turned off all power without warning or explanation.

He wasn't able to move the train for three hours. When he did get into the tunnel, the power went off again. When he got rolling again, the control center refused to allow the train to achieve test speed because they couldn't locate the operating procedures. Price didn't get out of the tunnel until 3 A.M. the following morning.

"I feared for my life in there," Price said. "I went over to the control center to talk to those people the next day. They had no spatial knowledge of the tunnel. They had never been down there. I pointed to the board, to the five-kilometer test track, and asked the guy if he could tell me how long it was. He held up his thumb and forefinger. 'About this far,' he said. They were computer whiz kids who didn't understand anything about the tunnel."

The queen and President Mitterand presided at splendid official opening ceremonies in May 1994, during which a celebratory banquet was served in the British crossover cavern. The celebration was premature; the *Wall Street Journal* greeted the gala with a headline saying the tunnel was "vulnerable to financial disaster."

No train would carry a paying customer until September, when a trickle of passenger shuttles yielded Eurotunnel's first revenue from operations. In March 1995, after months of struggling with the problems in the complex shuttle cars, Eurotunnel finally invited automobile and bus drivers to "show up and go." The Folkestone terminal was overwhelmed; police had to clear access roads barricaded by furious drivers. Full operations were delayed until the summer of 1995.

Each day in all those long months added £2 million in interest to Eurotunnel's debt. Each day seemed to bring a fresh crisis: There were rumors that the tunnel was leaking badly, reports that the banks were about to foreclose. Eurotunnel embarked on doomed lawsuits to collect damages from British Rail, SNCF and Transmanche-Link (Lemley estimated that the shared loss to the ten contracting companies in TML was between £600 million and £800 million).

Eurotunnel reported that operating revenues exceeded operating expenses from March 1995 onward, but the debt created stupefying bottom-line losses: £925 million in 1995 alone. In September 1995, Morton stopped paying interest on most of Eurotunnel's bank debt, which then stood at nearly £8 billion.

But these fantastic numbers had the odd effect of preserving Eurotunnel. The banks simply could not afford to write off such enormous sums. So when Eurotunnel suggested that they accept shares of stock rather than cash as repayment, the banks could do little more than grumble and agree. So debt was restructured, and equity redistributed, and the venture lurched and stumbled on toward an ever-receding day of profitability.

This does not diminish at all the extraordinary work done by Morton, whose confidence and sheer nerve seemed to keep the vultures from settling on something very like a carcass.

By buying time, Morton (who providentially left Eurotunnel a few weeks before the fire) allowed the Channel Tunnel to fulfill the single essential hope of the people who had planned and built it: It quickly drew unto itself a dominant share of the cross-Channel market. The Eurostar passenger service, just before the fire, was carrying between 60 and 70 percent of passenger traffic between London and Paris. The shuttles were carrying half of the Dover-Calais automobile traffic, 39 percent of the buses and 47 percent of the freight.

On November 19, 1996, Frank and Izaline Davidson awoke in their apartment on the rue de Varenne in Paris to news reports of the tunnel fire. Frank had some business in London that day, and he called to reserve a seat on the Eurostar. The agent said he couldn't sell any tickets.

Davidson, who had once taught a class on failure at MIT, was philosophic. "It doesn't really matter," he told a visitor later. "The tunnel is built. People will see. It will succeed."

Izaline smiled.

INDEX

Abbots Cliff, 39
accidents, 80
Adit A1, 218
Adit A2, 218, 219
Agent Banks, 129, 130, 132
    and Eurotunnel financing,
        302–313, 317, 318
    and Protocol, 373
air spade, 295
Aitken, Jonathan, Thanet member,
    147
Alcatel Alsthom compagnie générale
    d'électricité, 244
Alexander, Henry Clay, lawyer, 58–59
Alsthom, 104
Amiens, 33
Amsterdam-Rotterdam Bank
    (AmRo), 130
Anderson, Joe, engineer, 232–236
    on signaling and train-control
        system, 243
Arlberg Tunnel, 13
Armand, Louis, head of SNCF, 61
Army, Navy & Air Force Gazette, 50
Arranging Banks, 129, 130
Ashford, 156
Assemblée nationale, 85
Assheton, Nina, 181

Associated British Ports, 104
Atkins-SETEC, 206–207
    role in Project Implementation
        Division (PID), 208

Balfour Beatty, 6, 7, 81
    and English Channel Tunnel
        Group, 96–97
Ball, George, undersecretary of state,
    57
bank(s)
    and Eurotunnel/Transmanche-
        Link relationship, 259–260
    and funds for Eurotunnel, 368
    and loan funding, 257–258
    and Protocol, 372–373
    and tunnel opening delay,
        362–363
    underwriting, 201
Bank of England, 174
Banks, Lawrence, investment banker,
    171
Banque indosuez, 93, 129
Banque nationale de Paris, 93, 129,
    177
Banque nationale du commerce et de
    l'industrie, 71
Banque paribas, 104

Barclays, 104
Beaumont, Frederick E., 42–45
Bechtel Corporation, 62, 112–113
Bechtel, Stephen, head of Bechtel
    Corporation, 62
Bechtel, Steve, Jr., 145
Behr, Pete, Bechtel senior vice presi-
    dent, 143–145, 163–164
    and Clause, 67, 245
Bénard, André, cochairman of the
    Channel Tunnel, 151–154, 162
Bertrand, Alain, 315, 316
Billecocq, Pierre, French transport
    minister, 85–86
Black Monday, 213–214
Blériot, Louis, 32
Blériot-Plage, 32
Board of Trade, 40
Bombardier of Canada, 277
Bonny, Jack, head of Morrison
    Knudsen, 62
Boothroyd Airship Company of
    Bournemouth, 117
boreholes, 183, 184–185
Bouygues, Francis, engineer, 99–101,
    105, 107
Bouygues S.A., 99–101
Brandenburg, 30
Breda Construzione Ferroviaria, 277
bridges, 70–71, 72
Bristow, Isaac George, president of
    Barge-Builders' Trades Union, 45
Britain, geographical history, 27–28
British issues
    compromising with French on tun-
        nel size, 238–239
    and Kent, 220
    logistical difficulties of Channel
        Tunnel project, 219–221
    problems within management, 271
    and rabies, 363–364
    race with French to finish tunnel,
        348–349, 354

British Channel Tunnel Company, 76
    and American investors, 76
    and investment banks, 76
British government
    and opposition to tunnel, 85, 86
    and privatization of businesses,
        175–176
    and tunnel financing, 94
British isolationism, 82–84, 91
British Marine Service Tunnel
    tunnel-boring machine, 247
British Petroleum, 209
British press, and tunnelers, 290
British Rail, 76, 86–87
    and catenary, 207
    and the Mousehole, 92
    and Rail Usage Contract, 162, 231
    use of tunnel, 125–126, 182–183
British rings, 295–296
British Steel, 95, 104
British Telecom, 104
Broakes, Sir Nigel, EuroRoute chair-
    man, 103
Brown & Root, 62
Brown, David, engineer, 118–120,
    139–140, 182
    tunnel path optimization, 183
Brown, George, 62
Brunel, Marc Isambard, French
    engineer, 12–13
Bull, Sir William, 48, 50–52
bullet trains, 330–331
bull's prick, 224
Burley, Baron of. *See* Shackleton,
    Edward Arthur Alexander
Burnett, Andrew, 156–157
Byatt, Roger, NatWest executive, 161

Caisse des dépôts et consignations,
    145
Calais, 32
Calderon, Daniele, secretary, 165,
    360–361

Callaghan, Ian, 127–128, 192, 201–203
Canadian National Railways, 110
Cap Blanc Nez, 27, 33
Cap Gris Nez, 32
Cargo, Steve (The Snail), British engineer, 25
Castle Hill, 340
Casualty Union, 319
catenary, 207, 365
Catto, Lord, 173
Catto Room, 173
CGE-Developpement, 89, 90
chalk marl, 33, 64, 183
    under Channel Tunnel, 185–186
Chalks, the, 33
Channel, the
    chalk marl, 64
    and chalk marl dumping, 220
    geological studies of, 63–65
    history of, 4
Channel Expressway, 117–118, 120–122
Channel Islands, 27
Channel Tunnel
    adits, 218–219
    and American financing, 146
    announcement of, 126
    attempt to stall bill, 147
    and Beaumont, Frederick E., Royal Engineers, 42–45
    beginning construction of, 177–180
    breakthrough, 341–343, 345–346, 354–357
    breakthrough celebration, 341–343, 346–348, 351
    British celebration, 347–348
    and British tourist trade, 50–51
    chalk marl, 185–186
    chambers in, 10
    choosing path for, 185
    civilian sentiments toward, 66
    complexity of, 8–9, 10
    composition of, 8–9
    construction railway, 325–331
    cooling system, 241
    cost of delay, 8
    cost issues, 131–132, 141–142, 264–268
    cracks in, 336–337
    crossover cavern breakthrough, 337–339
    cross-passages, 10, 77–78, 333, 340
    and Davidson, Alfred, 56–57
    and Davidson, Frank, 56–57
    and Doll, Izaline and Henriette, 55
    and dumping of spoil, 220–221
    Dunn's plan for, 67, 70
    1856 proposal for, 36
    engineers, 206
    England's financial troubles with, 86
    and English Channel Tunnel Group, 96–98
    English opposition to, 130
    financing of, 90, 127–130
    and fire, 158–159, 280
    first train passengers, 386
    French celebration, 346–347
    geological issues, 63–65, 186
    government commitment to, 81–82
    handing over of, 371–379
    hazards to tunneling, 183–184
    history of, 35–54
    humidity in, 329
    and importance of completion, 4
    infilled valleys, 64, 65
    Invitation to Promoters, 103
    and Japanese banks, 322
    and Kings Cross station, 215–216
    land tunnels, 339–340
    lighting during construction, 17
    linking process, 20–21

Channel Tunnel (*Continued*)
  and loan funding, 257–258
  main power to, 365
  and Mathieu, Jacques-Joseph,
    35–36
  and Means, Jr., Cyril, 56
  Mousehole, 90
  opening ceremonies, 386
  opposition to, 82–84
  original proposal for, 35
  peak traffic hour design, 81
  physical characteristics, 5
  piston relief ducts, 10
  plans for digging, 77
  political sentiments toward, 65–66
  portrayal to investors, 9–10
  precast plant, 222–223
  previous work on, 221–222
  proposed construction phases,
    82
  and rabies traps, 364–365
  rail tracks, 358–360
  raising money for, 82
  and Royal Commission, 51
  safety concerns, 80–82
  and sea level measurement, 16
  as security threat, 46
  service tunnels, 69, 78–79,
    256–257, 351–352
  shuttle system, 77–82
  signaling system, 80–81, 242–244
  size of project, 3
  and stock market crash, 213–214
  surveying complications, 17–18
  television broadcast of break-
    through, 343, 347
  temperatures in, 79–80
  terminal tracks, 365–367
  and Thomé de Gamond, Aimé,
    35–39
  train fire, 381–385
  trains, 10
  treaty, 86–88

  and tunnel design problems,
    231–232
  and tunneler safety, 297–298
  tunnel segments, 221–227
  tunnel size, 238–239
  and underwriting banks, 201
  water leakage in, 79
Channel Tunnel bills, 44–45, 46,
    50–51, 75, 86–88, 140, 147,
    155–156
  Select Committee revisions to, 181
Channel Tunnel Company, 39, 46,
    72–73
  continuing role in project, 76
  and d'Erlanger, Baron Emile
    Beaumont, 46, 48
  and d'Erlanger, Leo, 53
Channel Tunnel Group (CTG)
  bid for Channel Tunnel, 103,
    105–106
  business opposition to, 104–105
Channel Tunnel Group/France
    Manche (CTG/FM), 109–112
  and Submission to Government,
    114–116
Channel Tunnel Height Datum
    1986, 16
Channel Tunnel Opposition Associa-
    tion, 83–84
Channel Tunnel Study Group,
    62–63, 73
  and British Channel Tunnel
    Company, 76–77
Channel Tunnel treaty, signing of,
    130
Chapman and Scott, 70
chef de train, 321
Chemin de fer du nord, 39
Chetwood, Sir Clifford, Wimpey's
    chairman, 261
Chevalier, Alain, head of Louis
    Vuitton-Moët et Chandon, 151
Clause 67, 245–247

Clay, Tom, American engineer, 372

Coindreau, Pierre, Banque nationale de Paris employee, 148–149
  on Eurotunnel, 154

Colquhon, Brian H., consulting engineer, 59–60

Colville, Sir John, private secretary, 84

Comité de sécurité, 280

commissioning, 369–370

Committee of the Members of the House of Commons in Favour of the Construction of a Channel Tunnel, 48

Compagnie française d'entreprises, 70

concrete, 330–331

concrete cancer, 222

construction railway, 325–331
  bullet trains, 330–331
  and cement transportation, 330
  and operations board controllers (OBCs), 329–330
  removal of, 351–354
  signaling system, 329
  and water transportation, 329

contractors
  money disputes with Eurotunnel, 229–231
  See also Transmanche-Link

coordination par projet, 166

Coquelles, 9, 371

Corbett, Graham, Eurotunnel managing director for finance, 312

Costain Civil Engineering, 91–92, 96

cover ratio, 257

Cozette, Philippe, tunneler, 21, 345–346

The Crack, 286, 288
  and Tim Green, 326

cranes, 226–227

Credit Agreement, 214–215, 217

Crédit lyonnais, 71, 129, 130

Crighton, Gordon, tunnel engineering director (British), 3–4
  and Channel bid, 6–7
  engineering experience, 5, 6
  and Laurent Leblond, 7, 8
  personal history, 6
  relationship with French and British, 7
  tunnel impact on reputation, 8
  on water seepage in tunnel, 248

Crosland, Tony, head of Department of the Environment, 86, 87

Cross Channel Contractors, 81

Crossley, Nick, engineer, 76

customs
  and firearms, 279
  on-train checks, 279–280

Davidson, Alfred, 56–57, 59

Davidson, Frank, 55, 56–59, 65, 66, 73
  contribution to tunnel, 75
  and EuroRoute, 96
  and reviving Channel Tunnel project, 89–116

Deacon, Chris, Midland Bank executive, 128–129, 148, 149–150, 159

De Dietrich, 282, 315, 323

DeFenoyl, Christian, Banque nationale de Paris senior executive, 160

de Gaulle, Charles, 66

de la Rochefoucauld, François, French nobleman, 31–32

De Leuw Cather, 63

demarcation, 296–297

Demeillat, Jean-Yves (Le Capitaine), 346

de Moleyns, Bishop Adam, 29

Denman, David, service tunnel manager, 22, 25
  and The Crack, 286, 288

d'Erlanger, Baron Emile Beaumont,
46, 47, 48, 50, 51–52
d'Erlanger, Baron Frederick Emile,
45–46
d'Erlanger, Leo, 52–53, 60–61, 82
Descenderie, The, 77
Des Landes, Daniel, Euroshuttle
project director, 316
Deutsche Bank, 130
de Vitry D'Avaucort, Count Arnaud,
55
Dherse, Jean-Loup, Eurotunnel chief
executive, 162–163
on stopping the Channel Tunnel
project, 208
Dickens, Charles, 32
Dillon Read, 55, 75
Disneymobile, 351
Dixon, Sir Pierson, British ambassador, 66
Doll, Henriette, French heiress,
55–56
Doll, Izaline, French heiress, 55, 57
Dorman Long, 70
Dover Strait, 27, 28–33
balloon crossings of, 32
and conquerors, 28
geographical makeup, 28
geological makeup, 27, 33
hazards of traveling, 30–31
and inclement weather, 30, 31–32
and *The Libell of Englyshe Polycye*,
29
and Napoleon, 29
ship traffic on, 29–30
and seasickness, 31–32
and smuggling, 29
and supertankers, 31
swimming, 32
and Thomas à Becket, 29
travel of, 28–33
unusual crossings of, 32
and Varne Bank, 30

wartime importance of, 29, 32
Weald-Artois anticline, 33
Driver, Brian, executive director of
Transmanche-Link, 278–279
Dumez S.A., 99
Duncan, Val, engineer, 76
Dunn, Charles Putnam, civil engi-
neer, 67, 69–70, 72–73
and modification of tunnel plans,
77
Dunsany, Admiral Lord, 40–42, 45
Durand-Rival, Pierre, deputy chief
executive for technical matters,
163–164, 230–231, 240–241

East London Railway, 13
Eastware Point, 36
Edmund Nuttall, 81
Edward, William, the Second Vis-
count Harcourt, 77, 84–85
elephant's foot, 224
engineer(s)
Anderson, Joe, 232–236
and backup system for train signal-
ing, 81
Bouygues, Francis, 99–101, 105,
107
British, 6, 7
British view of, 7
Brown, David, 118–120
Brunel, Marc Isambard, 12–13
Cargo, Steve, 25
Clay, Tom, 372
Coindreau, Pierre, 148
Colquhon, Brian H., 59–60
Crighton, Gordon, 5–8
Crossley, Nick, 76
and determining sea level, 16
Duncan, Val, 76
Dunn, Charles Putnam, 67
Durand-Rival, Pierre, 163–164
Frame, Alistair, 76
French, 6, 7

French views of, 7
Gueterbock, Tony, 99
Hamlen, John, 249
Heydon, Howard, 137–139
Jolivet, François, 164–166
Keitel, Peter, 138
Leblond, Laurent, 7–8
Lemley, Jack, 268–274
and Marquis of Granby, 5
Mathieu, Jacques-Joseph, 35
McDowall, Andrew, 97–99
Nattrass, Helen, 249–252
and piston relief ducts, 77–78
and problems with trains, 78–79
Ridley, Nicholas, 101
and Safety Authority, 280
of Simplon Tunnel, 14–15
Thomé de Gamond, Aimé, 35–39
and tunnel size, 206
English precast plant, 224, 226, 227
English Channel, 27, 28
    See also Channel
English Channel Tunnel Group, 95
    and EuroRoute, 96
    and French companies, 99
    See also Channel Tunnel Group
English, Thomas, 44
Equity 1, 140, 162
Equity 2, 140, 141, 148, 155
    and Bank of England, 176
    pathfinder prospectus for,
        171–177
    problems with, 173–174
Equity 3, 140, 177, 209, 211, 268
Equity 3
    and advertising, 210
    postponement of, 193–195
    prospectus for, 210, 214
Essig, Philippe, chairman of SNCF,
        118, 263–268
    on fire safety, 198–199
Étoile de Varne, 36, 38
Eurobridge, 118

European Investment Bank, 201,
        317
EuroRoute, 95–96, 102
    acceptability to British govern-
        ment, 124
    bid for Channel Tunnel, 103–104
    as CTG/FM competitor, 113
    drawbacks, 120
    member companies of, 104
Euroshuttle, 323
Euroshuttle Consortium Shuttle
        Group, 277, 316
Eurostar passenger service, 387
Eurotrain, 372
Eurotunnel (ET), 9, 118, 122–126
    and bank control, 128–130
    and the British press, 318
    and Channel Tunnel financing, 194
    and Clause 67, 245–246
    commissioning of system,
        369–370
    and cooling system, 361
    Credit Agreement, 214–215
    disputes with Transmanche-Link,
        240
    easing of financial crisis, 321–323
    Equity 3 postponement, 193–194
    expenses, 131
    and financing, 302–313, 317
    and fire safety, 198–201
    headquarters, 160
    and heavy goods vehicles, 350–351
    hurdles of, 126–127
    investors in, 210
    and lack of meeting privacy, 179
    and lump-sum differences, 362
    and market research, 210, 216
    money disputes with Transmanche-
        Link, 229–231
    and negotiations, 160–164
    and optimization, 183
    overrun costs of transportation
        system, 264–268

Eurotunnel *(Continued)*
  problems created by privatization,
    175–176
  Project Implementation Division
    (PID), 208
  public information center, 130
  public relations, 209–210
  and Rail Usage Contract, 231
  and railroads, 182–183
  and Safety Authority findings,
    158–159
  scheduled sales of shares,
    140–141
  and Shakespeare Cliff seawall,
    228
  and share selling, 201–203,
    209–211, 349
  and shuttle wagons, 349
  and signaling system, 242, 243,
    274
  stock prices, 268
  and Transmanche-Link, 136
  and tunnel debt, 386
  and tunnel opening delay,
    362–363
  and tunnel size, 206–207
  See also Channel Tunnel
    Group/France Manche
Eurotunnel PLC, 210
Eurotunnel S.A., 210

Fagg, Graham, tunneler, 21,
    343–344, 346, 347
Fahri, François, French businessman,
    133
Farthingloe Village, 289–290
faults, 183–184, 186
Fell, Arthur, member of Parliament,
    48
Fermin, Jacques, assistant construc-
    tion director, 271
Fiat Ferroviaria, 277
Field of the Cloth of Gold, 278

fire safety, 198, 319–320, 321
  and first tunnel fire, 381–385
  and halon, 281
  and testing of heavy goods vehi-
    cles, 281
First Boston and White, 76
Fitzgerald, Michael, Queen's
    Counsel, 155–156
Five-Bank Report, 93–94
Flexilink, 104–105
flooding, 80
Foch, Marshal, 48
Folkestone, 5, 322
Fond Pignon, 178, 199, 227
Fos, 163
Fosse Dangeard, 27
Frame, Sir Alistair, engineer,
    Eurotunnel board member, 76,
    162
France Manche, 106
Franklin, John, Morgan Grenfell
    executive, 144, 171–173, 177
Freeman, Roger, Transmanche-Link
    chief lawyer, 246, 361
Fréjus Tunnel, 13
French issues
  and Channel Tunnel legislation,
    199
  compromising with British on
    tunnel size, 238–239
  and Equity 2, 176
  and funding of Channel Tunnel,
    176
  management organization,
    271–272
  precast plant, 224–227
  race with British to finish tunnel,
    348–349, 354
  reaction to British default, 87–88
  tunnel-boring machines, 253, 272
French Marine Service Tunnel
    tunnel-boring machine, 272
French rings, 295, 296

Gabriel, Jean, Banque nationale de Paris executive, 144
Gault Clay, 335–336, 340
GEC-Alsthom, 243–244, 274, 303
General Electric Company (British), 244
George Wimpey Ltd., 97
Georges-Picot, Jacques M.C., Suez Canal Company president, 61
Gibb, Frank, chairman of Taylor Woodrow, 261
graben, 249
granite, 223
Green, Jim, construction railway operator, 286, 326–331, 351–354
grout, 272
GTM, 104
Gueterbock, Tony, civil engineer, 99
Guinness Peat, 191

Hades Hotel, 13
halon, 281
Ham Street Road Study Group, 156–157
Hamlen, John, Transmanche-Link engineer, 249
hand-tunnel gang, 332–333
Harcourt, Lord. *See* Edward, William, the Second Viscount Harcourt
Harding, Harold B. J., Institution of Civil Engineers vice president, 63
Harvey-Jones, John, ICI executive, 187
Hawker Siddeley, 110
Headon, Walter, chief economist Port of New York Authority, 63
Heads of Agreement, 308
Health and Safety Executive, 372
heavy goods vehicle (HGV), 277, 279
and fire testing, 281

Henderson, Sir Nicholas, British ambassador, 96, 102
Herald of Free Enterprise, 192
Hessig, Jean-Jacques, Crédit lyonnais representative, 113
Hester, Alabama, tunnel superintendent, 18
Hester, John, tunneler, 7, 18–20, 291
Hester, John
and ritual of linking tunnels, 21
on tunnel-boring machines, 292
Heydon, Howard, engineer, 137–139, 203, 204–206
Hill Samuels, 84
Holland, Don, chairman of Balfour Beatty, 119
Holywell Coombe, 180, 285
and Gault Clay, 340
Hoo Peninsula, 223
hot air balloon, 32
House of Commons Select Committee on the Channel Tunnel Bill, 155–156
concerns by ferry owners and port authorities, 157–158
hearings on environmental damage by Channel Tunnel, 180–181
and public interest, 156, 157
House of Lords' Select Committee on Channel Tunnel Bill, 181
fire safety, 198
hearing petitions, 195
House of Morgan, 55, 73
Hutter, Roger, SNCF deputy director-general, 89, 90

Industrial Bank of Japan, 130
Industrial Reorganisation Corporation (IRC), 187, 188
infilled valleys, 64, 65
Institut géographique national, 15, 16

Intergovernmental Commission
(IGC), 130–131
  Comité de sécurité, 280
  and heavy goods vehicles approval,
    279
  and passenger shuttles, 283
International Engineering Company,
  67
Irish tunnelers, 289
Isle of Grain, 222, 223
Isle of Guernsey, 282

Japan, 203
Joint Accord, 259, 260, 264, 265,
  268
Jolivet, François, French director-
  general of Transmanche-Link,
  164–170
  on tunneler training, 293
Jurassic bedrock, 64–65

Kander River, 64
Kane, Frank, 368
Keitel, Peter, engineer, 138
Kent, 220
  and tunnelers, 289
Kent Fire Brigade, 200–201, 320
King, John, director of U.K. tunnel-
  ing, 271, 297
Kirkland, Colin, Eurotunnel techni-
  cal director, 210
Kirkpatrick, Sir Ivone Augustine,
  diplomat, 62–63
Kleinwort Benson, 104
Knowles, James, editor, 46. *See also*
  The Nineteenth Century
Koeberg nuclear power station, 165

La Compagnie financière de suez, 62
La directive pour la conduite des
  grands projets, 166
La fédération routière, 62

Lahmeyer International, 133
Lamont, Thomas Stilwell, House of
  Morgan, 58, 59
Land Service Tunnel, 288
land tunnels, 339
Leblond, Laurent, tunnel engineer-
  ing director (French), 7–8
  tunnel impact on reputation, 8
Leigh-Pemberton, Rubin, governor of
  Bank of England, 174–175
Lemley, Jack, American construction
  engineer, 268–274, 299
Le Pont sur La Manche, 71
le puits de Sangatte, 177, 178
Libell of Englyshe Polycye, The, 29
Litten, Donald Ivor, 180
Lloyd, Elizabeth Pollard, 195–196
Lloyd's of London, 50
loading wagons, 275
Lobourg Channel, 28
locker rooms, 253–254
locomotive, diesel, 327
locomotives, electric, 327
London Interbank Offer Rate
  (LIBOR), 214
Lötschberg Tunnel, 13, 64
Louis Berger Associates, 132–133
Louis Berger International, 203
Lower Chalk, 33, 69
The Lump, 289
Lyonnaise des eaux-dumez, 99

MacGregor, Ian, industrialist, 96
Macnamara, Rory, of Morgan
  Grenfell, 194
Maggiemobile, 351
maître d'oeuvre (MdO), 132,
  143–144, 206–208, 280
Malcor, René, former chief engineer
  of port of Marseilles, 63, 64
Marine Running Tunnel North, 354
Mark I Hunslett locomotive, 327

Marquis of Granby, 5

Marsh, Richard, British Rail chairman, 86–88

Martin, Bryan, chairman of the Safety Authority, 281, 282

Massigli, René Lucien Daniel, secretary-general at Quai D'Orsay, 62

Matheron, Pierre, Transmanche-Link construction manager, 168–169

Mathieu, Albert. *See* Mathieu, Jacques-Joseph

Mathieu-Favier. *See* Mathieu, Jacques-Joseph

Mathieu, Jacques-Joseph, 35–36, 38

Maurin, General Philippe, 77

McCullouch, M. L., 117

McDowall, Andrew, construction engineer, 97–99, 225–226, 241

McMillan, Ian, Midland Bank executive, 137, 160–162

Means, Cyril, Jr., arbitration director of New York Stock Exchange, 56, 59, 60, 66

Memorandum of Understanding, 259–260, 261–262

meta-règles, 166

Michel, Serge, 313

Midland Bank, 93, 107, 112
and Equity 2, 176–177

Mitterand, François, 92, 93

Moch, Jules, 70–72

Mochida, Dr. Yutaka, 133

Montagner, Phillipe, 100, 106–107

Montague, Adrian, lawyer, 161

Montgolfier brothers, 32

Montgomery, Viscount, 65–66

Mont-Saint-Hubert, 178

Morgan Stanley, 75, 76

Morris, Quentin, Eurotunnel financial executive, 127–128

Morrison Knudsen, 19, 20, 62

Morton, Alastair, Eurotunnel British cochairman, 187–189, 191–195, 375, 386–387

mountain bikes, 352

Mountbatten, Lord Louis, 65

Mousehole, 89–90

Nadin, Mark (Pykie), operations board controller, 330

Napoleon, 29

National Westminster Bank, 86

Nattrass, Helen, senior geotechnical engineer, 249–252

NatWest, 128, 130
and contract problems, 147
and Equity 2, 176

Naylor, George, 76

Neerhout, John, 310–311

New Austrian Tunneling Method (NATM), 219, 340

1984 Five Bank Report, 268

1986 Concession Agreement, 242

The Nineteenth Century, 40–42, 44–46

The Nineteenth Century and After, 46

Nomura Securities, 176

Nord-Pas de Calais, 92–93

Noulton, John, chairman of Intergovernmental Commission, 93, 279
on rail travel safety, 320–321

Nova Zapatana, 185

operations board controllers, 329–330

optimization, 206, 264

Ordnance Datum Newlyn, 15, 16

organisation matricelle, 166

Orient Express coaches, 372

Osborne, Alan, Tarmac representative, 135

Ove Arup, 98

overbreak, 247–248

Pahl, Till, of Deutsche Bank, 146
Paracas, 30
Parayre, Jean Paul, French chairman of Eurotunnel, 152
Paris Metro, 71
Parliamentary Channel Tunnel Committee, 59
Parsons-DeLeuw Cather, 204
passenger shuttles, 275–276, 278
  and fire, 280–281
  pass door requirements, 275–278, 281–282, 315–316, 319–320
Pavot, Bernard, 319
Pennock, Lord Ray, 135–136
Perlowski, Stan, lawyer, 161
piston relief ducts, 10, 77–78, 79
point M, 346, 351
polygon, 13–14
polytechnicien, 98, 369
  Armand, Louis, 61
  Bénard, André, 152
  de Vitry D'Avaucort, Count Arnaud, 56
  Dherse, Jean-Loup, 162–163
  Essig, Philippe, 260–261
  Moch, Jules, 70–72
Pompidou, Georges, 66–67
Powell, Christopher, secretary of Parliamentary Channel Tunnel Committee, 59
precast plant, 222–223, 224–227
Price, Keith, of Morrison Knudsen, 360–361
Priestley tunnel-boring machine, 87
prime movers, 326
Project Implementation Division (PID), 208, 233
Protocol, 372–373
pump stations, 333

rabies, 181, 196–197
  and traps, 363–365

Radcliffe, Eric, chief surveyor, 10, 15, 16
  and surveying complications of Channel Tunnel, 17
  and tunneling crews, 17–18
Rail Usage Contract, 162, 231–236
railroads
  Channel Tunnel agreement, 172
  optimization of path for, 183
  and train timetables, 231–232
RATP, 265
Rawlinson, Charles, investment banker, 171
Reeve, John, 92, 110, 136
Reflex Maxibor, 23, 24
Reinach, Joseph, 45
Renault, Jean, Spie representative, 99, 162
Richborough, 28
Ridley, Nicholas, civil engineer, government Minister, 101, 121–122
Ridley, Tony, Eurotunnel managing director, 215–216, 260–261
Rio Tinto Zinc, 75, 77
  and British Channel Tunnel Company, 76
  difficulties with Mousehole, 90
  train signaling system, 80–81
Rose, Charles, chief of railway safety, 158–159
Rotherhithe, 12
Rothschild Frères, 39
Royal Assent, 199
Royal Commission, 51
Royal Westminster Hotel, 160
running-tunnel machines, 207, 272–273, 322
Running Tunnel North, 374

Safety Authority, 130, 131
  Comité de sécurité, 280

and fire, 280–281
and halon, 281
and signaling system, 274–275
Safety Committee, 280
St. Gotthard Tunnel, 13
Salomon Brothers, 176
Sangatte, 9, 77, 218, 325
   beginning of Channel Tunnel construction, 177–180
   and Spanish Armada, 29
Saracen, 352
Sarmet, Marel, of Crédit lyonnais, 93, 94, 162
Sea Containers, 105
seasickness, 31–32
seawall, 220–221
seepage, 79
service tunnels, 78–79, 256
   use of rubber tires in, 352, 354
   ventilating system, 327
SETEC, 132
714 Certificates, 289
SG Warburg, 194
Shackleton, Edward Arthur Alexander, 76
Shakespeare Cliff, 9, 22, 219–220, 325
   spoil dumping, 220–221
Shakespeare Cliff seawall
   cost of, 227–228
Sherwood, James, 105, 116, 117, 120–121, 123–125
Shotcreting, 219
Shuttle, the, 374
   systems in, 321
shuttle rakes, 275–276
signaling system, 242–244
   awarding of contract for, 274
   bids on, 243–246
   and Clause 67, 244–247
   and 1986 Concession Agreement, 242

and rabies traps, 364–365
and Sofrerail, 367
and trackside signaling, 366–369
signal lights, 80
Simes, David, 298
Simms, Neville, Transmanche-Link chairman of members assembly, 367
Simplon Orient Express, 373
Simplon Tunnel, 13–15
6A material, 335
SNCF (French national railways company), 77
   and bid for tunnel rail tracks, 359–360
   and catenary, 207
   Rail Usage Contract, 162, 231
   and signaling system, 242–243, 274
   and signaling system bid, 244
   use of tunnel, 125–126, 182–183
Société auxiliare d'enterprises (SAE), 102–103
Société d'étude du pont sur la manche, 70
Société d'études techniques et économiques (SETEC), 63
Société du chemin de fer sous-marin entre la france et l'angleterre, 39
Société française du tunnel sous la manche, 77
Société générale, 71, 104
Société generale d'enterprises (SGE), 103
Sofrerail, 367–369
Solmer steel mill, 163
Sonneville block, 359
Sparker, 64, 65
Spie Batignolles, 97
spoil, 328
spoil dumping, 220–221

Stannard, Colin, of National Westminster Bank, 91, 93, 162
   addressing concerns of Rail Usage
      Contract, 232
Stansted Protocol, 115
steel reinforcing cages, 224–226
Sterling, Sir Jeffrey, P&O executive,
   187
stock market crash, 211, 213–214
Strait of Dover. *See* Dover Strait
Submarine Continental Railway
   Company, 46
Submission to Government, 136
Suez Canal Company, 60–61, 63
Summerly, Felix, 32
sumps, 333
surveying, 13–14
   complications of, Channel Tunnel,
      17
   difficulty of, 18
   and refraction, 14–15, 18
   and sea level measurements, 15–16
   technology used in, 14–15
surveyor
   Radcliffe, Eric, 10, 15, 16, 17–18
   Reeve, John, 92
   of Simplon Tunnel, 14–15
Sykes, Allen, insurance expert, 94–95

Tarmac, 97, 223
Taylor, Frederick Winslow, 166
Taylor Woodrow Construction, 81
   and English Channel Tunnel
      Group, 96–97
Tebel-Darchem, 315
Technical Studies, 55, 61–62, 75
   benefits of tunnel project revival,
      89
   and British Channel Tunnel
      Company, 76–77
   and civilian sentiments toward
      tunnel, 66

   and political sentiments toward
      tunnel, 65–66
Texaco Caribbean, 30
TGV Atlantique, 242, 366
TGV Nord, 367
TGV systems, 242–243
Thames Barrier, 91–92
Thames Tunnel, 12–13
Thanet, 147
Thatcher, Margaret, 92, 93, 96, 101,
   102
30th Peak Hour, 81
Thomé de Gamond, Aimé, 35–39
   Channel dive, 37–38
   plans for other tunnels, 38
Tontine House, 130
track-to-train transmission, 242
Trades Union Congress, 86
Trafalgar House, 104, 176
train(s)
   breakdown of, 80
   and catenary, 207
   for Channel Tunnel, 77–78
   on construction railway, 327–331
   derailment of, 320–321
   and driver error, 320
   and fire safety, 198–199, 319–321
   fires in, 80
   passenger shuttle, 275
   shuttle builders, 277
   shuttle doors, 275–277
   signaling system, 80–81, 242–243
   signaling system and rabies traps,
      363–365
   terminal tracks, 365–367
   track-to-train transmission,
      242–243
   and trackside signaling, 366–367,
      368–369
   and tunnel design problems,
      231–232
   and tunnel temperatures, 79–80

TVM300, 242
TVM400, 242–243
train captain, 321
train drivers, 326
Translink, 108
Translink JV, 237
Transmanche Construction, 237
Transmanche g.i.e., 108
Transmanche-Link (TML), 108–112,
    127
  and boreholes, 185
  and Clause 67, 245–247
  and construction contract, 159,
    181, 245–246
  contract problems, 136–150
  cooling system, 241, 361
  disputes with Eurotunnel, 240
  engineering staff, 237–239
  and Eurotunnel's looming financial
    default, 302–313
  and fixed equipment costs,
    357–358
  and lump-sum differences, 362
  management of, 237–241
  management problems of, 164
  money disputes with Eurotunnel,
    229–231
  and optimization, 181–182
  problems with Channel Tunnel
    Bill, 181
  and Shakespeare Cliff seawall,
    228
  and signaling system, 242–244
  and spoil dumping, 220–221
  and tunnelers, 289, 290
Transmission Voie Machine
    (TVM300), 242
  diameter of, 206–207
  surveying, 13–14
  water seepage, 43
tunnel-boring machine (TBM), 5, 8,
    251–253

and Beaumont, Frederick E., Royal
    Engineers, 42–45
and breakthrough, 342
British, 5, 345, 355
British marine service tunnel, 286
computers in, 292
and David Denman, 22
English, 295–296
first use of, 217
French, 295, 296
French "Brigitte," 5, 8, 25
French "Europa," 354, 355
French grouting procedures, 272
French land service tunnel, 285
French marine service tunnel, 286
and grout injection, 257
Land Running Tunnel South, 323
operator, 332
Priestley, 87
and Reflex Maxibor, 23
and rock, 17
Running Tunnel North, 337–338
and Sangatte shaft, 285
testing of, 23–25
and tunnel-linking process, 20–21
U.K. land service, 285
tunnelers
  and air spades, 295
  British, 286, 289, 290
  and British press, 290
  and ceremonial handshake, 21
  and chalk marl, 33
  Cozette, Philippe, 21
  The Crack, 286
  Denman, David, 22, 25
  and drinking water, 329
  Fagg, Graham, 21
  and Farthingloe Village, 289–290
  French, 295
  French training program, 293
  hand-mining, 295
  Hester, Alabama, 18

tunnelers *(Continued)*
  Hester, John, 7, 18–20
  and humidity in tunnels, 329
  and *Independent* article, 290–291
  Irish, 289, 295
  and keystone, 296
  logistics of, 331–340
  and The Lump, 289
  makeup of, 288–289
  and mountain bikes, 352
  payment of, 289, 290
  and 714 Certificates, 289
  single-line working, 329
  and traveling, 291
tunneling, 247
  history of underwater, 11–12
  horizontal, 200
  and overbreak, 247–248
  and railroads, 13
  regulations, 296–297
  and water problems, 247–248
tunnel refraction, 14–15, 18
Tunnel Signal Group, 303
tunnel spoil, 227
Tunnel Tigers, 290
tunnel treaty, 86
Turner, Sir Alfred, 46
Turner, Mark, Rio Tinto Zinc deputy
  chairman, 75, 76
TVM300, 242
TVM400, 242–243
TVM430, 244, 274

Underwriting Banks, 129
une descenderie, 77
Union Bank of Switzerland, 130
Usinor, 104

Varne Bank, 30
Vickers, 110
Victoria, Queen (of England), 38, 39
Victoria Station, 371
Victoria Street, 59–60

Walker, Sir David, Bank of England
  executive director, 171,
  174–175
Wapping, 12
War of the Lump Sum, 358, 362
Watkin, Sir Edward, cotton
  merchant, 39–40, 45
Weald-Artois anticline, 33
Weld & Company, 76
Well of Sangatte, 177, 178
White Cliffs of Dover, 27, 33
Winton, John, U.K. construction di-
  rector, 271
Wolf, Derish, president of Louis
  Berger International, 137
Wolseley, Sir Garnet, 40, 41–42
wrongful act or admission (WAO),
  245–246
W. S. Atkins, 132

Zunz, Sir Jack, head of Ove Arup, 98